OLD FAMILIES OF

LARNE

& DISTRICT

Larne, reproduced from *The scenery and antiquities of Ireland (I)*, illustrated from drawings by W.H. Bartlett, literary content by N.P. Willis and J. Stirling Coyne, published, London 1842.

GRAVESTONE INSCRIPTIONS
COUNTY ANTRIM
VOLUME 4

OLD FAMILIES OF
LARNE
& DISTRICT

from
Gravestone Inscriptions, Wills
and
Biographical Notes

◆

compiled by
GEORGE RUTHERFORD

and edited by
RSJ CLARKE

ULSTER HISTORICAL
FOUNDATION

First published in 2004
by Ulster Historical Foundation
12 College Square East, Belfast, BT1 6DD
www.ancestryireland.com
www.booksireland.org.uk

Printed by Biddles Ltd

ISBN 1-903688-19-1

CONTENTS

LIST OF ILLUSTRATIONS

Coats of arms reproduced from the *Ulster Journal of Archaeology*
(GRANT see page 69-70)

INTRODUCTION

The site of Larne, with its south-pointing spur known as The Corran, has been occupied since Late Mesolithic times. The raised beach, composed largely of gravel provides evidence for a flowering of a flint tool-making industry in this period. The Corran, stretching into Larne Lough, also gave a safe anchorage to early man.

The name of Larne is derived from the sub-kingdom of *Latharne*, "the descendants of *Lathar*". According to legend King *Ugaine Mor* divided Ireland among his twenty-five children, one of whom was *Lathar*. The river now known as Larne River was anciently Ollar, and this may have been corrupted by the Norsemen to form their name for the Lough — Ulfrek's Fiord. A Viking grave three-quarters of a mile from the town and seventy yards from the seashore was found in 1840. It yielded a bone comb, bronze ringed pin, iron spearhead and double edged sword, which suggest a late ninth or early tenth century date. Einar Wry-Mouth, Earl of Orkney, followed the Viking tradition of plundering expeditions. In 1018 he came to Ireland and met King Conchobar in a great battle in Ulfreksfiordr. He lost nearly all his men and all the spoils they had already taken. The earl fled with one ship back to Orkney. He attributed his defeat to the Norwegians who had fought on the side of the Irish king, principally Eyvind Aurochs-Horn.

After the invasion by the Norman knight John de Courcy in 1177 the area was brought into the Earldom of Ulster. (There are mottes in Kilwaughter Demense and Rory's Glen.) In 1198 while de Courcy was ravaging parts of Tyrone, Hugh O'Neill sailed to Latharna with five ships and burned part of the town. During the fighting eighteen English were killed against five of Hugh's men.

In 1210 King John granted to Duncan Fitz-Gilbert of Carrick (Ayrshire) and his heirs, the Town of Wulfrichford and all the land from Wulfrichford to Glynarm. Duncan's son Neil died in 1256 leaving as heiress his daughter Marjorie, mother of Robert Bruce, who was to become king of Scotland. However, the Bisset family had gained the lordship of the Glynns at some time during the thirteenth century and the Macdonnells took a leading role when Margery Bisset married John Mor Macdonnell about 1399.

Edward Bruce landed at Larne with a Scottish army in 1315 on his way to conquer Ireland and become king. His brother Robert, king of Scotland, made another landing here in 1327 but does not seem to have gone beyond the present county Antrim and withdrew after a few months.

In 1592 Moses Hill of Carrickfergus received a lease of the ruinous Castle of Olderfleet and the 180 acres belonging to it. The ward of Olderfleet Castle was sold to the Scots on 9th December 1597 by Robert Strabridge and John Wright. Moses Hill, still the constable, had been wounded on the 4th November when Sir John Chichester, Governor of Carrickfergus, and many of his soldiers had been killed in a battle with the McDonnells "on the road to Olderfleet". Those stationed at Olderfleet must have felt very vulnerable. Randal McDonnell secured from James I a grant of land stretching from Coleraine to Larne (excepting Olderfleet), was raised to the peerage as Earl of Antrim, and began settling lowland Scots on his Irish lands. The Agnews of Lochnaw, Wigtonshire, began their acquisition of Kilwaughter at this time with leases obtained from Lord Antrim. In 1608 Arthur Bassett (nephew of the Lord Deputy, Arthur Chichester) received a grant of lands in Larne including the church and townlands of Gardenmore and Greenland.

In 1683 Larne was described as a single street of thatched houses, a market town, yet no market was kept, only two fairs yearly. Almost all the inhabitants were Scottish and Presbyterian and the port was a major entry point for continuing immigration. Horses were exported to Scotland and coal imported. Linen was established as the major trade. It became a significant embarkation port for emigration to North America in the eighteenth century. The *Friends Goodwill* made the first of these Atlantic crossings in 1717.

On 7th June 1798 two hundred and fifty insurgents took on an officer and twenty soldiers stationed in the town and supported by a few loyalist residents, most notably Dr. Casement. In the exchange of fire there were about six fatalities, but the rebels did not press their advantage and the insurrection soon faded.

By 1800 Larne had two neighbourhoods: Old Town which was a tangle of narrow streets to the north of the bridge, and New Town which was a long straight street stretching eastward (later named Main Street). Following the enactment of the Poor Law of 1838, Larne became the centre of a Poor Law district and the Workhouse began functioning in 1843. Larne became a municipality in 1858. The Local Government Act (1898) produced the Larne Urban and the Larne Rural District Councils. A Royal Charter in 1939 raised the status from Urban District to Borough but reorganisation in 1973 created a new entity with the Borough of Larne containing urban and rural areas.

Linen was important in both Inver and Millbrook, Kilwaughter, in the seventeenth century, but cotton proved more profitable early in the new century and a new factory opened in Craiganorne. By the 1830s cotton was failing and linen revived with the Larne Weaving Company as a major employer in the town from 1889 to 1971. Another local industry was salt refining which was carried on from 1725 to 1825. Rock salt was imported from the Chester mines and the finished product exported to northern Europe.

The Antrim Coast Road was built 1832-1842 and opened up Larne to trade with the north. The broad gauge railway reached Larne from Carrickfergus in 1862 and the narrow gauge operated to Ballyclare (and Ballymena) 1877-1950. After repeated efforts the Larne to Stranraer passenger ferry began operating on a regular basis in 1872. After obtaining a lease of the Curran from Lord Donegall in 1823, William Agnew had built a harbour and quays facing Islandmagee. In 1866 his interest was bought by James Chaine who diligently improved the harbour and promoted Larne as a port and from 1873 the trans-Atlantic liners of the State Line called at Larne. Opportunities opened by these improved communications were grasped by Henry McNeill (1836-1904), the father of tourism, who acquired several hotels in Larne and ran day excursions in char-a-bancs, and package holidays.

Other industries which have flourished include the pottery 1842-57, iron ore mining in Larne and Kilwaughter 1848-79, boat and shipbuilding 1879-1922; paper making 1885-1999, alumina production 1895-1961 and Kane's Foundry 1887-1986. After World War II, inward investment established large factories in heavy and light engineering, B.T.H. manufacturing turbines and Pye radios, but by the end of the century the development of many small firms was more successful in maintaining employment.

The ecclesiastical history of Larne begins with the Taxation of Pope Nicholas in 1306. This lists four entries in or about Larne: the chapel of St Mary of Ynver 20 shillings, the rector of St Cedma of the same 60s, the vicarage of the same 20s, and the church of Dunales 33s 8d (see Reeves: *Ecclesiastical Antiquities* (1847)). St Mary's of Inverbeg is believed to have stood at the corner of Bridge Street and Point Street. At this time the rectory of St Cedma`s belonged to Bangor Abbey, and they still had possession at the dissolution of the monasteries. The present parish church of Larne and Inver is believed to stand on the site of the old church of Invermore, dedicated to St Cedma. As St Comgall, founder of the monastery of Bangor was born in Magheramorne in 517, Monsignor O'Laverty (*Diocese of Down and Connor* (1883)) conjectured that the dedication of St Cedma represents Comgall's father, Setna. The parishes of Invermore and Inverbeg were united in 1622 with the Dean of Connor as rector. As the dean was normally resident in Carrickfergus, he would appoint a curate for Larne. Scottish Presbyterian ministers filled the role of parish clergy in 1627-37 and 1646-61, but by 1670 the Presbyterians of Larne had organised as a distinct congregation and had built their own meeting house. During the 1641 Rebellion St Cedma's parish church was used as a refuge for the settlers of Larne and Kilwaughter and its defence was organised by Captain Agnew. The church of Dunales was later in the possession of the Premonstratensian Abbey of Woodburn near Carrickfergus, and the same hill was chosen by Sir Hugh Smiley in 1872 when he began building his mansion of Drumalis. Since 1930 it has been occupied by the Sisters of the Cross and Passion, who now run it as a retreat and conference centre. In modern historic times Larne has been a civil parish of ten townlands and was united, for practical purposes, with the smaller parish of Inver, which lay on the south side of the river.

This volume covers the composite parish of Larne and Inver, together with the small adjoining parish of Kilwaughter. The largest and oldest of the graveyards is round St Cedma's Parish Church, with a gravestone dating from 1677. The register of baptisms dates from 1806, marriages from 1817 and burials from 1826, with the vestry book running from 1763.

The first Presbyterian Meeting House was built about 1668 on the site of the present Larne and Kilwaughter Non-Subscribing Presbyterian Church and was also known as the "Head of the Town" (HOTT). The congregation divided in 1715 over the choice of a non-subscribing versus orthodox minister, and the HOTT joined the Presbytery of Antrim on its formation in 1726. The orthodox section erected a new church (First Larne) beside the Inver bridge and later a new congregation (Gardenmore) was formed. The oldest stone in the HOTT graveyard only goes back as far as 1827 and the First Presbyterian church had only one grave (of 1867) which has now been moved. The McGarel Cemetery also dates from 1867 and the oldest stone in St McNissi`s graveyard dates from 1895. This indicates that all denominations used St Cedma's well into the nineteenth century, but as the grave plots were filled up the other graveyards were opened. The original Presbyterian church, did however keep a baptismal register which has survived from 1720 and marriage register from 1721 and the First Presbyterian Church registers date from 1813 and 1846 respectively, but most of these have gaps of some years. The Second Presbyterian registers date from 1861 (baptisms) and 1846 (marriages), while those of St McNissi's Roman Catholic Church date from 1821.

The small parish of Kilwaughter is to the west of Larne and just to the north of the main Larne-Ballymena road. The church is mentioned in the 1306 Taxation, but was in ruins by 1622 and 1657. Only a fragment of the old building remains in a corner of the graveyard, which is now among the outbuildings of the ruined Kilwaughter Castle. The castle itself was designed by John Nash and built in 1807 for Edward Jones Agnew. However, it is on the site of a 17th century castle built for an earlier Agnew and incorporated into Nash's mansion. The last of the family moved out during the 1920's and the castle was used by American soldiers during World War II. Finally, the roof was removed for the value of its lead and slates in 1951 (Dickson 1901; McKillop 2000). The newer cemetery in the parish was opened after a meeting in 1876, though some of the gravestones refer to earlier deaths.

We are grateful to members of the Larne and District Historical Society for their work in copying gravestones during the 1990's, in particular to Edith Dempsey, Ann Harris and Tom Norrell. Thanks are due to the Ulster Folk and Transport Museum for permission to reproduce the photograph of the Chaine Memorial (W.A.G. 536) and to the Public Record Office of Northern Ireland for permission to reproduce the photographs of Inver Church (W.L. 2182) and Kilwaughter Castle (W.L. 1574). The valuable summary guide to documentary sources has been compiled by William Roulston of the Ulster Historical Foundation.

GEORGE RUTHERFORD

RICHARD CLARKE

BIBLIOGRAPHY

ANON: *Gardenmore Presbyterian Church Bazaar, July 26, 27, &28 1894: Historical Sketch of the Gardenmore Presbyterian Church, Larne 1769-1894.* Belfast, 1894.

ANON: *Historical Sketch of the Old Presbyterian Congregation of Larne and Kilwaughter.* Belfast, 1889.

Army List

BAILIE, W.D. (ed.): *A History of Congregations in the Presbyterian Church in Ireland 1610 - 1982.* Belfast, Presbyterian Historical Society, 1982.

BASSETT, G.H.: *The Book of Antrim.* Dublin, 1888 (reprinted by Friar's Bush Press, 1989.

Belfast and the Province of Ulster Directory.

BENN, G. *A History of the Town of Belfast.* Belfast, Vol. II, 1880.

BIGGAR, F.J.: "Armorial Stones" in *Handbook of Larne Grand Fete 19th - 22nd July 1893: Historical Sketches* pp. 75 - 85.

BRETT, C.E.B.: *Buildings of County Antrim.* Belfast, 1996.

BURKE, SIR BERNARD: *Genealogical and Heraldic History of the Landed Gentry of Ireland.* London, 1912.

BURKE, SIR BERNARD: *Genealogical and Heraldic History of the Landed Gentry of Ireland.* London, 1958.

BURKE, SIR BERNARD: *Peerage and Baronetage.* London, 1938.

BURTCHAELL, G.D. and SADLEIR, T.U. *Alumni Dublinenses.* London, 1924.

CLOSE, M. The Chaine Memorial Tower. *The Coran* 1987, No. 42, p. 7 and 1988, No. 48, p. 12.

CORCORAN, D.: *A Tour of East Antrim.* Friar's Bush Press, 1990.

Corran, The. Published quarterly by the Larne and District Folklore Society, from 1976.

DAY, ANGELIQUE and McWILLIAMS, PATRICK: *Ordnance Survey Memoirs of Ireland,* Vol. 10, 1991, Institute of Irish Studies, Queen's University, Belfast (parishes of Carncastle and Killyglen, Island Magee, Kilwaughter, and Larne).

Debrett`s Peerage. London.

DICKSON, J.M. The Agnews in County Antrim. *Ulster Journal of Archaeology,* Second Series, 1901, 7, 166-171.

Dictionary of American Biography. London, 1933.

Dictionary of National Biography. London, 1909.

FAIR, J.A.: *To This You Belong.* Belfast, Northern Whig, c 1979.

FISHER, J.R. and ROBB, J.H. *Royal Belfast Academical Institution. Centenary Volume, 1810-1910.* Belfast, 1913.

FROGGATT, P. Two neglected Belfast medical professors: James Lawson Drummond (1783-1853) and James Drummond Marshall (1808-1868). In Gray, J. and McCann, W. (eds.) *An Uncommon Bookman*. Belfast, 1996.

HARVEY, W.J. *The Head Line*.

HEATLEY, F. and DIXON, H. *Belfast Scenery in thirty views 1832, Drawn by Joseph Molloy, Belfast and engraved by E.K. Proctor, London*. Published with a modern commentary by the Linen Hall Library, Belfast 1983.

Journal of the Association for the Preservation of the Memorials of the Dead in Ireland known as *Memorials of the Dead* or *M.D.*

KEANE, E., PHAIR, P.B. and SADLEIR, T.U. *King`s Inns Admission Papers 1607-1867*. Dublin, 1982.

KNOX, G.: *A History of Larne Methodist Church*. 1985.

Larne Weekly Reporter, Larne Reporter and *Larne Times*.

LESLIE, J.B. *Clergy of Conor, from Patrician Times to the present day*. Belfast, 1993.

McCONNELL, J. and McCONNELL, G. *Fasti of the Irish Presbyterian Church, 1613-1840*. Belfast, 1951.

McCREARY, A.: *A Vintage Port: Larne and its People*. Greystone Press, 2000.

MEHAFFIE. F.G.: *The Short Sea Route*. T. Stephenson & Sons Ltd., 1975.

McILRATH, R.H.: *Early Victorian Larne*. 1991, Braid Books.

McILRATH, R.H.: *Larne Grammar School: the first 100 years*. The Universities Press, 1985.

McKILLOP, F.: *History of Larne and East Antrim*. Ulster Journals, 2000.

McNEILLY, D.J.: *Gardenmore: A Record of the History and Tradition of Gardenmore Presbyterian Church*. 1953.

Medical Directory

Navy List

O'LAVERY, J.: *An Historical Account of the Diocese of Down and Connor,* Volume 3. Dublin, 1884 (reprinted, Davidson Books, 1981).

O'NEILL, D.: *The Parish of Larne: a short history*. 1994.

PORTER, C., McILRATH, R.H. and NELSON, J.W.: *Congregational Memoirs of the Old Presbyterian Congregation of Larne and Kilwaughter*. New edition, 1975.

REEVES, W.: *Ecclesiastical Antiquities of Down, Connor, and Dromore*. 1847, reprinted 1992 by Braid & Moyola Books.

SMYTH, A. *The Story of Antrim*. Antrim, 1985.

STEWART, D. *The Seceders in Ireland, with Annals of their Congregations*. Belfast, 1950.

STURGESS, H.A.C. *Register of Admissions to the Honourable Society of the Middle Temple*. London, 1949.

Ulster Journal of Archaeology, Second Series.

YOUNG, R.N. and PIKE W.T. *Belfast and the Province of Ulster.*. Brighton, 1909.

LIST OF ABBREVIATIONS

A.D.	Anno Domini
AE	Aetatis (aged)
A.M.	Master of Arts
A.M.D.G.	Ad Majorem Dei Gloriam
B.A.	Bachelor of Arts
B.C.L.	Bachelor of Civil Law
B.L.	Bachelor of Law
C.B.E.	Commander of the Order of the British Empire
C.E.F.	Combined Expeditionary Force
C.M.G.	Commander of the Order of St Michael and St George
D.B.E.	Dame Commander of the Order of the British Empire
D.D.	Doctor of Divinity
D.L.	Deputy Lieutenant
D.N.B.	Dictionary of National Biography
D.S.O.	Distinguished Service Order
F.I.C.E.	Fellow of the Institute of Civil Engineers
F.R.C.V.S.	Fellow of the Royal College of Veterinary Surgeons
G.N.	Grave North
H.M.S.	Her Majesty's Ship
H.O.T.T.	Head of the Town
I.H.S.	Iesus Hominum Salvator or In Hac (cruce) Salus or In Hoc Signo vinces
Ills.	Illinois
Inst	Royal Belfast Academical Institution
I.O.W.	Isle of Wight
J.P.	Justice of the Peace
K.B.E.	Knight Commander of the Order of the British Empire
K.C.B.	Knight Commander of the Order of the Bath
L.O.L.	Loyal Orange Lodge
L.R.C.S.	Licentiate of the Royal College of Surgeons
M.A.	Master of Arts
M.B.	Bachelor of Medicine
M.B.E.	Member of the Order of the British Empire
M.C.	Military Cross
M.Ch.	Master of Surgery
M.D.	Doctor of Medicine
M.D.	*Memorials of the Dead*
M.O.D.	Ministry of Defence
M.P.	Member of Parliament
M.R.C.S.	Member of the Royal College of Surgeons
M.Sc.	Master of Science
N.B.	North Britain (Scotland)
N.E.	North East
N.I.	Native Infantry

N.J.	New Jersey
N.S.W.	New South Wales
N.W.	North West
O.B.E.	Officer of the Order of the British Empire
O.S.	Ordnance Survey
P.P.	Parish Priest
R.A.	Royal Artillery
R.A.F.	Royal Air Force
R.A.M.C.	Royal Army Medical Corps
R.B.A.I.	Royal Belfast Academical Institution
R.B.P.	Royal Black Preceptory
R.C.C.	Roman Catholic Curate
R.D.C.	Rural District Council
R.D.F.	Royal Dublin Fusiliers
R.E.	Royal Engineers
R.F.A.	Royal Field Artillery
R.I.C.	Royal Irish Constabulary
R.I.P.	Requiesca(n)t in Pace
R.I.R.	Royal Irish Rifles
R.N.	Royal Navy
R.N.R.	Royal Naval Reserve
R.U.I.	Royal University of Ireland
S.E.	South East
S.W.	South West
T.D.	Territorial Decoration
U.J.A.	*Ulster Journal of Archaeology (Second Series)*
U.S.A.	United States of America
V.F.	Vicar Forane

CHAINE PARK

This is in the townland of Curran and Drumaliss, the parish of Larne and the barony of Upper Glenarm and wholly within a public park. Four grave plots are surrounded by a bank which is enclosed by iron railings five and a half feet high, mounted on the granite coping of a low wall of squared basalt. The sub-circular enclosure is set on the edge of a cliff looking northeast across the North Channel to Scotland and marked on the O.S. map as on the site of an antiquity, "fort". A bronze plaque on the gate tells us "These railings enclose the private burial ground of James Chaine Esq. M.P., late of Cairncastle Lodge, Larne, and of his family and heirs".

CHAINE

[Headstone and enclosure of polished pink granite.] James Chaine died 4th May 1885. Henrietta Chaine died 21st Dec.1913.

[The will of James Chaine, late of Ballycraigy, county Antrim, esquire, M.P., who died 4 May 1885 at Larne Harbour in said county, was proved at Belfast 15 July 1885 by Donald MacDonald of Larne Harbour, civil engineer, one of the executors. Effects £62,681 . 3s. 6d.

James Chaine was the son of James Chaine of Ballycraigy House, Muckamore, and Maria Whittle, daughter of Francis Whittle of Muckamore. He was grandson of William Chaine of Ballycraigy House, who owned extensive linen works at Muckamore. In 1863 he married Henrietta Creery, daughter of Charles A Creery. He bought Cairncastle Lodge, Carnfunnock from James Agnew in 1865. He also bought the harbour area in Larne from the Agnew family in 1866 and greatly improved its primitive quays and facilities. In 1871 the Larne and Stranraer Steamship Company was established and in the following year the first sailing took place. The next logical step was to extend the railway to the harbour in 1878 and, to provide travellers with accommodation, he opened the Olderfleet Hotel in the same year. As a result he probably did more for trade in Larne than anyone else in the nineteenth century. Sadly, it was while waiting to receive the Prince of Wales (later King Edward VII) and Princess Alexandra, that he caught a chill and died in his hotel. He was buried upright in his yachting uniform, and the monument (see p. 3) was erected in 1887.

James` eldest son, William Chaine, J.P., D.L., continued with his father`s enterprises and when he died, in 1937, Cairncastle Lodge was sold to Sir Thomas Dixon, who lived at Cairndhu nearby, and demolished (except for the front door which still survives in Carnfunnock Park). William`s property passed to his cousin Augustus Alexander Nickson (see below). See Burke: *Landed Gentry of Ireland* (1912 and 1958); Brett: *Buildings of County Antrim* (1996), p. 296; Close: *The Corran*, No. 42 (1987), p. 7 and No. 48 (1988), p. 2; McKillop: *History of Larne and East Antrim* (2000); Smyth: *The Story of Antrim* (1985), 73-74]

CHAINE

[Headstone and enclosure of polished pink granite.] James Chaine died 22nd Nov.1910. Christina Chaine died 7th Sep. 1911. [See Young and Pike (1909).]

CHAINE

[Headstone and enclosure of polished pink granite.] William Chaine died 3rd May 1937.

CHAINE-NICKSON

[Headstone and enclosure of polished pink granite.] Rachel Halley Chaine-Nickson O.B.E., dearly loved wife of Augustus Chaine-Nickson O.B.E., died 8th December 197(2). Also the said Augustus Chaine-Nickson O.B.E., died 10th February 1974. Both of Balrath, Co. Meath.

[Augustus Alexander Chaine-Nickson O.B.E. (1937) of The Grove, Balrath, Co. Meath, formerly with the Liverpool Cotton Association, was born 2 February 1886, son of Augustus Abraham Nickson, and Alexandrina Mary Henry of Rathescar, Dunleer, Co. Louth. He assumed the additional name of Chaine by deed poll in 1938, on succeeding to the property of his cousin, William Chaine. He was educated at Sedbergh School, and married on 22 April 1913, Rachel Halley, O.B.E. (1945), 2nd dau. of Sir Richard Hampson of Brown Howe, Coniston, Lancs. They had issue:

1. Augustus Terence T.D. was born 15 Feb. 1916
2. Michael Henry Chaine was born 21 Sept. 1918 and was killed in action 27 July 1944.
3. Denys Sophia was born 16 Dec. 1924 and married Lieut.-Colonel Horace Rollo Squarey Pain, M.C., of Hartley Witney, Hants.)

See Burke: *Landed Gentry of Ireland*, (1958).]

James Chaine, junior, younger son of James Chaine, M.P.
(from Young and Pike: *Belfast and the Province of Ulster*, 1909).

CHAINE MEMORIAL

O.S. Antrim 40. Grid Ref. D414029

Eight hundred metres south-east of the burial ground, and in the same townland, stands this granite replica of an Irish round tower with its foundations in the tidal water. It was built in 1887 to designs by S.P. Close. Navigational lights were installed on the seaward side in 1899. The inscription is on a tablet above the door.

CHAINE
This tower was erected and the road leading to it made by the contributions of every class in this mixed community irrespective of creed or party all cordially united in esteem and affection for the memory of James Chaine of Ballycraigy and Cairncastle, County Antrim, who represented this county in the Imperial Parliament of Great Britain and Ireland from February 1874 till the 4th of May 1885, when his early and lamented death in the 44th year of his age deprived his native county of one who had worked indefatigably for its interests especially in developing and improving the natural capabilities of the harbour of Larne and establishing its connection with Great Britain, the United States of America and with the inland parts of this county. *"Si monumentum requiris circumspice."*

Chaine Memorial Tower (reproduced by permission of the Ulster Folk and Transport Museum/MAGNI, W.A.G. 536).

DROMAIN GRAVEYARD

O.S. Antrim 35. Grid Ref. D373044

This is in the townland of Dromain and Grange of Killyglen, barony of Upper Glenarm. The family plot is enclosed by a wall of local stone surmounted by iron railings and is approached by a concrete path leading from the clachan. The land was owned by the McFall family but came down to the Gordons after Jeannie McFall married Alexander Gordon, who was buried in Larne Cemetery in 1945.

McFALL

[Sandstone standing in centre of plot.] Archibald McFall in memory of his mother Jane McFall who died 2nd May 1845 aged 59 years. Also his brother Robert who died 16th February 1848 aged 18 years. His sister Nancy McFall who died 1st July 1885 aged 44 years. His father John McFall who died 9th May 1861 aged 74 years.

[The will of John McFaul [sic], late of Dromaine in the county of Antrim, farmer, who died 9 May 1861 at same place, was proved at Belfast 6 November 1861 by the oath of John McFaul of Dromaine and Archibald McFaul of Ballyloran, Larne, both in the county of Antrim, farmers, the executors. Effects under £200.

Death: June 4th, at his residence, Dromaine, John McFall, aged 67. *Larne Reporter*, 11 June 1887.]

McFALL

[Large granite stone towards west of plot.] In memory of Archibald McFall who died 7th June 1884 aged 73 years. His beloved wife Maria who died 8th July 1869 aged 48 years. Also their children – Robert who died 23rd November 1882 aged 25 years; Maggie died in infancy; John Clarke McFall who died 11th May 1921 aged 67 years; Jeannie Gordon who died 26th October 1950 aged 91. Eileen Dickey Gordon died 5th April 1978 aged 81 years.

"So He giveth His beloved sleep." Psalms CXXVII, 2.

[The will (with one codicil) of Archibald McFall, late of Ballyloran, county Antrim, farmer, who died 7 June 1884 at same place, was proved at Belfast 15 September 1884 by John Clarke McFall of Ballyloran, farmer, and Hugh George Younge of Larne in said county, draper, the executors. Effects £2,256 . 19s. 6d.

Letters of administration of the personal estate of Robert McFall, late of Clifton Park Avenue, Belfast, builder, who died 23 November 1882 at same place, were granted at Belfast 3 January 1883 to Archibald McFall of Ballyloran, Larne, county Antrim, farmer, the father. Effects £2,968 . 5s. 10d.]

KILWAUGHTER CEMETERY

O.S. Antrim 40. Grid Ref. D357006

This is in the townland of Rory's Glen, civil parish of Kilwaughter, and barony of Upper Glenarm and about two hundred yards north of Kilwaughter cross roads.

A public meeting in Kilwaughter Orange Hall on 8th May 1876 was advertised for all those interested in establishing a new cemetery for Kilwaughter. The land was donated by Mr. Baillie for a burial ground and the enclosing wall built at his expense. It has been managed by trustees ever since. A shield mounted on the caretaker's dwelling bears the legend, "Built by David Nelson Esq., J.P., of Larne, 1887." This was sold by the trustees some years ago.

All stones with dates of death before 1900 have been copied.

AGNEW
   See CALDWELL and MAGEE

ALEXANDER
   See COBAIN

ALLEN
   See MAXWELL

APSLEY
   [Limestone headstone and enclosure.] In loving memory of Robert Apsley, Ballyrickard, who died 12th February 1904 aged 65 years. Also his son William Robert who died 22nd June 1899 aged 27 years. Also his mother Ellen McNAIR who died 3rd June 1879 aged 75 years. Also his father William Apsley who was interred in Inver church yard. And his wife Isabella D. BUCHANAN died 25th December 1935 aged 90 years. Annabella Apsley died 6th Dec.1946 at Rorysglen, Kilwaughter. Charles Apsley died 1st March 1955. Mary Agnes CRAWFORD died at Temora, N.S.W., 22nd May 1937. James Apsley died at Sydney 22nd June 1945. His daughter Ellen NELSON died 2nd November 1935 aged 56 years. His daughter Jane MORRISON died 2nd Jan. 1973 aged 92 years.
   [Marriage: 15th inst. in Raloo Presbyterian Church, by Rev. James Whiteford, Mr. William McFall of Ballyrickard, to Miss Martha Anne Apsley of same place. *Larne Weekly Reporter*, 18 Nov. 1865.]

BAILEY
   [Polished granite headstone within iron railings.] Erected by Ann Bailey in memory of her husband Robert Bailey, Rorysglen, who died 24th Sept. 1881 aged 74 years. The above-named Ann Bailey died 25 May 1885 aged 78 years.
   [The will of Robert Bailey, late of Kilwaughter, county Antrim, farmer, who died 24 September 1881 at same place, was proved at Belfast 6 March 1882 by Hugh Bailey of

Kilwaughter, farmer, and John McNinch of Larne in said county, merchant, the executors. Effects £1,147 . 6s. 5d.]

BAILIE

[Limestone headstone.] Erected by Margaret Watt Bailie in memory of her husband James Bailie, who died 24th May 1895, aged 82 years. And her daughter Mary Bailie, who died 3rd February 1860, aged 1 year & 6 months. And her son Samuel Bailie who died 11th December 1870, aged 2 years & 5 months. The above-named Margaret Watt Bailie died 1st March 1896, aged 68 years. Edith Bailie, grand-daughter of above-named died 13th March 1905 aged 8 years. James Bailie, eldest son of above, died 7th December 1934, aged 77 years. Also his wife Margaret HAMILTON died 10th March 1936, aged 69 years. Elizabeth Bailie, nee McGAREL, wife of Joseph R. Bailie, died 5th November 1954 aged 50 years. Joseph Rocke Bailie died 8th January 1974 aged 72 years. Holden, Larne.

[The will of James Bailie, formerly of Kilwaughter and late of St. John's Place, Larne, county Antrim, farmer, who died 24 May 1895 at latter place, was proved at Belfast 7 August 1895 by Robert McNinch of Hightown and Lennon Knox of Lealies, both in said county, farmers, the executors. Effects £415 . 16s. 10d.

The will of Margaret Bailie, late of St. John's Place, Larne, county Antrim, widow, who died 1 March 1896, was proved at Belfast 24 April 1896 by James Bailie of Larne, labourer, and Robert Burns of 65 Mount Street, Ballymacarret, county Down, brass finisher, the executors. Effects £58 . 11s. 2d.]

BAILIE

[Tapering pillar of polished granite surmounted by draped urn, in granite enclosure. Arms:- engrailed, barry, a semee of estoiles. Crest:- an estoile of eight points. Motto:- nil clarius astris. SW face:-] 1881. The under-mentioned Hugh Bailie, born 18th March 1833, died 9th Novr. 1904. His wife Jane MOLYNEUX born 5th Sept. 1840, died 4th Jany. 1925. Sarah Molyneux Bailie, born 3rd May 1874, died 20th Decr. 1931. The burying place of Hugh Bailie, Kilwaughter. [SE face:-] Mary Howard, daughter of Samuel Molyneux Bailie born 2nd Feby. 1903, died 26th Sept. 1913. His wife Tillie Howard DAVISON born 21st Aug. 1870, died 9th July 1938. The above named Samuel Molyneux Bailie, died 25th August 1954. [NW face:-] In memory of the children of Hugh Bailie. Hugh died 23rd Nov. 1875 aged 6 months. Robert Hill died 18th Jan. 1879 aged 6 years. Hugh Arthur died 20th July 1881 aged 4 months. William Bailie born 20th August 1867, died 1st April 1921. Evelyn Jane Bailie, born 9th Feb. 1881, died 13th May 1970. HWG Bailie, born 15th Aug. 1915, died 24th Sept. 1980.

[On a low headstone on the enclosure.] In everlasting memory of Peter Charles DAVIES, of Goodwick, Pem., died at Seabank, Larne, 5th June 1924.

[Lead lettering on enclosure.] S.M.B. 20-12-31. E.J.B. 13-5-70. W.B. 1-4-21. H.W.G.B. 15-8-1915, 24-9-1980. H.B. 9-11-04. J.M.B. 4-1-25. R.H.B. 18-1-79. M.H.B. 26-9-13. T.H.B. 9-7-38. S.M.B. 25-8-54.

BAILIE

[Polished granite table stone with arms:- wavy, a semee of estoiles. Crest:- an estoile of eight points. Motto:- Nil clarius astris.] In affectionate remembrance of Robert Hill Bailie of Summerhill, Muckamore, died at Larne 31st March 1908 aged 75 years. And his wife Jane FERGUSON died 28th March 1887. Erected by the children of his brother Hugh Bailie.

BARR

[Limestone.] Erected by Robert Barr in loving memory of his wife Jane Barr, who died 13th Dec. 1918 aged 57 years. His son Robert, who died 17th March 1906 aged 8 years. Also his son Robert, who died 6th Jan. 1886 aged 1 year. The above Robert Barr died 20th July 1940. Their son-in-law William Rainey STEWART, died 28th November 1961. Also Annie Stewart died 12th Nov. 1973. J. Bell, Larne.

BARR

See LYTLE

BAXTER

See LYTLE

BEGGS

[Lead lettering in limestone headstone, decorated with dove holding a trefoil leaf in its beak.] Erected by Jane Beggs in memory of her husband William Beggs who died 23rd Sept. 1885 aged 72 years. Also their son Patrick who died 7th March 1867 aged 15 years. Also their son Thomas who died 27th Nov. 1880 aged 38 years. Also their daughter Eliza, who died 30th Oct. 1881 aged 41 years. The above-named Jane Beggs, died 17th Feb. 1904 aged 84 years.

[The will of William Beggs, late of Ballykeel, Kilwaughter, county Antrim, farmer, who died 23 September 1885 at same place, was proved at Belfast 20 January 1886 by William Stewart Beggs of Larne, merchant, Patrick Gingles of Kilwaughter, farmer, and Thomas Campbell of Killyglen, farmer, all in said county, three of the executors. Effects £406 . 17s. 6d.

The will of William Beggs, lare of Ballykeel, Kilwaughter, county Antrim, farmer, who died 23 September 1885 at same place, was proved at Belfast 2 July 1886 by William McMaster of Duffshill, Carrickfergus, farmer, one of the executors (double probate). Former Grant 20 January 1886. Effects £383 . 17s. 6d.

Letters of administration of the personal estate of Thomas Beggs, late of Kilwaughter, county Antrim, farmer, who died 28 November 1880 at same place, were granted at Belfast 7 January 1881 to Letitia Beggs of Kilwaughter, the widow of said deceased. Effects under £300.]

BEGGS

[Sandstone headstone within railings.] In memory of Ella, daughter of Thos. & Margaret Beggs, Lealies, Kilwaughter who died 6 Jany. 1881 aged 11 months. The above Thós. Beggs died 3rd February 1917. Also his wife Margaret died 14th May 1933. Their grandaughter Ella died 27th June 1940. Their daughter-in-law Mary Ellen died 10th October 1955. Their son Edwin died 18th February 1978.

BEGGS

[Lead lettering in limestone headstone.] Erected by William Beggs in memory of his wife Abigail Beggs, who died 30th May 1886 aged 46 years. Also his daughter Mary Ellen who died 15th January 1885 aged 3 years. Holden, Larne.

BEGGS

[Lead lettering in white limestone.] Erected by Agnes Beggs in memory of her husband Thomas Beggs who died 21st Jan. 1894. Also her son Thomas Beggs who died 17th Dec. 1924. Holden, Larne.

BEGGS
[Sandstone, probably of late nineteenth century.] Erected by Stuart Beggs.

BELL
See WALLACE

BOYD
[Headstone of hammered granite with polished face and enclosure.] Erected by Joseph C. & Agnes Boyd in loving memory of their daughter Agnes who died 5th Sept. 1880 aged 14 years. The above Joseph Boyd died 5th May 1906 aged 80 years. Also their son Joseph Boyd who died 12th May 1911 aged 49 years. Sadly missed. The above-named Agnes Boyd died 21st May 1913 aged 87 years. Also her grandson Robert John Boyd who died 28th Sept. 1917 aged 18 years. Also their great grandson, Josias Clugston Boyd, who died 11th March 1924 aged 4 years. Mary Jane McNEILL, wife of the last named Joseph Boyd, died 28th Aug. 1953 aged 86 years. T. Holden, Larne.

BOYD
[Polished granite headstone in a cement enclosure.] Erected by James Boyd, Ballytober, in memory of his youngest son Archie who died 18th August 1909 aged 18 years. Also his son Samuel, who died 18th July 1884 aged 1 year. Also the above named James Boyd who died 23rd Aug. 1933 in his 90th year. Also his wife Jane Boyd died 6th March 1940 in her 96th year. Also his son Hugh Boyd died 3rd Aug. 1939 in his 67th year. Thomas Boyd, dearly loved husband of Cassie Boyd, died 6th May 1968 aged 79 years. The above Cassie died 14th Dec. 1974 aged 81 years. Also Mary Ann died 29th April 1950 aged 76 years, wife of Hugh Boyd.

BOYD
[Limestone headstone with granite enclosure.] Erected by Jane Boyd in memory of her husband Samuel Boyd who died 17th Decr. 1895 aged 50 years. Also their son John, who died 6th Decr. 1890 aged 14 years. And their three children viz. Matthew, Joseph & Agnes, who died in infancy. Also their daughter Elizabeth, who died 26th Jany. 1900 aged 16 years. Also their son Robert, who died 12th Feby. 1900 aged 11 years. The above-named Jane Boyd, died 5th March 1928, aged 72 years. Also her son William Boyd, died 3rd Oct. 1946, aged 68 years. Also her daughter Mary Jane (Boyd) died 6th Dec. 1946 aged 66 years. Also her son Samuel Boyd, died 26th Oct. 1950 aged 65 years. Also his wife Elizabeth Boyd, died 22nd March 1964 aged 78 years. Jenkins.
[The will of Samuel Boyd, late of Lealies, Kilwaughter, county Antrim, farmer, who died 17 December 1895, was proved at Belfast 10 June 1896 by Robert Boyd of Ballycraigy, Larne, and Joseph Boyd, junior, of Lealies, farmers, executors. Effects £499 . 1s. 1d.]

BOYD
See CALDWELL and McCONNELL

BUCHANAN
See APSLEY

CALDWELL
[One limestone headstone flanked by two smaller polished granite headstones.] Erected by James Caldwell in memory of his parents William Caldwell who died 11th July 1855

aged 84 years. He was a class-leader in the Methodist Society 50 years. His mother Margaret HILL who died 18th February 1859 aged 88 years who like Mary sat at the Master's feet. Also his dearly beloved wife Jane BOYD who died 20th October 1878 aged (5)5 years. His son Wesley who died 9th July 1878, aged 25 years. And two children who died young. The above-named James Caldwell died 24th September 1897 aged 87 years. Also his grandson George Arthur AGNEW died 11th Feby 1888, aged 1 year and 6 months. Also John JAMISON, the beloved husband of Mary Jane Jamison, died 28th Octr. 1904 aged 57 years. "And I heard a voice from heaven saying unto me write, blessed are the dead which die in the Lord. From henceforth, yea saith the spirit that they may rest from their labours, and their works do follow them." Rev. 14 &13. Mary Jane Jamison, wife of the above-named John Jamison and daughter of James Caldwell, who died 10th March 1935 aged 87 years. G. Rankin, York St.

In memory of Herbert H. DAVIS died 10 July 1984 aged 70 years, son of Elizabeth and Joseph S. Davis.

In memory of Elizabeth Creighton Davis died 26th August 1984 aged 95 years, niece of Jane Jamison and widow of Joseph S. Davis, killed in France 1918. Erected by her sons Leslie and Tommy. Capt. Lesley Patterson Davis, RAF/KLM, died 14th Sept.1988, cremated Holland.

[Probate of the will of James Caldwell, late of 14 Mount Collyer Road, Belfast, retired packer, who died 24 September 1897, granted at Belfast 1 November 1897 to William Campbell of 4 Hurst Street, Belfast, architect. Effects £57 . 6s.]

CALDWELL
[Limestone headstone.] Erected by Ann Caldwell in memory of her beloved husband Thomas Hill Caldwell who died 27th March 1892 aged 75 years. And his granddaughter Susan died 1899 aged 4 months. The above-named Ann Caldwell died 9th April 1910 aged 84 years. Gone, but not forgotten. T. Holden, Larne.

CALDWELL
[Polished granite headstone with concrete enclosure.] Erected by John Caldwell in loving memory of his daughters, Elizabeth who died 7th April 1894 aged 13 years, Rebecca who died 28th Nov.1905 aged 4 years, and Elizabeth who died 11th May 1914 aged 19 years. The above-named John Caldwell died 19th Aug. 1933 aged 82 years. And his wife Jane died 16th Aug. 1942 aged 83 years. And his daughter Mary Ann Caldwell died 18th November 1972 aged 89 years.

CLEMENTS
[Tapering monument of polished granite surmounted by draped urn, within iron railings. NE front:-] Erected in memory of David Clements who departed this life 7th June 1880 aged 62 years. Also his wife Jane Clements who departed this life 27th April 1917 aged 88 years. Also their son David who departed this life 30th June 1916 aged 52 years. Also their daughter Margaret who departed this life 2nd Nov. 1921 aged 69 years. Also their daughter Agnes who died 25th April 1932.

[SE side:-] Also their granddaughter-in-law Maggie Jane Clements, who departed this life 26th Sep. 1918 aged 25 years. Also their grand-daughter Martha Jane Clements, who departed this life 25th Oct. 1921 aged 21 years.

[NE side:-] Also their son Andrew Clements, who departed this life 25th March 1924 aged 74 years. Also his daughter Margaret Agnes who died in infancy, and his wife Isabella who departed this life 19th March 1942 aged 82 years. And his son John Clements, 26th September 1959.

COBAIN

[Lead lettering in white marble on sandstone plinth within iron railings.] Erected by Nancy Cobain in memory of her husband Thomas Cobain, who departed this life 8th August 1886 aged 82 years. The above-named Nancy Cobain died 27th June 1890 aged 73 years. Also Margaret HOGG, died 11th February 1955 aged 78 years. Also June ALEXANDER, died 20th September 1970 aged 4 years. The burying place of Thomas Cobain, Kilwaughter.

COOK

[Sandstone headstone.] Erected by John Cook to the memory of his son William who died 23rd Decr. 1881 aged 26 years.

COOKE

[Polished granite headstone.] Erected by Martha Cooke in loving remembrance of her children. Edith died 1st Dec. 1911. Martha died 4th Jan. 1923. Her husband Thomas died 15th Dec. 1944. Also the above Martha Cooke died 21st Nov. 1960. Her youngest daughter Marjorie died 24th March 1978. May died 16th Sept. 1985. Thomas Cooke killed in action Neuve Chapelle 27th Oct. 1914. Andrew Cooke died 14th June 1884. Rachel Cooke died 18th Oct. 1893. Their son Robert Cooke died 22nd Dec. 1925.

CRAIG

See NELSON

CRAWFORD

See APSLEY and HOLDEN

CRAWLEY

See ERSKINE

CROOKS

See SMYTH

CRYMBLE

[Limestone headstone with lead lettering.] Erected by William Crymble in memory of his wife Rose Ann DAVIDSON who died 11th April 1880 aged 41 years. Also his daughter Maggie who died 30th January 1898 aged 22 years. The above-named William Crymble died 24th May 1902 aged 62 years. Eliza HERON, second wife of W. Crymble, who died 6th July 1925. Also her grandson Thomas Hill Crymble died 2nd Jany. 1927. T. Holden.

DAVIDSON

See CRYMBLE and NELSON

DAVIES

See BAILIE

DAVIS

See CALDWELL

DAVISON

See BAILIE

DICKEY
See GREENLEES

DRUMMOND
[Polished granite with stone enclosure.] Erected by John Drummond in memory of his wife Agnes McILWAINE who died 30th October 1883 aged 29 years. Also his daughter Sara Nelson ROBINSON who died 7th April 1898 aged 23 years. His daughter Charlotte who died 25th April 1904 aged 26 years. His grand-child Kathleen Robinson who died 15th Decr 1905 aged 8? years. His son David Nelson Drummond who died 25th March 1917 aged 36 years. The above-named John Drummond died 29th Dec. 1919 in his 69th year.
[Marriage: Aug. 28, at Ballynure Presbyterian Church by Rev. William Kerr, John Drummond, Larne, to Agnes, second daughter of Mr. Robert McIlwaine, Kilwaughter. *Larne Weekly Reporter*, 29 Aug. 1874.]

DRUMMOND
See NELSON

DUNBAR
[Lead lettering in white limestone panel set into sandstone.] Erected by James Dunbar, in memory of his beloved daughter Margaret Emma, who fell asleep in Jesus 24th June 1880, aged 22 years. Also his beloved wife Isabella, who fell asleep in Jesus, 10th Jany. 1892, aged 54 years. Also his beloved son James, who fell asleep in Jesus, 25th June 1924, aged 63 years. Also his youngest daughter Sarah Russell Dunbar, who died 27th November 1954 in her 81st year. A. Jenkins.

ERSKINE
[Limestone headstone.] Erected by Samuel Erskine in memory of his father James Erskine, who died 11th Feby. 1885 aged 60 years. And his mother Agnes Erskine, who died 4th March 1901 aged 73 years. Also Jane, wife of John H. Erskine, who died 16th July 1913 aged 48 years. "Gone, but not forgotten". The above named John H. Erskine died 20th January 1929. Edith CRAWLEY, daughter of above John H. Erskine, who died 1st May 1940. "Be ye also ready". Also Minnie, died 5th Feb. 1980. John, died 9th Aug. 1980. Sam, died 23rd Sept. 1980. Maud, died 7th March 1981. Lily Erskine born 4th March 1892, died 8th April 1988.

ESLER
[Granite headstone and enclosure.] In memory of Robert Esler, born March 1850, died July 1927. Also his wife Agnes NELSON, born 1868, died 1936.
[Written on the enclosure.] Also his daughter Mary, born 1886, died 1889. Also his son David Nelson who died in infancy. Also his grandson Joseph Boyd Esler, born 1922, died 1924. Also his grandson Kennedy Esler who died in infancy.

FERGUSON
See BAILIE

FULLERTON
[Limestone headstone and enclosure.] 1899. Erected by Agnes Fullerton in loving memory of her husband, Edward C. Fullerton who died 22nd October 1898 aged 45 years. The above Agnes Fullerton, died 28th June 1938. And Isabella, wife of William

Fullerton, died 21st June 1956. The above William Fullerton, died 1st September 1957. Jean, wife of Thomas Fullerton, died 18th June 1944. T. Holden, Larne.

[Administration of the estate of Edward Coey Fullerton, late of Ballysnodd, county Antrim, farmer, who died 22 October 1898, granted at Belfast 16 January 1899 to Agnes Fullerton of Ballysnodd, the widow. Effects £519 . 3s. 4d.]

GARDNER
    See NELSON

GILLIES
    [Sandstone headstone with stone enclosure.] Erected by Robert Shiriff Gillies in memory of his beloved wife Mary Jane Shutter Gillies who departed this life on 22nd August 1886 aged 62 years. The above-named Robert Shiriff Gillies died 23rd Sept. 1904 aged 82 years. Also their daughter Jane McNeill died 5th Dec. 1927 aged 82 years.

GINGLES
    [Granite headstone with stone enclosure.] Erected to the memory of William Gingles, Hightown, died 5th Feb. 1888 aged 71 years. Also his wife Agnes Gingles, died 5th Jan. 1899 aged 80 years. Also of their family

Thomas	died	22nd May 1882	aged	31 years.	
William	"	30 Aug. 1896	"	50	"
Matilda	"	29 Mar. 1912	"	69	"
John	"	30 Jun. 1917	"	53	"
Patrick	"	7 Jun. 1927	"	76	"
James	"	2 Jun. 1927	"	69	"
Margaret	"	17 Nov. 1929	"	75	"

. T. Holden, Larne.

[The will of William Gingles, late of Hightown, county Antrim, farmer, who died 7 February 1888 at same place, was proved at Belfast 18 October 1888 by Agnes Gingles and Patrick Gingles, farmer, both of Hightown, the surviving executor. Effects £554 . 19s.

Probate of the will of Agnes Gingles, late of Hightown, Kilwaughter, county Antrim, widow, who died 5 January 1899, granted at Dublin 26 May 1899 to John Gingles of Cross Street, Larne, county Antrim, spirit merchant. Effects £1,098 . 5s. 10d.

Probate of the will of Agnes Gingles, late of Hightown, Kilwaughter, county Antrim, widow, who died 5 January 1899, granted at Dublin 14 August 1899 to William S. Beggs of Larne in said county, merchant. (Former grant 26 May 1899.) Effects £1,113 . 18s. 10d.]

GINGLES
    [Polished granite obelisk surmounted by draped urn.] Erected by Mary Jane Gingles in memory of her husband Thomas Gingles who died 15th Oct. 1910 aged 49 years. Also her son John Drummond who died 18th Nov. 1900 aged 3 years. Samuel M.D. Gingles died 14th October 1923 aged 31 years. Andrew Gingles died Ills., U.S.A., 9th June 1925 aged 39 years. John D. Gingles died 6th December 1930 aged 30 years. The above Mary J. Gingles, born 1866, died 1949, interred Glenview, Ills., U.S.A. Also her daughter Elizabeth, born 1889, died 1949, interred Glenview, Ills., U.S.A. Holden.

GINGLES
    See McNINCH

GRAHAM
    See McCANN

GRAY
    See SMYTH

GREENLEES
    [Limestone.] Erected by Eliza Greenlees in memory of her husband Andrew Greenlees, who died 1st March 1875 aged 57 years. Her daughter Jane, died 1st March 1870 aged 15 years. Her daughter Matilda, died 26 Augt. 1872 aged 19 years. Her daughter Ellen, died 26th Octr. 1875 aged 28 years. Her son Andrew, died 29th Nov. 1880 aged 23 years. And her son Thomas, died 9th Decr. 1887 aged 36 years. Also Thomas MOORE, who died 3rd April 1913 aged 56 years. T. Holden.

    [Letters of administration (with the will annexed) of the personal estate of Andrew Greenlees, late of Ballyedward, county Antrim, farmer, who died 28 February 1875 at same place, were granted at Belfast 31 May 1876 to Eliza Greenlees of Ballyedward, the widow and a legatee. Effects under £200.

    The will of Andrew Greenlees, late of Hightown, county Antrim, farmer, who died 7 October 1882 at same place, was proved at Belfast 1 November 1882 by Thomas Beggs and Andrew Greenlees, both of Kilwaughter in said county, farmers, the executors. Effects £252 . 1s. 6d. NOTE: This is presumably one of the same family.]

GREENLEES
    [Polished granite headstone with enclosure.] Erected by Samuel Greenlees in memory of his father Andrew, 1812-1881. His mother Mary, 1817-1906. His wife Jane, 1875-1915. The above Samuel Greenless 1853-1941. Jenny, wife of Thomas Greenlees, 1902-1948. Bell, Larne.

GREENLEES
    [Sandstone headstone with lead lettering on inset panel of limestone.] Erected by Andrew Greenlees in memory of his beloved wife Elizabeth who died 15th Nov. 1882 aged 31 years. Also his daughter Jenny DICKEY and Agnes Greenlees. His sons David & Thomas. The above-named Andrew Greenlees died 25th September 1906. His twin daughters Lizzie and Maggie who died in Douglas, Nebraska, U.S.A. And his wife Letitia who died 1st July 1944 aged 86 years. And his son Andrew. Also his daughters Mary and Martha who died in North America.

    [Polished granite slab laid flat on same grave plot.] Also daughter Letitia 1890-1978. John Greenlees 1896-1975. James McC. Greenlees 1897-1980. His wife Nance Greenlees 1898-1976 and son Andrew 1926-1969.

    [Lead lettering on granite enclosure.] Samuel Greenlees died 24th April 1961, aged 68 years. Margaret Greenlees 1892 - 1974, wife of Samuel.

GREGG
    [Small headstone.] In memory of Hannah Gregg, who died 15 Octr. 1888, aged 18 years. "Safe in the arms of Jesus."

HAMILTON
    See BAILIE

HAYES
    [Plain granite cross with inscription on base.] In memoriam Hannah Hayes born 9th October 1817, died 7th January 1902. Mary Hayes, born 6th Nov. 1814, died at Kilwaughter Castle 20th March 1886.

HEDGE
See NELSON

HERON
See CRYMBLE

HILL
See CALDWELL

HOGG
See COBAIN

HOLDEN
[Limestone headstone with enclosure.] In memory of Robert Holden, Kilwaughter, who died 23rd October 1887 aged 91 years. Ellen Holden, died 9th May 1893, aged 86 years. Also his grandson Robert James Holden, who died 17th July 1905 aged 3 years and 11 months. Also his wife Agnes Holden, who died 20th Nov. 1912 died 84 years. And his daughter-in-law Eliza Jane Holden, who died 1st Sept. 1938 aged 69 years. And her husband James Holden, who died 17th Oct. 1938 aged 79 years. Also John G. CRAWFORD, died 30th Sept. 1953. Agnes Holden, died 22nd October 1980. Also her brother Robert James Holden died 28th March 1989 aged 80 years.
[The will, with one codicil, of Robert Holden, late of Ballyedward, county Antrim, farmer, who died 23 October 1887 at same place, was proved at Belfast 21 November 1887 by John Arnold and Samuel Holden, both of Browndodd in said county, farmers, the executors. Effects £180 . 10s.]

HOLDEN
[Limestone.] Erected by William Holden, Kilwaughter, in memory of his beloved wife, Agnes NELSON, who died 4th Decr. 1893 aged 60 years. The above-named William Holden died 30th April 1901 aged 68 years. "To be with Christ which is far better." Eliza Holden. T. Holden.
[Letters of administration of the personal estate of Agnes Holden, late of Lealies, Kilwaughter, county Antrim, who died 4 December 1893 at same place, were granted at Belfast 19 July 1895 to William Holden of Dundonald, county Down, farmer, the husband. Effects £325.]

HUMPHREYS
[Sandstone headstone.] In affectionate remembrance of my beloved husband David Humphreys who died 13th Jan. 1892 aged 83 years. His wife Agnes Humphreys died 3rd Jan. 1896 aged 73 years. Also their daughter Jane McKEE died 11th Mar. 1938, aged 79 years. And Thomas McKee husband of the above Jane McKee died 28th Nov. 1942 aged 83 years. And also his brother William who died 8th Dec. 1891 aged 77 years. Jenkins.
[The will of David Humphrey [sic], late of Lowtown, Kilwaughter, county Antrim, farmer, who died 13 January 1892 at same place, was proved at Belfast 14 March 1892 by Alexander Clements of Craiganorne, Kilwaughter, farmer, one of the executors. Effects £362 . 10s.
The will of William Humphries, late of Lowtown, Kilwaughter, county Antrim, retired farmer, who died 8 December 1891 at same place, was proved at Belfast 2 March 1892 by Robert Apsley of Kilwaughter Road, contractor, and Robert McKinstry of Craiganorne, said county, farmer, the executors. Effects £88 . 3s. 10d.]

IRVIN

[Sandstone headstone.] Erected by Susan Irvin in memory of her beloved son James Alexander who died 28th Nov. 1883 aged 13 months.

Oh not lost but gone before us
He can never be forgot.
Heaven's bright mansions shall restored
In sweet ties that perish not.

IRVINE

[Sandstone with limestone panel inset.] Erected by John Irvine in memory of his beloved wife Margaret who died 16th June 1880 aged 57 years. "Sorrow not, even as others who have no hope. Jesus died and rose again." 1 Thess. 13 & 14. A. Jenkins, Larne.

JAMISON

See CALDWELL

LAING

[Polished pink granite with grey granite enclosure.] Erected by Edwin J. Laing in memory of his mother Agnes Laing, died 6th Dec. 1885 aged 56 years. His daughter Agnes died 23rd July 1887 aged 10 years. His father John P. Laing, died 7th April 1901 aged 80 years. His daughter Jenny, died 18th March 1903 aged 24 years. His wife Mary Ann Laing, died 7th March 1910 aged 59 years. William Robert Laing, died 8th Feb. 1929, aged 46 years. Edwin John Laing, died 27th April 1936 in his 82nd year. Edwin Laing, died 26th November 1939 aged 59 years. Samuel Laing, died 16th March 1941 aged 31 years. Sarah Laing, died 3rd July 1945. John Alexander Laing, died 3rd June 1960 aged 80 years. Letitia (Lottie) Laing died 23rd Jan. 1991 aged 80 years.

LYTLE

[Limestone headstone and enclosure.] Erected by Jane BAXTER in memory of my beloved mother Elizabeth Lytle, died 2nd Sept. 1925 aged 73 years. Also her son Thomas, who died 4th May 1896 aged 18 years. Her daughter Sarah, who died 20th Aug. 1898 aged 14 years. Her grand-daughter Margaret J. BARR, who died 24th Aug. 1917 aged 10 years.

MACAULEY

See MOORE

McCANN

[Limestone headstone.] Erected by James McCann, in memory of his beloved wife Mary GRAHAM, who died 8th January 1927 aged 78 years. Also their son Albert Edward, who died November 1883. Also their son Luke Livingstone, who died January 1924 aged 40 years, and interred in Ballycarry. The above James McCann, died 21st December 1933 aged 77 years. Also his son William James, died 16th January 1965. Samuel McCann, died 7th September 1969. Also Margaret Jane McCann died 26th January 1982. T. Holden, Larne.

McCONNELL

[Lead lettering in limestone.] Erected by Joseph McConnell in memory of his mother Margaret McConnell, who died 2nd Sep. 1878 aged 79 years, his brother James who died 5th Nov. 1888 aged 64 years, and his aunt Jane BOYD, who died 10th Oct. 1871 aged

75 years. The above-named Joseph McConnell, died 24th Decr. 1911 aged 85 years. Jenkins.

McCONNELL
See McFERRAN

McCULLOUGH
[Two limestone headstones.] Erected by John McCullough in memory of his wife Jenney NELSON who died 1865 aged 67 years. And their son William who died 1869 aged 33 years. William Nelson who died 1882 aged 64 years. And his wife Isabella Nelson who died 1888 aged 75 years. Also their son and daughter John & Lizzie. Also his wife Jane McCullough of Rorysglen who died 23rd April 1910 aged 86 years. And the above-named John McCullough of Rorysglen who died 9th Dec. 1901 aged 93 years.

In memory of William Nelson who died 6th May 1923 aged 79 years. Also his sons William and Joseph who died in infancy. Also William McILROY who was killed in France. Also his wife Catherine Nelson, who died 4th April 1931 aged 74 years. Also his son William Alexander Nelson, who died 15th September 1933, aged 43 years. "Peace, perfect peace." Erected by his loving wife & family.

McDOWELL
[Lead lettering in limestone headstone, dove with trefoil leaf between sprays of roses.] Erected by William McDowell in loving memory of his son John McDowell who died 1st June 1884 aged 10 years. Also his wife Agnes SNODDY who died 6th July 1901 aged 58 years. Also his daughter Nellie who died 11th Nov. 1914 aged 28 years. The above William McDowell died 1st Sep. 1931 aged 81 years. Also his son Robert who died 29th Dec. 1954 aged 77 years. Also his James McDowell died 16th March 1957 aged 78 years. And his daughter Elizabeth McDowell died 12th May 1957 aged 80 years. T. Holden, Larne.

McDOWELL
[Lead lettering in limestone headstone.] Erected by Martha McDowell, in memory of her husband William McDowell who died 13th May 1895 aged 29 years. Jenkins.

McDOWELL
See WALLACE

McFERRAN
[Limestone headstone with lead lettering, laid flat within a granite enclosure.] 1893. Erected by John McFerran in memory of his dearly beloved daughter Charlotte who died 9th Feb. 1893 aged 20 years. Also his son Robert who died 13th May 1876 aged 16 years. Also his three children who died in infancy. Also his wife Catherine HOLDEN who died 22nd July 1924. The above named John McFerran who died 22nd March 1927. Also his daughter Ellen who died 31st March 1928. Also his daughter Sarah who died 2nd August 1942. His son William James died 7th May 1956. His daughter Margaret died 4th April 1964. Also his daughters Annie died 20th April 1967. Mary McCONNELL died 27th Sep. 1967. "Safe in God's keeping". Jenkins, Larne.

McGAREL
See BAILIE

McGEE
[Sandstone headstone.] Erected by William McGee, Moordyke, in memory of his daughter Agnes who died 7th Sept. 1890 aged 7 years. Also his son William John who died 30th Oct. 1890 aged 12 years. And two children who died in infancy. Also his wife Janet McGee who died 3rd Oct. 1898 aged 52 years. "Thou are not forgotten, nor ever wilt thou be – so long as life & memory last, we'll ever think of thee". By her son Henry. The above William MAGEE, who died 19th June 1922 aged 78 years.

McGOOKIN
[Limestone headstone.] Erected by John McGookin, in loving memory of his daughter Matilda, who died 3rd September 1887. Also his son Henry, who died 22nd April 1915. Also his son Joseph K. McGookin, who died 17th May 1919 aged 27 years. Also his beloved wife Nancy McGookin, who died 24th Nov. 1921 aged 73 years. Also the above named John McGookin who died 17th May 1926 aged 76 years. T. Holden, Larne.

McILROY
See McCULLOUGH

McILWAINE
[Polished granite headstone.] Erected by Charlotte McIlwaine in memory of her husband Robert McIlwaine who died 5th Novr. 1905 aged 81 years. Also her son Robert, who died 20th April 1905 aged 44 years. And her son Edward who died 1st Jany. 1869 aged 2 years. The above-named Charlotte McIlwaine who died 22nd July 1910 aged 82 years. Also her grand-daughter Ella May McIlwaine died 7th August 1937 aged 21 years. Also Edward, son of Charlotte and Robert McIlwaine, died 9th March 1955 aged 85 years. Also Margaret, wife of above Edward, died 1st November 1956. T. Holden, Larne.

McILWAINE
See DRUMMOND and WORKMAN

McKEE
See HUMPHREYS

McKINSTRY
[Granite headstone with enclosure.] Erected by Joseph Alexander McKinstry in memory of his father Robert, died 2nd December 1938. Also his mother Martha, died 15th August 1899. Interred in Rashee Cemetery. Also his stepmother Rose Ann, died 7th April 1972. Also the above named Joseph died 4th July 1975. Also his sister Agnes, died 4th July 1977. Margaret A., died 26th September 1981. Also Robert died 19th January 1983.

McNAIR
See APSLEY

McNEILL
See BOYD and GILLIES

McNINCH
[Four granite headstones in stone enclosure.] John McNinch, Hightown, died 20th July 1887. Ann Jane his wife, 2nd January 1894. Isabella, 4th May 1873, buried in Old Cemetery. George, 12th May 1909. Robert, 22nd January 1928. T. Holden.

William McNinch, Belfast, died 17th February 1919. Anna Bella his wife, 2nd Oct. 1880. Anna Bella his daughter, 26th March 1916. Mary Josephine his daughter, 2nd November 1936. T. Holden.

Joseph McNinch M.D., Larne, died 3rd June 1902. And his wife Sarah died 14th October 1953. William McNinch, younger son, died 25th March 1960 aged 62 years. Samuel George McNinch died 6th Feb. 1966 aged 70 years, elder son of Joseph and Sarah McNinch. T. Holden.

In memory of Robert Bailie McNinch, Larne, born 5th Feby. 1870, died 9th July 1908. Hugh Bailie McNinch born 6th Sept. 1875, died at Texas, U.S.A., 19th June 1909. Their mother Marianne, wife of John McNinch, Larne, born 25th May 1846, died 16th Feb. 1915. John McNinch, born 25th July 1873, died 2nd Dec. 1918, interred in City Cemetery. The above John McNinch, Larne, born 24th Jan. 1841 died 21st Jan. 1922. Isa McNinch, last surviving daughter of the above John and Marianne McNinch, died 22nd August 1948. Jenkins.

[The will of John McNinch, late of Hightown, Kilwaughter, county Antrim, farmer, who died 20 July 1887 at same place, was proved at Belfast 9 March 1888 by John McNinch of Larne, merchant, and Robert McNinch of Hightown, farmer, both in said county, the executors. Effects £102 . 6s. 1d.

Joseph McNinch was born on 24 January 1856, son of the above John McNinch of Kilwaughter. He studied medicine at Queen's College, Belfast, graduating M.D. in 1883. He practised first in Ballyclare and from c 1890 in Pound Street, Larne. He married on 7 October 1892 Sarah Smiley, daughter of Samuel Smiley, farmer, of Dromaine, Larne.]

McNINCH
[Inscription on base of granite Celtic cross.] In memory of Robert McNinch, born 25th Aug. 1881, died 8th June 18(9)9. James Watt McNinch, born 22nd March 1888, died 14th Septr. 1911. Harry J. McNinch, born 1st July 1890, died 18th April 1925. Hugh McNinch born March 1883, died Feby. 1936, interred at Yanderra, N.S. Wales.

McNINCH
[Granite obelisk.] Erected by John McNinch, Seamount, in memory of his wife Barbara GINGLES, born 8 Oct. 1840, died 27 Aug. 1902. The above named John McNinch, born 24th Sep. 1839, died 20th June 1925. Mary McNinch, born Aug. 1871, died June 1937. Andrew McNinch, born 9th June 1869, died 28th May 1941. Ellen Watt McNinch, born 13th Nov. 1873, died 6th April 1959. John McNinch, born Feb. 1878, died Nov. 1929, interred in Battleford, Canada. John E.W. McNinch, born May 1900, died May 1974. Robert McNinch, born 27th June 1867, died 7th Oct. 1873.

MAGEE
[Limestone headstone.] Erected by Jane Magee in memory of her beloved husband William Magee who died 18th November 1882 aged 75 years. And their daughter Lizzie MENEELY who died 5th Feby. 1901. The above-named Jane Magee died 4th May 1904. And her granddaughter Maudie TAYLOR who died 25th March 1908. And her daughter Margaret AGNEW who died 21st Oct. 1909. Also of Thomas Agnew who died 24th September 1923.

MAGEE
See McGEE

MAGILL
[Polished granite headstone.] In memory of William A. Magill, Kilwaughter, born July 1883, died March 1897. His father William Magill, born Feb. 1839, died July 1927. Margaret, wife of above-named William Magill, died 18th December 1936. Their daughter Margaret Magill died 19th December 1950. Their daughter Mary Magill died 26th December 1955. Their daughter Nellie Magill died 5th Feb. 1957. Jenkins.

MAGILL
[Polished granite headstone.] Erected by Sarah Magill in memory of her husband Hugh Magill, who died 28th Nov. 1925 aged 77 years. The above named Sarah Magill who died 18th Jany 1928 aged 78 years. Also her grand-daughters Martha & Charlotte, who died in infancy. Also her son William James who died 7th June 1973 aged 84 years.

MAGILL
See NELSON

MAXWELL
[Lead lettering in limestone headstone.] Erected by Samuel Maxwell in loving memory of his daughter Elizabeth, who died 21st May 1894 aged 6 years. Also his wife Lizzie, who died 6th February 1910 aged 58 years. The above-named Samuel Maxwell, died 11th Nov. 1919 aged 68 years. "God's will be done." Also his daughter Agnes ALLEN died 24th May 1949, interred in Cairncastle. Holden.

MEHAFFEY
[Limestone headstone.] Erected by Matthew Mehaffey, in loving memory of his mother Matilda Mehaffey, who died 11th July 1890 aged 38 years. Also his father Robert Mehaffey who died 28th April 1922 aged 74 years. Also his son Matthew, who died 12th June 1963 aged 38 years. And his son Robert James who died 27th April 1983. Precious memories of a dear son and brother Jason Robert Gilbert died 3rd March 1997 aged 26 years. J. Bell, Larne.
  [Flower vase on grave] Mehaffey, L.O.L. 1297, R.B.P. 47.
  [The will of Matilda Mehaffey, late of Hightown, Kilwaughter, county Antrim, wife of Robert Mehaffey, who died 11 July 1890 at same place, was proved at Belfast 22 September 1890 by Hugh Bailie of Rory's Glen, Kilwaughter, farmer, the sole executor. Effects £23 . 15s.]

MEHARG
[Sandstone headstone.] Erected by John Meharg junr. in memory of his father John Meharg who died 2nd Sept. 1900 aged 60 years. Also his brother William Hood Meharg who died 13th November 1913 aged 46 years.
  [Administration of the estate of John Meharg, late of Browndod, Larne, county Antrim, farmer, who died 2 September 1900 at Ballyhampton, Larne, granted at Dublin 8 June 1901 to James Meharg, farmer. Effects £391 . 13s. 4d.]

MENEELY
See MAGEE

MILLER
See SMYTH

MOLYNEUX
See BAILIE

MOORE
[Limestone headstone with granite enclosure.] Erected by John Moore, Drumsough, in memory of his daughter Emily, who died 26th Sept. 1888 aged 19 years. Also his daughter Maggie, who died 29th March 1890 aged 29 years. And his wife Jane Moore who died 26th Feby. 1902 aged 69 years. The above-named John Moore, died 15th June 1912 aged 80 years. Maria Ellen Moore, born 9th Jan. 1874, died 7th Sept. 1916. And his daughter Mary Moore died 12th Nov. 1951 aged 89 years. His son James Moore, born 15th Aug. 1864, died 30th May 1952. His daughter Elizabeth MACAULEY, born 17th Oct. 1866, died 21st March 1957. T. Holden, Larne.

MOORE
[Lead lettering in white limestone.] In memory of William Moore who died at Larne Harbour, 27th October 1892. And his two sons William and Robert. Also his wife Jenny Betty WALLACE who died 9th November 1907. T. Holden, Larne.

MOORE
See GREENLEES

MORRISON
See APSLEY and RAINEY

MULLEN
[Limestone.] Erected to the memory of Sarah Mullen of Ballyboley, Larne, who died 21st March 1892 aged 82 years. And her daughter Ann who died 4th Sept. 1897 aged 66 years. "Gone to Christ"

NELSON
[Limestone monument with granite enclosure. Front, southwest] A.D. 1885. In memoriam WN & TN. Erected by William Hugh and Thomas Nelson in memory of their uncle Thomas Nelson who died 16th Sep. 1884 aged 62 years.
    [Northwest] Also of their father William Nelson who died 22nd April 1865 aged 35 years. Also his son Thomas who died 2nd October 1899 aged 35 years. Interred in Strabane Cemetery. Also his son-in-law Wm. H. CRAIG who died 8th July 1934 aged 72 years.
    [Southeast] William Hugh Nelson, born 3rd Novr. 1859, died 18th May 1891. Also Maggie J. Craig, born 2nd December 1896, died 24th July 1929. Margaret, wife of Wm. H. Craig, died 27th August 1940. William HEDGE 1899-1981. Molly Hedge 1899-1982.
    [Death: Apr. 22, at his residence, Mill Street, Larne, William Nelson, carpenter, aged 34 years. *Larne Weekly Reporter,* 29 Apr. 1865.]
    [The will of Thomas Nelson, late of Larne, county Antrim, spirit merchant, who died 16 September 1884 at same place, was proved at Belfast 6 October 1884 by James Morrow, manager of Ulster Bank Branch, Patrick Crawford and William Hugh Nelson, spirit merchants, all of Larne, the executors. Effects &,848 . 8s. 11d.
    The will of William Hugh Nelson, late of Larne, county Antrim, gentleman, who died 19 May 1891 at same place, was proved at Belfast1 July 1891 by James Morrow, bank manager, and Patrick Crawford, spirit merchant, both of Larne, the executors. Effects £6,513 . 2s. 4d.]

NELSON
[Square column of polished granite surmounted by draped urn. Front, southwest] Erected by David Nelson, Esq., J.P., Larne, to the memory of the following who are interred in Kilwaughter Old Graveyard viz. his mother Agnes Hill Nelson who died 31st Jany. 1868 aged 75 years. His father William Nelson who died 17th July 1871 aged 83 years. The above-named David Nelson, died 31st March 1896 aged 66 years and is interred here. David McKee Nelson, born 2st October 1900, died 27th March 1995.

[Northwest] Also to the memory of his sister Jenny Nelson who died 10th Augt. 1839 aged 16 years. His sister Rachel Nelson WALLACE who died 17th Augt. 1879 aged 59 years. Her husband William Wallace who died 30th June 1867 aged 62 years.

[Southeast] Also to the memory of his brother, Robert Nelson, who died 8th Octr. 1854, aged 27 years. His sister Sarah Nelson DRUMMOND, who died 4th June 1853 aged 28 years. Her husband William Drummond, who died in Australia, 1853. Their son William N. Drummond who died in infancy. Bessbrook Granite Co.

[The will of William Nelson, senior, late of Rorysglynn [sic], Kilwaughter, county Antrim, farmer, who died 17 July 1871 at same place, was proved at Belfast 7 August 1872 by the oaths of Andrew Nelson of Ballyhempton, Larne, farmer, and David Nelson of Larne, woollen draper, both in county Antrim, the executors. Effects under £800.

The will of David Nelson, late of Inver Lodge, Larne, county Antrim, draper, who died 31 March 1896, was proved at Belfast 29 June 1896 by John Drummond, spirit merchant, David A. Nelson, draper, and John McNinch, grocer, all of Larne, executors. Effects £31,304 . 7s. Re-sworn £31,676 . 1s. 6d.

The will of Rachel Wallace, late of Kilwaughter, county Antrim, widow, who died 17 August 1879 at same place, was proved at Belfast 3 May 1880 by the oaths of Andrew Nelson of Ballyhempton, farmer, David Nelson of Larne, woollen draper, and John Drummond of Larne, publican, all in said county, the executors. Effects under £800.

The will of William Wallace, late of Kilwaughter, county Antrim, farmer, who died 30 June 1867 at same place, was proved at Belfast 13 August 1867 by the oath of David Nelson of Larne in said county, woollen draper, one of the executors. Effects under £800.]

NELSON
[Granite with polished face.] Erected by Hugh Nelson in memory of his beloved wife Mary MAGILL who died 18th Sep. 1871 aged 28 years. His son Thomas died 26th Nov. 1882 aged 11 years. His son Robert died 1st July 1887 aged 10 years. His daughter Jemima died 19th May 1891 aged 6 years. His daughter Margaret died 2nd March 1892 aged 12 years. His daughter Jenny died 9th March 1897 aged 18 years. His daughter Mary A. died 11th April 1897 aged 10 years. Also his wife Mary A. Nelson, who died 8th Decr. 1809 aged 52 years. His son Andrew, Irish Guards, killed in action 13th Sept. 1916 aged 19 years, buried at Combles, France. His son David died 24th March 1919 aged 27 years. The above-named Hugh Nelson died 7th Oct. 1921 aged 86 years. T. Holden.

NELSON
[Granite headstone and enclosure.] Erected by Andrew Nelson, Ballyhempton, in memory of his beloved wife Jane DAVIDSON who died 26th Jany. 1882 aged 56 years. Also their son Matthew who died 24th Feby. 1880 aged 15 years. Their son Thomas Davidson who died 27th Novr. 1888 aged 18 years. Their daughter Agnes who died 17th June 1893 aged 26 years. The above-named Andrew Nelson died 6th March 1904 aged 81 years. Their son William Robert who died 21st Aug. 1931 aged 77 years. Also their daughter Annie who died 27th Nov. 1937 aged 78 years.

[Marriage: December 31 in Ervey Presbyterian Church, Co. Cavan, by the Rev. John Wilson, William Robert eldest son of Andrew Nelson, Loughview House, Ballyhempton,

Larne, to Annie third daughter of George R. Archibald, Deescart, Carrickmacross, Co. Monaghan. *Larne Reporter*, 3 Jan. 1891.]

NELSON

[Lead lettering in limestone headstone.] In memory of John Nelson, Rorysglen, who died 15th Dec. 1891 aged 52 years. His father James Nelson, who died 8th Nov. 1880 aged 68 years. His mother Margaret Nelson, who died 14th Dec. 1891 aged 72 years.

[The will of John Nelson. late of Rorysglen, Kilwaughter, county Antrim, no occupation, who died 15 December 1891 at same place, was proved at Belfast 3 May 1892 by Hugh Nelson of Rorysglen, farmer, and John Drummond of Larne in said county, spirit merchant. the executors. Effects £250 . 4s. 2d.

Letters of administration of the personal estate of James Nelson, late of Kilwaughter, county Antrim, farmer, who died 8 November 1880 at same place, were granted at Belfast 29 November 1892 to Margaret Nelson of Kilwaughter, the widow of said deceased. Effects £300.

Letters of administrationof the personal estate of Margaret Nelson, late of Rorysglen, Kilwaughter, county Antrim, widow, who died 14 Decembed 1891 at same place, were granted at Belfast 15 June 1892 to William Nelson of Moordyke, Kilwaughter, farmer, the son. Effects £147 . 3s.]

NELSON

[Polished granite headstone. Arms:-barry, three dexter hands. Crest:- a hand holding a spear.] Erected by William Nelson in loving memory of his wife Eliza Nelson, died 14th October 1909 aged 62 years. His daughter Agnes died 27th July 1908 aged 36 years. His daughter Mary died 1880. And his grandson Stafford GARDNER died 27th August 1915. Also the above named William Nelson died 24th March 1933 aged 92 years. J. Bell, Larne.

NELSON

[Polished granite headstone with enclosure.] Erected by William Nelson, Burnside, in memory of his father William Nelson, who died 16th Feb. 1885 aged 66 years. And his mother Jane Nelson who died 15th April 1901 aged 82 years. Also his sister Sarah who died 1st May 1901 aged 43 years. The above-named William Nelson died 6th December 1914 aged 67 years. T. Holden.

[The will of William Nelson, late of Lealies, Kilwaughter, county Antrim, farmer, who died 16 February 1895 at same place, was proved at Belfast 22 July 1885 by David Nelson of Larne in said county, draper, John Nelson of Holywood, county Down, commercial traveller, and William Nelson of Lealies, farmer, the executors. Effects £1,178 . 5s.]

NELSON

[Polished granite headstone.] Sacred to the memory of Alexander Nelson, who died 6th Feby 1891 aged 70 years. Also his wife Jenny Locke Nelson who died 24th Feby 1908 aged 84 years. Also their son Samue who died at Ballygally 1st Augt. 1911 aged 61 years. Also their daughter Isabella WILSON who died 12th June 1919 aged 52 years. Also their son James who died 5th March 1921 aged 70 years. Also their daughter Sarah who died young. Also their daughter Mary, died 8th Decr. 1927 aged 72 years. Also their daughter Jane who died 3rd April 1943 aged 78 years.

[Death: Feb. 6 at his residence, Ballysnodd, Larne, Alexander Nelson, aged 70 years. Funeral on Sunday evening at half past two o'clock. *Larne Reporter,* 7 Feb. 1891.]

[The will of Alexander Nelson , late of Ballysnodd, Inver, county Antrim, farmer, who died 6 February 1891 at same place, was proved at Belfast 29 July 1891 by James Nelson of Ballywillan and Samuel Nelson of Ballysnodd, both in said county, farmers, the executors. Effects £887.]

NELSON

[Polished granite headstone with concrete enclosure.] Erected by Robert A. Nelson in memory of his sister Lizzie who died 15th Nov. 1891 aged 36 years. Also his father James Nelson who died 10th June 1901 aged 72 years. Also his mother Rachel Hill Nelson who died 9th Feb. 1902 aged 71 years. The above-named Robert A. Nelson died 12th Aug. 1917 aged 54 years. And his wife Martha died 12th Nov. 1935 aged 69 years. His sister Sarah Jane died 16th Mar. 1919 aged 66 years. Also his grand-daughter Martha Gibson (Maureen) Nelson who died 28th Feb. 1937 in her 12th year. [T. Holden.]

[Small headstone on enclosure.] In memory of James Nelson, J.P. died 4th April 1977, beloved husband of Henrietta, who died 12th May 1987.

NELSON

[Polished granite headstone.] In loving memory of Annie Jane Nelson who died 8th August 1897. Also her father David Nelson who died 22nd May 1906. Hastings, Larne.

NELSON

[Granite headstone.] Erected by Alice M. Nelson, Co. Monaghan, in memory of her husband James Nelson who died 11th April 1913 aged 50 years. Their son Andrew who died 26th Sep. 1897 aged 2? years. Their son David Arthur who died 4th June 1917 from wounds received in action in France aged 20 years.

NELSON

[Granite headstone.] Erected to the memory of Robert Nelson who died 12th January 1919 aged 66 years. Also his daughter Janey who died 22nd January 1898 aged 5 years. Also his son Samuel W. Nelson who died from wounds received in action 31st August 1916 aged 20 years. Interred in Souvenier Cemetery, St. Omer, France. Also his wife Mary Nelson died 16th April 1937 aged 73 years. T. Holden, Larne.

NELSON

See APSLEY, ESLER, HOLDEN and McCULLOUGH

RAINEY

[Dove in flight with trefoil leaf in its beak. Lead lettering in limestone headstone, in a polished granite enclosure.] Erected by William Rainey in memory of his son Robert James Beggs who died 10th May 1881 aged 8 years. Also his son John who died 1st Decr. 1883 aged 17 years. And of his brother Thomas Rainey, Chief Officer of the ship *Louis Walshe*, who died at sea 19th Aug. 1888 aged 42 years. Also his wife Mary Rainey who died 7th Feby. 1909 aged 75 years. Also his grand-daughter Madge Rainey who died 1st Aug. 1916 aged 18 years. The above-named William Rainey died 8th April 1921 aged 78 years. Also his grand-daughter Mary Rainey who died 5th March 1922 aged 21 years. Also his youngest son Isaac who died 5th Jan. 1930 aged 52 years. Also his youngest daughter Letty MORRISON who died 11th June 1931 aged 56 years interred in Handsworth New Cemetery. Also his eldest daughter Mary Rainey who died 21st Jan. 1945 aged 76 years. Also his eldest son Henry Rainey who died 27th Dec. 1952 aged 82 years. Also his grand-daughter Helen Rainey who died 19th Jan. 1977. Also his grand-son William Rainey who died 30th May 1986, interred Bellevue Cemetery, California, U.S.A. Jenkins.

RAINEY

[Polished granite in a matching enclosure.] Erected by Isaac Rainey in loving memory of his father Isaac Rainey who died 2nd June 1897 aged 85 years. His mother Jane Rainey died 13th Nov. 1900 aged 81 years. His sister Eliza Jane died 24th Jany. 1915 aged 65 years. His wife Mary Rainey died 28th February 1931 aged 73 years. The above-named Isaac Rainey died 7th July 1948 aged 97 years.

[Limestone monument lying flat.] In loving memory of Norman Allan Rainey who died 12th April 1966 aged 28 years. Also his father Hugh who died 2nd October 1982 aged 87 years.

REA

[Polished granite headstone and enclosure.] Erected by Alexander & Patrick Rea in loving memory of their father Thomas Rea who died 23rd June 1915 aged 69 years. Also their mother Ann Jane Rea who died 28th April 1921 aged 70 years. Also their brother Robert who died 14th April 1887 aged 1? years. Also their grandmother Mary Rea who died 10th Nov. 1894 aged 74 years. Also Elizabeth, died 17th September 1959 wife of Alexander Rea. The above Alexander Rea died 17th November 1966. Martha Rea who died 16th January 1985, wife of William Nelson Rea. The above William Nelson Rea died 17th June 1987. T. Holden.

REA

[Lead lettering in limestone headstone with concrete enclosure.] Erected by Thomas Rea in memory of his father Thomas Rea died 3rd Jan. 1893. His mother Jane died 2nd May 1904. And his nephew John, died 27th July 1895. Also his sister Jane, died 25th September 1929. The above Thomas Rea, died 6th May 1946 aged 92 years.

REA

[Lead lettering in limestone headstone.] Erected by John Rea, in memory of his wife Mary Rea who died 9th March 1898 aged 60 years. The above-named John Rea died 31st Dec. 1901 aged 61 years. T. Holden, Larne.

ROBINSON

[Lead lettering in limestone headstone.] Erected by Margaret Robinson, in memory of her beloved husband John Robinson who died 4th Jany. 1885 aged 79 years. Also her son James Thomas died 17th Decr. 1890 aged 19 years. And her brother-in-law Samuel Robinson who died 9th Feby. 1894 aged 83 years. The above-named Margaret Robinson died 4th May 1915 aged 76 years. Also her son Robert who died 1st May 1930. T. Holden, Larne.

[The will with one codicil of Samuel Robinson, late of Ballyhampton, Kilwaughter, county Antrim, farmer, who died 9 February 1894 at same place, was proved at Belfast 27 April 1894 by Hugh Wilson of Drumaho and John McNinch of Seamount, Knocknagulliagh, both in said county, farmers, the executors. Effects £55 . 4s. 3d.]

ROBINSON

See DRUMMOND and WALLACE

SERVICE

[Polished granite headstone.] Erected by Robert Service, Gogry, in memory of his father John Service who died 2nd June 1882 aged 87 years. His mother Margaret Service who died 17th Aug. 1886 aged 80 years. His brother Thomas who died 2nd Oct. 1871 aged 41 years. His sister Margaret who died 6th June 1899 aged 71 years. His wife Mary Eliza

Service who died [blank]. The above-named Robert Service died 25th Sept. 1916 aged 81 years.

SHAW
See WHITE

SMYTH
[Sandstone with inset panel of limestone.] Erected by Hugh Smyth in memory of his wife Isabella MILLER who died 25th Feby. 1885 aged 48 years. Also of his children, Henry died 17th May 1870 aged 2 years, Mary died 18th May 1870 aged 5 years, Daniel died 26th Feb. 1880 aged 9 years. The above Hugh Smyth, died 31st Oct. 1889 aged 52 years.

SMYTH
[Limestone.] Erected by Samuel Smyth in loving memory of his mother Sarah CROOKS who departed this life 2nd Augt. 1900 aged 65 years. His sister Charlotte who died 25th April 1883 aged 22 years. And his brother Robert John died 19th Oct. 1891 aged 19 years. T. Holden, Larne.

SMYTH
[Limestone, beside and similar to foregoing.] Erected by Samuel Smyth, in loving memory of his wife Ellen GRAY, who departed this life 12th Oct. 1900 aged 42 years. Also their 3 daughters Charlotte, Elizabeth, Eliza Jane, and Susana. The above-named Samuel Smyth, died 28th Aug. 1917 aged 63 years. T. Holden, Larne.

SNODDY
See McDOWELL

STEWART
See BARR

TAYLOR
See MAGEE

WALLACE
[Polished granite headstone surmounted by draped urn, with enclosure.] Erected by Sarah Nelson McDOWELL in memory of her grand-father William Wallace who departed this life 30th June 1867 aged 62 years. Her grand-mother Rachel Wallace who departed this life 17th Augt. 1879 aged 59 years. The above-named Sarah Nelson McDowell departed this life 8th Decr. 1893 aged 30 years.
[The will of William Wallace, late of Kilwaughter, county Antrim, farmer, who died 30 June 1867 at same place, was proved at Belfast 12 August 1867 by the oath of David Nelson of Larne in said county, woollen draper, one of the executors. Effects under £800.
The will of Rachel Wallace, late of Kilwaughter, county Antrim, widow, who died 17 August 1879 at same place, was proved at Belfast 3 May 1880 by the oaths of Andrew Nelson of Ballyhempton, farmer, David Nelson of Larne, woollen draper, and John Drummond of Larne, publican, all in said county, the executors. Effects under £800.
The will, with one codicil, of Sarah Nelson McDowell, late of Lealies, Kilwaughter, county Antrim, spinster, who died 8 December 1893 at same place, was proved at Belfast 2 February 1894 by David Nelson, J.P., and John Drummond, merchant, both of Larne in said county, the executors. Effects £152 . 10s.]

WALLACE
[Polished granite.] Erected by Susan Wallace in memory of her father Robert Wallace (Moordyke) who died 24th August 1882. Her mother Mary Wallace, died 19th Dec. 1899. Also her brother John Wallace died 4th Feb. 1932. And her two neices Mary ROBINSON and Agnes BELL. H. Bell, Larne.

[The will of Robert Wallace, late of Moordyke, Kilwaughter, county Antrim, farmer, who died 24 August 1882 at same place, was proved at Belfast 25 September 1882 by John Drummond of Larne, spirit merchant, and Robert Nelson of Rorysglen, Kilwaughter, farmer, both in said county, the executors. Effects £97.]

WALLACE
See MOORE and NELSON

WHITE
[Lead lettering in limestone headstone.] Erected by Agnes White in memory of her husband William White died 11th June 1892 aged 86 years. The above-named Agnes White died 2nd Novr. 1906 aged 86 years. Also their grandson George Anson Shaw White, died 6th January 1921. Also the dearly loved wife of William James White, Martha Samima SHAW, who died 6th January 1931 and devoted mother of above named George. The above named William James White died 14th September 1940. T. Holden.

[The will of William White, late of Ballyrickardmore, Raloo, county Antrim, farmer, who died 10 [sic] June 1892 at same place, was proved at Belfast 25 July 1892 by John White of 16 Mayne Street, Belfast, grocer, and Matthew McRoberts of Ballygowan, Raloo, farmer, the executors. Effects £191 . 17s. 6d.]

WILSON
[Polished granite headstone and enclosure.] In loving memory of Hugh Wilson died 26th May 1916. And his wife Annie died 28th March 1924. Also their children Robert and Samuel died in infancy. James died 25th April 1884. Letitia died 1887. John B. died 10th Feb. 1945. Margaret died 11th Feb. 1948. Tillie died 23rd Nov. 1960.

WILSON
See NELSON

WORKMAN
[Lead lettering in limestone headstone.] Erected by Robert McILWAINE in memory of his grand-mother Mary Workman who died 11th March 1887 aged 76 years. Also his father John McIlwaine who died 29th October 1892 aged 69 years. His sister Mary who died 12th March 1899 aged 16 years. His brother Edward who died 21st May 1899 aged 19 years. His brother John who died 12th December 1899 aged 22 years. His brother Henry who died 23rd February 1903 aged 19 years. And his mother Ann McIlwaine who died 12th May 1903 aged 58 years. The above-named Robert McIlwaine died 28th October 1905 aged 33 years. His sister Sarah who died 11th January 1908 aged 23 years. T. Holden, Larne.

[The will of John McIlwaine, late of Craiganorne, county Antrim, farmer, who died 22 October 1892 at same place, was proved at Belfast 21 July 1893 by Robert McIlwaine of Craiganorne, and Henry McIlwaine, junior, of Headwood, both in said county, farmers, the executors. Effects £434 . 10s.]

KILWAUGHTER OLD GRAVEYARD

O.S. Antrim 40. Grid Ref. D356015

This is in the townland of Demesne, civil parish of Kilwaughter, and barony of Upper Glenarm. It is in the midst of a farmyard, being partly bounded by the stables of Kilwaughter Castle and partly by a purpose-built wall of black stone. Until it weathered into illegibility, a painted sign placed at the gate by the Poor Law Guardians displayed their conditions. Burials ceased here in the middle of the twentieth century and the graveyard has become very wild and overgrown. All inscriptions have been copied.

ADAMS
>Here lyeth the body of Robert Adams who died Sep. 4th 1756 aged 47 years. Also his son Robe(rt) who died Oct. 22d 1782 aged 36 years.

ADAMS
>[Sandstone headstone.] Erected in memory of Jane Adams, who departed this life March the 24th 1785 years aged 55 years.

ADRAIN
>Erected by Robert Adrain in memory of his mother Martha Adrain who died 5th March 1852 aged 73 years. Also his father Hugh Adrain who died 8th Novr. 1861 aged 73 years. Also his son Robert who died 10th Sept. 1868 aged 17 years. [Along upper edge] 1 grave north & 1 south.

Kilwaughter Castle (reproduced by permission of
the Public Record Office of Northern Ireland, W.L. 1574).

ADRIAN
>See WINNARD

AGNEW
>[Green slate next to Elizabeth Agnew d.1811.] Erected by W. Agnew in memory of his son William who died in infancy.

AGNEW
>[Large slate with arms:- a chevron, in chief two gillyflowers, in base three saltires couped barwise. Crest:- an eagle(?) displayed. Motto:- Concilio non impetu.] Erected by John Agnew in memory of Elizabeth Agnew who departed this life June the XIth AD MDCCCXI aged XV years.
>>O happy youth with graces blest
>>To whom the Lord has given rest.
>>Also his wife Margt. who departed this life May 1825 aged 66 yrs. Also John Agnew who died Mar. 1839 aged (78) yrs.

AGNEW
>[Fallen forward.] Erected by James Agnew of Cambridge St., Belfast, in memory of his beloved mother Margaret Agnew who departed this life on the 12th day of October 1863 aged 64 years. Also his beloved father Samuel Agnew who died on the 6th day of February 1871 aged 74 years. Also Samuel, James, & Mary Jane Agnew, 3 children of James Agnew, all of whom died in infancy.

AGNEW
>[Slate propped against north wall.] Agnes Agnew died 2nd June 1896 aged 82 years.

AGNEW
>See BAILIE

ALEXANDER
>[Sturdy grey-green slate with arms:- a chevron, in base a crescent, all counterchanged per pale. Crest:- a horse's head bridled and reined. Motto:- Ducitur non trahitur.] Here lyeth the body of Janet BOYD wife to James Alexander who died May the 19th 1762 aged 43 years. Agnes CRAIG died 1784 aged 7 years.

ALEXANDER
>See CALDWELL

ALLEN
>See CURREY

ANDERSON
>Mary Anderson who died young.

BAILIE
>[A monument comprising three panels of white limestone set into sandstone in a railed enclosure.] 1877. In memory of Hugh Bailie of Kilwaughter who died August 12th 1833 aged 72 years. And Agnes his wife who died April 1st 1826 aged 59 years.
> Robert Bailey of Larne who died March 25th 1857 aged 48 years. And Mary Ann his wife who died March 4th 1876 aged 72 years. Also their son Robert who died at New

Orleans October 7th 1849 aged 18 years.

William Bailie of Kilwaughter who died June 26th 1872 aged 73 years. And Agnes his wife who died March 29th 1870 aged 71 years. Also their son James who died Sept. 25th 1861 aged 26 years. And their grandson Hugh who died Nov. 23rd 1875 aged 6 months.

[The will of William Bailie, late of Rory`s Glen, Kilwaughter, county Antrim, farmer, who died 26 June 1872 at same place, was proved at Belfast 16 October 1872 by the oaths of Robert Hill Bailie of Shanoguestown, Dunadry, and Hugh Bailie of Kilwaughter, Larne, both in said county farmers, the executors. Effects under £4,000.]

BAILIE

[Lead lettering on white limestone panel set into sandstone, in a low railed enclosure.] Erected by Robert H. Bailie of Summerhill, Dunadry, in memory of his aunt Jane AGNEW, formerly of Richfield, Ohio, America, who died at Kilwaughter 30th April 1871 aged 77 years. Also her only child Jane who died at Richfield 2nd Jany. 1867 aged 29 years. Jenkins.

BALLANTINE

[Fallen, in railings with succeeding stone.] Sacred to the memory of William Ballantine of Craggyhill who departed this life 14th Nov. 1835 aged 77 years. Erected by his sons, viz. Thos. & Wm. Also his wife Janet who departed this life on the 19th of March 1849 aged 80 years. Likewise their son William who died 17th Jany. 1850 aged 49 years. And of their son Thomas of Ballyhempton who died 27th Decr. 1852 aged 63 years. Also Thomas son of the above Thomas Ballantine who died 10th May 1858 aged 30 years.

BALLANTINE

[Large tumbled stone within railings.] Erected to the memory of Willm. Ballantine late of Ballyhempton who departed this life 25th of March 1859 aged 33 years. Also his mother Matilda Ballantine who died 18th Feby. 1873 aged 74 years.

[The will of Matilda Ballentine [sic], late of Larne, county Antrim, widow, who died 18 February 1873 at same place, was proved at Belfast 26 March 1873 by the oaths of John Ritchie of Belfast, merchant, and William Barry Ritchie of the Grove, near Belfast, esquire, both in said county, the executors. Effects under £100.]

BALLENTINE

[Arms:- A stag's head in profile couped between three crosses crosslet fitchee disposed.] Here lyeth the body of Mary the wife of John Ballentine who died Apr. 2d 1763 aged 56 years. Also John Ballentine Junr. who died May 10th 1781 aged 36 years.

The mother & the son here lies
Whose virtues rise above the skies
Faithfull & just you did them find
In their connections with mankind
Their souls thus to their God return
While here their friends lament and mourn.

BALLENTINE

[Arms:- a stag's head in profile couped between three crosses crosslet fitchee.] Here lyeth the body of William Ballentine who died 28th July 1788 aged 43 years. Also 3 of his children viz. Margaret aged 1 year & William died Oct. 3d. 1791 aged 6 years & a 2d. Margaret died Octr. 7th 1791 aged 9 years.

BALLINTEN
See FERGUISON

BEGGS
[Sandstone in south of graveyard.] Erected by Hugh Beggs in memory of his father John
Beggs who died June 28th 1812 aged 52 years. His mother Sarah Beggs died January 15th
1856 aged 89 years. Also his John Beggs died February 18th 1865 aged 45 years.

BELL
[Sandstone, now broken. Arms:- in chief two bells (?), in base as many crosses patee
fitchee. Crest: an animal's head (deer/llama).] Erected by John Bell in memory of his
father John Bell who died March 14th 1783 aged 77 years. Elizabeth Bell died 6th June
1796 aged 84 yrs. Andrew Bell died July 20th 1796 aged 2 yrs. Margret Bell died Janry.
19th 1779 aged 26 years. Also Nancy Bell who departed this life in July 1837 aged 77
years. Also Serra MILLER who departed this life in March 1838 aged 50 years. And James
Bell who departed this life in June 184(.) aged 58 years.

BLAIR
Erected by Hugh Blair in memory of his daughter Margaret who died 10th Feb. 1868
aged 1 month. Also his daughter Jane who died 13th April 1870 aged 4 years.
  [Marriage: in First (Unitarian) Presbyterian Church, Larne, on Tuesday 10th inst. by
Rev. C. Porter, Mr. Hugh Blair, Headwood, to Miss Margaret Stevenson, Millbrook.
Larne Weekly Reporter, 14 Oct. 1865.]

BLAIR
See MOOR and ROSS

BOYD
[Small broken stone decorated with a marigold, lying loose near John Boyd, 1752.] Here
lyeth the body of Mary Boyd who de(......d) this life the 20th .... age....... Also
....

BOYD
Here lyeth the body of John Boyd who died in Augt 1752 aged 51 years.

BOYD
[Sandstone with arms:- a fess chequy, in the base a cross moline. Crest:- a hand in
benedicton couped. Motto:- confido.] Here lyeth the body of Agness Boyd who died 8th
Jan. 1792 aged 75 years. Also James Boyd who departed this life 17th Jan. 1792 aged 67
years. Also Janet Boyd who died 2d Feb. 1796 aged 75 years. Also Jenny Boyd who
departed this life January 3rd 1832 aged 71 years. Also Wm. NELSON who departed this
life March 3rd 1841 aged 82 years.

BOYD
[Large sandstone, tilting, in east of graveyard.] Erected by Grace Boyd to the memory of
her husband William Boyd of Larne who departed this life on the 18th of August 1842
aged 42 years. During life he was much esteemed and his death deeply lamented by all
who knew him. Here also are deposited the remains of his brother Robert Boyd who died
on the 7th February 1829 aged 35 years.

BOYD

[Red sandstone next to Wm Boyd, d.1842.] Erected by Joseph Boyd, Ballycraigy, in memory of his father Robert Boyd who died 28th April 1829 aged 73 years. Also his sister Jenny who died 24th June 1860 aged 71 years. Also his son Samuel who died 7th March 1879 aged 27 years. Also the above-named Joseph Boyd who died 22nd Dec. 1879 aged 75 years. Also his sister Agness CAMPBELL who died 25th Jan. 1880 aged 83 years. Also Nancy, wife of the above-named Joseph Boyd, who died 20th June 1894 aged 83 years. Also his daughter Mary Eliza Boyd who died 6th Sep. 1900 aged 53 years.

[Administration of the estate of Mary Eliza Boyd of 26 Castle Street, Lisburn, county Antrim, spinster, who died 6 September 1900, granted at Belfast 13 February 1901 to Robert Boyd, farmer. Effects £350.]

BOYD

[Square & compass enclosing 'G' at top of stone.] Erected by Captain Samuel Boyd in memory of his father Thomas Boyd who departed this life 23rd June 18(9.) aged 73 years. Also his sister Janet who died October 1841 aged 22 years. Also his mother Agnes Boyd who died 30th November 1871 aged 85 years.

BOYD

[Fallen and weathered stone.] Erected (by) Mary Boyd in (memory of her husband) John Boyd (who died 22nd) Novr. 1(859 aged) .... Also of her .... daughter Mary Jane Bo.......... August (4th) 1869 aged 26 years.

Happy the youth with graces blessed
To whom the Lord hath given rest.

Also of her daughter Margaret .... died 6th Marc........ Also the above-n(amed) ....d who died (-)th .... years.

BOYD

See ALEXANDER, DUNCAN and NELSON

BREEN

[Blue slate.] Thomas Breen departed this life the 12th March 1798 aged 17 years.

BYLY

[Small loose stone.] Robt. Byly.

CALBON

[Loose blue roofing slate.] Ewd. Calbon aged 46: 1724. Also Samuel Calbon July 1st 1809 aged 9.

CALDWELL

[Sandstone in west of graveyard with arms:- three piles, in base a barry wavy of five. Crest:- a fat bird displayed. Motto:- In Domino Confido.] Here lyeth the body of John Caldwell who departed this life on the 12th May 1787 aged 32 years and his father John who died 23d May 1790 aged 85 years. And also the body of Mary ALEXANDER wife to the firstnemed John Caldwell who departed this life on the 15th Febr. 1824 aged 75 years.

CAMPBELL

See BOYD

CLIELAND

[Slate near centre of graveyard.] Here lyeth the body of Martha NIELSON who died 1st May 1788 aged 66 years, wife to Thos. Clieland.

COBAIN

Erected by Thomas Cobain in memory of his father Robert Cobain who departed this life in the (yea)r 1831 aged 80 years. Also his mother Margaret Cobain who died in the year 1839 aged 78 years.

COBAIN

Erected by John Cobain in memory of his son Thomas who died 1(6)th September 1870 aged 4 years and 4 months.

COEY

[Table stone.] Dedicated by JW & E Coey to the memory of James Coey their father who departed this life at Larne 3rd June 1807 aged 40 years. Also three of his children who died in infancy. Likewise their mother Agnes FULLERTON who died 1st August 1854 aged 77 years.

CRAIG

See ALEXANDER and WINNERT

CRAWFORD

[Lying within railings of William Simpson Crawford (1841). Arms:- A fess ermine between three crows. Crest:- a garb. Motto:- God feeds the crows.] Here lieth the remains of Eliza ESTLER wife to William Crawford of Ballytober who departed this life the 20th of March 1787 aged 46 years. Also their son William Crawford who departed this life the 26th of March 1808 aged (..) years. Also the above named William Crawford her husband who departed this life the 12th of September in the year of our Lord 1815 aged 72 years. And James Crawford their son in whom meekness, charity and unaffected piety were equally and eminantly conspicuous. He was beloved through life at death much lamented. He departed this life the 3rd of June in the year of our Lord 1822 in the 54th year of his age.

CRAWFORD

[Large stone with railings.] Sacred to the memory of William Simpson Crawford, the eldest and dearly beloved child of John and Elizabeth Crawford born 20th Jany. 1833, died 14th Jany. 1841. Also their daughter Jane born 5th May 1849 died 15th Oct. same year. Also in memory of their father John Crawford, born June 1804, died 11th April 1851. And his mother Jane Crawford who died June 1824 aged 55 years. Also his wife Elizabeth (SIMPSON) Crawford who departed this life 19th Decr. 1890 aged 80 years. "The memory of the just is blessed."

[Letters of administration of the personal estate of Elizabeth Crawford, late of Edenvale, Larne, county Antrim, widow, who died 19 September [sic] 1890 at same place, were granted at Belfast 17 April 1891 to Elizabeth Peden Hay, wife of William Hay of Edenvale, the child. Effects £911 . 4s.]

CURREY

[Tilted sideways and partly buried. Arms:- a saltire, in the chief a rose. Crest:- a rose slipped. Motto:- (...... p)a(rat)us.] Here lyeth th(e bo)dys of ....Currey (who) died in (M)ay 1710 aged 35 years. Also Agne(ss) ALLEN who ...ed Mar. 1737 aged 55 years.

Agnes (Cu)rrey who died Febr. 1(.) 17(45) aged 9 years, daughtr. ... Robt Currey. Also William Currey who died May 30th 1773 aged 32 years. Also Robert Currey who died Oct. 16th 1773 aged 69 years. Also Elizabeth STUART who died Jan. 2 1789 aged 77 years.....John Currey who died t..... of July 1812 aged 74 years.

DUNCAN
[Sandstone in southwest of graveyard.] Hear lyeth the body of John Duncan who departed this life May the 10th A.D. 1819 aged 66 years. The body of his wife Matilda BOYD lyeth in Larn Church Yard. Also in memory of his son Patrick Duncan hows remains lieth in America & Stte. of Newyork. Underneth lieth the body of his daughter Mary who departed this life March the 10 A.D. 1810 aged 25 years. Also the body of his son John Duncan who departed this life July the 7th AD 1823 aged 38 ys. Likewise the body of his son James Duncan who departed this (life N)ovember the 26 AD 182(. aged) forty years.

EATON
[Arms:- a chevron between three roses (?). Motto:- virtue survives the ruins of the tomb.] Erected, through filial repect, to the memory of Hugh Eaton who departed this life Jany. the 1 1808 aged 52 years. Also his wife Mary KERNEY who died July 27th 1820 aged 58 years. Also James Eaton, son of the above, who died 22nd Feb. 1834 aged 40 years. And his wife Mary died 26th June 1835 aged 38 years. Also their daughter Mary Eliza Eaton who died 8th March 1839 aged 14 years. And their son John Eaton died 8th July 1840 aged 8 years.

EATON
[White limestone panel set in red sandstone.] In memory of Mary and Jemima, daughters of Alexander & Margaret Eaton. Mary died 2nd August 1877 aged 15 years & 10 months. Jemima died 14th May 1877 aged 11 years & 1 month.

ESLER
[Within iron railings together with larger broken stone.] In memory of M(a)ry Esler who departed this year of (of our Lord) 17(5)9 aged 6(5). Alexander Esler who departed in the year of our Lord 1786 aged 4(.).

ESLER
[Broken sandstone enclosed by railings with M(a)ry Esler d. 17(5)0.] Erected by Alexander Esler in memory of his daughter Ellen who died 1868 aged 11 years. Also his son Robert who died 1874 aged 28 years. Also his daughter Jane who died 1877 aged 17 years. The above-named Alexander Esler died 21st Feby. 1886 aged 63 years. Also his son William who died 7th Sept. 1887 aged 33 years. And his son John who died 21st March 1894 aged 29 years. Also his wife Martha NELSON (who di)ed 2(8)th Sept. 1898 aged 78 years.

[The will of Alexander Esler, late of Ballykeel, Kilwaughter, county Antrim, farmer, who died 21 February 1886 at same place, was proved at Belfast 29 March 1886 by John Esler and William Magill, both of Ballykeel, Kilwaughter, farmers, the executors. Effects £173 . 1s.

Probate of the will of Martha Esler, late of Ballykeel, Kilwaughter, county Antrim, widow, who died 28 August [sic] 1898, granted at Belfast 9 November 1898 to Robert Esler of Drumadonaghy, said county, farmer. Effects £312 . 15s. 4d.]

ESLER

[Lead lettering on white marble set into yellow sandstone.] Erected by John Esler in memory of his daughter Martha who died 17th June 1874 aged 26 years. His daughter Margaret Ellen who died 6th March 1875 aged 30 years. Also his wife Jenny Nelson who died 9th Novr. 1892 aged 79 years. The above-named John Esler died 2nd Feby. 1896 aged 80 years. Also his daughters Mary Ann who died 3rd May 1917 aged 72 years and Jenny who died 24th January 1922 aged 67 years. A. Jenkins, Larne.

ESTLER

See CRAWFORD

FERGUISON

[Arms:- A chevron, in chief two posthorns, in base a dove. Crest:- An hourglass.] Erected by Samuel Ferguison his wife. Here lyeth Mary BALLINTEN who died 27th Janry. 1808 aged 52 years. Also Samuel Ferguson hur son who died Agust the 5th 1801 aged 11 years. Also Mary aged 9 y. Also the above Samuel Ferguison who departed this life on the 7th of March 1835 aged 87 years. Also William Ferguison who departed this life the 5th of September 18(6)2 aged 88 years.

FULLERTON

[Sandstone headstone.] Sacred to the memory of Hugh Fullerton who departed this life in March 1805 aged 74 years. Erected by Samuel Fullerton his son. Also Rose Fullerton who died in 1808 aged [blank] years. Also the above Samuel Fullerton who departed this life the 26 Octr. 1845 aged 78 years.

FULLERTON

[Sandstone next to Hugh Fullerton d.1805.] Erected by William Fullerton in memory of his beloved wife Margt. Ann Fullerton who departed this life 3rd March 1867 aged 54 years. Also his son John Fullerton who departed this life 9th April 1(8)69 aged 28 years. Also the above Wm. Fullerton who died 1884 aged 76.

[The will of William Fullerton, late of Ballysnodd, county Antrim, farmer, who died 31 January 1884 at same place, was proved at Belfast 23 May 1884 by William Fullerton and Edward Coey Fullerton, both of Ballysnodd, and Robert Apsley of Ballyrichard in said county, farmers, the executors. Effects £906 . 3s. 6d.]

FULLERTON

See COEY and MOOR

GILLIS

[Sandstone headstone.] Erected by Robert Gillis in memory of his mother Jenny Gillis who departed this life 28th Januy. 1860 aged 62 years. [Along top edge:-] 2 graves north.

GINGLES

[Arms:- a saltire fleury, two flowers with four petals leafed slipped in pale and as many mullets in fess. Crest:- a dove holding an olive branch. Motto:- vincit omnia v(er)itas.] Erected by John Gingles in memory of his father John Gingles who died May 7th 180(5) aged 72 years. Also his wife Barbra HYNMAN who died March the 5th 1797 aged 60 years. And their son William who died Novr. the 10th 1808 aged 25 years. Also John Gingles who departed this life the 10th May 1814 aged 32 years. Also his son William who died in the year 1832 aged (2)1 years. And Andrew who died in the year 1841 aged 37 yrs.

GINGLES

[Sandstone.] Erected by John and Andrew Gingles in memory of their father Andrew Gingles who departed this life 21st August 1856 aged 78 years. And of their mother Mary who departed this life 27th July 1837 aged 35 years. Also their sister Mary who departed this life 16th September 1847 aged 13 years.

GINGLES

[Sandstone next to John Gingles d.1805.] In memory of Andrew Gingles of Lowtown, Kilwaughter, who died 13th Feb. 1841 aged 36 years. Also his daughter Margaret who died 24th Sept. 1854 aged 16 years. Also his daughter Mary who died 24th June 1859 aegd 22 years. Also his daughter Martha who died 16th Oct. 1859 aged 24 years. Also his wife Mary Gingles who died 29th March 1863 aged 53 years. Also his grand son Robert McNINCH who died 7th Oct. 1873 aged 6 years.

(GO)LBREATH

[Formerly set into west wall, now loose.] Erected in memory of William (Go)lbreath who departed this life April the 4th 1805 aged (3)7 years. Also his mother who departed this life November the 2d. 1803 [or 1805] aged 68.

GREENLEES

[Low steeply tilting stone.] Erected to the memory of Andrew Greenlees, Kilwaughter, who died 23rd Feby. 1842 aged 60 years.

HANEY

[Rough whinstone.] J Haney.

HILL

See NELSON

HOLDEN

[Tilting yellow sandstone in east of graveyard.] Erected by Nathaniel Holden in memory of his father William Holden who died 18th June 1872 aged 77 years. Also his wife Isabella who died 10th Oct. 1878 aged 38 years. Also his mother Margaret Ann Holden who died 3rd March 1881 aged 83 years. The above-named Nathaniel Holden died 6th Feby. 1911 aged 70 years. Also his grandson William MAGEE who died 6th May 1913 aged 4 years. Also his wife Jane Holden died 19th Feby. 1927 aged 86 years.

[The will of William Holden, late of Ballyedwards, county Antrim, farmer, who died 18 June 1872 at same place, was proved at Belfast 14 October 1872 by the oaths of Thomas Moore of Kilwaughter and Nathaniel Moore of Browndod, both in Larne, said county, farmers, the executors. Effects under £450.]

HUNTER

Here lyeth the body of Samuel Hunter who died the 28th June 1804 aged 71 years.

HYNMAN

See GINGLES

JOHNSTON

[Loose crumblimg red sandstone in northeast of graveyard.] (Erected) by .... Johnston ....y of her husband ...hn Johnston ......parted this life 8th ...... 1870 aged 54 years. .... her daughter .....ret Johnston .... 3rd March 1861 ....ar and 6 mon(ths.)

JOHNSTON

[Sandstone in north of graveyard.] Erected by Patrick Johnston in memory of his beloved father John Johnston who departed this life 8th April 1870 aged (5)4 years. Also his mother Agnes Johnston who died 19th October 1908 aged 93 years.

[Letters of administration of the personal estate of John Johnston, late of Kilwaughter, county Antrim, farmer, who died 8 April 1870 at same place, were granted at Belfast 25 July 1870 to Agnes Johnston of Kilwaughter, Larne aforesaid, the widow of said deceased. Effects under £300.]

KERNEY

See EATON

McCAREY

[Yellow sandstone in southwest of graveyard.] Erected (by) Jose(...McCa)rey (in) memory of .... daugh... Annie McCarey who departed this life 20th December 1865 aged 18 years. The above Joseph McCarey died 25th March 1888 aged 85 years. And his wife Margaret died 24th April 1894 aged 82 years.

[The will of Joseph McCarey, late of Browndodd, county Antrim, farmer, who died 25 March 1888 at same place, was proved at Belfast 20 July 1888 by James McCarey of Browndodd, farmer, one of the executors. Effects £260 . 5s.]

McCOMB

See McNEILL

McCULLOUGH

[Sandstone in north of graveyard.] Erected by Matthew McCullough in memory of his wife Mary McCullough who died 26th March 1869 aged 85 years.

McDOWAL

[Very steeply tilted. Arms:- a lion rampant. Crest:- a demi lion rampant in the dexter paw a dagger. Motto:- Pro r(e)ge in tyrannos.] Here lyeth the body of Janet the wife of Hugh McDowal who died Feb. 15th 1778 aged 80 years. Also 2 sons viz John and Hugh & 2 daughters. Also the abovenamed Hugh McDowal who died Oct. 1(3)th 1786 aged 96 years. Also their daughter Agness who died Augu... 12th 1787 aged 65 years.

McDOWELL

[White limestone set into sandstone with railed enclosure.] Erected by Margaret McDowell in memory of her beloved husband John McDowell who died July 4th 1857 aged 66 years.

Mourn not for me my wife so dear,
I am not dead but sleeping here;
My end you know, my grave you see,
Prepare yourself to follow me.

Also his brother Robert who died 11th July 1855 aged 59 years. And his wife Betty who died 25th Feby. 1882 aged 82 years. The above-named Margaret McDowell died 1st Jany. 1891 aged 86 years.

[The will of Elizabeth McDowell, late of Kilwaughter, county Antrim, widow, who died 25 February 1882 at Hightown, Kilwaughter, was proved at Belfast 3 July 1882 by James McDowell of Kilwaughter, and David Girvan of Ballysnod in said county, farmers, the executors. Effects £150 . 5s. 6d.

The will of Margaret McDowell, late of Hightown, Kilwaughter, county Antrim, widow, who died 2 January 1891 at same place, was proved at Belfast 11 February 1891 by William Craig of Carneal in said county, and Hugh Bailie of Kilwaughter, farmers, the executors. Effects £380 . 15s.

Death: Jan. 2, at Hightown, Kilwaughter, Mrs. Margaret McDowell, relic [sic] of the late John M'Dowell, aged 86 years. *The Larne Reporter,* 10 Jan. 1891.]

McDOWELL

Erected by Robert McDowell in memory of his brother John who died 10 April 1858 aged 13 yrs. His uncle Samuel McDowell who died 4 Sep. 1858 aged 54 years. His son John who died 10 Jany. 1872 aged 3 years. His son Samuel who died 23 April 1874 aged 15 years. His wife Jenney McDowell who died Jany. 1900 aged 63 years.

[The will of Samuel McDowell, late of Hightown in the county of Antrim, farmer, who died 5 September 1858 at same place, was proved at Belfast 24 November 1858 by the oaths of John McNinch of Hightown and Samuel Fullerton of Lealies, both in said county, farmers, the executors. Effects under £450.]

McF

[Low red sandstone, loose, with square & compass.] H. McF.

McFALL

[Small loose red sandstone with square & compass.] In memory of Henery McFall died Jay. the 2d (18)08 aged 28 yea.

McNEILL

[Sandstone held in concrete plinth.] Erected by William McNeill in memory of his father Andrew McNeill who died 8th May 1851 aged 88 years. And his mother Elisabeth McCOMB who died 4th June 1852 aged 78 years. Also their grand-daughter Martha who died 18th March 1874 aged 29 years. Also their son Andrew who died 28th Feby. 1880 aged 75 years. And Mary MAXWELL his wife who died 26th May 1897 aged 82 years.

McNINCH

[Red sandstone next to Hugh Eaton d.1808.] (Erected to) the memory of Jane ......(i)e wife to John McNinch ... departed this life J(une) ... 1766 aged (25) years. Also the above John her husband (who) departed this (life) .... 1795 aged 65 .... grandson J(ohn M) .... who departed (this life) .... 1810 aged 4 (years) .... sister Janet died .... agd. 20 yrs.

McNINCH

[White limestone set into sandstone in east of graveyard, fallen.] In memory of John McNinch who died 26th July 1795 aged 65 years. And his wife Jane WYLIE who died 21st Jany. 1766 aged 25 years. Also their grand-daughter Martha who died 15th June 1825 aged 10 years. David Gary McNinch born 31st March 1888 died 25th October 1893. Thomas Watt McNinch born 27th Nov. 1890 died 3rd May 1915. James Watt McNinch born 27th Nov. 1890 died 20th Oct. 1918. Also their father Thomas Watt McNinch, Ballymullock, born 10th February 1851 died 9th Nov. 1936.

McNINCH

[Sandstone.] Erected to the memory of John McNinch, Kilwaughter, who departed this life 6th July 1845 aged 83 years. Also his wife Martha who departed this life 10th Decr. 1865 aged 92 years.

McNINCH
See GINGLES

McTAGU(E)
[Broken slate, loose.] (He)re lies ... body of .... McTagu(e) ...o died the 3rd Sept. 1818 AE 19 ys.

MAGEE
[Sandstone propped against west boundary wall.] Erected by Alexr. Magee in memory of his beloved wife Susan who departed this life 14th March 1870 aged 84 years. Also the above-named Alexr. Magee who died 1st March 1879 aged 93 years.

MAGEE
[White limestone leaning against west boundary wall.] Erected to the memory of William Magee, Kilwaughter, who died 16th June 1903 aged 84 years. Also his son William who died 19th Feby. 1911 aged 48 years. Also Jane wife of the above-named William Magee died 12th June 1913 aged 89 years. T. Holden, Larne

MAGEE
See HOLDEN

MAGILL
Erected to the memory of John Magill who departed this life the 28th February 1812 aged 20 years.

MAGILL
[Small headstone next to John Magill.] Erected in memory of Mary NELSON, wife of Thomas Magill, who died 12th December 1866 aged 56 years. The above-named Thomas Magill died 19th March 1879 aged 76 years. [On upper edge:-] 3 north.

MAGILL
See NELSON and WILSON

MAXWELL
Erected by James Maxwell in memory of his daughter Janet who died 14th August 1855 aged 13 years.
    Happy the youth with graces blest
    To whom the Lord has given rest.
Also the above James Maxwell who died 30th July 1872 aged 68 years.

MAXWELL
See McNEILL

MEHARG
Erected in memory of Thomas Meharg who departed this life February 28th 1806 aged 60 years. And of Margaret Meharg his wife who died the 3d Decr. 1816 aged 68 years. Also their grandson Thomas Meharg who died 5th March 1821 aged 4 yrs.

MILLER
See BELL

MOFFAT
  See SMITH

MOOR
  [Arms:- a chevron between three mullets, in chief a crescent. Crest:- broken, but seems to include a human chin and neck. Motto:- (.............du)m onma.] Here lyeth the body of John Moor who died Janry. (the) 12th 1775 aged (5)(-) years. Also Elisabeth BLAIR wife to John Moor who died Decmbr. the 28d 1798 aged 64 yrs. Also Saml. Moor son to Thomos [sic] Moor who died Aug. 20th 1808 agd. 2 yrs. And Nathan Moor their son who died 18th March 1820 aged 53 years. Also John son of Nathan who died 17th Aug. 1828 aged 36 years. Also his wife Ann Jane FULLERTON who died 27 April 1871 aged 64. And their son's daughter Ann Jane died 27 Nov. 1873 aged 6 months.

MOORE
  [White limestone with lead lettering. Arms:- a chevron between three mullets, in chief a crescent. Crest:- a moor's head in profile, wreathed about the temples.Motto:- Deus munitio mea.]

John Moore,	born	[blank]	died	1764.
Wm. Moore,	"	1730	"	1775.
Wm. Moore,	"	1760	"	1835 and his wife
Janet SHAW, Ballygelly	"	1774	"	1862
John Moore,	"	1817	"	1895

  Monument renewed by Rev. Wm. Moore D.D., Ottawa, Canada, 1898.

MOORE
  [Arms:- a fess between three estoiles of seven on a chief indented and in the base a crescent. Crest:- a moor's head in profile wreathed about the temples. Motto:- fortis cadere cedere non potest.] Here lie the bodies of 2 children of John Moores, viz James who died 13th Aug. 1790 aged 2 years. Also Nathan who died 25th Feb. 1807 aged 6 years. Also Peggy Ann Moore who died the 27th April 1812 aged 9 years. Also the above John Moore who departed this life 15th April 1837 aged 74 years. Also his wife Margret Moore who departed this life on the 27th May 1854 aged 87 years. [Along top edge:-] 4 graves north.

MOORE
  [Sandstone next to John Moore d.1775.] Erected by Thomas Moore in memory of his mother Mary Moore who died Sept. 10th 1830 aged 51 years. Also his wife Rose Mary Moore who died July 22d 1859 aged 49 years. Also his son Samuel who died April 1st 1860 aged 22 years.

MOORE
  [Green slate next to Wm. Moore d.1764.] Erected to the memory of Wm. Moore who departed this life on the 28th May 1835 aged 75 years. And also to Mary his daughter who departed this life Sept. 17th 1830 AE 12 years and a son who died in infancy.

MOORE
  [Broken.] Erected by ...chd. & Ellen Moore of Larne in memory of their dearly beloved children, Jenny, Anne and James, who died in infancy. Also Thomas who died 2nd D(ec) 1856 aged (2)..... And James (who died 21st June 18.. aged 13 years.)

MOORE

Erected by John Moore in memory of his children Nathaniel Moore died 1st December 1864 aged 6 years. Elizabeth Moore died 19th October 1865 aged 9 years.

N

[Low whinstone near William Neilson (1801), no date.] R.N., I.N., A.N.

NEILSON

In memory of William Neils(o)n who died 15th October 1801 aged 29 years. Also his father Alexander Neilson who died 20th June 1805 aged 78 years. And his wife Elizabeth ORR, who died the 3d day of Sept. 1813 aged 70 years.

NEILSON

[Sandstone next to Agness Boyd d.1792. Arms:- three dexter hands couped. Crest:- In a dexter cubit arm a spear. Motto:- His regi servitium. Translation: "Subjection to these rulers".] Erected by Elizabeth Neilson in memory of her husband James Neilson son to William Neilson of Rorysglen who departed this life the 18th of July 1823 aged 38 years.

NELSON

[Fallen and broken beside Agness Boyd 1792.] Erected by William Nelson junr. of Rorysglen in memory of his uncle Andrew BOYD who departed this life June the 30th 1815 aged 51 years. Also his daughter Janet Nelson who died August 10th 1839 aged 15 years. Also his daughter Sarah Nelson who departed this life 4th June 1853 aged 27 years. And also his son Robert Nelson who departed this life Oct. 8th 1854 aged 27 years.

NELSON

[Sandstone.] Erected by William Nelson, Ballykeel, in memory of his daughter Margret Nelson who departed this life Janry. 9th 1836 aged 21 years. Also his daughter Ellen Nelson who departed this life Decr. 22nd 1830 aged 12 years.

NELSON

In memory of William Nelson, Rorysglynn who died 17th July 1871 aged 82 years. And his beloved wife Agnes HILL who died 31st January 1868 aged 74 years.

[The will of William Nelson, senior, late of Rorysglynn, Kilwaughter, county Antrim, farmer, who died 17 July 1871 at same place, was proved at Belfast 7 August 1871 by the oaths of Andrew Nelson of Ballyhempton, Larne, farmer, and David Nelson of Larne, woollen draper, both in county Antrim, the executors. Effects under £800.]

NELSON

[Fallen sandstone.] In memory (of Rober)t Nelson (......... who died 8th) Dec. 1869 aged (7.) years. Also his .... Jane Elizabeth Nelson who died (2nd) Dec. 1875 (74 years.) And .... Nelson wh.................. 1880 .... A. Jenkens.

NELSON

[Sandstone enclosed with Wm. Wallace d. 1867.] Erected by Hugh Nelson in memory of his beloved wife Mary MAGILL who died 1(8)th Sept. 1871 aged 28 years.

NELSON

See BOYD, ESLER and MAGILL

NICKLE

[Fallen sandstone.] Erected by Hugh Nickle in memory of his father and mother. Also the following two who was drowned at Brownsbay 4th August 1878 his son Hugh aged 10 years and his brother Robert aged 22 years. Also his wife Matilda who died 15th Nov. 1899 aged 52 years.

I long for household voices gone,
For vanished smiles I long;
But God hath led my dear ones on,
And he can do no wrong.

Their daughter Maggie died 5th Dec. 1902 aged 22 y.... Their daughter Lizzie died 8th April 1905 aged 1.......

NIELSON

See CLIELAND

ORR

See NEILSON

PEOPLES

[Small red sandstone.] Erected by George Peoples in memory of his son George who died 27th August 1851 aged 3 years. [Along top edge:-] South 1 Graves 3 North.

PEOPLES

Erected by Mary Peoples, Killyglen, in memory of her beloved husband James Peoples who departed this life 21st July 1863 aged 62 years. The above-named Mary Peoples who died 5th Aug. 1899 aged 88 years. Also their daughter Margaret who died 8th Feb. 1924 aged 70 years. [Along top edge:-] Three graves north.

PEOPLES

[White limestone enclosed with James Peoples d.1863.] Erected by James Peoples Senr., Killyglen in memory of his sister Margaret who died 8th Feby. 1924 aged 70 years. Also his brother W. J. Peoples who died 16th Nov. 1927 aged 77 years. Also the above named James Peoples who died 12th May 1929 aged 87 years. [Holden, Larne.]

PEOPLES

[White limestone – probably first half of twentieth century.] Erected by James Peoples sen. in memory of his grandparents James & Margaret Peoples. Also his uncles, James, David, Archie & Joseph. Also his aunt Ellen. And her daughter Ellen. And his cousin James. [2 G.S., 2 G.N.]

REID

[Arms:- Quarterly, in the first and fourth a chevron between in the chief three mullets in fess and in the base two crosses crosslets in pale, in the second and third a fess chequy. The crest is weathered away. Motto:- pr(o......ute.)] Here lyeth the body of Hugh Reid who died the 12th July 1772 aged 44 years. Also Hellen TWEED who died Sept. the 20th 1772 aged 8 years.

RITCHIE
Erected in memory of Rebecca Ritchie late of Killyglen who departed this life (2)(8)th
Octr. 18(4)4 aged (5)9 years. Also her husband Robert Ritchie who departed this life 1st
April 1857 aged 71 years. And his grandson R.J. Ritchie who died 17th September 1873
aged 20 years. Also his grandson John Ritchie who died 14th May 1876 aged 2 y.....

ROBINSON
[Sandstone.] Erected by Samuel Robinson of Ballyhempton in memory of his son Robert
Robinson, who departed this life 28th January 1854 aged 34 years. Also his beloved wife
Mary who departed this life 21st Decr. 1862 aged 80 years. Also the above Samuel
Robinson who departed this life 2nd Novr. 1869 aged 86 years. [On upper edge:-] 2N.

ROCKE
Erected to the memory of James Rocke, Kilwaughter, who died 12th August 1871 aged
59 years. Also his son Thomas who died 1st June 1861 aged 9 years. Also his daughter
Agnes who died 20th May 1865 aged 23 years. Also his daughter Jane who died 1st July
1867 aged 19 years. Also his brother John who died 22nd November 1870 aged 67 years.
Jenkins, Larne.
    [The will of James Rocke, late of Kilwaughter, county Antrim, farmer, who died 12
August 1871 at same place, was proved at Belfast 30 August 1871 by the oaths of Nancy
Rocke, widow, and John Rocke, farmer, both of Kilwaughter, and John McNinch of
Ballyboley, farmer, all in Larne, said county, the executors. Effects under £1,500.
    Death: Sep.1, at his residence, Kilwaughter, Mr. James Rocke, aged 80 years. *The Larne
Reporter*, 5 Sep. 1874.]

ROSS
[Arms:- a wolf's head between three chessrooks disposed. Crest:- A harp headed. Motto:-
constant & true.] Here lyeth the body of Margaret BLAIR who died in Mar. 1768 aged
54 years wife to Robert Ross who died 21st Mar. 1778 aged 67 years.

ROSS
[Small headstone of red sandstone.] Here lyeth the body of Samuel Ross of Carncastle
who departed this life the 5th March 1806 aged 84 years.

SHAW
See MOORE

SIMPSON
See CRAWFORD

SMITH
[Sandstone lying flat in front of Martha Esler d.1874.] In memory of John Smith who
died in December 1773 aged 35 years. Also his wife Jennet MOFFAT who died the 22d
day of May 1801 aged 63 years.

STEWART
Slate.] Erected by Andrew Stewart in memory of his brother Samuel Stewart who
departed this life October 6th 1806 aged 28 years.

STEWART
[Yellow sandstone next to foregoing.] Erected by Hugh Stewart of Carrickfergus in memory of his father Hugh Stewart who departed this life the 17th December 1837 aged 52 years.

STUART
See CURREY

TOOKE(Y)
[Blue slate, broken.] Mary Tooke(y) departed this life the 12th June 179(-) aged 16 ys.

TWEED
See RITCHIE

VARNOR
[Small stone with irregular inscription which includes a compass and square symbol.] E. by R. Varnor. Sarah do. d. young.

WALLACE
[Fallen forward.] Here lieth the body of Nathaniel Wallace who departed this life February 25th 1814 aged 70 years. James Wallace of Kilwaughter died at Larne 12th December 1893 aged 83 years. Letitia, wife of James Wallace, died at Kilwaughter 12th Jany. 1877 aged 67 years.
[The will (with one codicil) of James Wallace, formerly of Kilwaughter and late of Curran, Larne, both in county Antrim, gentleman, who died 6 [sic] December 1893 at latter place, was proved at Belfast 5 February 1894 by the Reverend James Kennedy of Larne. Presbyterian minister, and Jane Moore of Curran, Larne, married woman, the executors. Effects £131 . 1s. 8d.

WALLACE
[Fallen forward.] Erected by Robert Wallace in memory of his father Arthur Wallace who departed this life 11th Nov. 1850 aged 76 years. Also his mother Martha Wallace who departed this life 10th July 1851 aged 74 years. Also Robert Wallace who departed this life June 19th 1871 aged 68 years. Also Margaret Wallace who died 9th May 1890.
[The will of Robert Wallace, late of Lowtown, county Antrim, farmer, who died 19 June 1871 at same place, was proved at Belfast 21 July 1871 by the oaths of John Wallace of Lowtown aforesaid, farmer, and Thomas Holden of Larne, grocer, both in Larne, in said county, the executors. Effects under £300.
The will of Margaret Wallace, late of St. John`s Place, Larne, county Antrim, widow, who died 9 May 1890 at same place was proved at Belfast 6 June 1890 by the Reverend James Kennedy of Larne, Presbyterian minister, the sole executor. Effects £139 . 13s. 8d.]

WALLACE
[Enclosed with Hugh Nelson`s stone.] Erected by Rachel Wallace in memory of her beloved husband William Wallace who departed this life 30th June 1867 aged 62 years. The above-named Rachel Wallace who died 17th August 1879 aged 59 years.
[The will of William Wallace, late of Kilwaughter, county Antrim, who died 30 June 1867 at same place was proved at Belfast by the oath of David Nelson of Larne in said county, woollen draper, one of the executors. Effects under £800.

The will of Rachel Wallace, late of Kilwaughter, county Antrim, widow, who died 17 August 1879 at same place, was proved at Belfast 3 May 1880 by the oaths of Andrew Nelson of Ballyhempton, farmer, David Nelson of Larne, woollen draper, and John Drummond of Larne, publican, all in said county, the executors. Effects under £800.]

WHINNART
[The stone is rough, but the writing neat.] Erected in memory of John Whinnart who departed this life the 19th of Feburary [sic] 1811 aged 63 years.

WILSON
Erected by Hugh Wilson in memory of his beloved wife Mary MAGILL who died 18th Sept. 1871 aged 28 years.

WINNARD
[Sandstone next to John Whinnart d.1811.] Erected by James Winnard in memory of his daughter Margaret who departed this life on the 3d of October 1823, aged 12 years.

WINNARD
[Broken into two major pieces.] Erected by Jacob ADRAIN to the memory of his uncle Jacob Winnard who departed this life 17th Feb. 1845 aged 79 years.

WINNERT
[Red sandstone with arms:- a bend, on a chief an escutchion bearing a glove between two (mavis). Crest:- a fig leaf (this might be considered part of the mantling).] Erected by David Winnert in memory of his wife Agnes CRAIG who departed this life 18 July 1818 aged 64 years. Also 3 of his children viz Jennet and two named Mary. The erector David Winnert died 15th Decr. 1844 aged 92 years. And Ann Craig, wife of his son John, died 3rd Septr. 1852 aged 79 years.

WOODS
Erected by Samuel Woods to the memory of his son William who departed this life the 5th of August 1833 aged 21 years. Also 3 children. No person to open those 3 graves.

WYLIE
See McNINCH

[Badly flaked.] Ere(cted) by J(ohn) .... of........ bor(n) .... April .... w(as) ....

LARNE AND INVER OLD GRAVEYARD
ST. CEDMA'S

O.S. 40. Grid Ref. D397023

This is in the townland of Town Parks and parish of Larne, and is to be found at the end of Church Road just to the south of the Inver river and modern bypass to Larne Harbour. It is the only medieval burying ground in the combined parishes of Larne and Inver to continue in use to modern times.

The graveyard is well kept but a high proportion of the stones have been removed from their original setting and arranged round the outer wall. The oldest stone dates from 1677 and all inscriptions in the graveyard and memorials in the church building have been copied.

ADAMS
> [Sandstone set against north boundary wall.] Erected by Robert Adams in memory of his son William Adams who departed this life Nov. 17 1853 aged 1 year. Also his son James, November 1st 1863 aged 1 year. Also Eliza Jane, July 10th 1865 aged 10 years. Also Mary, March 8th 1866 aged 8 years. Also Robert, Sept. 4th 1868 aged 5 months.

ADAMS
> [Sandstone laid flat against east boundary wall, now breaking up.] Erected by Robert and Isabella Adams in memory of their son Samuel G. G. Adams who died 20 June 1883 aged ... years. (Al)s(o t)h(e above-named Is)a........... Also the above-named Robert Adams who died 7th Jan. 1915 aged 82 years.

ADAMS
> See FERRES and McCREADY

ADRAIN
> [Laid flat in front of Smiley monument (Jane Smiley d. 1859).] Erected by John Adrain in memory of his wife Christian SMILEY who died 10th Jan. 1821 aged 59 years. Also their daughter Mary who died 23rd Feb. 1822 aged 20 years. And three of their sons, viz. Samuel S. John & James who died young.

ADRAIN
> [Set against south wall of church.] Erected in memory of John Adrain who departed this life 12th February 1858 aged 60 years. Also Jane Adrain who died in infancy. Jane Adrain who departed this life 17th March 18(34) aged 21 years.

AGNEW
> [Table stone of polished granite in railed enclosure.] In memoriam Patrick Agnew of Larne and Kilwaughter died 25th October 1842 aged 84 years. Eliza McNEILL, his wife died 8th May 1851 aged 66 years. Anne WILSON Agnew their daughter died 23rd October 1887 aged 62 years. Jane CALWELL, their youngest daughter and the wife of

John MACAULAY of Red Hall, died 26th June 1899 aged 71 years and John Macaulay, formerly of Red Hall, died at Cheltenham 16th Sept. 1912 in his 90th year.

[Letters of administration, with the will annexed, of the personal estate of Anne Agnew, late of Larne Harbour, county Antrim, spinster, who died 23 October 1887 at same place, were granted at Belfast 3 February 1888 to Jane Callwell Macaulay of Red Hall in said county (wife of John Macaulay), the universal legatee. Effects £2,546 . 5s.]

AGNEW

[During work which began on the chancel in 1879 the four archangels, Michael, Gabriel, Uriel, and Raphael were painted in oils on the east wall by Cox, Buckley & Co., London. On a small unobtrusive shield appeared the memorial dedication. All is now gone. (See Fair: *To This you Belong*, p. 29.)] To the glory of God and in loving remembrance of Patrick Agnew of Ballysavage and Larne, died October 25 1842. Also of Eliza his wife died May 8 1851. And of their daughter Ann Wilson Agnew, died October 23 1887. And their son William Agnew, major general, Bengal Staff Corps, died August 12 1888. This memorial is placed by their daughters, Margaret St. Leger Mitchell, Hariette Robertson Cunningham, Matilda Agnew, and Jane Macaulay, 1889.

AGNEW

See OGILVIE

AIKEN

[Lead lettering on white marble set into sandstone.] In memory of Mary HAMILTON, wife of James KING, engineer, Carrickfergus, who died 27th October 1879 aged 32 years. Also her father James Hamilton who died 28th Feb. 1881 aged 66 years. And of his grandson George Hamilton Aiken who died 15th June 1874 aged 7 years.

AIKEN

See BOYD

ALEXANDER

[Ledger south-east of church.] Sacred to the memory of William Alexander who died 8th April 1842 aged 12 years. Also his sister Isabella who died in infancy. Children of Samuel Alexander of Larne. Also his son John who died 8th Octr. 1850 aged 15 years. Also his daughter Mary who died 8th March 1859 aged 22 years. And his daughter Ellen who died 5th April 1863 aged 19 years. Lisze KINDER his grand daughter who died 6th Feby. 1871 aged 9 years. Also his son Thomas Alexander who died in Demerara 22nd April 1871 aged 23 years. Also his daughter Sarah, wife of Charles Kinder, died at Birmingham on the 20th of November 1876 aged 45 years, interred at Kingsw(oo)d Chapel near Birmingham.

[Death: June 30, Kathleen Kinder, aged 36, eldest daughter of Charles Kinder of 6 Willow Road, Hampstead, London; and grand-daughter of the late Samuel Alexander, Larne. *The Larne Reporter*, 5 July 1890.]

ALEXANDER

[Sandstone in south-east of graveyard next to Alexander GRAHAM.] Erected by James Alexander of Larne in memory of his beloved daughter Mary Ann who departed this life 19th July 1850 aged 14 months.

ALEXANDER

See GRAHAM, KIRKPATRICK and ROWAN

ALLAN
See SMITH and SMYTH.

ALLEN
[*M.D.*, V, 2. Slate. A profile portrait is boldy carved in the typanum, holding a heart, and between a four petal rose and a tulip (?).] Here lyeth ye body of Janet HAR who died March ye 31 1754 aged 75 years, who was wife to Robert Allen of Ballycragie & he died in 1770 aged 94 years. Also his son Thomas Allen who died 15th Aug. 1804 aged 84 years. Also the remains of Martha Anne, widow of the late John BOYLE of Ballycraigy, died 7th January 1866 in the 93rd year of her age.

ALLEN
[*M.D.* IV (1899), 2, p.xxiv; *U.J.A.* VI (1900), p.41.   Arms:- a bend indented in the chief two crescents in the base a mullet. Crest:- a swan regardant. Motto:- virescit vulnere.] Erected in memory of Patrick Allen who died 6th June 1770 aged 47 years. Also his daughter Jennet who died 11th Janry. 1811 aged 47 years. Also Ann his wife who died 11th Decr. 1811, aged 80 years. Also their son Patrick Allen who died 26th Octr. 1828 aged 57 years. Also their daughter Ann Allen who died on the 12th May 1832 aged 68 years. Also their grand son Patrick Allen who died on the 17th January 1834 aged 29 years. Also their daughter Margaret who departed this life 21st December 1837 aged 70 years. Also their grandson John Allen, who died 13th April 1849, aged 42 years. Also Mary C. NICHOLSON, wife of the above John Allen, who died 17th June 1873, aged 78 years. Also their son Patrick Allen who died 5th March 1901 aged 66 years.
   [Death: Mar. 11th, at Ballycraigy, Larne, Fanny, beloved wife of Patrick Allen. *The Larne Reporter,* 14 Mar. 1891.]

ALLEN
[*U.J.A.* VI (1900), 42. Sandstone in southwest corner of graveyard with arms:- per bend indented, in chief two crescent in base a mullet. Crest:- a crescent. Motto:- I hope to speed.] Here lyeth the body of Robert Allen who died 28th Jan. 1781 aged 3 years. Also Elizth. Allen who died the 4th Oct. 1784 aged 4 years & Mary died 20th Sep. 1778. William died 17th June 1796. James Allen's children & his wi.. Jane who died 6th Aug. 179(7) (a)ged 44 years. Also Ja(ne A)llen daughter who died (16th) May 1800 aged 16 years. Also James Allen senior who died on 9th of (Apr)il 1816 aged 66 years.

ALLEN
[White limestone set against east boundary wall.] Erected to the memory of Neal Allen who died 17th July 1896, aged 68 years. Also his grandson Neal Allen DUFF who died in infancy. Also his grandson Robert Allen JELLIE. Also his grandson Neal Allen HYSLOP. Also his wife Mary HAGEN Allen who died 18th Dec. 1918 aged 97 years. Holden.

ALLEN
See McFAREN and McGAREL

ANDREOW
See MORDOC(H)

ANDREWS
See RUSSEL

ATKINSON
    See MOORE

BAINE
    See McNEILL and SMILEY

BARKLIE
    [Yellow sandstone tablet built into north boundary wall, revealed during the building of
    a new wing to the Sunday School. This area would have been formerly outside the
    curtilage.] Sting, for 12 years the faithful & favourite terrier dog of Thomas Barklie, died
    19th Feby. 1883.

BARKLIE
    [Ledger enclosed with Montgomery (1752). Crest:- The sun is splendour.] Thomas
    Barklie, Inver, eldest son of Archibald Barklie (see adjoining stone), born Oct. 22 1821,
    died Nov. 22 1894. And (his wife) Mary, daughter of James MARTIN Esq. of B....
    Galway, died 27th March 1902. "Her children a(rise up and call) her blessed". In the
    adjoining grave (south). Their only son Robert Martin Barklie, Colonel in the Royal
    Engineers, who was born in Dublin Jany. 30th, 1846, died at Inver, August 30th 1903.
    "Seek ye the honour that cometh of God only." "Whom the Lord loveth He chasteneth."
    And their only daughter Helen MONTGOMERY Barklie, born at Inver 27th Sept.
    1847, died 7th March 1916.
        [Thomas Barklie and William Eccles became the proprietors, in 1861, of Messrs. John
    and Archibald Barklie & Co., the bleaching dying and finishing works west of the
    churchyard — parts of which, such as the mill race, can still be seen beyond the football
    ground. The firm was established by Thomas Barklie of Cogry (near Doagh) in the third
    quarter of the eighteenth century and passed to his sons John and Archibald. Bassett:
    County Antrim, 1888.]

BARKLIE
    [Double lancet window depicting the last supper, in south wall of nave.] To the glory of
    God and in loving memory of Robert Martin Barklie of Inver, Colonel of Royal
    Engineers, died 30 August 1903 aged 57. Erected by his widow. "My peace I give unto
    you. There remainth therefore a rest for the people of God."
        [R.M. Barklie: Lieutenant, R. Eng., 10 July 1867; Capt. 13 Sep. 1879; Major 31 Dec.
    1886; Lt. Col. 1 July 1893; Brev. Col. 1 July 1897; Subt. Col. 5 Dec. 1898. Col. on the
    staff apptd. 22 Dec. 1898, station Gibraltar. War Service: Soudan Expedition, 1884-5 –
    Nile. Medal with clasp; bronze star. *Army List*, 1899.]

BARKLIE
    See McNEILL and MONTGOMERY

BARR
    See McADAM

BARRON
    See ROSS

BAXTER
    See CLEELAND

BAYLEE
See GILLMER

BEATTIE
[Brass plaque on book rest of choir.] To the glory of God and in memory of George Alexander Beattie, organist of this church 1946-1957 and 1970-1988, and of his daughter Mrs. Mavis HOBAN, chorister here for many years. The embroidered frontals of this choir gallery are the gift of the Beattie family 28 February 1998.

BEERS
See FERRES

BEGGS
[Sandstone south of chancel.] Erected by John Beggs in memory of four of his children viz. William who died 20th July 1828 aged 4 years, James who died 25th Feb. .... aged 16 years, Peggy Ann who died 16th D(ec 18..) aged 6 years, and Jemima who died in infancy. Also of his son John who died 18th Feby. 1849 aged 33 years.

BEGGS
[South of chancel.] Erected (by) Hugh & Thomas Beggs in memory of their beloved mother Mary MOORE who died 8th April 1853 aged 62 years. And of their grand parents Hugh Beggs who died 22nd Novr. 1845 aged 89 years. And his wife Elizabeth NICHOL who died 16th Jany. 1841 aged 84 years......o of Hugh's son Thomas....[continues below ground level].

BEGGS
[Lying flat beside Graham, left of pathway.] Erected (by) Hugh Beggs in memory of his father William Beggs of Larne who departed this life 18th May 1849 aged 73 years. His mother Elizabeth Beggs (who) departed this life 24th March 18(56) aged 64 years.

BEGGS
See FERRIS and SNODDY

BELL
See McCOMBE, MINFORD and PATTON

BLACK
[Buried sandstone with arms:- a chevron, in the chief two mullets in the base an increscent. Crest:- an increscent. Wear at the top of the stone may have removed a motto.] Here lyeth ye bodies of Ro...rt Black who died Apr. ye 15, 1727 aged 39 years. Also his wife Rose FER(IE)S died July ye 17, 1737 aged 50 years.

BLAIR
[Large thin slab of carboniferous limestone propped against north boundary wall, probably from a dismantled monument.] This monument was erected by John Blair and his wife Elizabeth in memory of their two sons, viz. James who departed this life in the sixth year of his age, and in the year of our Lord 1813 and John who, after his return from college, departed this life in the 20thd [sic] year of his age and in the year of our Lord 1822 two [sic.]
Here sleeps in death a youthful pair,
That once were gentle kind and fair,

If Innocence ascend above,
Or virtue soar to realms of love,
T`is theirs in endless bliss to shine,
And bask in beams of love divine,
Then parents who should you deplore,
You'll meet your sons to part no more.

BLAIR
[Loose sandstone in south west of graveyard.] In memory of James Blair, son to George
Blair, who died the (3d) May 1813 aged 6 years. Also James MILLER, died 4th January
1893 aged 80 years.

BLAIR
[Sandstone laid flat, south of church.] Erected in memory of Susanna Blair who died
Decr. 1836. aged 39 years. Also of her husband surgeon Randal Blair who died April 1837
aged 45 years. (Also) the remains of their esteemed friend Nancy PALMER who departed
this life 15th October 1862 aged 87 years. And her husband James Palmer who died 23rd
November 1877 aged 92 years.
    [He was involved in treating the cholera epidemic of 1833. See McKillop (2000).]

BLAIR
See OGILVIE and ROGERS

BOYD
[Set against south wall of church, stone almost smooth.] (He)re lyeth (the body of) Mary
McNINCH who ...d March ye 2 171(9) wi... to Alexander Boyd.

BOYD
Here lyeth the body of Sarrah SMITH who died in 1744 aged 80 years, wife to James
Boyd who died in year 1755 aged 105 years. Also their daughter Mary AIKEN who died
Oct. 10th 1795 aged 84 years.

BOYD
[Two slate panels in sandstone frame, only one panel inscribed, laurel wreath in typanum,
south of church. Now removed to church hall.] Sacred to the memory of James Boyd and
Margaret his wife who departed this life, the former on the 17th Dec. 1833 aged 42 years,
and the latter on the 6th May 1838 aged 48 years. Also their second son James who died
the 1st Jan. 1831 aged 71 years.
    [James Boyd married Margaret Thompson. He was steward of the Methodist Society
and Superintendent of the Sunday School at the time of his death. He had been
instrumental in having the Methodist Chapel built in Pound Street and his body was laid
to rest in a vault beneath its floor, as was his wife. Years later, "for sanitary reasons", they
were removed to this churchyard. See Knox: *History of Larne Methodist Church* (1985), p.
9. *Larne Weekly Reporter*, 5 Sep. 1874.]

BOYD
[Window of two lights depicting Christ meeting Mary and Martha, in the south wall of
the nave.] To the memory of the Rev. Andrew Boyd M.A., Rector of this Parish 1906 -
1925, who died in the vestry after preaching at divine service on Sunday evening, June 14
1925. "For I know that my Redeemer liveth and that He shall stand at the latter day upon

the earth." "I am He that liveth and was dead and behold I am alive for evermore." 1927. W.M. Geddes.

[The Rev. Andrew Boyd was born in January 1863, near Kilrea, county Londonderry, son of George and Mary Boyd, and was educated at Coleraine Academical Institution. He graduated B.A. (R.U.I.) with first class honours in 1886 and M.A. in 1889, teaching for a period at Campbell College, Belfast. He was ordained in 1899 as curate of Antrim 1899-1901, and was curate of Drumbeg 1901-3, of Christ Church, Lisburn 1903-4, rector of St. Barnabas, Belfast 1904-6, and of Inver 1906-25. See Leslie: *Clergy of Connor* (1993).]

BOYLE
See ALLEN

BRIDGMAN
[Loose sandstone in south-west of graveyard.] Er(ect)ed by William McCALMONT Senr. in memory of Ellen Bridgman who died 18th Feb. 1838 aged 88 years. [On edge:] 1 gra(ve) north.

BROWN
[Sandstone in north-west corner of graveyard.] ....art ....parted t(his life) aged 14 ...... Also to her sister E(llen ....) who died 27th Novr. 1855 aged .... Also to their brother John ...... who died 23rd Octr. 1858 aged 22 years. Also to their brother Ephraim James who died 18th March 1865 aged 22 years. Also to their mother Mary Brown who died 1st Feby. 1873 aged 62 years. And her beloved husband Lawrence Brown who died 18th July 1873 aged 65 years. Also their son Captain Thomas Brown who died at sea 13th June 1877 aged 32 years. Also two grandchildren of the above Mary and Lawrence Brown viz. John Henry DAWSON who died 1st March 1868 aged 2 years & 3 months and John Henry Dawson died in infancy. Also Robert J. Dawson who died in infancy and Mary A. Dawson died 5th Sep. 1886 aged 24 years. Also their mother Annie E. Dawson who died 27th [blank] 1889 aged 49 years.

[Sandstone plinth, probably base of previous monument].

(His handsome) form and modest worth,
Long graced, the church that's nigh,
And Lawrence Brown's intrinsic worth
Was registered on high.
The churchyard path he ever trod,
When Sabbath mornings came
(And at) the foot stool of his God,
Adored his saviour's name.
This sad memorial lettered stone,
Two sorrowing daughters rai(sed)
To one that made the happiest home,
For childhood's happy days.

BROWN
See BURNS and SHANNON

BRUCE
[Lead lettering on white limestone set against south boundary wall.] Erected by Annie R. Bruce in memory of her father William Bruce who died 10 Sept. 1867 aged 62 years. Her brother Alexander who died 28 July 1872 aged 26 years. Her brother William who died at New Orleans 23 Aug. 1890 aged 47 years. Her brother Samuel who died 6 Sept. 1891.

Her mother Annie Bruce who died 9 June 1895 aged 85 years.
[Death: Aug. 23rd, at New Orleans, U.S.A., William Bruce, formerly of Point Streer, Larne, aged 47 years. The deceased was a member of Masonic Lodge, No. 41, Larne, for many years. *The Larne Reporter*, 13 Sep. 1890.]

BURNEY
[*U.J.A.* VI (1900), 40. Laid flat, east of church. Arms:- a fess; in chief a bow and arrow, in base three legs barwise. Crest:- a lion's head erased. Motto:- sapere aude indipe.] Here lyeth the body of Samuel Burney who departed this life 31st Decr. 1800 aged 22 years. Also John Burney who departed this life the 13th February 1821 aged 83 years.

BURNEY
[*U.J.A.* VI (1900), 39. Sandstone laid flat, deside foregoing. Arms:- a fess; in chief a bow and arrow, in base three legs barwise. Crest:- a lion's head erased. Motto:- sapere aude indipe.] Here lyeth the body of Margaret (B)urney who (d)e(p)arted thi(s l)ife (2)8th (Ju)ne 1804 aged (24)

BURNEY
See PATRICK and THOM

BURNS
[*U.J.A.* VI (1900), 40. Sandstone south of church, with arms:- a hunting-horn stringed, in chief two mullets. Crest:- an increscent. Motto:- gradatim plena.] Here lyeth the body of Elizabeth BROWN who died Mar. 6th 1769 aged 32 years wife to William Burns & Isabel their child. Also the above named William Burns who died 16th Mar. 1793 aged 60 years. Also his son Willm. Burns who died on the 17th May 1834 aged 52 years. And Ann Burns his wife who died on the 18th of January 1845 aged 60 years.

BURNS
[*M.D.* III (1895), 2; *U.J.A.* VI (1900), 40. Set against north boundary wall. Arms:- a hunting horn stringed, in chief two mullets. Crest:- on a wreath an increscent. Motto:- (Gradatim) plena.] Here lyeth the body of one child of John Bur(ns) viz. Mary Ann who died Feb. 2d 1785 aged 1 year.

BURNS
[Propped against Agnew enclosure.] Erected to the memory of Martha Burns who departed this life August 1849 aged 62 years. Also her son John who died Feb. 1860 ae 47 years. Also Marianne & Elizabeth (S)YMINGTON her grandchildren who died in infancy.
    [Letters of administration of the personal estate of John Burns, late of Ballylig in the county of Antrim, writing clerk, who died 14 February 1860 at same place, were granted at Belfast 2 March 1860 to Maria Anne Symington (wife to Daniel Symington of Wilmslow in the county of Chester in England, missionary), the sister, one of the next of kin of said deceased. Effects under £450.]

BURNS
Erected by John Burns in memory of his beloved daughter Mary who departed this life the 8th Sept. 1846 aged 8 years. Also his son James aged 19 years who departed this life 12th Jan. 1851. And of his beloved wife Martha who departed this life 11th of May 1853 aged 46 years. Also his beloved John who died 31st Octr. 1865 aged 22 years. The above-named John Burns 2nd June 1874 aged 68 years.

BUTLER
[Probably a re-used stone, north of church.] In memory of Daniel Butler who died 29th June 1866 aged 82 years. He was for 66 years the faithful and attached servant of the late M. McNEILL Esq. of the Curran by whose family this stone is erected.
[Lettering on the top edge.] One grave (sou)th ..... north of this.

BUTTLER
See WALSH

CALDWELL
[Loose sandstone set against south wall of nave.] Erected by Hannah Caldwell in memory of her husband Robert who died 29th April 1888. Also her dear and only son Robert, chief officer S.S. Bengore Head who died at London 29th Augt. 1886 aged 30 years and his remains were interred in this grave. Also her grandson Samuel McGAREL who died in infancy.
[The *Bengore Head* was built for the Ulster Steamship Co. by A. & J. Inglis, Glasgow and launched in March 1884. It was sunk by a torpedo from German submarine U60 on 20 June 1917 on a voyage from Sydney to London with a general cargo. See Harvey: *Head Line*, p.70]

CALDWELL
[*U.J.A.* VI (1900), 43. Arms:- three piles, in base a barry of three. Crest:- a bird displayed. Motto:- (In domino confido).] Here l(yet)h ye bodys of 2 children of John Caldwell viz. Ealenor aged 3 years & Janet 1 year died both in Nov. 1762.

CALDWELL
See SMYLY, TERBERT and WILSON

CALWELL
See AGNEW

CAMPBELL
[*M.D.* IV (1899), 2, p. xxviii; *U.J.A.* VI (1900), 41. Against south boundary wall, now in three pieces. Arms:- invected, a boar's head couped, in the base two swords in saltire, on a canton an estoile. Crest:- a (wolf's) head erased.] Erected in memory of Samuel Campbell who departed this life on the 1st of April 1823 aged 75 years. Also Jane HAWTHORN, wife to the above Samuel Campbell, who departed on the 9th of May 1823 aged 77 years.

CAMPBELL
[Beside James Campbell d. 1883.] Erected by Jane Campbell in memory of her beloved husband John Campbell who died 21st July 1881 aged 63 years. Also his father Patrick Campbell who died 29th April 1858 aged 82 years. The above-named Jane Campbell died 24th March 1890 aged 67 years. Also her grand-daughter Mary Jane Campbell who died 5th October 1890 aged 5 months. And her son John Campbell who died at Nottingham 20th Decr. 1900 aged 42 years. Also her son Thomas Campbell who died 22nd Jan. 1924 aged 69 years. Also his wife Mary G. Campbell who died 30th Dec. 1932 aged 84 years.

CAMPBELL
Erected by William Campbell in memory of three of his children who died in infancy. Also his daughter Agnes who died 2nd Jany. 1869 aged 16 years. And his beloved wife

Margaret died 13th Oct. 1879 aged 63 years. The above-named William Campbell died 20th Aug. 1884 aged 70 years.

CAMPBELL

[Beside path.] Erected by Robert Campbell, Inver, in memory of his son James who died 25th Jany. 1883 aged 22 years. His only daughter Annie who died 3rd June 1885 aged 22 years. His son William died in Pensacola 17th Jany. 1911 aged 44 years. The above-named Robert Campbell died 9th Novr. 1911 aged 80 years. His wife Jane Campbell died 29th Dec. 1914 aged 88 years. Their grandson James Campbell died 19th Aug. 1912 aged 14 years. Their grandson John Campbell died 3rd April 1927 aged 19 years.

CAMPBELL

See ROGERS

CAMPBLE

[Headstone in east of graveyard.] Here lieth the body of Margret Campble who departed this life the 25th July 1787 aged 55 years.

CARLEY

[*U.J.A.* IV (1900), 44. Ledger with crest:- two dragon heads addorsed. Motto:- Humilitate.] Erected by James Carley, in memory of his father Alexander Carley who departed this life on the 24th of March 1813 aged 51 years. Underneath are also interred three children of the latter viz – William who died on the 21st of January 1790 aged 3 months, Nancy 6th of April 1792 aged (one) year, and Alexander 8th of Novr. (17)93 (aged) 9 m(onths). And his daughter Ma(rg)are(t HOL)MES who (died Feby. 16th 183(6) aged 4(5) years. Also Jane, relict of the said Alexander Carley, who died April 24th 1848 aged 86 years. And the above(-nam)ed James Carley who died M(ay) 9th (1852) aged 62 years. Also the remains of Margaret Holmes who (died) in Liverpool on the 7th Jany. 1856 aged 37 yea(rs,) daughter of the above-named Margar(et Holmes) and Alexander Holmes, buried in Rio de Janeiro April 1826. Also (the) remains of Elizabeth, daughter of the said Alex(an)der Carley, who died on the 4th of June 1862 aged 66 years. And of Jane, daughter of the said Alexander Carley, who died on the 7th of June 1862 aged 64 (years). And of Anne, daughter of the said Alexander Carley, who died on the 9th of June 1881 aged 80 years. And of Ellen, daughter of the said Alexander Carley, who died on the 7th of May 1884 aged 82 years.

CARRUTHERS

See MANSON

CARSON

[East of church, white limestone with lead lettering, set in a sandstone frame.] Erected in affectionate remembrance of William Carson who died 28th Sept. 1884 aged 70 years. Also his son James who died in infancy, and his wife Isabella Carson who died 10th Decr. 1901 aged 82 years.

[The will of William Carson, late of Larne, county Antrim, overseer, who died 28 September 1884 at same place, was proved at Belfast 14 November 1884 by William John Dale of Ballyrudder, Cairncastle, and William Hill of Knowhead, Islandmagee, both in said county, farmers, the executors. Effects £220 3s. 6d.]

CASEMENT
[Recumbent granite cross enclosed with MONTGOMERY (1752).] Edmund
McGildowny Casement of Invermore, son of John M. Casement, died 24th April 1876
aged 63. Jane Casement died 28th February 1886. John Montgomery Casement of
Invermore died 24th October 1839 aged 83. Mary McGildowny Casement, wife of
above, died 22nd November 1844 aged 63. Grace Casement died 30th December 1888.
    [The will, with two codicils, of Grace Casement, formerly of Invermore, Larne, county
Antrim, and late of 8 Marguerite Terrace, Ballynafeigh, in the city of Belfast, county
Down, spinster, who died 30 December 1888 at latter place, was proved at Belfast 24
April 1889 by Edmund McGoldowney Hope Fulton of Pelham Lodge, Bray, county
Wicklow, esquire, of the Indian Civil Service, one of the executors. Effects £1,672 0s. 1d.
    The first of the Casements to settle in Inver was Dr. George Casement, R.N., who
leased 99 acres from the Marquis of Donegall in 1780. He was the son of Hugh Casement
of Ballinderry. He married (1) Elizabeth Montgomery and had two sons: John
Montgomery Casement of Invermore House; and Major-General Sir William Casement,
K.C.B., (1778-1844), who died in India. He married (2) Matilda Montgomery, daughter
of Hugh Montgomery of Inver.
    John Montgomery Casement, J.P., married Mary McGildowney, only daughter of John
McGildowney of Clare Park, Ballycastle, and had 2 sons and 6 daughters. Of their
children: Lieut. George died aged 19; Edmund McGildowney Casement (1812-1876)
inherited the property and was chairman of the Larne Board of Guardians. He died
unmarried. His sister Anne married General George Anson McCleverty; Jane and Grace
never married and when they died, Invermore House was sold to John Howden. Grace
Casement died at Ballynafeigh, Belfast, in her 71st year. *Larne Weekly Reporter*, 5 Jan.
1889. See Burke: *Landed Gentry of Ireland* (1912); McKillop: *History of Larne and East
Antrim* (2000).]

CASEMENT
See McCLEVERTY and MONTGOMERY

CATHERWOOD
See HOLDEN

CHICHESTER
[*U.J.A.* VI (1900), 42, sandstone, now smashed. Arms:- chequy, a chief vair, impaling
three (dog?) heads. Crest:- a heron holding in the beak a snake. Motto:- Invitum sequitur
bonos or honor sequitur fugientem.] Here lieth the body of David Chichester who
departed this life the 20th of April 1787 aged 45 years. Likewise Spenser Chichester, his
son, who departed the 9th of Oct. 1787 aged 2 years. And Mary his wife who departed
this life the 14th of January 1821 aged 75 years. Also Isac Chichester who departed this
life the 6th of July 1851 aged 69 years. Also Isabella, wife of Isaac Chichester, who
departed this life 8th June 1863 aged 70 years.

CHICHESTER
[*M.D.* IV (1900), 2, p. xxviii; *U.J.A.* VI (1900), 43. Sandstone, set against south
boundary wall. Arms:- chequy, a chief vair, impaling three (dog?) heads. Crest:- a heron
holding in the beak a snake. Motto:- Invitum sequitur bonos or honor sequitur
fugientem. Along the top edge is carved, "From this to south wall one grave north".] Here
lieth the body of Margaretann SNODY, wife to Arthur Chichester, who departed this life
April 25th 1807 aged 38 years. Also George Chichester aged 19 years. Also Margt HILL,
2nd wife to the above Arthur, who departed this life the 12th of March 1822 aged 55 yers.

Also the said Arthur Chichester, who died 14th Novr. 1844 aged 75 years. Also his son James, who died 29th July 1823 aged 19 years. And of his daughter Margaret who died the 23rd June 1829 aged 29 years.

CHICHESTER
[Red sandstone, against west bounday wall.] Two graves in length. This is the last resting place of the late Hamilton Chichester of Browndodd and Larne, a freeholder of the county Antrim, certificate no. 2144 dated at Carrickfergus 25th Oct. 1832, died 23rd Oct. 1835 aged 50 years. Also his wife Mary KEARNEY Chichester who died 12th July 1857 aged 70 years. Also his son David Chichester who died in infancy. Also his daughter Elizabeth Chichester who died 18th Jany. 1836 aged 18 years. Also his daughter Jane Chichester who died 24th June 183(8) aged 25 years. In memory of his sons David Chichester, John Chichester, Hamilton Chichester & James Chichester who all died abroad and are not interred here.
[Along top edge.] 2 graves north.
[Death: June 24, at the bank House, Ballycastle, Mary Chichester, eldest daughter of the late Hamilton Chichester, of Ballysnodd, relic the the [sic] late Samuel Kirkpatrick of Larne, *The Larne Reporter*, 28 June 1890.]

CHICHESTER
See PATON

CLARK
[Set against south wall of chancel.] In memory of Isabella SHUTTER, wife to William Clark, who died the 29th of Aug. 1778 aged 43 years. And three of their children, James, Hugh, and Robert. Also the above named William Clark, who died 1st Decer. 1827 aged 95 years.
[On top edge of stone:-] Two graves north of this.

CLEELAND
Erected by Henry Cleeland, Belfast, 18(3)8 in memory of his (mot)her Elizab(eth) Cleeland who died 1st J(un)e 18(3.) aged 52 years. H(is ..st(er ....)y who died 10(th F...) 184(0) aged 26 years. (H.....)ster J(a)ne who died 3rd Nov. 18(44) aged 23 years. His father James Cleeland who died 21st Feb. 1858 aged 76 years. Also his brother and sister who died infancy. Also his brother Samuel who died 19th August 1859 aged 33 years. Also his sister Elizabeth wife of James BAXTER, who died 27th May 1867 aged 48 years.

CLEMENTS
[Lead lettering on modern granite stone and low surround, south of church.] In loving memory of our dear father Robert Clements called home 15th May 1917. Also our dear mother Mary Clements called home 14 Oct. 1944. They left no will but goodwill and that to all mankind.

CLUGSTON
[Now flaking badly. Illegible portions (within brackets) have been supplied from *Porter: Congregational Memoirs*, p.82.] (Hic jacent omnia quae dissolvi potuerunt d)uoru(m virorum reverendorum,) viz. Josiae (Clugston et Roberti) SINCLAIR, quorum (utterque caetus anti)quior(is Protestantium Dissentientium apud Larne fuerat minister, prior quinquaginta octo annos, cum decesserit 80 annos natus 10 die Augusti 1775; alter triginta novem annos cum) mortem (obierit) 70 annos natus 20 (die) Februarii, 1795. Hi amicitia conjuncti, literarum periti, sancti, humani, religionem christianam doctriana et

moribus pieque, probeque illustrarunt. Renewed 1858, Classon Porter, minister. [The Latin as translated by H.G. Calwell:- Here lies all that was subject to dissolution of two reverend men viz. Josias Clugston and Robert Sinclair, of whom the one was minister of the old congregation of Protestant dissenters at Larne for fifty-eight years until his death at the age of 80 years on the 10th day of August 1775; the second for thirty-nine years before his death at the age of 70 years on the 20th day of February 1795. These men, joined in friendship, skilled in letters, holy, humane, showed forth the Christian religion by their teaching and their characters, piously and uprightly.]

[The Rev. Josias Clugston was the fifth minister of the Old Presbyterian Congregation of Larne and Kilwaughter, from 1717-1755. He was born c. 1695 near the town of Antrim but nothing further is known of his origins. He was one of the original members of the (Non-Subscribing) Presbytery of Antrim, founded in 1726, and seems to have been supported by his congregation in his religious views. He lived at Ballyboley, married and had 2 sons, one of whom died in 1732, while the other was the reverend James Clugston of Bandon, county Cork. He retired in 1755 and did not die until 10 August 1775.

The Rev. Robert Sinclair was born in 1725, son of William Sinclair, farmer, of near Tobermore, and brother of the reverend John Sinclair of Ballyhalbert and the reverend William Sinclair of Newtownards. He was ordained minister of the Larne Old Congregation in 1755 and lived for many years in Kilwaughter House (Castle) with the family of William Agnew, the local landlord. He graduated M.A. of Glasgow in 1766. He later married Elizabeth, daughter of Robert Allen and widow of William Jackson, and moved into Larne, but lived finally at Drumahoe, in the parish of Kilwaughter, where he died on 20 February 1795. Their son John emigrated to America and their daughter Fanny married a Mr. Williamson. See Porter: *Congregational Memoirs* (1929).]

COBAINE
[Sandstone in two pieces set against east boundary wall.] Erected by Samuel Cobaine in memory of his wife Barbara who died 22nd Feb. 1889 aged 79 years. Also their children viz. Edward, who died 1863, John, who died 1868, Rachel, who died 1868, Ellen, who died 1872.

[He had a bakery in Mill Street, later changed to Baine.]

COEY
[Sandstone set against south boundary wall.] Erected in memory of John Coey of Ballylorn who departed this life on the 26st [sic] of June 1843 aged 74 years. Also his son John Coey died on the 27th of August 1850 aged 33 years. Also his son James who died 11th November 1861 aged 48 years. And his wife Elizabeth who died 29th December 1861 aged 82 years.

COOPER
See COWAN

COWAN
[Loose sandstone set against the south wall of the church.] Erected by Agnes COOPER In memory of her mother, Ann Cowan, who died 25th Dec. 1861 aged 64 years. Her aunt Mary Ann SIMPSON who died 9th Nov. 1880 aged 96 years, interred in Borough Cemetery, Belfast. Also her uncle Samuel SIMPSON who died 24th Feb. 1870 aged 73 years.

[The will of Samuel Simpson, late of Larne, county Antrim, master mariner, who died 24 February 1870 at same place, was proved at Belfast 21 March 1870 by the oath of Elsie Simpson of Larne aforesaid, the widow and one of the executors. Effects under £800.]

COWAN
    See YOUNG

CRAWFORD
    See SMILEY and WOODSIDE

CREIGHTON
    See McMUNN

CROOKS
    See HOOD

CUBITT
    See SMYTH

CULBERT
    See ROBINSON

CUMMING
    See MACAULAY

CUNNINGHAM
    [White limestone with lead lettering, against south boundary wall.] In memory of David
    Cunningham who died in 1854. Also his wife Eliza Cunningham who died 2nd Dec.
    1879 aged 82 years. Their son Thomas who died 27th May 1905 aged 79 years. Their
    daughter Isabella who died 19th June 1907 aged 76 years.

CUNNINGHAM
    [Sandstone south of chancel. Along top edge is carved "(......grave so)uth".] Erected by
    James Cunningham in memory of his beloved parents John Cunningham & Ja(net
    N)ichol. Also his brother('s ... John who) died ... Feb. 18(4)0 a(ged 61) years. And (.....
    who d)ied) 13th July 1840 aged 59 years.

CUNNINGHAM
    [Laid flat near south boundary wall, south of chancel.] Erected by James Cunningham in
    memory of his beloved wife Ann Cunningham who departed this life 30th October 1845
    aged 67 years. Also the above named James Cunningham who departed this life the 10th
    June 1846 aged 57 years.

CUNNINGHAM
    See McCUSACK

CURRY
    [South of nave.] Erected in memory of Montgomery H. Curry who departed this life the
    4th Decr. 1814 aged 42 years. Also his beloved wife Mary who died 17th Feb. 1854 aged
    77 years. Their son James 16th Dec. 1828, 22. His wife Margt. 10th April 1830, 22.
    Their son Robert in 1829, 20 daughter Agnes 17th Nov. 1832, 28. For they alone are held
    in everlasting memory whose deeds partake of heaven.

CURRY
    See MORDOC(H)

DARCUS
[White marble tablet in carved sandstone frame attached to boundary wall beside door to church hall. Arms:- a chevron between three lion heads erased. Crest and motto damaged.] Sacred to the memory of Solomon Darcus who died at Gardenmore, November 29th 1849 aged 66 years. J. Robinson.
[Solomon Darcus was second son of Henry Darcus of Castle Fin, county. Donegal, deceased., one of the Surveyors of the Revenue, and Mary Speer. He was educated in Dublin (according to an affidavit by Solomon Speer, Michaelmas 1802) and became an attorney to the Exchequer, 1810). See Keane, Phair and Sadleir: *King's Inns Admission Papers, 1607 - 1867*]

DARCUS
[A table-stone beside door to church hall.] Beneath this stone are the earthly remains of Letitia Darcus, eldest daughter of Solomon and Anne Darcus, who died at Larne on Monday the 3rd day of October 1831 aged 19 years and 10 months. Trusting to a happy meeting with her family at the resurrection of all, through her blessed redeemer the Lord Jesus the Saviour of all who believe and trust in him. Also the remains of her youngest brother Richard Speer Darcus, an infant aged 10 months and 14 days, who died on Sunday the 18th day of December 1831. "The Lord gave and the Lord hath taken away. Blessed be the name of the Lord." Also beneath the same stone lie the remains of Mr. William WALSH, late of Glenarm, their granduncle who died at Larne on the 9th day of November 1828 aged 74 years. There also lie the remains of Henry John Darcus, eldest son of said Solomon and Anne, who died at Gardenmore 5th November 1837 in the 16th year of his age after a long and painful illness which he bore with Christian patience and submission to the divine will.

DARCUS
See WALSH

DAWSON
See BROWN

DIAMOND
Here was interred John Diamond who died the 22(nd) October 1793 aged 78 & his wife Elizabeth DOE who died the 22nd July 1785 aged 80. Also 5 grand children, viz. John Diamond 8 months old died Aug. 1785 & Lucy the 4th May 1802 aged 3 years & James the 8th April 1804 aged 4 years & Mary the 26th January 1812 aged 23 years & John the 11th June 1813 aged 20 years. Also his son Jno. & father of the above children who died the 29th Novr. 1819 aged 70.

DICK
[Set against south wall of church.] In memory of James Dick who died (........ 1824 aged .. years .... mother (C)a(th)a(rine) Dick departed this life 2(6th De.......) aged (4)7 years. Also his brother Campbell Dick who died 23rd June 1868 aged 64 years.

DICKEY
See MOORE

DIXON
[White limestone and sandstone monument (in a high railed enclosure) northwest of church. At the top a female figure in a halo of fourteen stars holds with outstretched arms a scroll bearing the legend "ever let love and truth prevail".] Sacred to the memory of Thomas Dixon who died 31st July 1868 aged 63 years. And of his eldest son Francis McCambridge Dixon who died of sunstroke at Westpoint US 25th June 1866 aged 30 years. Also two of his children Thomas and Sarah who died in infancy. And Sarah, wife of the above named Thomas Dixon, who died 4th September 1873 aged 62 years. Also their youngest son Alexander McCambridge Dixon who died 28th May 1926 aged 80 years and Harriett Elizabeth wife of Alexander McCambridge Dixon who died 22nd June 1940 aged 89 years.

[The will of Thomas Dixon, late of Larne, county Antrim, merchant, who died 31 July 1868 at same place, was proved at Belfast 7 September 1868 by the oaths of Thomas Stewart Dixon and Daniel Dixon, late of Belfast, and Alexander Dixon of Larne (all in said county), merchants, the executors. Effects under £5,000.

Thomas Dixon, timber merchant and ironmonger and one of the first Town Commissioners in 1854, was the son of Thomas Dixon (1770-1849) of Bun-na-Mairge, Ballycastle, and Mary McNeill (c. 1775-1827). He married Sarah McCambridge and one of their sons was Sir Daniel Dixon, D.L., (1844-1907); shipowner and timber merchant; Mayor of Belfast 1892; Lord Mayor of Belfast 1893, 1901-3, 1905-6; M.P. for North Belfast (Conservative) 1905-07; created a baronet 1903; married firstly Lizzie Agnew (d.1868), secondly Annie Shaw (d. 1918). His son, Sir Thomas James Dixon (1868 - May 1950) married Edith Clarke, D.B.E., (c.1872-1964), daughter of Stewart Clark of Dundas, Linlithgow, and Annie Smiley, sister of Sir Hugh Smiley, bart. Sir Thomas was a member of the Northern Ireland Senate 1924-50 and became the first mayor of Larne 1939-41. He was succeeded by his half-brother Herbert (1880 - July 1950); M.P. (Unionist) at Westminister 1918-39; M.P. at Stormont 1921-50; created Lord Glentoran of Ballyalloly, 1939. He was succeeded by his son, Lt. Col. Daniel Stewart Thomas Bingham Dixon, K.B.E., (1912-95); second Baron and fourth Baronet; M.P. at Stormont 1950-61; N.I. Senate 1961-73; married Lady Diana Mary Wellesley 1933. He was succeeded by his elder son, Major Thomas Robin Valerian Dixon, C.B.E., D.L.; third baron; born 21 April 1935; Olympic Bobsleigh Gold Medallist 1964; resident at Drumadarragh House, Doagh. See McKillop: *History of Larne* (2000); *Debrett's Peerage* (1964). *Burke's Peerage & Baronetage* (1999).]

DIXON
[Double lancet window depicting storm and Jesus walking on water, in south wall of nave.] To the glory of God and in loving remembrance of Thomas and Sarah Dixon and of their sons Francis McC. and Thomas S. Dixon.

DOE
See DIAMOND

DOOLE
[White limestone with lead lettering, laid flat in north-east of graveyard.] Erected by Mary E. Doole in memory of her husband James Doole died 21st May 1912. Their daughter Rachel died 20th Aug. 1902 aged 13 years and his father James Doole died 14th Oct. 1877.

[The will of James Dool [sic], late of Carnduff, county Antrim, late a farmer, who died 14 October 1877 at same place, was proved at Belfast 19 November 1877 by the oaths of

Hugh Walker, auctioneer, and John Kane, surgeon, both of Larne, same county, the executors. Effects under £450.]

DOORIS
[Sandstone, against east boundary wall.] Erected by James Dooris in memory of his father John Dooris who died the 31st August 1871 aged 59 years. Also Rose MONTFORD his grand mother who died June 1st 1860 aged 79 years. Also his mother Jane Dooris who died 2nd August 1873 aged 70 years. The above-named James Dooris who died 26th February 1903 aged 69 years. Also Mary Montford, wife of James Dooris, died 14th Jan. 1906 aged 78 years.

DRUMMOND
See GETTY

DUFF
See ALLEN and LEWIS

DUGAT
SeeMONTGOMERY

DUNCAN
[Laid flat, east of church.] Erected to the memory of Margaret Duncan who departed this life the 6th day of June 1838 aged (18) years. Also her mother Margaret Dun... who died 27th De....... aged 76 yea...

EARL
[Very low stone.] Erected by (J)ames Earl (in) memory of Mary (his) wife who died 16th De(c.) 1831 aged 53 years.

EARL
[Laid flat near east boundary wall.] Sacred to the memory of Mary, wife of James Earl, who died 16th Decr. 1831 aged 58 years. Also the above-named James Earl who died 19th Jany. 1847. Also their daughters, Betsy who died 2nd June 1883, Mary who died 11th March 1886.
[Betsy Earl died at Cooper's Lane, Larne, 2 July 1883 aged 64 years. *Larne Weekly Reporter*, 7 July 1883, p.2.]

EARLS
[Sandstone set against south boundary wall, southwest of church.] Erected by Mary Earls in memory of her husband John Earls who died 29th Augt. 1854 aged 53 years. Also her second son Thoms. who died 28th January 1858 aged 23 years. And of her eldest son Alexr. who died 11th March 1859 aged 26 years. The above Mary Earls died 5th April 1884 aged 75 years. Also her daughter Jane who died 24th Feby. 1894 aged 62 years.

ECCLES
[*U.J.A.* VI (1900), 46. The arms were doubtless the same as on the succeeding stone. Only part now remains.] Here lyeth the body of Margery, wife of Samuel Eccles, who departed this life May 6th 1789 aged 35 years. Also of the said Samuel Eccles who departed the 21st of Decr. 1805 aged 53 years. Also of Eleanor his second wife who died 4th Decr. 1825 aged 62 years.

ECCLES

[*U.J.A.* VI (1900), 45. Laid flat before east window. In a roundel are the arms:- or, two halberts saltireways. Crest:- an arm embowed, in the hand a broken halbert. Motto:- se defendendo.] Here lie the remains of Thomas Eccles who died on the 11th of September 1860 aged 47 years. And of his sons James who died 7th December 1851 aged 10 years. And Thomas who died 18th February 1851 aged 1 year & 7 months. A(lso of h)is father & mother, James Eccles who died 25th May 1850 aged 77 years. And Anne Eccles who died 15th March 1850 aged 74 years. A(nd of his) daughter Margaret (who) died 22nd October 1874 aged 20 years. And of his (wife) Anne Munro FERRES who died 20th (Febry.) 1889 aged 75 years. And of his son Robert, M.A., M.D., M.R.C.S., Eng. who died 18th August 1891 aged 40 years.

[Dr Robert Eccles was born on 11 July 1851 at Larne, son of Thomas Eccles, educated at Belfast `Inst` and studied arts and medicine at Q.U.B. He graduated B.A. (R.U.I.) 1872, M.A. 1873, M.D. 1875 and M.Ch. 1876, also taking his M.R.C.S. England in 1876. He became a surgeon and general practitioner in Kensington, Liverpool, where he died on 18 August 1891. See *Medical Directory.* and QUB records.]

ECCLES

[Single lancet window depicting the revival of Jairus' daughter, in south wall of chancel.] To the glory of God and in memory of Margaret Glasgow Eccles, born Oct. 14 1854, died Oct. 22 1874. Erected by her brother. "She is not dead, but sleepeth." St. Luke VIII, 52.

If Thou shouldst call me to resign
What most I prize, it ne'er was mine.
I only yield Thee what is Thine.
Thy will be done.

E(CC)L(E)S

See MATEER

ELLIOT

[Laid flat beside next stone.] Erected by .... Elliot .. (Bally.........).

ELLIOTT

[Laid flat, appears on a Lawrence photograph.] Erected by John Elliott in memory of his father David Elliott who died 27th August 1877, aged 78 years. The above-named John Elliott died 30th December 1920 aged 77 years. Also his daughter Anna Maria Elliott who died 8th July 1938 aged 55 years.

[The will of David Elliott, late of Kilwaughter, county Antrim, farmer, who died 21 August 1877 at same place, was proved at Belfast 19 December 1877 by the oaths of Houston Ballantine junior, and John Elliott, both of Headwood, Kilwaughter, Larne, same county, farmers, two of the executors. Effects under £800.]

ENGLISH

Erected by Ellen English to the memory of her father Matthew English who died 18th October 1836 aged 69 years. Al(so) her mother Nancy who died .... Febr(u....) 18(47) aged 9(1 years.) T(he above..........e)n (..ng)lis(h died 18th M.. 1890 .... 94) ye(ars.)

[Death: May 18th, at her residence, Inver, Larne, Ellen English, aged 94 years. *The Larne Reporter*, 31 May 1890.]

ENGLISH

See McNEILL

ERWIN
   See FEE

ESDEL
   [*U.J.A.* VI (1900), 50. Arms:- a chevron between three swords. (Crest:- a bird, in the
   dexter talon a javelin(?)] Here lyeth the body of Janet Esdel who died Oct. 20 1772 aged
   52 years. Also Janet Wylie who died 11th Apr. 1776 aged 1 year. Also Mary WYLIE........

ESLER
   See FERRIS

FAIR
   [Large single lancet window in south wall of nave. The church of St. Cedma's is depicted
   at the centre of a cross with "To this you belong" written across the arms. The four
   apostles are represented in the quarters by borrowings from the Book of Kells. At the top
   are arms:- azure, three crosses patonce argent, on a chief or a lamb trippant of the second.
   Above this is the date 1609 and encircling all is the legend:- Salvatoris Connorensis
   Decanus et capitulum sancti. At the bottom left of the window are the arms of the see of
   Connor:- azure three crosses patonce or between the Agnus Dei argent with the banner
   of victory, on a chief of the second two crosiers in saltire of the third.] To the glory of
   God and in grateful memory of James Alexander Fair, M.A., Rector of Larne and Inver
   1968-1995 and Dean of Connor 1990- 1995. Revelation 14:13. Lead Lines & David
   Esler Studio, 1977.
      [The Reverend James Alexander Fair was born on 4 May 1926 in Glasgow, son of James
   Alexander Fair, J.P. of Ballygawley, county Tyrone, and Jane Wilson of Ballygawley. He
   was educated at the Royal School, Dungannon, and graduated B.A. and M.A. of T.C.D.
   He was curate of Monaghan 1949-52, and of St. Mark`s, Portadown 1952-56, rector of
   Woodschapel 1956-60, dean`s vicar of St. Anne`s Cathedral, Belfast 1860-62, curate-in-
   charge of Rathcoole 1962-68, rector of Larne and Inver 1968-95, prebend of Cairncastle
   1982-84, treasurer of Connor 1984-86, chancellor of Connor 1986-90 and dean of
   Connor 1990-95. He married on 6 September1956 Marcella Jane Thompson of
   Portadown and had 1 son and 3 daughters. See Leslie: *Clergy of Connor* (1993).]

FAIRIES
   See McTIER

FEE
   [Loose sandstone, broken at bottom, in southwest corner of graveyard.] Here lyeth the
   body of Janet Fee who died (22)d Jan. 1777. Also A(n)...ew (Fee) who died (J)uly ..
   17(8)6 aged (.) years and ... m(o)nths. Al.. their ..... Sarah ERWIN who died Mar. 1788
   aged 43 years. And likewise their father Andrew Fee who died 9th of Feb. 1790 aged 49
   years. Also his brother-in-law Owen McGERRALD who died Novr. 2d. 1800 a
   ....

FERGUSON
   [Sandstone in south west of graveyard. Broken stone, bottom missing.] In memory of
   (Jen)ny Ferguson (wif)e to David (Fer)guson who died J(un)e 19th .... 10) aged (63)
   years. (As a wi)fe, a mother and a fri(end sh)e faithfully performed her duty and left this
   world in the faith and hope of a Christian. Also her grand-daughter Jennet Ferguson died
   13th Augt. 1833 aged 19 years. Also her husband David Ferguson died 2nd March 1838

aged 75 years. And daughter Mary Ann Ferguson who departed this life 26th Jan. 1842 aged 53 (years. A)lso their s(on ....) (One grave at each side of this stone).

FERGUSON

[Loose sandstone set against south wall church tower.] In memory of John Ferguson who died 12th Nov. 1833 aged 2 years. Eliza Ferguson died 27th Oct. 1836 aged 19 years. And Mary Ann Ferguson their sister departed this life 28th April 1838 aged 16 years. Also Elizabeth Ferguson who died 9th Feb. 1878 aged 85 years.

FERGUSON
See MITCHEL

FER(IE)S
See BLACK

FERRES

[*U.J.A.* VI (1900), 48. Recumbent, east of church, with arms:- three fish in pale naiant. Crest:- a horse's head couped. Motto:- gaudium adfero.] Underneath this monument (Erected by Samuel Ferres) is the remains of his father Charles Ferres who departed this life the 27th of Sepr. 1794 AEt 70.Likewise the remains of five of S. Ferres's children of whome Jas. B. S. Ferres departed this life the 26th of Octobr. 1811 AEt 19 yrs. Underneath this monument was likewise formerly deposited, the remains of Jno. MILLAR (grandfather to Charles Ferres) who died the 12th May 1732 AEt 76. His wife Elizabeth ADAMS who died 4th May 1752 AEt 90 and their son Chas. Millar who died 7th of Novr. 1763 AEt 76. Here also is deposited the remains of Dorathea BEERS, wife of the above named Samuel Ferres, who departed this life the 12th of June 1818 AEt 50 years. Here also is interred the remains of the above named Samuel Ferres who died on the 28th day of May 1827 aged 68 years.

[Samuel Ferres (also spelt "Ferris") was an apothecary and surgeon in Larne, son of Charles Ferres, distiller. Samuel helped to establish the Larne Savings Bank in 1816 and sold the premises for the Methodist Church in 1827. See McKillop; *History of Larne and East Antrim* (2000).]

FERRES

[Recumbent, beside the foregoing.] Dedicated by Charles Ferres, surgeon, in memory of his father the late William Ferres of Larne who departed this life 29th July 1831 aged 69 years. Also two of his sons, viz. Thomas J.M. who died 20th Feby. 1847 aged 9 years and 10 months. And William who died 4th March 1847 aged 4 years and 5 months. Also to the memory of his mother Margaret Ferres who died 7th Septemr. 1849 aged 76 years. And his son William born 31st May 1850, died in infancy. Also his sister Jane McCAUGHEY who died 1st Decr. 1852 aged 42 years. The above-named Charles Ferres died 4th Nov. 1870 aged 58 years. His son James McD. died 2(.)th Sept. 1871 aged 27 years. And his sister Margaret who died 19th June 1879 aged 72 years.

[Letters of administration of the personal estate of Charles Ferris [sic], late of Larne, county Antrim, surgeon, who died 4 November 1870 at same place, were granted at Belfast 18 January 1871 to Letitia Ferris of Larne aforesaid, the widow of said deceased. Effects under £2,000.

Charles Ferres qualified with the LRCS Edinburgh in 1836 and was medical officer of health and medical officer of the workhouse. Two nephews were also medical doctors: Hugh Smiley Kane, d. 1872 aged 33; and John Kane medical officer of health for the

Larne Union, d. 1883 aged 42. See McKillop: *History of Larne and East Antrim* (2000); *Medical Directory.*

Death: April 21st, at Groomsport, Annie McDonald Ferres, third daughter of the late Doctor Ferres, of Larne. *The Larne Reporter,* 3 May 1890.]

FERRES
See ECCLES

FERRIS
[Recumbent stone, east of church.] Erected by Charles Ferris in memory of his parents John and Fannie Ferris. Also his son William who died 6th Jany. 1861 aged 36 years. And Jane, wife of Alexander HA(MILTON), died June 8 1863 aged 28 years. John died 13th Jan. 1874 aged (44) years. And six of his grand-children namely Nancy Ferris, Robert Ferris, William Ferris, (Ja)ne Ferris, Jane Hamilton, and Ann McCAREY. All died young. And of his beloved wife Nancy who died 8th D(ece)mber 1877 aged 73 years. Maggie ESLER died 29th Novr. 1878 (ag)ed 22 years. Also her two children (Joh)n Ferris died 22nd April 1879 aged 3? years. And Martha died 18th August 1880 aged 3 years. Robert John (died) 12th April 1881 aged 19 years. The above-named Charles Ferris who died 2nd August 1894 aged 92 years. Also Mary Ferris, wife of the above John who died 30th May 1898 aged 69 years.

[The will of John Ferres [sic], late of Larne, county Antrim, grocer and builder, who died 13 January 1874 at same place, was proved at Belfast 29 June 1874 by the oath of Mary Ferres of Larne aforesaid, the widow, the sole executrix. Effects under £200.

Death: Oct. 29, at Railway Terrace, Larne, Jane, infant daughter of Mr. Alexander Hamilton, aged 3 years. *Larne Weekly Reporter,* 4 Nov. 1865.]

FERRIS
[Polished granite stone in the shape of a hipped roof decorated with dove bearing a laurel branch and on a scroll the motto:- gaudium adfero.] Erected by James Ferris in memory of his mother Margaret Ferris, who died 28th Aug. 1905 aged 84 years. Also his sister Agnes, who died 29th Dec. 1879 aged 24 years. His sister Eliza BEGGS, who died 21st Oct. 1882 aged 21 years.

FINLAY
[*U.J.A.* VI (1900), 49. Set against south boundary wall. Arms:- a lion passant, on a chief a boar's head between two mullets.] Here lyeth the body of Hugh Finlay who died June 11th 1786 aged 64 years after 3 days ilness but we hope not unprepared for his end as he was a sincere Christian, an affectionate husband and indulgent parent & a faithful friend. Also his wife Mary NAESMITH who departed this life on the 22nd of Jany. 1823 in the 91st year of her age.

FINLEY
[*U.J.A.* VI (1900), 49. Laid flat east of church alongside the Barklie enclosure. Arms:- a chevron between three roses. Crest:- an arm, in the hand a sword. Motto:- (Invitum seuitur bonos or honor sequitur).] (Her)e lyeth the body (of) Jean Fi(n)ley w(ife to T)homas F(inley) who depar(te)d this life (the 11th of) January (1806 ag)ed 58 years. (Al)so the above named Thomos Finley who departed this life the 25th of April 1811 aged 78 years. Also Thomas Finley who departed this life the 29th of March 1851 aged 73 years. [Along the top of this stone is cut:-] Erected by Thomos Finley in memory of his father and mother.

FISHER
[Small stone next to William PATTON d. 1880. On the front is a face (skull?) and on the back is a similiar face and an hourglass.] Memento mori. Here lyeth the body of (Ma)grat Fisher wife to E(r)gh(.e) Mv(rr.. F)o(r.tne..............) and o(f) a(ge a.o..8)0 (vh)o d(ep)arted this life the 6 of Ivn 1708.

FISHER
[*M.D.* IV (1899), 2, p.xxviii, illustrates arms for Fisher. These are the same as appear on the Ferres stone, but no existing Fisher stone has been found with arms. The *M.D.* entry is probably a mistake.]

FITZSIMONS
See McKEOWN

FLECK
[*U.J.A.* VI (1900), 45. Slate set against north boundary wall. Arms:- a barry of six. Crest:- a garb. Motto:- Virtus semper viridus.] Here lyeth ye bodies of 2 children of Robert Flecks viz. Mary, who died August ye 20th 1738 & Helen died May ye 8th 1751. Ye aforsed Robert Fleck died Novr. ye 22 1757 aged 53 years.

FLECK
[White limestone with anchor carved in a roundel, north-west of church.] Erected by G. & T. Fleck to the memory of their brother John who died 4th Novr. 1897 aged 51 years. Also their father & mother Thomas & Rose Fleck and of their aunt Nellie Fleck. Also Ellen, daughter of the above T. Fleck, who died in infancy and was buired [sic] in Castlereagh.

[Administration of the estate of John Fleck, late of Larne, county Antrim, mercantile manager, who died 4 November 1897, granted at Belfast 24 November 1897 to Thomas Fleck of 51 Westmoreland Street, Belfast, commission agent, the brother. Effects £616 10s.]

FLECK
See NEILSON

FOSTER
[Set against east boundary wall.] To the memory of Arabella Letitia Foster who died Febuary 1826 aged 6 months.

FOSTER
See GETTY

FOR(RE)ST
[Lying flat in east of graveyard.] H... lyeth the body of .....t For(re)st (who) died ... Augt. 1779 aged (45) yea(rs).

FULLERTON
[Large bookstand on holy table.] Presented to Larne & Inver Parish Church by David Fullerton, J.P., People's Churchwarden, July 1919.

FULLERTON
See GAWN

GAWN

[Lead lettering in white limestone, laid flat in south-west of graveyard. Top half of stone only.] Sacred to the memory of John Hill Gawn who died 25th December 1885 aged 80 years. Ellen WILSON, his wife, who died 31st March 1890 aged 84 years. Also their children James Wilson Gawn B.A., Curate of Trowbridge, Wilts., who died 26th October 1860 aged 33 years. Elizabeth Jane FULLERTON, ...

[The will of John Hill Gawn, late of 22 Main Street, Larne, county Antrim, gentleman, who died 25 December 1885 at same place, was proved at Belfast 13 January 1886 by the Rev. John Douglas Gawn of Rookervilla, Whally Bridge, Stockport, England, clerk, and David McQuillan of Mill Street, Larne, merchant, the executor. Effects £814 15s.

John Gawn was teacher and town clerk in 1861 and was still town clerk in 1884. *Belfast and Province of Ulster Directory.*]

GETTY

[Recumbent stone, east of church.] Here lyeth the body of Robert Getty who died May the 13 1698 aged 89 years, with his wives Margaret FOSTER & Margaret PORTER & 13 children. & also the 5 children of John Getty:- Robert who died Feb. 18 1722 aged 10 years, Hugh who died Apr. 30 1718 aged 4 years, Mary who died Sep. 4 1722 aged 1 year, John who died Sep. 13 1725 aged 2 years, Margaret who died Mar. 10 1726 aged 1 mon. Also John Getty who died 8th Mar. 1756 aged 81 years. Mary McPEAKE his wife who died 31st Dec. 1771 aged 84 years. Elisabeth Getty who departed this life the 14th of Novbr. 1817 aged 55 years. Jane Getty, wife to James L. DRUMMOND M.D., who died on the 8th Feby. 1831 aged 40 years.

[Jane Getty was the first wife of Dr. James Lawson Drummond, one of the great driving forces of intellectual life in early 19th century Belfast. She married him on 30 March 1824 in Rosemary Street Presbyterian Church, Belfast. He was born in Larne in 1783, the son of William Drummond, naval surgeon (died of typhus, 1783 in Ballyclare) and Rose Hare, and graduated M.D. of Edinburgh University in 1814. His main appointments were as professor of anatomy and physiology at Belfast `Inst` 1818-49 and first president (dean) of the Faculty of Medicine at `Inst` 1835-37 and 1844. He was also one of the founders and first president of the Belfast Natural History Society (forerunner of the Ulster Museum) and a president of the Belfast Literary Society. He married twice later but had no children by any of his wives. He died in College Square North on 16 May 1853 and was buried in Ballybollen, Ahoghill. His elder brother William Drummond (1778-1865), also born in Larne, was minister of Belfast Second Presbyterian Church and of Strand Road, Dublin, and a poet. See Calwell: The Drummonds of Larne, *The Corran,* Winter 1982/83, pp. 2-3; Benn: *History of the Town of Belfast* (1880); *D.N.B.*; Fisher and Robb: *R.B.A.I., Centenary Volume* (1913); Froggatt (1996).

GETTY

[Recumbent stone, next to the above.] Here lyeth the body of Robert Getty who departed this life 26th Ma(r.17.. a)ged 33 years. Al(so his ...)nd - daughtr. Mary Getty who died 15th June 1801 aged 11 years. Ma(ry) Getty, wife ...... above Robert Getty died (23rd) Febry. 1823 aged 82 years. Also their son John Getty who died on the 25th Sept. 1832 aged 62 years. Also their daughter Margaret Getty who departed this life the 28th of May 1846 aged 75 years.

GETTY

[Large sandstone with two panels, beside and north-east of church. First panel:-] Here lieth the body of Elizabeth Getty wife of William Getty who died 1st April 1791 aged 66 years. Also one son, a child. Also his daughter Elizabeth who died 17th March 1800 aged

36 years. Also William Getty who died 27th Jan. 1807 aged 84 years. Also his son Robert Getty who died 8th May 1815 aged 63 years. And Mary Getty, wife of said Robert Getty, who died 8th April 1827 aged 62 years. Also Robert Getty, son of the above Robt. & Mary Getty, died 20th Jan. 1854 aged 67 years. Also John Getty, last surviving son of the above named Robt. & Mary Getty, who died at his residence, Beechpark, Belfast, on the 10th day of April 1874 aged 76 years.

[Second panel:-] Erected in memory of Elizabeth Getty, wife of Hugh SMILEY, who died suddenly on the 29th day of September 1827 aged 38 years. Also Ann Getty who died 20th Jan. 1828 aged 65 years. Also Jane Getty who died 4th Dec. 1828 aged 73 years. Also Francis Getty who died 5th Dec. 1830 aged 65 years.

GETTY
   See MATEER

GILLIS
   See LEARMOR

GILLMER
   [Table stone, bottom missing.] Here lyeth the body of George Gillmer Esqr. late surveyor of the Port of Larne who departed this life on the 22d October 1775 aged 53 years. Also are deposited the remains of James WHITE Esqr., successor to the late Geoe. Gillmer, Surveyor of Larne, who departed this life suddenly on the 4th of July 1781 aged 35 years. Also the remains of Henry Wm BAYLEE Esqr. C(o.....) of (Cust....................).

GLASGOW
   [*M.D.* IV (1899), 2, pp.xxvii and xxx; *U.J.A.* VI (1900), 47. Loose slate headstone now in church hall. Arms:- on a mount a tree, in the dexter fess point a salmon naiant with a ring in its mouth, in the sinister fess point a bell. Crest:- a bird rising with a branch in its beak. Motto:- I wait my time] Here lyeth the bodies of XI children of Hugh Glesgow towit Jane ye first who died Janr. ye 8th 1733 & Hugh ye last died Novr. ye 30th 1756 aged XI years. Hugh Glasgow their father who died the 8th of July 1767 aged 62 years. Also his wife Ann Glasgow who died the 8th June 1786 aged 75 years. And James Glasgow their son who died the 14th of April 1802 aged 64 years. Also his wife Jane Glasgow died 21st July 1820 aged 79 years. And of Ann Glasgow, daughter to the last named, who died the 25th May 1832 aged 64 years.

GLASGOW
   [*U.J.A.* VI (1900), 47. Loose sandstone set against south wall of church. Arms:- on a mount a tree, in the dexter fess point a salmon naiant a ring in its mouth, in the sinister fess point a bell. Crest:- a bird rising with a branch in its beak. Motto:- I wait my (time).] Erected by William Glasgow to the memory of his daughter Jane SHUTTER Glasgow who departed this life the 21st day of April 1799 aged nine months. Also the above Willm. Glasgow died 5th Octr. 1816 aged 53 years. His wife Elizth. died 17th Sept. 1832 aged 60 years. Also their daughter Eliza who died 25th April 1839 aged 37 years. And their daughter Mary who died 18th Octr. (1844) aged 37 years.

GLASGOW
   [Arms:- on a mount a tree, in the dexter fess point a salmon naiant with a ring in its mouth, in the sinister fess point a bell. Crest:- a dove with a laurel branch in its beak. Motto:- I wait my time.] William Glasgow departed this life 19th April 1783 aged 7(4) years. Also James Glasgow who died the 25th July 1831 aged 58 years.

GLASS
[Small stone, south wall.] Wm. Glass.

GLEGHORN
Erected by Samuel MARTIN in memory of the Gleghorn family. One grave south, one grave north.

GLEGHORN
See McFAREN

GRAHAM
[Red sandstone set against east boundary wall.] Erected by Margaret KIRKPATRICK in memory of her mother Margt. WOODSIDE, wife of Alexr. MEHARG, who died 5th Dec. 1814 AE 72 years. Hugh Graham, her great-grand-father in July 1736 AE 72. And of Agnes HENDERSON his wife in Sept. 1738 AE 57 years.

GRAHAM
[Tall sandstone in southeast of graveyard beside James ALEXANDER.] Sacred to the memory of Alexander Graham who died at Larne July 24, 1857 AE 77 years. And of four of his children who also are interred in this place (viz.) Ellen Graham who died March 1, 1839 aged 19 years. Jane Graham who died Octr. 14, 1843 aged 20 years. And Mary and John Graham who died in infancy. His three other sons died and were interred abroad, viz. Alexander Graham who died at Vera Cruz June 15, 1845 aged 19 years. James Graham who died at George Town, Demerara, January 22, 1849 aged 27 years & William D. R. Graham who died at Cincinnati, U.S., March 22, 1856 aged 30 years. His widow and four surviving daughters before leaving their native town for America inscribe this stone to the memory of the beloved relatives whose names are thereon recorded.

GRAHAM
[White limestone set in sandstone beside path.] Erected by Gawn and Sarah Graham in loving remembrance of their dear and only daughter Ellen, who died 5th December 1874 aged 25 years. Also their dear and only son William who died 5th December 1875 aged 28 years. The above-named Gawn Graham died 28th May 1892 aged 71 years. The above-named Sarah Graham died 6th Feby. 1898 aged 77 years.

[Letters of administration of the personal estate of Gawn Graham, late of Larne, county Antrim, saddler, who died 28 May 1892, granted at Belfast 30 September 1892 to Sarah Graham of Larne, widow. Effects £135.

Deaths: Jan. 16 at the residence of her parents, Park Street, Larne, Margaret Jane, only daughter of Mr. Gawn Graham, aged 13 months. *Larne Weekly Recorder*, 27 Jan. 1883.]

GRAHAM
See ALEXANDER and WOODSIDE

GRANT
[*M.D.* III (1895), 1, 3; *U.J.A.* VI (1900), 46. Flaking sandstone southeast of church. A family group is carved at the top of the stone – mother and four children. A further two children may be represented by the cot and the coffin. Corinthian columns flank the inscription and arms:- a mullet between three antique crowns within a bordure ermine. Crest:- a dexter arm vambraced embowed, in the hand a sword. Motto:- Stand sure. Supporters:- two savages each holding a club.] Here lyeth ye body of Cath(e)rine

McDON(A)LD l(a)t(e) wife to (William Grant) who died Feb. ye 15 1740 aged 36 (years. Also 6 children.)

GRANT
   See RUSSEL

GRAY
   [Laid flat beside gate.] Erected by Robert MARTIN in memory of his aunt Mary Gray who died 12th Jany. 1883 aged 70 years. Also his neice [sic] Lizzie McCALLISTER who died 24th Jany. 1888 aged 2 years.

GWYNN
   [Inscription around three sides of polished limestone platform for font.] A.D. 1878. For the service of God in this church and in memory of Stephen Gwynn, incumbent of the same 1816 - 1836, and of Mary (STEVENSON) his wife this font is dedicated by their children & kindred.

HADDAN
   [*U.J.A.* VI (1900), 51. Sandstone in southwest of graveyard. Arms:- a chevron between three garbs.] Here lyeth the body of John Haddan who died 24th June 1797 aged 74 years. Also his daughter Sarah aged 12 years and his son John aged 15 years. Also Jane SMYLIE, wife to the above named John Haddan senr. She departed this life the 10th of June 1821 aged 83 years. Also his son Samuel HOLDEN who departed this life 1st Feb. 1836 aged 78 years. Also Mary Holden, wife of the above-named Samuel Holden, who departed this life 29th March 1865 aged 84 years.
   [The will of Mary Holden, late of Ballyrickard, in the county of Antrim, widow, who died 29 March 1865 at same place, was proved at Belfast 1 July 1865 by the oaths of William Pennel and Thomas Holden, both of Ballyrickard (Larne) aforesaid, farmers, the executors. Effects under £20.
   Death: Mar. 29, at Ballyrickard, Mary, relict of late Samuel Holden, aged 83 years. *Larne Weekly Reporter,* 8 Apr. 1865.
   Bigger (*U.J.A.* above) comments that the change from "Haddan" to "Holden" represents two forms of the same name.]

HADDEN
   [*U.J.A.* VI (1900), 51. Sandstone set against south boundary wall with arms:- a chevron between three garbs.] In memory of Thomas Hadden who died Nov. 13th 1802 aged 77 years. Also his daughter Mary who died April 3d 1793 aged 24 years. Also 3 children who died in infancy. Also Margaret his wife who died 4th Nov. 1833 aged 89 years.

HAGEN,
   See ALLEN

HALL
   Here restes in the Lord the body of the Reverend and Great Master Thomas Hall, who continued a very worthy and faithfull pastor of this parish and a considerable pillar and ornament of this church for about 50 years, who though he died Anno Dom. 1695 and of his age 75 yet is most worthy to live in the memory of posterity to whom he hath left a rare example of faithfullnes, gravity and wisdom as a minister of integrity and solid piety as a Christian of constancy as a sufferer in all vicissitudes of times for the truth and simplicity of the gospel of Christ and, after all, of crowning his great virtues with most

admirable humility and modesty and so lived an eminent blessing to the world and departed therefrom much desired in it. The above inscription was renewed by the first Presbyterian Congregation A.D. 182(1)-.J.C. LEDLIE, Minister.

[The Reverend Thomas Hall was born in Scotland in 1820, graduated M.A. at Glasgow University in 1642, and was ordained minister/vicar of Inver (Larne) in August 1646, officiating in the parish church. (The presbyterian meeting house was not built until 1668.) He had to return to Scotland when he refused to take the republican "Engagement" in 1649-50 and 1651-54 and was minister first at Erskine and then at Kirkmalcolm. He was re-instated in Inver from 1654 to 1661, but was again expelled for non-conformity. In 1658 he was one of three Ulster ministers sent to Dublin to confer with Henry Cromwell. He was imprisoned in 1663 for alleged complicity in Blood's plot. He was Moderator of the General Synod 1691-2 and died in 1695. His book *A Plain and Easy Explication of the Assemby's Shorter Catechism* was published in 1697 in Edinburgh. See McConnell: *Fasti of the Irish Presbyterian Church* (1951); Porter, McIlrath, & Nelson: *Congregational Memoirs*, pp. 16-29.]

HAMILL
    See SMILEY

HAMILTON
    Erected by William Hamilton in memory of three of his children, viz:- Ann who died 30th April 1832 AE 5 years, John who died 4th Septr. 1832 AE 3 years, John who died 30th June 1842 AE 5 years. James his son died in America 22nd Decr. 1858 aged 37 years. Also his beloved wife Agnes who died 27th August 1859 aged 65 years. Also his son William who died on his passage from India 23rd May 1861 aged 29 years. Also the above William who erected this stone died on the 22nd Jany. 1875 aged 87 years.

HAMILTON
    See AIKEN and HOLDEN

HAR
    See ALLEN

HARE
    Here lyeth ye body of James Hare apothecary who died in Mar. 1747 aged 46 years & Samuel Hare who died Mar. 9th 1755 aged 61 years.

HARE
    See HOUSTON

HAR(L)ES
    [Basalt, south of chancel.] Margret Har(l)es died May 17 1763.

HARVEY
    [Laid flat east of church.] Erected by Ellen Harvey in memory of her husband Samuel Harvey who departed this life the 25th Decr. 1849 aged 60 years. Also her son William Harvey who departed this life 17th Novr. 1856 aged 22 years. And of her daughter Mary who departed this life 6th March 1858 aged 25 years. And her daughter Ellen Harvey who died 26th July 1866 aged 24 years. Also the above named Ellen Harvey who departed this life 29th Decr. 1870 aged 74 years.

[The will of Ellen Harvey, late of Larne, county Antrim, widow, who died 29 December 1870 at same place, was proved at Belfast 15 February 1871 by the oaths of William Hill of Kilcoan, Islandmagee (Larne), farmer, and William Carson of Larne, mill manager, both in said county, the executors. Effects under £200.]

HAWTHORN
See CAMPBELL

HAY
[Sandstone against west boundary wall.] Here are deposited the remains of John Hay who died 17th June 1826 aged 77 years. And of Margaret his wife who died in 1807 (aged 5)3 years. Also eleven of (their) children.

HENDERSON
See GRAHAM

HILL
See CHICHESTER and SIMPSON

HOBAN
See BEATTIE

HOEY
See JACKSON

HOGG
See McGAREL

HOLDEN
[Sandstone in south-west of graveyard.] Erected by Eliza Holden in memory of her mother Eliza Holden who departed this life 28th Jany. 1823 aged 39 years. Also her father James Holden who died 5th March 1862 aged 83 years.

HOLDEN
[Sandstone in south-west of graveyard between John Hadden and south boundary wall.] Erected by Thomas Holden in memory of his mother Rose Holden who departed this life 16th February 1855 aged 74 years. Also his father John Holden who died 3rd Febry. 1860 aged 83 years. Also his sister Sarah Jane Holden who died 27th Novr. 1862 aged 40 years. Also his nephew John Holden who died 5th May 1877 aged 34 years. Also his sister Mary B. Holden who departed this life 21st April 1881. Also his sister Eliza Holden, wife of James HAMILTON, Larne, who departed this life 20th January 1885 aged ..... Also his sister Margaret Holden otherwise C(AT)H(ERW)OOD who died 26th Feby. 18(85) aged 67 years. [Along top edge:-] 3 graves north. [On back of stone:-] 1882, 5 graves north.
[The will of John Holden, late of Ballyrickartmore, in the county of Antrim, farmer, who died 3 February 1860 at Ballyrickartmore aforesaid, was proved at Belfast 16 April 1860 by the oaths of Thomas Holden of Ballyrickart and Bryce McMurtry of Ballysnodd, both in said county, farmers, the executors. Effects under £200.
The will of John Holden, late of Ballydonaghy, county Antrim, farmer, who died 5 1877 at same place, was proved at Belfast 11 July 1877 by the oaths of Thomas Holden of Ballyrickard (Larne), farmer, and Thomas Holden of Larne, merchant, both in same county, the executors. Effects under £200.

Letters of administration, with the will annexed, of the personal estate of Margaret Holden, late of Larne, county Antrim, widow, who died 26 February 1885 at same place, were granted at Belfast 22 April 1885 to John Holden Hamilton of Larne, grocer, one of the residuary legatees. Effects £833 16s. 6d.

Letters of administration, with the will and codicil annexed, of the personal estate of Margaret Holden otherwise Catherwood, late of Larne, county Antrim, widow, who died 26 February 1885 at same place, left unadministered by John Holden Hamilton, one of the residuary legatees, were granted at Belfast 22 March 1886 to Alexander Hamilton of Larne, mechanic, one other residuary legatee. (Former grant 22 April 1885.) Effects unadministered £150 19s. 8d.]

HOLDEN
[Two panels of polished granite held in sandstone. South panel:-] Erected by Agnes Holden, Ballyrickard, in memory of her beloved husband Thomas Holden who died 9th Nov. 1882 aged 69 years. Also the above-named Agnes Holden who died 14th March 1891 aged 60 years. Also her mother Leah MARSHALL who died 22nd Nov. 1892 aged 92 years.

[North panel:-] Also of their daughter Agnes who died 19th Feb. 1882 aged 14 years. Their daughter Sarah Jane who died 7th April 1882 aged 12 years. Also their daughter Rose Mary, wife of The Rev. Robert J. MILLAR, who died 15th Jany. 1893 aged 28 years.

HOLDEN
See HADDAN

HOLMES
See CARLEY

HOOD
[Ledger laid flat. The missing parts of the inscription are supplied from *Historical Sketch of the Old Presbyterian Congregation of Larne and Kilwaughter*, 1889, and placed in round brackets.] (Here lys) the body of the Reverand James Hood (M.A. m)inister of the congregasion (of Larne). He was a youth of consi(derable) abilities, which afor(ded a ple)asing prospect of his (future ser)uices in the church(: a good preacher) and diligent in (his short l)abours, a faithfull (friend, cheer)full, affable and of a co(urteous mi)nd and winning behaviour. He (had muc)h at heart the peace of (the Ch)urch, bewaild devisions amongst Protestants and the intemperate hearts of men of all (pers)vasions and w(ha)t finished (his c)haracter was his unaff(ected) piety for he aimed rather (to be) than appear religious (and his extens)ive charity for men (of differen)t sentiments from (himself being) of catholic (principles, and) not of a party sp(irit confining re)ligion to his (own side. He lived) just to shew (himself to the world an)d died (lamented in the) year of (his age 30, October 12) Anno (D. 1716, having laboured) in the (Gospel in this place) one year and about four months. Renewed A.D. 1858 Classon PORTER, Minister.

[The Reverend James Hood was born near Carrickfergus in 1687, graduated M.A. of Glasgow University in 1707, and was ordained as the fourth minister of the Old Presbyterian Congregation of Larne and Kilwaughter in June 1715. He was the choice of the non-subscribing majority of the congregation at the time of "the split" in 1715. He died on 12 October 1716. See Porter: *Congregational Memoirs* (1929).]

HOOD
[Against north wall of church.] Erected by William Hood in memory of his mother Margaret Hood who died 9th Nov. 1847 aged 82 years. Also of his father Alexander Hood

who died 14th April 1848 aged 80 years. Also of his wife Margaret who died 3rd March 1861 aged 54 years. And of his daughter Letitia Darcus Hood who died 11th April 1867 aged 18 years.

HOOD

[Laid flat east of church.] Erected by John Hood, Curran, in memory of his beloved wife Martha who died Dec. 20th 1872 aged 56 years. Also their son John who died July 1st 1848 aged 18 months. Also their daughter Margaret who died Feby. 17th 1863 aged 21 years. Also their grand-son William CROOKS who was accidently drowned at Curran 21st Octr. 1881 aged 20 years. The above-named John Hood died 26th Feby. 1891 aged 77 years.

HOUSTON

[*M.D.* IV (1899), 2, pp.xxix and xxx; *U.J.A.* VI (1900), 50. Against north boundary wall. Arms:- five arrows upon a chevron between three quatrefoils. Crest:- an hourglass. Motto:- In time.] Here lyeth the bodys of 2 children of Robert Houston, viz Jane who died Octr. 12th 1755 & John who died Octr. 16th 1762. Robert Houston died April 29th 1782 aged 62 years. Martha his wife died Aug. 25th 1794 aged 77 years.

HOUSTON

[*M.D.* V, 3. *The Corran*, Summer 1981. Sandstone against north boundary wall. Composite columns at either side of inscription.] Here lyeth the body of James Houston who died September the 20th 1725 aged 48 years & Rose HARE, wife to said James Houston, who died June 13th 1759 aged 76 years.

HOUSTON

[The upper part and reverse of this grey sandstone have now weathered into illegibility. Southeast of church.] The remains of the late Mr Sam. Houston who died (24th Novr. 182)7 aged 74 y(ears are interred here.) This monument also marks the (buryin)g ground of his forefathers for nearly two centuries (as the surrounding) headstones testify. Also his wife Martha KIRK who died May 10th 1847 aged 72 years. Also their son Samuel Houston who died 13th May 186(6) aged 63 years. Also his sons David Houston who died 23rd j(an. 1874) aged 29 years. And John Houston who died 24th Novr. 1875 aged 28 years. Margaret Houston wife of the above-named Sam. Houston who died 25 Nov. 1886 aged 77 years. And their son Samuel Houston who died 16th May 1888 aged 45 years. Also Mary Houston who died 29 May 1890 aged 85 years and Matilda Houston who died 7 June 1896 aged 90, the daughters of Samuel Houston who died in 1827. Here also are interred the remains of Jane Houston who died 1835 aged 75 years and Robert Houston who died 1837 aged 73 years, brother and sister of Samuel Houston senior. It also records the death of his son John Houston who died at New Orleans 1844 (aged) 42 years.

[Letters of administration with the will annexed, of the personal estate of Samuel Houston, late of Richmond, Belfast, in the county of Antrim, merchant, who died 13 May 1866 at same place, were granted at Belfast 9 August 1866 to Margaret Houston of Richmond, Belfast aforesaid, the widow and a legatee. Effects under £6,000.

The will of Margaret Houston, late of 3 Fortwilliam Terrace, Belfast, widow, who died 25 November 1886 at same place, was proved at Belfast 23 March 1887 by Elizabeth Houston of 3 Fortwilliam Terrace, spinster, one of the executrixes. Effects £1,088 18s. 6d.

The will of Samuel Houston, late of Fortwilliam Terrace, Belfast, gentleman, who died 16 May 1888 at same place, was proved at Belfast 30 July 1888 by Thomas Stewart Dixon of York Street, Belfast, merchant, the surviving executor. Effects ££,716 16s. 7d.

Letters of administration with the will annexed, of the personal estate of Mary Houston, late of 65 Eagleson Place, Duncairn Street, Belfast, spinster, who died 29 May 1890 at same place, were granted at Belfast 19 September 1890 to Elizabeth Houston of 3 Fortwilliam Terrace, Belfast, spinster, the attorney of Mary McKean, the surviving executrix. Effects £1,480 19s. 7d.

Probate of the will of Matilda Houston, late of 143 Duncairn Street, Belfast, spinster, who died 7 June 1896, granted at Belfast 20 July 1896 to Mary McKean, wife of E. McKean, of Rosaville, Fortwilliam Park, Belfast. Effects £641 6s. 2d.]

HOUSTON

[Against north wall of church.] Erected by Thomas Houston in memory of his father William Houston, who died 12th Feb/ 1835 aged 70 years. Also his mother Mary who died 30th April 1847 aged 77 years. Also two of his sons, Thomas and Nathaniel, who died in infancy, and his beloved wife Priscilla, who died 20th Octr. 1869 aged 58 years. Also his daughter Margaret who died 9th July 1872 aged 18 years. And his son James who died 26th September 1873 aged 26 years. The above-named Thomas Houston died 19th Sept. 1900 aged 98 years. [4 graves east].

[Probate of the will of Thomas Houston, late of Glenarm, county Antrim, retired farmer, who died 19 September 1900, was granted at Belfast 7 December 1900 to James Foster, merchant. Effects £265 11s. 5d.

Death: July 9 at Ballysnod, near Larne, Margaret, youngest daughter of Mr. Thomas Houston, aged 19 years. *Larne Weekly Reporter*, 13 July 1872.]

HOUSTON

[Double-light window depicting the healing of the paralytic and the healing of man at the gate of the temple by the apostles, in north wall of nave. Arms:- Or, a chevron chequy, sable and argent, between three martlets of the second.] To the glory of God and in memory of the Hovston family who lived in Larne for many generations and now sleep in the Chvrchyard ovtside these walls. "Arise take vp thy bed and go to thine hovse." "In the name of Jesvs of Nazareth rise vp and walk."

HOUSTON

See SMILEY

HUME

[Sandstone laid flat near east boundary wall.] Here lyeth the body of Mary Hume wife to John Hume who departed this life the 18th of Aug. 1803 aged 58 years. Also John Hume who departed this life the (-5)th of March 1806 aged 62 years.

HUNTER

In memory of Isabella WATT, wife of Wm. Hunter of Ballywillian, who died 14th Jan. 1818 aged 44 years. Their son Wm. 15th May 1836 aged 27 years. Erected by their daughters viz. Agnes & Ann Jane. Also their daughter Agnes Hunter who died March 29th 1868 aged 57 years.

HUNTER

[Laid flat east of church.] The burying ground of Samuel Hunter of Ballymullock 1825.

HUNTER

[Set against south boundary wall. Emblems:- compass and square.] Erected by Jane Hunter in memory of her husband Charles Hunter who died 5th Nov. 1872 aged 72 years. Also her son John who died 5th March 1873 aged 37 years. Also her son Matthew who died 8th Novr. 1885 aged 40 years. The above-named Jane Hunter died 21st Novr. 1889 aged 81 years. Also her grandson Thompson REID who died in infancy.

[The will of Jane Hunter, late of Mill Brae, Larne, county Antrim, widow, who died 21 November 1889 at same place, was proved at Belfast 29 January 1890 by the Reverend James Kennedy of Larne, presbyterian minister, the sole executor. Effects £83 . 4s.]

HUNTER
[Set against south wall of chancel.] Erected by Thomas Hunter in memory of his two grand children viz. Thomas who died 10th July 1885 aged 6 years, James who died 31st Augt. 1885 aged 6 years. The above-named Thomas Hunter died 29th Jany. 1893 aged 77 years. Also his wife Mary Hunter who died 5th June 1894 aged 69 years.

HUNTER
See SMYTH

HUSTON
[In the east of the graveyard.] Erected by James Huston in memory of his father James Houston who died 11 July 1883 aged 55 years. His mother Margaret Huston who died 18 Jany. 1891 aged 62 years. [1 G.N.]

HUSTON
See SMILEY

HUTTON
[White limestone with lead lettering, set in sandstone, in a granite enclosure, in the south-east of graveyard.] Erected to the memory of James Hutton who departed this life 12th January 1874 aged 75 years.Also his wife Mary who departed this life 21st July 1879 aged 72 years. Also in loving memory of Louisa, wife of G.R. Hutton who departed this life on 11th September 1888 aged 31 years. Her remains are interred in the Parish Church Yard, New Haven, Sussex. And their only child Eva who departed this life on 28th April 1889 aged 8 months. W. Graham, Belfast.

[Letters of administration of the personal estate of James Hutton, late of Larne, county Antrim, rate collector, who died 12 January 1874 at same place, were granted at Belfast 27 April 1874 to George Richard Hutton of Larne aforesaid, woollen draper, the son of said deceased. Effects under £200.]

HYSLOP
See ALLEN

JACKSON
[Sandstone laid flat, southeast of church.] Erected in memory of William Jackson, Larne, who died 5th April 1829 aged 76 years. And of Jane HOEY his wife who died 11th Dec. 1823 aged 56 years. Also their son John who died 7th April 1797 aged 4 years. And Edward Jackson their grand-son who died in infancy. Also of John Jackson their son who departed this life 26th Septr. 1843 aged 40 years. And his wife Elizabeth Jackson who departed this life 21st December 1863 aged 60 years. Also their grandson Danl. McCAIMBRIDGE who died in infancy.

JACKSON
[Against north boundary wall.] Sacred to the memory of Ann Jackson who died on the 31st May 1847 aged 14 years.

JACKSONE
[Small sandstone with inscription on recessed panel facing east boundary wall.] Here lyeth the body of William Jacksone who departed this life Decr. II 1697. [Inscription on other side:-] Here lyeth the body of Janet McN(I)SH who died April (the 1)0 1730.

JEFFERIES
[Set against south boundary wall.] Erected by William Jefferies in memory of his wife Catherine Jefferies who died 1(5)th Feby. 1816 aged 17 years.

JEFFERIES
See MITCHEL

JELLIE
See ALLEN

JONES
[Lead lettering on white limestone against north boundary wall.] Catherine Jones died 13th September 1912.

KAIN
See WOODSIDE

KANE
[Set against south boundary wall.] Erected by Margaret Kane in loving memory of her husband James Kane who died 23rd April 1894 aged 78 years. The above Margaret Ann died 16th July 1901.

KANE
See WYLIE

KELLY
[*U.J.A.* VI (1900), 52. Laid flat in east of graveyard. Arms:- a saltire fleury. Crest:- a dexter hand holding a hammer/mallet.] In memory of Mary SILEYMAN wife to William Kelly who died 29th Decr. 1802 aged 36 years. Also her 3 children viz. Margt. Kelly aged 9 years, (Jo)hn & Alexr. Kelly each 9 months. Also the above Wm. Kelly who died the 30th of May 1812 aged 48 years.

KERR
[Sandstone decorated with hourglass, skull and crossbones. Set against south wall of church.]
MEMENTO MORI. Heir lyes the corps of Iean Karr daughter to Robert Kerr who died the 7 day of Appryl 1701 aged 8 years.

KERR
See SMYTH

KINDER
See ALEXANDER

KING
See AIKEN

KIRK
[Ledger flush with ground level, chipped and worn.] Here are deposited the remains of Hugh Kirk who died the 11th April 18(1-) aged 80 years. Also his first b(o...) in(terre)d in the tomb of her father. Of his second wife Jane ...NTER who died 26th Feby. 17(-5) aged (33) years. And of his third wife (Eli..a MI)LLER who died 2nd June (181-) (aged) 48 years. (Also) four of (their chil)dren.

KIRK
See HOUSTON

KIRKPATRICK
[*U.J.A.* VI (1900), 52. Laid within railings of Thomas Kirkpatrick d. 1864. Arms:- a saltire, on a chief three cushions. Crest:- a hand couped at the wrist holding a sword, point downwards. Motto:- I make sure.] Here lyeth the body of Thomas Kirkpatrick who died Oct. 30th 1786 aged 3 years. Also Elinor Kirkpatrick died 8 April 1788. Also their mother Elinor Kirkpatrick who died 1st April 1797 aged 47 years. And their father Thomas Kirkpatrick who died 20th March 1803 aged 50 years. Rose Kirkpatrick, sister to the last named Thomas Kirkpatrick, died the 24th March 1824 aged 70 years. And John Kirkpatrick his son departed this life 5th September 1833 aged 48 years.

KIRKPATRICK
[To east of church.] Erected by Thomas John J. and Alexander H. Kirkpatrick in memory of their beloved brother William Johnston who departed this life 21st August 1839 aged 44 years. Also their mother Mary Kirkpatrick who died 19th Jany. 1840 aged 62 years. Also Ellen wife of Samuel ALEXANDER who died 27th October 1871 aged 66 years. Also Samuel Alexander who died 14th September 1874 aged 84 years. And their son William Alexander who died 23rd February 1890 aged 45 years. And their son Thomas Alexander who died in Demerara, Feb. 1871 aged 23 years.

[The will with two codicils of Samuel Alexander, late of Larne, county Antrim, gentleman, who died 14 September 1874 at same place, was proved at Belfast 21 October 1874 by the oaths of John Maxwell, gentleman, David Nelson, draper, and Alexander Fleming, merchant, all of Larne, the executors. Effects under £7,000.

The will, with one codicil, of Thomas Kirkpatrick Alexander, formerly of Larne, county Monaghan [sic, recte Antrim] and late of Montrose Cottage, county Demerara, Colony of British Guiana, merchant, who died 22 April 1871 at Montrose Cottage aforesaid, was proved at the Principal Registry 7 September 1871 by the oaths of David Nelson, merchant, and the Reverend Classon Porter, presbyterian minister, both of Larne aforesaid, the general executors (save as regards property in Demerara). Effects under £600. NOTE – This is presumably the Thomas Alexander on the gravestone.]

KIRKPATRICK
[Laid within railings of Thos. Kirkpatrick d.1864.] Sacred to the memory of Sarah Kirkpatrick daughter of John Kirkpatrick who died 29th April 1837 aged 23 years. And of her uncle William Kirkpatrick who died 28th March 1842 aged 61 years.

KIRKPATRICK
[White limestone and sandstone set against east boundary wall.] Erected by Thomas Kirkpatrick M.D. to the memory of his mother Margaret who departed this life on the 8th day of May 184(3) aged 61 years. Here also are interred the remains of his beloved child Joseph TWEED who died on the 24th day of June 184(3) aged 9 months. Also the remains of the above named Thomas Kirkpatrick M.D. who died at Torquay in Devonshire 20th March 1867 aged 62 years. Robinson.

[The will with two codicils of Thomas Kirkpatrick, formerly of Larne, county Antrim, and late of Torquay, county of Devon, medical doctor, who died 20 March 1867 at Torquay aforesaid, was proved at the Principal Registry 17 June 1867 by the oaths of the Reverend Classon Porter, presbyterian minister, and William Eccles, merchant, both of Larne aforesaid, two of the executors. Effects under £1,500.

Dr. Kirkpatrick graduated M.D. Edinburgh in 1827 and practised medicine in Larne, where he was also an active member of the committee of Larne National Schools. At his suggestion land was leased as a Model Farm to give the pupils a knowledge of the theory and practice of Agriculture. After the Irish Board of Education set up an Agricultural Department Dr. Kirkpatrick was appointed the first inspector of Model Agricultural Schools in 1848. He retired about 1864 due to failing health and sought a milder climate in Torquay. See Dempsey: *The Corran*, Summer 1988, pp. 11-12; McKillop: *History of Larne and East Antrim* (2000); *Medical Directory.*]

KIRKPATRICK
[Sandstone in pieces set against south boundary wall, south of chancel.] Erected by John A. Kirkpatrick in memo(ry) of his father David who died 15th Sep(r.) 1882 aged 73 yea... Also his mother Mary who died 12th October 1856 aged 48 years. (Thr)ee graves north.

KIRKPATRICK
[White limestone framed in sandstone within iron railings, south of church. Crest:- a dexter hand couped at the wrist holding a sword in pale point upwards. Motto:- I mak sicker.] Erected 1864 in memory of Thomas Kirkpatrick of Larne & Demerara, who died at Larne 9th January 1864 aged 55 years. And of his wife Margaret Kirkpatrick who died 11th March 1895 aged 78 years. Also of his brother John Johnston Kirkpatrick of Ballyclare & Larne who died 5th September 1895 aged 85 years.

KIRKPATRICK
[Granite hogback.] In memory of Samuel Kirkpatrick of Larne who died at New York on 18th Jan. 1868 and was buried there aged 54 years. Buried here his two children who died in infancy. His son Arthur CHICHESTER Kirkpatrick who died on 29th Jan. 1874 aged 24 years. His wife Mary CHICHESTER Kirkpatrick who died on 12th July 1900 aged 75 years.

KIRKPATRICK
[Lead lettering in white limestone set against south wall of chancel. Anchor in roundel.] Erected by John Kirkpatrick in memory of his father James Kirkpatrick who died 1st Octr. 1910 aged 62 years. The above-named John Kirkpatrick died 21st March 1921 aged 37 years. Also his mother Margaret Kirkpatrick died 5th June 1926. Margaret Kirkpatrick.

[John Johnstone Kirkpatrick, J.P., Ballyclare, second son of J.J. Kirkpatrick, Esq., Larne, married Cecilia (Cecil) Gordon, only child of S. Gordon Esq., Landsdowne Road, Dublin, in St. Bartholomew's Church, Dublin, on 16 Aug. 1887. *Larne Weekly Reporter,* 20 Aug. 1887.]

KIRKPATRICK
See GRAHAM and McNEILL

LAMONT
[Loose slate now placed against office wall. Arms:- two halberds saltireways, in the chief the crown imperial. Crest:- a ship in sail. Motto:- ne pereas nec spernas.] Here lieth the children of Patrick Lamont viz two Margrets & Robert. As also Jean Lamont who died Jany. the 28th 1760 aged 7 years.

LANAUZE
[Sandstone set against south boundary wall.] Sacred to the memory of Daniel Lanauze who departed this life on the 22nd January 1839 in the 73rd year of his age. Also to that of Anne his wife who died in the 72nd year of her age on the 16th February 1838.

LANGTRY
See POWELL

LAVERTY
[Against north boundary wall.] Erected by Robert Laverty in memory of his daughter Jane who died 12th Jany. 1885 aged 24 years.

LEARMOR
[*M.D.* III (1895), 1, p.2; *U.J.A.* VI (1900), 53. Laid flat in southwest of graveyard. Arms:- quarterly; 1st and 4th, on chevron three lozenges; 2nd and 3rd, on a fess three cinquefoils. Crest:- a gillyflower. Motto:- spero.] Here lyeth (the body of William Learmor who died Janr. the 8th 1725 and his wife Mary GILLIS died Feb.) the 14th 1728. Also 4 children viz. (John wh)o died Novbr. ye 3rd 1706 and Mary died Apr. ye 28th 1718, William died May ye 28th 1718, Janet died Febry. ye 1st 1734. Also Robert Learmor who died 3d April 1782 aged 80 years.

LEDLIE
See HALL

LEE
See WOODSIDE

LEWIS
[Red sandstone south of church.] Erected by Ann E. Duff in memory of her father Samuel Lewis who deid 8th Decr. 1873 aged 74 years. Also her aunt Mary RAINEY died 12th March 1881 aged 74 years. Also her husband Samuel DUFF who died 15 April 1888 aged 73 years. And her mother Ellen Lewis who died 22nd Jany. 1895 aged 88 years.

LOUGHRIDGE
[*M.D.* IV (1899), 2, p.xxix, illustrates the arms without providing an inscription. No existing Loughridge stone has been found.]

(L)UNN
[Sandstone laid flat near east boundary wall.] Erected in memory of George (L)unn a native of Bandbridge who departed this life (24th) Jany. 18(2)3 aged 44 years.

LUSK
Erected by Robert Peden Lusk in memory of his father James Lusk who died 5th Augt.
1880 aged 86 years. Also his mother Margaret Peden Lusk who died 2nd April 1886 aged
79 years. And his son Robert James who died in infancy. Also his wife Ellen Lusk who
died 19th Dec. 1907 aged 72 years. Also his sister Jane who died 25th May 1923 aged 96
years. The above named Robert Peden Lusk who died 11th Jan. 1924 aged 90 years. Also
his brother John who died 14th April 1924 aged 86 years. Also John youngest grandson
of the above named Robert Peden Lusk who died 23rd May 1942 aged 2 years.
    [R.P. Lusk advertised as "family and ship bread baker, Cross Street, Larne". *Larne
Weekly Reporter,* 18 Mar. 1865. He stood for election to Larne Rural District Council in
Kilwaughter Division in 1899 and later served as vice-chairman of the RDC. *Belfast &
Province of Ulster Directory,* 1906, 1907.]

M
[M.D. V, 1. "This stone bears neither arms nor inscription, only the initials and date as
given. At the top of the stone it bears the initials I.E."] E.M. 1688.

McADAM
[Laid flat east of church.] Erected by Jane McAdam in memory of her father John
McAdam died 4th Mar........ aged 40 years. Also her mother Janet BARR who died 18th
Sept. 1832 aged 73 years. Also her brother Francis McAdam who died 22nd August 1879
aged 88 years.

McALISTER
[Sandstone against east boundary wall.] Erected by John McAlister in memory of his
father & two brothers.

McALISTER
[South of church.] Erected by Robert McAlister in memory of (two) of his children viz
Robert who died 10th June 182(4) aged 3 (mon)ths. And Robert who died 12th March
1830 aged (5) years.

McALISTER
See PATTON

MACAULAY
[Table stone of polished granite within railings. The inscriptions are arranged around a
latin cross in three quadrants.] In Memoriam. Robert Macaulay Esq., of Larne died 12th
January 1864 aged 76 years. Helena, wife of Robert Macaulay, died 28th January 1867
aged 80 years. Elizabeth CUMMING, fourth daughter of above, died 11th October 1854
aged 38 years.
    [The will, with one codicil, of Robert Macauley, late of Larne in the county of Antrim,
merchant, who died 12 January 1864 at same pl;ace, was proved at Belfast 10 March 1864
by the oaths of James Macaulay and Jasper Macaulay, both of Belfast aforesaid, and John
Macaulay of Larne aforesaid, merchants, the executors. Effects under £60,000.]

MACAULAY
[The lower wall of the chancel is adorned with encaustic tiling. Recorded on one of the
tiles is the following:] To the glory of God and in loving remembrance of Robert
Macaulay of Larne, died January xii, mdccclxiv aged lxxvi; and Helena his wife, daughter
of Jasper White of Limerick, died January xxviii, mdccclxvii aged lxxx years. This

memorial was placed by their sons Jasper Macaulay of Leigh Hill House, Cobham, Surrey, and John Macaulay of Red Hall in this County.

[Robert Macaulay of Larne was son of James Macaulay, J.P., flour miller, of Benveagh, Crumlin (died 1839), and Jane Hyndman (died 1842), daughter of Thomas Hyndman of Ballyronan, county Londonderry. Robert bought the Inver flour mills at Larne in 1854 and became one of the most successful millers in the North of Ireland. He married in 1807 Helena White, daughter of Jasper White of Limerick, and had issue (as well as 3 daughters):-

1. Jasper Macaulay of Leigh Hill House, Cobham, Surrey, married 1865 Sarah Boyd of Newry and died 19 March 1893 aged 72.
2. John Macaulay was born 23 June 1823 and married 1 February 1853 Jane Callwell Agnew, daughter of Patrick Agnew of Kilwaughter (see AGNEW above). In 1864 he bought Red Hall, Ballycarry, from David S. Ker and sold it in 1902. They had issue (as well as 3 daughters):-
    a. Robert Helenus Macaulay, born 21 November 1854.
    b. Agnew McNeil Macaulay, born 31 July 1858.

See Burke: *Landed Gentry of Ireland* (1912); McKillop: *History of Larne and East Antrim* (2000).]

MACAULAY
   See AGNEW

McCAIMBRIDGE
   See JACKSON

McCALLISTER
   See GRAY

McCALMONT
   Erected by William McCalmont junr., printer, Larne, in memory of his beloved wife Jane who departed this life 1st March 1840 aged 31 years. His grandson Henry W. McCalmont who died in infancy. His son John S. McCalmont, born 4th June 1844, entered into his eternal rest 13th Novr. 1909. Mary, wife of above, died 30th Sept. 1939. Also her daughter Caroline STUART McCalmont died 21st August ..... "Till He Come".

McCALMONT
   See BRIDGMAN, MONTGOMERY, NICKLE and RITCHIE

McCAMMONT
   [Set against north boundary wall.] Erected by Helen McCammont to the memory of her husband John McCammont who died 23rd March 1825 aged 32 years. Also their daughter Elizth. who died in early life.

McCAREY
   See FERRIS

McCARTNEY
   [Laid flat in north east of graveyard.] Erected by Charles MILLAR in memory of Robert McCartney aged 56 years. Also his widow Jane who departed this life the 28th January 1889 aged 74 years. And of his .... Maggie MILLAR who died (2..th ....) 1890 aged 8

years. Al(so .....) Jane who died (10.....189)2 aged .. years. A(l .... Lettie) who di(ed 27.......... ye)ars.

McCAUGHEY
See FERRES

McCLESTER
[Sandstone with cherub carved at top. Set against south wall of church.] Here lyeth the body of James McClester who departed this life April 11th 1781 aged 65 years.

McCLEVERTY
[White marble tablet on north wall of nave under gallery.] In memory of Anne McGildowney, wife of Lieut. General Wm. Anson McCleverty, Commander in Chief of the Madras Army, and daughter of John Montgomery CASEMENT, Esqre., of Invermore in this parish. She died at Ootacamund, East Indies, 26th July 1868 aged 48 years, beloved of a sorrowing husband and six children. Faith, hope, and charity.

[William Anson McCleverty was the son of Major General Sir Robert McCleverty C.B. K.C.H. (Royal Marines, died 1838); born 11 Feb. 1806; Ensign 26 Mar. 1824; Lt. 26 Aug. 1825; Capt. 21 May 1829; Major 23 April 1841; Lt. Col. 19 Dec. 1845; Col. 20 June 1854; Maj. Gen. 4 May 1860; Lt. Gen. 22 Nov. 1868. Col. of 108th Regt. of Foot (Madras Infantry) "Central India", 27 Mar. 1868. He served in the campaign against the Rajah of Coorg in April 1834, with the 48th Regiment commanded the troops in New Zealand during the native disturbances in 1847 and repulsed 400 natives in their attack at Wanganui on 19th July, which resulted in a peace undisturbed till 1860 (Medal). *Army List*, 1873, pp. 9, 354.]

McCLOY
[South of church.] Erected by David McCloy in memory of his wife Agnes WILSON who died on the 13th Decr. 1867 aged 48 years. Also his son John Wilson McCloy M.D. M.S.Q.C.B. who died 20th March 1868 aged 25 years. The above-named David M'Cloy died 5th Sept. 1883 aged 73 years.

[Letters of administration of the personal estate of John Wilson McCloy, late of Larne, county Antrim, medical doctor, a bachelor, whodied 20 March 1868 at same place, were granted at Belfast 5 June 1868 to David McCloy of Newtownards, county Down, manager of the Scrabo Stone Quarries, the father and sole next of kin of said deceased. Deceased died domiciled in Ireland. Effects in Great Britain and Ireland under £450.

Dr John Wilson McCloy was born on 1 February 1843 in Mill Street, Larne, was educated at Belfast `Inst`, and graduated M.D. at Queen`s College, Belfast, with first class honours, in 1863 at the exceptionally early aged of 20. He was subsequently medical officer to the Liverpool Infirmary and Cholera Prevention Committee and surgeon on the SS *Great Eastern*. He wrote a paper on cholera and, more famously, a number of poems about his home territory. He died of cholera and a lingering fever at Mill Street, Larne. A selection of his poems was published by W.G. Baird, Belfast, in 1877. See McKillop, *History of Larne and East Antrim* (2000); *Medical Directory; The Corran*, Spring 1984, pp. 6-7.]

McCLURKEN
[Sandstone in south-east of graveyard.] Erected by Robert McClurken in memory of his son Samuel who died 10th August 1874 aged 33 years. Also his wife Agnes McClurken who died 20th March 1884 aged 86 years. The above-named Robert McClurken died 24th July 1884 aged 90 years. Robinson, Belfast

McCOLLOUGH
   See WORKMAN

McCOLOCH
   See MORDOC(H)

McCOLOUGH
   See SNODDY

McCOMBE
   [Sandstone, set against north boundary wall.] Erected by Hugh McCombe in memory of
   his wife Ellen who departed this life 25th February 1862 aged 60 years. Also his daughter
   Margaret who died 14th October 1842 aged 10 months. Also the above Hugh McCombe
   M.D. who died 20th December 1873 aged 77 years. Also his daughter Eliza BELL, who
   died 8th Feby. 1885 aged 54 years. Also his daughter Ellen, who died 22nd Sept. 1887
   aged 61 years.
   [The will, with one codicil, of Ellen McComb [sic], late of Larne in the county of
   Antrim, wife of Hugh McComb of same place, who died 25 February 1862 at same place,
   was proved at Belfast 16 May 1862 by the oath of Thomas McComb of Antrim in the
   county of Antrim, surgeon, one of the executors. Effects under £300.
   The will of Eliza Bell, late of Belfast, widow, who died 8 February 1885 at same place,
   was proved at Belfast 18 March 1885 by Matilda Jane Kelso of 2 Bayview Terrace,
   Strandtown, county Down, widow, the sole executrix. Effects £295 8s. 6d.
   Letters of administration of the personal estate of Ellen McCombe, late of Larne,
   county Antrim, spinster, who died 22 September 1887 at 89 Agnes Street, Belfast, were
   granted at Belfast 14 October 1887 to Matilda Jane Kelso of Bayview Terrace,
   Strandtown, county Down, widow, a sister. Effects £223.]

McCORMICK
   [Loose stone propped against Kirkpatrick stone.] Erected by John McCormick in memory
   of Mary his wife who died 9th May 1828 aged 57 years.

McCREADY
   [Loose stone propped against Kirkpatrick stone.] Sacred to the memory of Margaret
   ADAMS wife of James McCready who died 21st Jan. 1826 AE 70 years. Also of their
   children viz. James John & Margt, who died young. Also their son James who died 20th
   July 1842 aged 4 years. Also James McCready senr. who died 30th Feb. 1845 aged 85
   years.

McCULLOCH
   [Laid flat near path.] In memory of John McCulloch who died the 30th day of March
   1825 [1825 and 1815 occupying same space - stonecutter's error] AE 64 and Jane his wife
   who died the 7th day of August 1831 AE 60. Here also were formerly deposited the
   remains of Mary Ann, wife of John McCulloch, who died in 1741 AE 66; John
   McCulloch, 20th February 1754 AE 84; Dorothea Margaret, daughter of Patrick
   McCulloch, 8th October 1768 AE 16; Patrick McCulloch, 2nd November 1792 AE 82;
   Mary his wife, 2nd January 1793 AE 72; and Mary McCulloch, 27th June 1826 AE 84.
   William McCulloch M.D., second son of the above named John & Jane McCulloch, died
   on his passage from Demerara to Halifax, N.S., on the 23rd May 1838 in the 33rd year
   of his age. Also John McCulloch, the eldest son of the said John & Jane McCulloch, who
   died on the 4th day of November 1840 aged 37 years.

McCULLOCH
[Set against north boundary wall. The decoration includes a flaming urn between two feathered birds, two faces, and roses.] In memory of Hilley McCulloch who departed this life 30th of January 1800 aged 66 years. Also Rosey McCulloch, daughter to Wm. McCulloch, who died on the 9th of Feburary [sic.] 1832 aged 4 years and 4 months. And Nancey who died the 18th of Mary 1842 aged 3 years and 5 months. And James who died 6th Feburary 1844 aged 3 & 4 months. [On top edge:-] Two graves south.

McCULLOCH
[Lead lettering on white limestone set against south boundary wall.] Erected by William McCulloch of New Zealand in memory of his father & mother William & Margaret McCulloch of Inver. Also his sister Maggie McCulloch, born May 1862, died Aug. 1910.

McCULLOCH
See MORDOC(H) and YOUNG

McCUSACK
[Close to south boundary wall in south-east of graveyard.] Erected by Mary McCusack in memory of her husband Robert McCusack who died 15th March 1827 aged 33 years. Also the above-named Mary who departed this life 8th Dec. 1870 aged 90 years. Also their daughter Margaret CUNNINGHAM who departed this life 21st Feb. 1898 aged 71 years. Elizabeth, daughter of the above Margaret Cunningham departed this life 23rd July 1915. "Blessed are the dead which die in the Lord."
    [Probate of the will of Margaret Cunningham, late of Main Street, Larne, county Antrim, widow, who died 21 February 1898, granted at Belfast 19 September 1898 to Elizabeth Cunningham of Larne, spinster. Effects £226.]

McDONALD
[Flaking sandstone against east boundary wall.] Erected by (Marg.....) Mc(Donald) in memory of her beloved husband (...h)n McDonald, Capt. of the ship *Irene* of Liverpool, who was unfortunately drowned with 10 of his crew by the upsetting of his ship in the River Mersey on the 26th February 1853 aged 35 years. His remains were found and interred in this grave.
    [*Lloyd's List*, 28 Feb. 1853: The Irene for Valparaiso, having drifted from her anchors during the night, was taken in tow by a tug to be docked, but catching the tail of the bank which extends into the river from the Coburg Dock, she capsized; Master, Chief Mate, and eight men drowned; the vessel lies on her broadside, fills with the tide, and is half immersed at low water. See Duffin: "A Sea Tragedy of Long Ago", *The Corran*, No. 11, Summer 1979, p.11.]

McDONALD
See GRANT

McDONNELL
See MONTGOMERY

McELH(E)GO
[Set against east boundary wall.] Here lieth the body of Agnes McElh(e)go who died July the 27th 1819 aged 17 years. Also two of her brothers viz. George and James.

McFAREN

[*M.D.* V (1901), 1, 2. Set against north boundary wall.] Here lyeth the bodys of Patrick & Mary, children to David McFaren who deceased in Febrvary 1689. Also Elizabeth ALLEN who died Oct. 31st 1771 aged 22 years. And Elizabeth GLEGHORN died in June 1772.

McFAUL

[Laid flat beside Macaulay enclosure.] Erected by James McFaul in memory of his beloved wife Jane McFaul who died 6th June 1879 aged 56 years. Also his daughter Margaret who died 16th Nov. 1847 aged 4 years. Also his infant son John who died 22nd March 1851. And his youngest daughter Matilda who died 25th March 1879 aged 14 years. The above-named James McFaul died 2nd June 1885 aged 66 years.

[Letters of administration of the personal estate of James McFall [sic], late of Ballysnod, county Antrim, farmer, who died 2 June 1885 at same place, were granted at Belfast 10 July 1885 to James McFall of Ballysnod, farmer, a child. Effects £183.]

McFEE
See NICKLE

McGAREL

[Laid flat, south of chancel.] Sacred to the memory of Charles McGarel, Larne, who died (2... of) February 1831 aged 86 years. Also Catharine McGarel, mother of Charles McGarel, who died the 2nd of May 1791 aged 79 years. And Catharine ALLEN, daughter of Charles McGarel, who died the 15th of January 1816 aged 38 years. Also Hannah, wife of Charles McGarel, who died on the 7th March, 1839 aged 97 years. And ajoining [sic] this stone on the south side are deposited the remains of William Allen grand-son of Charles McGarel who died on the 28th of July 1812 aged 32 years. Here also are deposited the body of John McGarel, eldest son of the above-named Charles McGarel, who died on the 16th of October 1832 aged 73 years. Also Peter McGarel son of the above Charles McGarel who died 28th (of) June (18)59 aged 79 years. Also Mary, daughter of the above Charles McGarel, who died 11th July 1872 aged 84 years. Also of Charles McGarel, son of the above Charle(s McGarel), Magheramorne, who died 10th Oc(tober 1876 aged 88 years). Also Helena, wife of the above-(named ....) who died 30th April 1882 a(ged 86 years).

[The will of Peter McGarrell. Death 28 June 1859. Grant of probate herein from Principal Registry, London, dated 1 August 1859. Resealed at Principal Registry, Dublin, 6 August 1859. Effects under £49,195 in Ireland.

Charles McGarel, late of 2 Belgrave Square, county Middlesex, and of Magheramourne, county Antrim, esquire, died 10 October 1876. Probate granted herein from Principal Registry, London 7 November 1876. Resealed at Principal Registry, Dublin, 20 December 1876. Effects in Ireland £67,750 0s. 9d.

The will of Helena McGarel, late of Larne, county Antrim, widow, who died 30 April 1882 at same place, was proved at Belfast 12 July 1882 by Malcolm McNeill of the Curran, Larne, and John Macaulay of Redhall, Ballycarry, in said county, esquires, the executors. Effects £18,575 10s.

Mary McGarel died on Thursday 11 July at The Manse, Glenarm, whither she had removed for the benefit of her health. *Larne Weekly Reporter*, 27 July 1872.

The first record of the McGarel family in Larne is of a lease to Charles McGarel in 1743 (McKillop, 2000) and another Charles McGarel was apparently proprietor of the Antrim Arms Hotel or McGarel`s Inn in 1789. This refutes the popular belief that the McGarel family came to Larne from Raloo only c 1815. Charles McGarel (c 1745-1831) and his wife Hannah had 4 sons, John, Peter, William and Charles. John, William and Charles went out to seek their fortune in Demerara, South America, where William died in 1810. The other two subsequently returned home and, like Peter, established successful businesses, Charles McGarel's being in the City of London. Peter was prominent in the formation of a Board of Town Commissioners in 1858, but died in the following year. Charles lived in London but his fortune enabled him to buy the estate of Mageramorne from John Irving, MP, in 1842. He was made a High Sheriff for County Antrim in 1848. In 1862 he gave a plot of land to the town for the McGarel Cemetery. He funded the building of Larne Town Hall, at the junction of Main Street and Cross Street, in 1869 and the McGarel Almshouses in 1876. The Town Hall remained the centre of council business until 1955 but has survived, but the Almshouses were removed in 1971. Charles died childless at his home in Brighton on 10 October 1876 at the age of 88.

Charles McGarel had married in 1856 Mary Rosina Hogg, second daughter of Sir James Weir Hogg, baronet, of Lisburn, but had no children. When he died his property at Glynn and Magheramorne was left to his wife's brother Sir James Hogg, (second baronet), MP, who in 1877 assumed the name of McGarel-Hogg and in 1887 became first Baron Magheramorne. Sir James and his brother Quintin Hogg (father of the first Lord Hailsham) erected the memorial window in Inver Church (see below). The title became extinct on the death of the 4th Baron in 1957. See Burke's *Peerage, Baronetage and Knightage* (1938 edition); McKillop, *History of Larne and East Antrim* (2000); O'Laverty, *Diocese of Down and Connor*, III, p. 163; *The Corran*, Spring 1984.]

McGAREL
    See CALDWELL.

McGARELL
    [White limestone with lead lettering, in two pieces set against east boundary wall. Dove with fern leaves.] Erected by Mary McGarell in memory of her beloved husband William McGarell who died 4th September 1879 aged 40 years. And the above named Mary McGarell who died 18th May 1924 aged 72 years. Holden.

McGAREL
    [East window depicting the Ascension.] This window was erected in memory of Charles McGarel Esq. of Magheramorne by Sir James McGarel Hogg, Bart., and Quintin Hogg, Esq., 1878.

McGARRIAGHER
    Erected by William McGarriagher in memory of his father James McGarriagher who died 6th Feby. 1847 aged 45 years. His mother Anne McGarriagher who died 24th Feby. 1890 aged 84 years. Also his niece Agnes McGarriagher who died 14th Nov. 1914 aged 41 years.

McGEREL
    [Rough basalt at south-east corner of church.] Margt. McGerel died 1770. Hugh McREV died July 13 1807 aged 88 years.

McGERRALD
    See FEE

McGIVERON
[Laid flat east of church.] Erected in memory of Charles McGi(veron) who died (14)th
March 1832 aged 78 years. Also (Agnes) his wife who died 14th Jany. (183)6 aged (7)5
years. Also his son Fe(lix) McGiveron who died 6th Feby. 1872 aged 89 years. And
Martha Mc(Giver)on who died 1st April 1874 aged 70 years.
    [The will of Martha McGivren [sic] otherwise Hunter, late of Larne, copunty Antrim,
widow, who died 2 April 1874 at same place, was proved at Belfast 13 May 1874 by the
oaths of the Reverend Classon Porter, Presbyterian Minister, and Robert English, grocer,
late of Larne aforesaid, the executors. Effects. under £100.]

McGUGIN
[Against north boundary wall.] Erected by Mr. H. McGugin R.N., Chief Officer of Coast
Guard, in memory of his beloved daughter Anne who died 14th May 1867 aged 19 years.
Also his beloved daughter Maggie who died 11th May 1882 aged 27 years. The above
named Hugh McGugin died 12th August 1887 aged 65 years. Also his daughter Jane who
died 7th Feby. 1891. Also his wife Anne McGugin who died 6th Jany. 1902 aged 75 years.
    [The will of Hugh McGugin, late of Glenarm, county Antrim, retired officer of Coast
Guards, who died 12 August 1887 at same place, was proved at Belfast by Ann McGugin
of Glenarm, widow, the sole executrix. Effects £265 1s.
    Navy List 1871, p. 213, Coast Guards: Hugh McGugin, Chief Officer 2nd Class,
seniority 31 Jan. 1867, Glenarm.]

McHARG
[*U.J.A.* VI (1900), 93. Against north boundary wall. Arms:- a dexter hand couped at the
wrist holding a dagger in pale point downwards between two mullets.] Here lyeth the
bodies of three children of Alexander McHarg viz. John a child & Margaret who died
April 29th 1776 aged 5 years. Also a 2d John. Also their father Alexr. MEHARG departed
this life 25th Septr. 1812 aged 72 years.

McHENRY
[*M.D.* V (1901), 1, 2. Polished granite between Samuel Smiley (1797) & Smiley
monument. A cross patee is carved on the headstone in a recessed circle.] In memory of
Mary SMILEY (wife of George McHenry) born 1765, died June 2 1827 and of her son
James McHenry M.D., author of "O'Halloran" & c., born Dec. 20 1795, died July 21
1845.
    [James McHenry was born 20th December 1785 at Livingstone's Court, Dunluce
Street and died 21st July 1845, also in Larne. He studied first for the Presbyterian
ministry, then medicine in Belfast and Glasgow, practised in Larne and Belfast, emigrated
to U.S.A. with his wife and infant son in 1817, and settled in Philadelphia in 1824. There
he became a draper. He was a poet, novelist, and editor of the *American Monthly
Magazine*. In 1842 or 1843 he was appointed U.S. consul in Londonderry. His son James
was a well-known financier and died in 1891 at Kensington. His daughter Mary married
J. Bellargee Cox of Philadelphia. See *D.N.B., Dictionary of American Biography* and *The
Corran* (Summer 1980, p. 11).]

McILROY
[Sandstone in south-west of graveyard.] Erected by Hugh McIlroy in memory of his wife
Mary who died 12th Jany. 1856 aged 66. Also the abovenamed Hugh McIlroy who died
8th July 1866 aged 81 years. Also his grandson William D. WRIGHT who died 21st
Feby. 1868 aged 15 years.

McKEE

[Laid flat in south east of graveyard.] Here (lys) the body of James McKee who died the 6th February 1808 aged 26 years. Also his father Thomas McKee who died the 15th October 1808 aged 60 years. Also Jane McKee, wife to the above Thomas McKee, who departed this life the (1)5th October 1815 aged 6(0) years. Also Ellen McKee who died 10th Jany. 1895 aged 74 years.

McKEOWN

[South wall.] Erected by James (McKeown in memory of ....) viz (Jan)e (..........F)eb. 1829 aged 2 years & 9 months and John who died 13th Decr. 1836 aged 2 years & 5 months.

McKEOWN

[Sandstone set against north boundary wall.] Erected by Daniel McKeown of Larne to the memory of his beloved child Mary who departed this life 10th April 1858 aged 6 years. Also his sister Catherine FITZSIMONS who died 14th June 1876 aged 55 years. And her husband Matthew Fitzsimons who died at Belfast 24th Jany. 1881 aged 76 years.

McKEOWN

See McQUOWN and MITCHEL

McKINSTRY

Erected by Robert (McKinstry) in memory of his children viz........... who died 10th June 18(..) aged 3 months and Robert who died 12th March 1830 aged (3) years.

McMANUS

[Set into west boundary wall with low railed enclosure.] In memory of Ellen McManus who died 7th Jan. 1870 aged 56 years. Also her husband Alexander McManus who died 19th Jan. 187(.) aged 66 years. Their son James who died 27th September 1890 aged 49 years. And his wife Eliza who died 1(3)th Decr. 1913 aged 69 years.

[The will of James McManus, late of Main Street, Larne, county Antrim, blacksmith, who died 27 September 1890 at same place, was proved at Belfast 21 November 1890 by Elizabeth McManus of Main Street, Larne, widow, the sole executrix. Effects £215 . 5s.]

McMEEKIN

[White limestone in sandstone, close to south boundary wall, laid flat.] Erected by William & Agnes McMeekin in affectionate remembrance of their beloved children, Elizabeth died 29th Sept. 1873 aged 1 year, and David NELSON died 15th October 1875 aged 15 months. Also their daughter Annie who died 1st Sept. 1901 aged 32 years. The above-named Agnes McMeekin died 25th March 1912 aged 76 years. Also the above-named William McMeekin died 8th April 1926 aged 83 years. Also their son Alexander HOLMES McMeekin died 22nd November 1934 aged 58 years.

McMULLEN

See PETERIE

McMUNN

[M.D. III (1895), 1, 3; U.J.A. VI (1900), 95. Sandstone set against north boundary wall, with arms:- a chevron between three anchors. Crest:- a ship. Motto:-hold sure.] Her(e) lyeth the bo(dy) of Mary McMunn who died Aug(t. 21)st (177)0 aged (30 ye)ars (&) Andrew McMunn who died Ap(ril) 12th 1771 aged 70 years also 4 children of his viz.

Sarah, James & 2 Andrews. Catherine CREIGHTON died 6th December 1902.
[Along top of stone:-] 3 graves breadth northward.

McMURDY
[Small uneven sandstone south of church in front of Smyth of Duneira.] Here lyeth John
McMurdy who died in Jan. 17..

McMURRAY
[Set against north boundary wall.] Erected by ... Graves McMurray, Purser, Royal Navy,
in memory of his beloved wife Jane who departed this life on the 28th November 1840
aged 58 years.
    [The *Navy List* of 1841, p. 308, includes Thomas G. McMurray as a purser with
seniority date of 30 Oct. 1813. Note: Thomas Graves was Rector of Larne 1802-1811.]

McNEILL
[Two limestone panels inlaid on sandstone. The arms given in *M.D.* IV (1899), 2, p.xxvii,
under McNeal, 1757, are probably from an earlier stone, removed in 1868. They are:- on
a fess between, in chief a dexter hand couped and appaumee fesswise, and in base a lion
rampant, a fish naiant, impaling on a fess between, in chief a lion rampant in base a galley,
sails furled, three mullets. Crest:- an arm vambraced embowed holding a dagger. The arms
on the existing monument given in *U.J.A.* VI (1900), 96, have the charges differently
arranged. Arms:- the field is divided one, two, one; first quarter, three mullets fesswise;
second quarter, a lion rampart, third quarter, in chief a sinister hand appaumee, in base a
fish naiant; fourth quarter, a lymphad. Crest:- a dexter arm flexed, in the hand a dagger.
Motto:- sincere aut mori.] 1868. The burying place of Malcolm McNeill Esq., The
Corran. Here lie the remains of John McNeill of The Corran who died 25th June 1757
aged 45 years. Also his wife Margt. McNeill who died 21st January 1794 aged 73 years.
Also his grand-daughter Matilda BARKLIE who died 6th January 1809 aged 21 years.
Also his daughter-in-law Margaret McNeill who died 15th August 1816 aged 58 years.
Also his son Malcolm McNeill who died 5th November 1818 aged 72 years. Also his
daughter Isabella McNeill who died August 1830 aged 76 years.
    [Second panel.] Here also lie the remains of his grand-son Malcolm McNeill, son of the
above-named Malcolm McNeill, who died 14th Septr. 1866 aged 75 years. Also his
daughter Helena Louisa McNeill who died 3rd March 1851 aged 6 years. His son John
McNeill died 28th April 1868 interred at Charlton, Kent. Also his sister Isabella McNeill
who died 25th January 1875 aged 81 years. Also his wife Lucy McNeill who died 15th
January 1884 aged 81 years.
    [The will of Malcolm McNeill, late of Curran, near Larne, in the county of Antrim,
gentleman, who died 14 September 1866 at same place, was proved at Belfast 29 October
1866 by the oath of Edmund McGildowney Casement of Inver, Larne, in said county,
esquire, the surviving executors. Effects under £2,000.
    Letters of administration of the personal estate of Isabella McNeill, late of Larne,
county Antrim, spinster, who died 25 January 1875 at same place, were granted at the
Principal Registry 3 May 1875 to Helena McGarel of same place and Jane Montgomery
of Corran near Larne, widows, the sisters of said deceased. Effects under £200.
    The will of Louisa [sic] McNeill, late of The Corran, Larne, county Antrim, widow,
who died 15 January 1884 at same place, was proved at Belfast 25 February 1884 by
Malcolm McNeill of The Corran, Larne, esquire, one of the executors. Effects £4,246.
    Alexander McNeill of T.C.D., aged 22, youngest son of Malcolm McNeill of the Conan
[sic], Larne, esq., admitted to Middle Temple 12 Nov. 1864; called to the bar 6 June
1868. See Sturgess: *Register of Admissions to the Middle Temple* (1949).]

McNEILL

[Granite obelisk with inscriptions on three sides. East side] In memory of Rachel ENGLISH (BAINE) who died 28th Octr. 1873 aged 49 years. Also her mother Jane McNeill who died 17th Decr. 1844 aged 41 years. Also her grand-mother Rachel MAGEE who died 26th Sept. 1850 aged 78 years.

[South side] Also her husband John English who died 6th Sept. 1854 aged 30 years.

[North side] Also her husband George Baine who died 30th Sept. 1885 aged 45 years.

[Death: October 28, at Main Street, Larne, Rachel, the beloved wife of Mr. George Baine. *Larne Weekly Reporter*, 1 Nov. 1873.

George Baine, Mount Pleasant, baker, was elected to Larne Urban District Council on 16 Jan. 1899. *Larne Times*, 21 Jan. 1899, p. 3.]

McNEILL

[White limestone tablet on south wall of nave. Crest:- an arm embowed (the hand is missing). Motto:- Vincere aut mori.] In memory of John McNeill, Esquire, Captain, R.A., born 22nd July 1834, died 28th April 1868. Erected by his brother Duncan.

McNEILL

[Brass plaque attached to front of organ, purchased 1881.] To the glory of God and for the honour of his service this organ was erected. The cost being defrayed by the loving and devoted exertions of Mrs. William Walsh McNeill, Larne. As a record of the gratitude of the congregation who worship in the parish church the Select Vestry have caused this tablet to be inserted.

[W.W. McNeill, son of William Walsh McNeill, solicitor, of Larne, educated at Birkenhead; went to Australia 1853; (affidavit of John Martin, cousin, 1857). His father, William Walsh (son of John McNeill, attorney, Dublin, and Catherine Walsh), had served his time to his uncle, Mr. Walsh, solicitor and seneschal of the manor, and became a partner in the firm renamed Walsh & McNeill. His father took control on the death of Mr. Walsh, and on his own death the practice went to his eldest son George Hill McNeill. On his death it passed to a cousin John McNeill, who died in 1865, when W.W. McNeill took over. While returning from a business meeting in London he took ill and died in Stranraer on 11 September 1883 aged 49 years. His funeral passed from his home in Main Street to St. Cedma's, where he had been churchwarden, and after a service the body was buried at Carncastle. A subscription list was opened to provide a memorial in St. Cedma's. See *Larne Weekly Recorder*, 15 & 22 October 1883; Keane, Phair and Sadleir: *King's Inns Admission Papers*.

Death: April 1 at Rathmines Road, Dublin, John McNeill, Esq., solicitor, aged 37 years. *Larne Weekly Reporter*, 8 Apr. 1865.]

McNEILL

[Small window depicting Jesus and children, in north wall of nave.] To the glory of God and in loving remembrance of Mary Georgina, George Hill, and Jane, this window is erected by their mother Martha McNeill, 1892. "Svffer little children to come vnto me." Cox, Son, Buckley & Co., 1892, London, Youghal, & New York.

McNEILL

[White limestone tablet on black limestone backing on south wall of nave.] In memory of the McNeill family who lived at The Corran, Larne Harbour, for nearly 300 years. Many of them worshipped in this church. Some of them rest beside its walls. This tablet was placed here in 1969 by Lucy E. KIRKPATRICK, the sole survivor.

[Lucy Edith McNeill, daughter of Col. Duncan McNeill (see McGarel Cemetery) married on 19 June 1919 the Rev. Robert Kirkpatrick (1877-1966), Vicar of Glynn, 1920-50. See Leslie: *Clergy of Connor* (1993).]

McNEILL
See AGNEW, BUTLER, MAGILL and MONTGOMERY

McNINCH
See BOYD

McNISH
See JACKSONE and ROBINSON

McPEAKE
See GETTY

McQUILLAN
[Monument south of church in the form of a hipped roof, with lead lettering in white limestone.] In loving memory of Margaret H. McQuillan who departed this life 2nd Jan. 1881 aged 57 years. Also her husband Thomas McQuillan who departed this life 4th Jan. 1883 aged 63 years. "For ever with the Lord". In loving memory of David McQuillan who departed this life 27th March 1909 aged 52 years. Also his wife Grace McQuillan who departed this life 11th January 1916 aged 58 years. "Lo, I am with you alway."
[The will of Thomas McQuillan, late of Larne, county Antrim, merchant, who died 2 January 1883, was proved at Belfast 14 March 1883 by David McQuillan, grocer, and William Baxter, auctioneer, both of Larne, the executors. Effects £527 0s. 1d.
Thomas McQuillan, grocer, died after a short illness, at his residence in Mill Street. He was a sunday school teacher in the Methodist Church and had been superintendent from 1871. David, grocer, meal and flour merchant, Mill Street, became the Sunday school superintendent in 1900. He was the last chairman of Larne Town Commisioners and the first chairman of the Urban District Council in 1899. See: *Directory for the Province of Ulster*, 1861, 1884, 1900; Knox: *Larne Methodist Church*; *Larne Weekly Recorder*, 6 Jan. 1883. *Larne Times*, 28 Jan. 1899.
Robert, youngest son of Thomas McQuillan, married Mary, eldest daughter of George Smyth, Larne, at the Second Presbyterian Church on 2 June 1881.See *Larne Weekly Recorder*, 4 June 1881.]

McQUILLAN
[South of church.] Erected by Thos. McQuillan in memory of his daughter Mary who died 27th March 1864 aged 6 years. Also two children who died in infancy.

McQUOWN/McKEOWN
[Set against south boundary wall.] Erected by Nicholas McQuown, Blackcave, in memory of his wife Janet McQuown who died 29th Sept. 1827 aged 55 years. Also four of their offspring, viz. Neal who died 15th June 1811 aged 5 years. Adam aged 18 years was drowned 27th June 1818 near the M(aiden Rock)s. Robert who died 28th March 1(83)3 aged 26 years & William who died 24th Sept. 1825 aged 30 years. Also Mary McKeown who died 18th Octr. 1880 aged 63 years. And her husband George McKeown who died 8th April 1901 aged 85 years. [On upper edge of stone:-] 2 graves south.

McREV
    See McGEREL

McTIER
    [*U.J.A.* VI (1900), 97. Slate – parts broken off and missing. Arms:- a cross bordured, impaling a paly of six, a canton ermine. Crest:- a dove, in its beak a laurel branch. Motto:- Gaudium adfero.] Here lyeth ye bodies of Janet FAIRIES who died Mar. ye 3d 17(53) aged 32 years, late wife to (Hugh) McTier. Also 4 children viz (Robert), Margret, Ann, & Janet.

McWILLIAM
    Erected by Jane McWilliam in memory of her husband (Hugh McW)illiam of Larne who departed this life on the 5th of August 1831 aged 40 years. The above named Jane McWilliam died on the 18th March 1862 aged 74 years.

MAGEE
    See McNEILL

MAGILL
    [White limestone, broken in three, set against east boundary wall.] In memory of William H. Magill who died 10th March 1904 aged 69 years. Also his wife Mary Jane McNEILL who died 15th April 1911 aged 69 years. Also their daughters & sons:- Martha 27th Nov. 1869 aged 2, Harry 28th June 1877 aged 8, William 30th Oct. 1884 aged 3, Wilhelmina 19th June 1890 aged 16, Maggie 11th Jan. 1905 aged 26.

MAGILL
    [White limestone with lead lettering, south-east of church.] Erected by Johny [sic] Magill, Ballytober, in memory of his beloved wife Nancy Magill who died 30th January 1904 aged 70 years. The above-named John Y. Magill died 29th April 1911 aged 75 years. T. Holden, Larne.

MAGILL
    [Laid flat in east of graveyard.] Erected by Ch(arles Magil)l to the (memory of his daug)ht(er Marg)ar(e)t who d .... Francis and Is(a...........ed .... The above-named Ch.......... died 5th .... Also his grandch...........who d(ied i)n infa(ncy). Also his gr(andso)n Harry (who died) 31st January 1915 a(ged ..) ye.... Also his dau(ght)er-in-law Mary Magill who died 15th May 1(.)3(.) aged 73 years. And his son Henry Magill who died 27th May 1932 aged 77 years.

MALLUM
    [Sandstone set against east boundary wall.] Erected (by ....n) Mallvm w(idow) of (....n) M(a)llum (late 1st mate the) sloop *Nancy* of Port Glasgow in Scotland perished with his crew in Larne Loch on the night of the 17th Nov. 1789 aged 43 years.

MANFOD
    [*M.D.* IV (1899), 2, p. xxviii; *U.J.A.* VI (1900), 90. Slate, now cracked with part missing. Had been set against north boundary wall, now against south wall of nave. Arms:- a lion rampant with two tails. Crest:- a garb. Motto:- Audacia et industia.] Here lyeth ye bodies of Hugh Manfod who died Oct. ye 15th 1751 aged 75 years. Also his first wife (E)lizabeth SNODEY died Aug. ye 12 (17)26.

MANSON

[*U.J.A.* VI (1900), 53. A lion rampant within a floral border.] (Thomas) Manson (departed) this life (31st Octr.) 1801 aged (5)9 years. (Three of) his children (viz. Jane, Nanc)y, & Th(omas died when) young. (His son James di)ed at Cambray (in France 3)0(th) March 1812 aged 26 years. Mary CARRUTHE(RS) wife of Thomas (Man)son died 28th Sept. 1822 AE 62.

MANSON

[Against north boundary wall.] Erected in memory of Jane SMYTH, wife to Antony Manson, who departed this life 1824 aged 68 years.

MARSHALL

[In several pieces in church porch.] Sacred to the memory of Chas. H. Marshall, Lieut. R.N., who died 22nd Sept. 1835 aged 44 years. He entered the navy at the age of 11 and was actively engaged at the Battle of Trafalger. This stone is erected by his widow as a tribute of respect to the remains of an affectionate husband.

[Marshall, Charles Henry; rank, lieutenant; seniority, 14 June 1813. See *Navy List*, 1828, p. cliii.]

MARSHALL

See HOLDEN

MARTIN

[Slate in sandstone frame against east boundary wall.] Erected by Samuel and Mary Ann Martin of Larne in remembrance of their only and dearly beloved daughter Rose Anne, born 20th July 1858, died 15th March 1875. Also his father Samuel Martin who died 25th March 1847 aged 54 years. And of his mother Rose Ann who died 22nd March 1855 aged 62 years. Also of their only and dearly beloved son Samuel, born 14th July 1862, died 13th March 1881. The above-named Samuel Martin, born 3rd Feby. 1825, died 15th May 1881. A. Jenkins, Larne.

[The will of Samuel Martin, late of Larne, county Antrim, relieving officer, who died 1 [sic] May 1881 at same place, was proved at Belfast 26 September 1881 by John Kane, M.D., and David Nelson, draper, both of Larne, the executors. Effects £424 15s. 10d.]

MARTIN

See BARKLIE, GLEGHORN, GRAY and ROBINSON

MATEER

[Laid flat, north of church.] Erected by Margaret Mateer in memory of her beloved son Wm. John Mateer who departed this life 27th Dec. 1867 aged 3(4) years. Also his son Saml. Jas. E(CC)L(E)S Mateer who died 12th June 1868 aged 18 months.

Ma(y) yo(u) and I in glory meet,
And cast our crown at Jesus feet.

Also the abo(v)e Margaret Mateer died (4)th July 1874 aged 70 years. Also (her daugh)ter M(ar)y GETTY (wh)o died .... May 1888 (aged 63 y)ears. And her hu(sband ....tty) who died 20th (aged 73 yea)rs.

MAYBERRY

[A small plaque with "arms" of the Parish of Larne and Inver.] Awarded posthumously to Mrs. Mary Joan Mayberry, much loved sextoness, killed by a motor car on her way home from church 19th January 1980.

MEARNS

[*U.J.A.* VI (1900), 91. Enclosed with Macaulay of Red Hall. Arms:- a chevron between in chief two mullets in base an increscent impaling per pale a wreath counterchanged(?). Crest:- a demi lion rampant.] Here lyeth the body of Margaret SNODY first wife to Robert Mearns who died Nov. the 13 1709 and his 2 sons viz. John who died May the 25 1717 and Thomas died July the 15 1729 & his grand child Martha WILLSON died Feb. the 28 1733. Also the above Robert Mearns, tanner in Larne, died Feb. the 7 1734 aged 76 years. Thomas Willson died June 28 1750 aged 28 years. James Willson died 16 November 1750 aged 60 years. Robert Willson died 25 December 1759 aged 44 years. Also John Willson who died Dec. the 27 1766 aged 4(3) years. Likewise Jean Willson who died March the 23rd 1768 aged 71 years.

MEHARG

[Slate broken into several pieces.] ....nders .. who .... in Sepr. 17(-)8 a(g.....) years. Also his g......ught... Margaret Wo..s..e w(ife) to Alexande(r) Meharg who died the 5th Decr. 1814 aged 72 years.

MEHARG

[Slate against west boundary wall.] Erected by Samuel Meharg in memory of his beloved wife Elizabeth who died 8th July 1825 aged 33 years. She faithfully discharged the various duties of life, & supported by a rational belief in the religion of Jesus, submitted to the will of God with resignation & hope. Samuel Meharg died 22nd May 1871 aged 75 years. And Sarah, second wife of above Samuel Meharg, died 1st April 1874 aged 74 years.

[The will of Samuel Meharg, late of Larne, county Antrim, merchant, who died 22 May 1871 at same place, was proved at Belfast 23 December 1872 by the oath of John Alexander Bowman of Larne aforesaid, woolen draper, one of the executors. Effects under £300.

Death: Sarah, relict of Samuel Meharg, aged 74 years, at Wesley Place, Larne. *The Larne Reporter*, 4 Apr. 1874.]

MEHARG

[White limestone set against south boundary wall.] In memoriam. Ellen Meharg, Larne, who died 25th June 1877 aged 61 years. Also her husband Joseph Meharg who died 30th June 1883 aged 66 years. And two of her children who died young. Also their daughter Mary who died 28th Nov. 1904 aged 58 years.

MEHARG

[Small loose sandstone, set against south boundary wall.] In memory of Thos. Meharg who died 20 Aug. 1881 aged 74 years. Also his wife Mary who died 27 Feb. 1889 aged 77. Their daughter Ellen died 2 May 1889 aged 49.

[Thomas Meharg died suddenly at his residence, Ballymena Road, Larne. *Larne Weekly Reporter*, 27 Aug. 1881.]

MEHARG

See GRAHAM and McHARG

MICHELL

See MOORE

MILER

[Small sandstone laid flat, east of church.] May 14 1700 Wiliam Miler.

MILLAR
See FERRES, HOLDEN and McCARTNEY

MILLER
See BLAIR and KIRK

MINFORD
[Memorial plaque on south wall of baptistry.] To the glory of God and in loving memory of Margaret Minford nee BELL who was an active guide and guider for thirty years: October 11th 1953. This memorial was placed here by her guides and friends of the Larne District.

MITCHEL
Erected by Rose FERGUSON in memory of Jenny JEFFERIES (Mitchel) who died 19th Nov. 1823, aged 57 years. Also Mary Mitchell who died 27 Feby. 1882 aged 70 years and William Mitchell who died 1st Oct. 1888 aged 72 years. Also of her husband Alexander Ferguson who died 16th July 1884 aged 53 years and her daughter Elizabeth McKEOWN who 19th March 1892 aged 24 years. The above-named Rose Ferguson who died 18th June 1900 aged 68 years.

MONTFORD
See DOORIS

MONTGOMERY
[*U.J.A.* VI (1900), 92. Ledger within railed enclosure, east of church. Arms:- per fess, a sword in pale overall, point uppermost; 1st and 4th quarters, three fleur-de-lis; 2nd and 3rd, three gem-rings. Crest:- a ship in sail. Motto:- Garde bien.] Here lyeth the body of Jane DUGAT wife to John Montgomery, merchant in Larne, who died October the 28 1752 aged 43 years. Also 4 children to witt Margaret, Robert, Hugh and Mary. Likewise Jane their daughter who died May the 13 1760 aged 19 years & James who died 8 April 1762 aged 25 years. On the 24 Feb. 1782 died the above named John Montgomery aged 72 years. Archibald BARKLIE of Inver, born July 22 1780, died July 27 1861. His wife Helen, grand-daughter of the above John Montgomery, born Decr. 1786, died Sept. 18 1861. Also their sons. John Montgomery, born Sept. 13 1823, died July 9 1831. James McDONNELL, born March 12 1825, died at Rome, April 13 1861 and buried in the English Cemetery there. Hugh McCALMONT born Jany. 22 1827, died July 26 1866, buried at Rashee in this county.

MONTGOMERY
[Sandstone ledger, east of church, with arms:- per fess a sword in pale overall, point uppermost; first and fourth quarters, three fleur-de-lis; second and third quarters, three gem-rings. Crest:- a ship in sail.] Here lyeth the body of William Montgomery who died Dec. 9th 1755 aged 98 years. Also Hugh Montgomery son to the said William died Sep. 14th 1772 aged 64 years. Also Martha Montgomery, Hugh's wife who died (the) 20th of Feb. 1800 aged 76 years. Doctor George CASEMENT who died 4th October 1834 aged (.)9 years. And Martha his wife, daughter of the above-named Hugh Montgomery, who died 11th April 1840 aged 88 years. And of Jane, widow of Fredk. Montgomery and youngest daughter of the late Malm. McNEILL, Esqre., at the Corran, born 1st Jany. 1800, died 11th May 1891 in her 92nd year.
[The will of Jane Montgomery, late of Larne, county Antrim, widow, who died 11 May

1891 at same place, was proved at Belfast 1 February 1892 by John Macaulay of Redhall, Ballycarry, in said county, esquire, the surviving executor. Effects £6,539 12s.]

MONTGOMERY
[*M.D.* IV (1899), 2, p.xxviii; *U.J.A.* VI (1900), 93. Sandstone set against north boundary wall. Arms:- per fess, a sword in pale overall, point uppermost; first and fourth quarters, three fleur-de-lis; second and third, three gem-rings. Crest:- a ship. Motto:- Garde bien.] Here lye(th) the bo(dy of) Robert (Mont)gomery who departed this life 29th Jan. 1780 aged 80 years and 8 of his children. And to the memory of his grandson Samuel MORROW who departed this life on the 21st of December 1868 aged 84 years. Also his beloved wife Margaret Morrow who departed this life on the 26th of January 1837 aged 57 years.

MONTGOMERY
[Sandstone, laid flat east of church.] Erected to the memory of Mary Montgomery who departed this life 19th July 18(5)6 aged (41) years.

MONTGOMERY
See BARKLIE, CASEMENT and WATT

MOORE
[Recumbent, next to Thomas Moore d.1823.] Here lyeth the body of John Moore who died the 9(th) Jan(ry.) 1777 aged 39 years. Also Mary Moore his daughter born 25(th) May 1772, died Ma(..1)st 1793. Also his wife born (14th) Jun(e 1749 died ....)

MOORE
[Vertical monument with sockets to take railings, east of church.] In memoriam. Thomas Moore died 30th Augt. 1823 aged 79 years. Barbara Moore (nee DICKEY) died 11th Sept. 1830 aged 81 years. Jane Moore died 24th Feby. 1799 aged 23 years. David Moore died 1st May, 1809 aged 24 years. Rev. William Moore died 1st Feby. 1842 aged 64 years. Miles ATKINSON died 21st June 1863 aged 72 years. Anne Atkinson (nee Moore) died 3rd Feby. 1863 aged 73 years. Thomas Moore Atkinson died 15th June 1845 aged 28 years. David Atkinson died 12th Dec. 1824 aged 17 months. William Atkinson died 2nd July 1828 aged 13 months. Also three children of Wm. D. Atkinson, Willie, Annie, & May who died infancy. William David Atkinson, son of Miles Atkinson, died 1st March 1896. Jane Atkinson his wife died 5th March 1919. William A. M. Atkinson died 4th September 1946. Annie Moore MICHELL (nee Atkinson) died 25th November 1952. I give unto them eternal life.
    [Miles Atkinson was a linen and woollen draper in Cross Street.]

MOORE
[Broad sandstone set against south wall of church.] Jane Moore, wife to William Moore died 11th Feby. 18(0)(-) aged 38 years. She is inter'd here with her 3 children, viz. Mary, Elisabeth & Jenny, Moore. Also William Moore who died 20th October 181(3) aged 51 years. Also his son David Moore who died the 4th May 1817 aged 27 years. Also his grand-daughter Jane SNODDY who died the 23rd March 1835 aged 9 months. And of Andrew Snoddy her father who departed this life 31st Jany. 1843 aged 72 years. And also Sarah Snoddy, wife to Andrew Snoddy, who departed this life 1(9 April) 1857 ....

MOORE
See BEGGS

MORDOC(H)

[Set against south wall of church. Carved in typanum: a flower in profile and two in full face.] Here lyeth the body of Janet ANDREOW, wife to Ja(me)s Mordoc(h) who died April ye 30 1711 aged 77 years & Hugh McCULLOCH who died Fe(b. 21) of 1718 aged 34 years & Mary PEDY his wife who died Octr. 28th 1737 aged 60 years. & David CURRY who died (Au)g. 9(th) 1761 aged 25 (y)ear(s). [Carved on top edge:-] Jean McCOLOCH died Decmr. the 20 17(59).

MORGAN

[Brass plate on prayer desk.] Ad Dei gloriam, atque in usum hujus ecclesiae. Rev. T.P. Morgan, A.M., rectore, ambonem hunc donaverunt presbyteri sex Connorenses, A.D. MDCCCLXXIX. [Translation:- To the glory of God and for the use of this church, six priests of Connor have presented this prayer desk. *To This You Belong*, p. 32.]

[The Rev. Thomas Poole Morgan was born on 6 September 1821, son of James Morgan, merchant, of Cork, and Maria Townsend Poole of Mayfield. He entered Trinity College, Dublin, in 1840, graduating B.A. with Div. Test. in 1845 and M.A. in 1863. He was curate of Cork 1846, of Glengariff 1846-7, Whitechurch (Cloyne) 1847-55, Garrycloyne 1855-65, rector of Larne and Inver 1865-99, rural dean of Carrickfergus and chaplain to Larne Workhouse, precentor of Connor 1894-99. He married on 2 December 1868, in St. Peter`s, Drogheda, Elizabeth Woolfe Kelly, daughter of Richard Kelly, M.B., of Drogheda. They had 3 sons and 2 daughters. He died on 23 May 1904. See Burtchaell and Sadleir: *Alumni Dublinenses* (1924); Leslie: *Clergy of Connor* (1993).]

MORGAN

[Lancet window depicting the Resurrection, in south wall of chancel.] To the glory of God and in memory of Canon Morgan, rector of this parish 1866-1899. Erected by the parishioners, 1904. During his incumbency and largely by his instrumentality, good taste, and ecclesiastical knowledge, this church fabric was restored to its present very creditable state.

MORROW

See MONTGOMERY

MUIR

[Brass plaque attached to south wall of nave.] To the glory of God and in memory of G.H. Johnstone Muir, F.R.C.V.S., born 3 June 1847 at Kilmarnock, died 25 August 1908 at Shamrock Lodge. Erected by the veterinary staff of the Department of Agriculture and Technical Instruction for Ireland. [Sawier, Dublin.]

MUNRO

[*U.J.A.* VI (1900), 94; *M.D.* V (1901), 1, 1. The arms have eroded. They were indistinct by 1899, but G.V. DuNoyer provided a drawing in his *Antiquarian Sketches* IX (1868), 71, giving it the year 1772. Arms:- a bird displayed mounted on an open helmet affrontee unbarred. Crest:- an eagle's head erased.] Here (lieth) the body of William M(unr)o who departed this life .... aged 66 years. Al(so .... Jane PEYTO who dep(arted) this life Dec. 8th 1(7)97 (aged) 43 years. And his daughter Ann FERRES who died Jan. 20 1802 aged 44 (yea)rs.Also his son David (who) departed this life .... 1804 aged 48 years. .... wife Mary Munro who (depa)rted this life 19th July 1804 aged 90 years.

No more Munros shall cross the Tropick Line
Nor bid his crew defy the Polar Wave
Or spread more sail to leave their foe behind

Here lies the landlock's in the silent grave.
Also Nancy, wife of David Munro, who departed this life 28th Sept. 1814 aged 76 years.

MURDOCH

[Set against north boundary wall, the letter "M" is carved across the top of the stone four times to form a frieze.] Here rests the body of Iames Murdoch who departed this life Feb. 23 1677.

MURDOCH

[Small thick sandstone with inscriptions on recessed panel. "July 6" is carved vertically up frame on left side. Set against south boundary wall.] I.M. July 6 1708. Here lyeth the body of Heilen Murdoch daughter to Robert M(urdoc)h who departed (June) 10 1697 and Heilen Jan. 30 1700.

MURDOCH

[*U.J.A.* VI (1900), 95. Sandstone set against boundary wall. Arms:- per fess, in chief two birds statant vulned through the throat by a single arrow, in base a saltire engrailed between four roses. Crest:- a bird rising. Motto:- Omnia pro bono.] Here lyeth ye body of Robert Murdoch, merchant in Larne, who died Sept. ye 9(th) 1742 aged 85 years.

NAESMITH

[*U.J.A.* VI (1900), 96. Set against south boundary wall. Arms:- a hand couped at the wrist holding a sword in pale between two hammers with broken shafts. Crest:- a hand couped at the wrist holding a hammer with broken shaft. Motto:- Non arte sed marte.] Here lyeth the body of John Naesmith who died April 23d 1789 aged 88 years.

NAESMITH

See FINLAY

NEILL

[Set against south boundary wall.] Erected by Eliza Neill in memory of her husband William Neill who died 16th Decr. 1864 aged 44 years. Also five of their children who died in infancy. The above-named Eliza Neill died 25th October 1898 aged 73 years.

NEILSON

[Red sandstone against east boundary wall.] Here lyeth the body of Jane Neilson who departed this life the 1st May 1816 aged 19 years. Also the body of Wm. FLECK who died on the 27th Feber(u)ary 1829 aged 29 years.

NELSON

[Close to south boundary wall. White limestone with lead lettering on granite plinth.] Sacred to the memory of Robert Nelson who departed this life on the 18th February 1887 aged 92 years and of Frances his wife who died on the 18th April 1874 aged 71 years. Erected by their surviving children. Here also lies the remains of Robert, Elizabeth and Jane, their children who died in youth. And of Samuel their eldest son who died on the 27th March 1859 aged 34 years. And of Catherine, his wife who died on the 27th February 1868. "The Lord knoweth the days of the upright: and their inheritance shall be for ever." Psalms XXXVII, 18. Robinson, Belfast.
[The will of Robert Nelson, late of Drumalis Terrace, Larne, county Antrim, gentleman, who died 18 February 1887 at same place, was proved at Belfast 30 March

1887 by John McNinch, David Nelson and John McDowell, all of Larne, merchants, the executors. Effects £2,722 . 5s. 3d.

Letters of administration of the personal estate of Samuel Nelson, late of No. 20 Brougham Street, Belfast, who died 27 March 1859 at Drumnadrough in the county of Antrim, were granted at Belfast 10 October 1859 to Catherine Nelson of No. 47 Bentinck Street, Belfast, the widow of said deceased. Effects under £600.

The will of Catherine Nelson, late of Belfast, county Antrim, widow, who died 29 February 1868 at same place, was proved at Belfast 27 March 1868 by the oath of Robert Nelson of Magheramorne in said county, esquire, the sole executor. Effects under £300.]

NICHOL
    See BEGGS

NICHOLSON
    See ALLEN and PATRICK

NICKLE
    [Tall sandstone set against east boundary wall.] Erected in memory John Nickle who died 21st Aug. 1845 aged 76 years. Also his wife Mary McFEE who died 15th June 1813 aged 45 years. Their son John died in New York 18th August 1834 aged 30 years. Their daughter Jane McCALMONT who died 20th Novr. 1864 aged 58 years. Also their son Thomas Nickle who died 23rd Aug. 1870 aged 68 years. Also their son Malcolm Nickle who died 3rd March 1890 aged 81 years. And his wife Jane DUNCAN Nickle who died 30th Dec. 1899 aged 74 years. Also Robert McCalmont, F.C.S. who died 31st July 1890 aged 61 years and John McCalmont who died 5th Augt. 1898 aged 71 years – grandsons of above John Nickle. Matilda RODGERS, wife of John McCalmont, who died 5th Jany. 1908 aged 81 years.

    [The will of Malcolm Nickle, late of Main Street, Larne, county Antrim, bootmaker, who died 3 March 1890 at same place, was proved at Belfast 24 March 1890 by Jane Nickle of Main Street, Larne, widow, one of the executors. Effects £190 16s.

    Administration of the estate of John McCalmont, late of 17 Mill Street, Belfast, linen draper, who died 5 August 1898, granted at Belfast 25 November 1898 to Matilda McCalmont of 17 Mill Street, the widow. Effects £45 10s.]

O'BRIEN
    See SMYTH

OGILVIE
    [Lead lettering on white limestone framed with slate and set in sandstone. The limestone arms have now dissolved but in *U.J.A.* VI (1900), 97, are shown: a lion passant gardant crowned with the crown imperial. Crest: a lion rampant holding a staff.] Here are deposited the remains of Revd. William Ogilvie who died in 1712 and Jane AGNEW his wife. William Ogilvie who died 14th February 1780 aged 74 years. James Blair Ogilvie who died 22nd April 1785 aged 48 years. Elizabeth BLAIR, wife of the last-named William Ogilvie who died 21st May 1785 aged 87 years. And Margaret SHAW, wife by her first marriage to said James Blair Ogilvie, who died 19th March 1818 aged 72 years. This monument is erected by Dorothea Shaw Blair in memory of her beloved parents. MDCCCXX.

    [Rev. William Ogilvie was the third Presbyterian minister of Larne and Kilwaughter, 1699-1712. He was descended from a younger son of Lord Airlie, and married Jane, daughter of Patrick Agnew of Kilwaughter House, and thereby gained the townland of

Ballyloran. His son William Ogilvie married Elizabeth, daughter of Major James Blair, a veteran of the Seige of Derry who settled in Killyglen. Their son James Blair Ogilvie, R.N., married Margaret, daughter of William Shaw of Doagh, and had three daughters:- Elizabeth who died at Doagh; Dorothea Shaw, who married firstly James Blair of Merville and secondly Major John Rowan; Helen, who married Campbell Graham of Belfast and had a large family. See Porter, McIlrath, & Nelson: *Congregational Memoirs*, pp. 30-64; Heatly & Dixon: *Belfast Scenery*, Plate XIV.]

OHAVERON
[Set against south wall of chancel.] Here lyeth the body of Peter Ohaveron who died the 19th of April 1782 aged 78 years. Also John Ohaveron who died on the 25th of Feburary 1853 aged 68 years.

OLDERSHAW
[Oval slate set into heavy sandstone, laid flat next to south boundary wall.] Erected by Sarah Oldershaw in memory of her beloved husband John Oldershaw, late of Strelley, Nottinghamshire, Officer of Excise, who died at Larne 28th Sept. 1849 aged 29 years.

ORR
[Sandstone against west boundary wall.] Erected by George McCAUGHEY Orr in memory of his father William Orr who departed this life March 1843 aged 72 years. Also his mother Jane Orr who departed this life October 1844 aged 62 years.

ORR
[Set against south boundary wall.] Erected by William Orr in memory of his beloved son Robert Orr who departed this life July 2 1868 aged 21 years. Also his son David Orr who died 22 May 1873 aged 25 years. Also his beloved wife Mary Orr who died 5th Oct. 1875 aged 66 years. Also the above-named William Orr who died 20th April 1877 aged 75 years. Also his granddaughter (Mary) who died in infancy. Also his son John Orr who died 3rd March 1913 aged 70 years. Also Jane, wife of John Orr, who died 29th March 1926 aged 86 years.

PALMER
See BLAIR

PARK
See WATT

PATON / PATTON
[*U.J.A.* VI (1900), 98. Arms:- three crescents. Crest:- a bird displayed(?) Motto:- Virtute adepta.] Here lyeth the body of John Paton who departed this life 20th Augt. 1777 aged 55 years. Also his son James Paton born in 1748 who departed this life the 4th of April 1823. Also Ann, wife of James Patton, who departed this life 22nd Jany. 1827 aged 75 years. And of David CHICHESTER who died on the 25th June 1830 &c.

PATRICK
[*U.J.A.* VI (1900), 98. The stone was showing signs of wear even in 1900. Arms:- a saltire, on a chief (three?) cushions. Crest:- a hand grasping a sword, pointing downward. Motto:- ...... sure.] Here lyeth the body of Thomas Patrick who died the 3d of April 1767 aged 72 years. Also Isabel THOM who died 14th Octr. 1773 aged 72 years. Also Isabella BURNEY who departed this life 9th Febr. 1800 aged 23 years.

PATRICK
[Slate ledger, cracked.] In memory of John Patrick, Blackcave, who died 11th April 1773 aged 37 years. Also his wife Eliza and their son Thomas. Eliza Nicholson died A.D. 1800 aged 18 months. Her father Revd. John NICHOLSON, late minister of the Seceding Congregation, Larne, died 10th March 1814 aged 53 years.
"In him conspicuous shone,
Religion in her most arractive form,
Himself the model of the truths be taught."
His wife Annie died 28th April 1834 aged 63 years.
[The Rev. John Nicholson was born in Dumfries, Scotland, in 1761 and ordained minister of Second Islandmagee and Gardenmore, Larne, in 1785. He remained there until 1799, preaching in each church on alternate Sundays, and was subsequently minister of Crescent Presbyterian Church 1799-1814. While in Larne he also ran an academy and later taught classics in Belfast Academy. He married Anne Patrick of Black Cave and had several children, the last of his sons dying in 1 March 1894 aged 91. See Stewart: *The Seceders in Ireland* (1950).]

PATRICK
See WATT

PATTON
Erected by William Patton, Larne, in memory of his father & mother viz. Alexander Patton & Elizabeth SMITH, 1840. Also of Agnes Patton his daughter who departed this life on the 20th March 1844 aged 16 months. Also the said William Patton who departed this life 17 Novemr. 1847 aged 45 years. Also his daughter Ellen McALISTER who died 25th Sept. 1876 aged 46 years. And his wife Mary Patton who died 12th Dec. 1878 aged 75 years.

PATTON
[Lead lettering on white limestone in sandstone; on the white limestone cartouche, an anchor.] Erected by William Patton, Larne, in loving remembrance of his dear son William who died 13th July 1880 aged 16 years. Also his daughter Martha who died in infancy 5th Feby. 1874. Also his eldest and dearly beloved daughter Mary who died 13th March 1885 aged 22 years. Also his dearly beloved daughter Jane who died 12th Jany. 1886 aged 20 years. Also his dearly beloved daughter Agnes who died 22nd June 1888 aged 19 years. Also his dearly beloved daughter Annie BELL who died 22nd July 1897 aged 29 years. Also his dearly beloved wife Maggie who died 16th August 1901 aged 63 years. Also his dearly beloved daughter Sarah who died 12th April 1905 aged 31 years. The above-named William A. Patton died 6th Nov. 1911 aged 71 years. Also his dearly beloved daughter Margaret died 4th Feby. 1955. A. Jenkins. 3 graves.

PEDEN
[Lead lettering on white limestone set into heavy sandstone. Above is a draped urn decorated with a rose sprig and an hour glass with motto "time is short". Against south wall of church.] Sacred to the memory of Thomas L. Peden aged 40 years. He died of cholera, 1st Sept. 1854. This monument is erected by a few of his numerous friends, as a mark of their affectionate regard and esteem and of the deep regret they felt at his untimely and sudden death.

PEDEN
[Upper part of sandstone laid flat in internal angle of Macaulay enclosure, so badly damaged that most of the inscription is unreadable. Probably early Victorian.] Erected by Robert Peden of Cairncastle in grateful r(emembrance of his ..ther Robert P)ed..

PEDEN
See TERBERT

PEDY
See MORDOC(H)

PETERIE
[Heavy sandstone, had a lain face down, now re-erected in south east of graveyard.] In memory of Jane McMULLEN, the beloved wife of William Peterie, who died 19th Oct. 1875 aged 47 years. Also two of his grandchildren who died young. Also his son William who died 1st Dec. 1879 aged 33 years. Also his daughter Maggie Jane who died 15th Nov. 1883 aged 25 years. Also his daughter Grace who died 10th Dec. 1885 aged 23 years. Also his daughter Martha who died 4th Aug. 1894 aged 21 years. The above-named William Peterie who died 3rd Jan. 1902 aged 101 years. And his daughter Elizabeth died 7th July 1955 aged 96 years. Mary Peterie died 16th Dec. 1958 aged 93 years. "Blessed are the dead which die in the Lord"

PORTER
[Set against north boundary wall.] 1694. Hear layeth the body of Hvgh Porter marchant of Learne and his vif Katrin WILSON vho departied this life Ianvary the 8 day.

PORTER
See GETTY and HOOD

POWELL
[South of church.] In memory of Louisa, the dearly beloved wife of Frederick Powell, died 20th Novr. 1865 aged 22 years. And Edward LANGTRY, infant son of same.
    [Death: Nov. 5, at Inver Lodge, Larne, the infant son of Frederick Powell, Esq., aged 23 days. *Larne Weekly Reporter*, 11 Nov. 1865.]
    [Death: Nov. 20, at Inver Lodge, Larne, Louise, wife of Frederick Powell, Esq., late of the 49th Regiment, aged 22 years. *Larne Weekly Reporter*, 25 Nov. 1865.]

QUINN
[Ledger southeast of church.] Dedicated by George Quinn to the memory of his father the late George Quinn of Bank who died the 3rd August 1819 aged 59 years.

RAINEY
[Laid flat, east of church.] Erected (by) Mathew Rainey in ...... of his daughter ..... who died the 8th ......(r)y 18(3)0 aged 1(5) years. ... (also) of four of his infant children.

RAINEY
[Laid flat in south-west of graveyard. The capstone is missing and with it the beginning of the inscription.] In memory of his beloved wife Isabella Rainey born 1st May 1825 died 20th Aug. 1883. Also their daughter Martha who died in infancy. The above-named Thomas Rainey died 12th Novr. 1894 aged 76 years. Also his daughter Isabella died 8th December 1914.

RAINEY
  See LEWIS

RANKIN
  See RODGERS

REID
  Erected in loving memory of George C. Reid who died 1st February 1879 aged 39 years.

REID
  [Table stone in southwest of graveyard.] Sacred to the memory of John Reid who died 4th November 1846 aged 79 years and Sarah his wife who died 15th February 1846 aged 82 years. Also John Reid, son of the abovenamed John and Sarah Reid, who died 10th January 1852 aged 46 years. Also Sarah Reid, granddaughter of the above named John and Sarah Reid and daughter of Captain William Reid, who died 19th March 1848 aged 15 years. And in memory of Capt. John SMILEY Reid, son of Captain Wm. Reid, who died at sea 17th March 1869 in the 34th year of his age. Also Jane Reid, wife of Captain Wm. Reid, who died 14th April 1884 aged 83 years.
  [April 20 at the parish church, Walton-on-the-Hill near Liverpool, Captain J.S. Reid of this town married Emma, eldest daughter of A. Cartmel, Esq., Liverpool. *Larne Weekly Reporter*, 29 April 1865.]

REID
  See HUNTER

RENNIE
  See SMILEY

RITCHIE
  [Slate with chipped top, set against south boundary wall.] Erected by John Ritchie, Lar(n). in memory of ....oved son .... McCalmont Ritchie who died 6th November 1870 aged 23 years. Also his father James Ritchie who died 31st March 1865 aged 82 years. And of his mother Elizabeth who died 22nd October 1866 aged 84 years. His brother in law John McCALMONT who died 5th Nov. 1852 aged 26 years. The above-named John Ritchie died 10th October 1878 aged 54 years. Also his wife Mary McCalmont who died 5th April 1912 aged 88 years.
  [James Ritchie died at his residence, Kilwaughter, after a protracted illness, 31st March 1865 aged 81 years. *Larne Weekly Reporter*, 8 April 1865.]

ROBINSON
  [*U.J.A.* VI (1900), 99. "These arms are borne by the Robertsons of Muirtown; the crest being that of Robertson of Newbiggin, both in Scotland. In Scotch dialect, Robin and Robert are the same, and interchangeable." Set against south boundary wall. Arms:- three wolves' heads erased disposed between as many crescents in chevron. Crest:- a dexter hand appaumé thereon the crown imperial. Motto:- Virtutis gloria merces.] Here lyeth the body of Samuel Robinson who departed this life June 21st 1784 aged 59 years. Also Janet his daughter who died in Oct. 1779 aged 3 years & his grand child Samuel CULBERT who died 20th Janu. 1795. He maintained an untainted moral character was a loveing husband a tender parent faithful friend & we believed fulfiled the duties of a Christian. Also his wife Jane McNISH who departed this life June 18th (18)01 aged 69 years.

ROBINSON
[Laid flat, south of church.] Erected to the memory of James Robinson of Ballyboley who departed this life on the 19th of December 1827 aged 74 years. Also his daughter Jane, 10th June 1841 aged (44) years. Also his daughter Margaret who died 18th December 1828 aged 31 years. Also his daughter Agnes who died 19th July 1851 aged 47 years. And his wife Agnes MARTIN who died 27th February 1855 aged 83 years.

ROBINSON
[Loose, near south boundary wall.] Erected by William Robinson in memory of his son Robert who departed this life 23rd of Novr. 1835 aged 23 years. Also his son Thomas who died 26th Octr. 1850 aged 22 years. Also the abovenamed William Robinson who died 28th Septr. 1857 aged 70 years. And [the inscription was never continued beyond this.]

ROBINSON
[White limestone set against south boundary wall.] Erected by Jane Robinson in memory of her husband Hugh Robinson who departed this life 11th June 1878. Also her sons, John who died 18th Sep. 1907, and David who died 25th Feb. 1908.

ROBINSON
[Lead lettering in white limestone set against south wall of chancel.] Erected to the memory of Thomas Robinson, Ballynerry, who died 15th Octr. 1886 aged 84 years.
  [The will, with one codicil, of Thomas Robinson, late of Ballynarey, Ballynure, county Antrim, farmer, who died 15 October 1886 at same place, was proved at Belfast 22 December 1886 by Robert McNair senior of Bogtown near Ballynure, and Thomas Wilson of Ballylaggan, Ballynure, farmers, the executors. Effects £722 11s.]

RODGERS
[Laid flat beside path.] Erected by Margaret Rodgers in memory of her husband John Rodgers who died 11th July 1847 aged 52 years. Also their son Robert Rodgers who died 22nd January 1831 aged 7 years. Also three of their children who died in infancy. The above-named Margaret Rodgers died 1882 aged 84 years. And their grand-daughter Mary E. RANKIN who died 17th March 1889 aged 37 years. Also their daughter Mary E. Rodgers who died 8th Augt. 1910 aged 79 years. Also their grand-son Robt. R. Rankin who died 15th Jany. 1914 aged 54 years. Also their daughter Annie, wife of Captain T. Rankin, who died 14th April 1915.

RODGERS
See NICKLE

ROGERS
[*U.J.A.* VI (1900), 99. Arms:- a stag's head erased, in the dexter fess point a mullet; impaling, on a saltire indented, five mascles. Crest:- a stag sejant. Motto:- (Amo) probus.]
Here lyeth the body of Andrew Rogers who departed this life May 14th aged 62 years and Margaret BLAIR his wife, May 17th 1781 aged 63 years. Their daughter Mary Rodgers, (wife of John CAMPBELL), who died 17th March 1825. Also John Campbell who died 29th January 1864. And their son Capt. Robert Campbeel [sic] of Larne who died 11th August 1898.

ROGERS

[Laid beside John McCulloch d. 1825 – now grassed over.] Erected in memory of Andrew Rogers who departed this life on the 9th April 1817 aged 65 years. Also four of his children who died in infancy.

ROSS

[Built into west boundary wall with low railing.] Erected by James Ross of Inver in memory of his father Willm. Ross who died 28th March 1833 aged 60 & his mother Margaret who died 8th March 1837 aged 60. Also his wife Grace who died 10th of Feb. 1839 aged 26 years. Also his son William who died 22nd Feb. 1876 aged 29 years. Also his son John Barron who died 29th Sep. 1886 aged 43 years. The above named James Ross died 18th March 1889 aged 76 years. And his wife Eliza BARRON who died 29th Novr. 1889 aged 84 years. And his son James who died 23rd June 1915 aged 66 years. Also his daughter Margaret who died 17th Jan. 1933 aged 90 years. Also Eliza, wife of son James, who died 12th Aug. 1938 aged 78 years.

[Letters of administration of the personal estate of John Barron Ross, late of Inver, Larne, county Antrim, mechanic, who died 29 September 1886 at same place, were granted at Belfast 25 October 1886 to James Ross of Inver, Larne, clothier, the father. Effects £769 4s. 11d.

The will, with one codicil, of James Ross, late of Station Road, Larne, county Antrim, clothier, who died 18 March 1889 at same place, was proved at Belfast 26 April 1889 by John McNinch of Dunluce Street, Larne, merchant, one of the executors. Effects £4,412 18s. 10d.

Eliza Barron died at 29 Station Road. *Larne Weekly Reporter,* 30 Nov. 1889.]

ROSS

[Limestone with granite enclosure.] Erected by Robert Ross in memory of his mother Mary Ross who died 9th Feby. 1878 aged 75 years. His sister Margaret who died 14th Feby. 1887 aged 53 years. His brother John who died 30th Octr. 1887 aged 49 years. His father Robert Ross who died 16th Jany. 1890 in the 90 year of his age. The above named Robert Ross died 18th Jany. 1896 aged 63 years. Also his wife Jane Ross who died 29th Nov. 1904 aged 71 years.

[Letters of administration, with the will, of the personal estate of Robert Ross, late of 370 Newtownards Road, Belfast, butler, who died 18 January 1896, were granted at Belfast 28 February 1896 to Jane Ross of 370 Newtownards Road, Belfast, the widow. Effects £413 14s. 6d.]

ROWAN

[Set against south wall of chancel.] Sacred to the memory of Mary Rowan who died 9th of July 1822 aged 17 years. Also her sister Isabella wife of (Sa)muel ALEXANDER of Larne who died 1st March (1824) aged 27 years. And their father (James) Rowan who died 4th Jany. (1825) aged (59). And of their sister Eliz(a who departed) this life 5th July 1(843 aged ..2 years). And of Eliza Rowan (wife to above) James Rowan who died 23rd Jany. 18(5)6 aged (82 years).

RUSSEL

[Polished granite against south boundary wall.] Erected by George Russel, late Supervisor, Inland Revenue, in memory of his beloved wife, daughter, and grandson. Margaret GRANT died 15th Aug. 1857 aged 60 years. Janet Russel, wife of J. K. ANDREWS, Larne, died 18th April 1858 aged 22 years. Also their son George Russel died 19th May 1857 aged 16 months.

(SE)RVICE
[Badly flaking sandstone against west boundary wall.] Erected in memory of ....
(Se)rvice who died 4th J(any.) ..37 aged 63 years .... wife ..... (Servi)ce w....... July 1
.... (A)lso his .... May (................ars). (Also) his son Ge(o....... died ...)
May 180(2) age......... (Also ......a)ndson Robert S(TEWART) who (died in in)fancy 21st
Novem.......(35) ... his son James (who died ....) March 1883 a(ged ... years. Also his
da)ughter Ca(t......... died on .. Janu)ary 188(......... years. Also ... dau)ghter (Jane) who
died 16th .... 1... (aged ..6 years).

SHANNON
[Laid flat in front of the stone of James Shannon who died 1878.] Erected by James
Shannon of Ballytober in memory of his son Robert who departed this life 17th June
1854 aged 14 years. Also his wife Jane Shannon who departed this life 5th Decr. 1868
aged 59 years.

SHANNON
Erected by Mary Jane Shannon, Ballytober, in memory of her father James Shannon who
died 21st April 1878 aged 74 years. Also her mother Jane Shannon who died 5th Decr.
1868 aged 59 years. Her brother Robert who died 17th June 1854. Her brother Hugh
who died 10 Augt. 1892. Her brother James who died 2nd June 1895. Jenkins.
    [The will of James Shannon, late of Ballytober, county Antrim, farmer, who died 21
April 1878 at same place, was proved at Belfast 17 June 1878 by the oaths of Hugh
Shannon and Robert Ritchie, both of Ballytober (Cairncastle), in same county, farmers,
the executors. Effects under £2,000.
    Letters of administration of the personal estate of Hugh Shannon, late of Ballytober,
county Antrim, farmer, who died 10 August 1892 at same place, were granted at Belfast
26 August 1892 to James Shanon of Ballytober, farmer, a brother. Effects £2,282 12s. 5d.
    The will of James Shannon, late of Ballytober, Cairncastle, county Antrim, farmer, who
died 2 June 1895 at same place, was proved at Belfast 17 July 1895 by Robert Aicken of
Oldmill, Ballygally, Cairncastle, farmer, the sole executor. Effects £1,631 8s. 1d.]

SHANNON
[Sandstone against east boundary wall.] Erected by Agnes Shannon in memory of (her
beloved) mother Jane Shannon who died 25th Augt. 1874 aged (75) years. Also her
brother George who died 29th Sept. 1856 aged 27 years. Her brother David who died
15th Novr. 1857 aged 27 years. Her sister Jane BROWN who died 5th Decr. 1887 aged
50 years. The above-named Agnes Shannon died 24th March 1916.

SHAW
See OGILVIE

SHUTTER
[*U.J.A.* VI (1900), 100. Against north boundary wall. Arms:- A barry of five wavy, on a
chief a demi-lion (?) rampant. Crest:- a ship. Motto:- Mihi lucra pericla: nothing hazard,
nothing have.] Here are interred the remains of two of James Shutter's (mariner) children
viz. Hugh who died 15th September 1738 and Elisabeth who departed this life the 8th of
January 1757 aged 17 years. Also James, a son of the above named James, who died the
19th of January 1827 aged 79 years and James, a son of the last named, who died the 17th
June 1820 aged 33 years.

SHUTTER
[Slate set against south wall of church. Arms:- per fess, in chief a demi-lion rampart, in base a barry of six wavy. Crest:- a ship. Motto:- Mihi lucra pericla: nothing hazard, nothing have.] Here lye(th) the body of John Shutter who died the 13th of April 1766 aged 18 (y)ears.

SHUTTER
See CLARK and GLASGOW

SIMPSON
[The inscription was deliberately effaced where dots are given. This headstone had been lying loose, but in 1988 was re-erected to the south of the church tower.] All the ground from this to the steeple. Erected by John Simpson in memory of his daughter Mary who died Septr. 16 1807 aged 28 years. Erected by Eliza Simpson in memory of her late husband .... who died .... aged ..
[The other side is inscribed as follows:-] In memory of Mary Simpson, daughter to John Simpson, who died the 16th Sept. 1807 aged (28) years. Also Agness STUART, wife to John Simpson, who died the 26th of Jany. 1815 aged 62 years. Also the above John Simpson who departed this life the 2nd of March 1835 aged 88 years.

SIMPSON
[Built into west boundary wall.] This monument erected by William Simpson in memory of his son John who died 6th Decr. 1814 aged 3 years. Died 25th Decr. 1818 another son named John aged 9 months. His daughter Jane died 5th Feby. 1824 aged 3 years. John Simpson brother to Wm. died 19th March 1829 aged 56. Margaret, daughter of the above William Simpson, died 30th July 1842 aged 38 years.

SIMPSON
[Table stone within iron railing with foregoing.] Erected by Dan Peden Simpson in memory of his father Willm. Simpson who died 16th August 1848 aged 73 years. Also Isabella, daughter of Dan Peden Simpson, who died 18th January 1849 aged 5 years. Also Elizabeth Peden, relict of the above named William Simpson, who died 16th June 1850 aged 73 years. Here also are interred the remains of the above named Dan Peden Simpson who died 3rd July 1852 aged 45 years. Also of his sister Ellen Simpson who died 26th May 1871 aged 57 years. Also his daughter Mary HILL who died 27th March 1875 aged 37 years.

SIMPSON
[Pink granite stone south-east of church.] Sacred to the memory of Agnes youngest daughter of William Simpson of Larne who died 5th April 1901 aged 85 years.

SIMPSON
See COWAN

SINCLAIR
See CLUGSTON

SMILEY
[Headstone beside Smiley obelisk.] Here lyeth the body of Samuel Smiley who departed this life Decr. 27th 1797 aged 77 years.
[Samuel Smiley of Larne (1720-1797) married Christina Robinson. His eldest son:-

John Smiley of Larne married Martha Love. His third son:-
John Smiley of Larne (1796-1878), grain and coal merchant, shipowner and agent for Lloyd's, married Ann Reid, see inscription on obelisk, below. They had 3 sons and 4 daughters:-
1. John MacCullough Smiley (died 1916).
2. Sir Hugh Houston Smiley (1841-1909) was created a Baronet 13 October 1903, see *Burke's Peerage and Baronetage*, 105th edition (1970). He married Elizabeth Anne Kerr and had 3 sons and 1 daughter. He and his daughter, Eileen, had the stained glass windows inserted, see below.
3. Robert Smiley (died 1876) married Mary Taylor and had 1 daughter, see inscription on obelisk to Mary and their daughter.
4. Sarah Smiley (1825-1904) married James Coey, see Coey headstone in McGarel Cemetery.
5. Margaret Thompson Smiley (1827-1907) married Charles Howden, see Howden headstone in McGarel Cemetery.
6. Martha Love Smiley (1833-1904) married John Alexander Bowman, see Bowman headstone in McGarel Cemetery.
7. Anne Smiley (died 1907) married Stewart Clark, M.P., D.L., of Dundas, county Linlithgow, see *Burke's Peerage* under Stewart-Clark, Bart.]

SMILEY

[Recumbent stone, east of church.] Erected in memory of James Smiley of Inver- who departed this life on the 6th of February 1814 aged 55 years. And of his son Hugh HOUSTON Smiley, M.D. of Larne whose earthly existence terminated on the 27th of April 1838 aged 37 years. Also Martha Smiley, daughter of James Smiley, who died 29th January 1853 aged 58 years. And of Mary HUSTON [sic] wife of James Smiley who died 22nd November 1854 aged 90 years. Also George BAINE who departed this life 1st of October 1861 aged 53 years. And Isabella HAMILL, wife of Samuel J. Smiley, (w)ho departed this life 27th July 1823 aged 37 years. (Al)so Mary Ann Smiley, wife of George Baine, who departed this life 20th Nov. 1880 aged 77 years. Also Mary, daughter of said Samuel J. Smiley, who departed this life 31st May 1883 aged 56 years. Also Samuel, son of the said Samuel J. Smiley who departed this life 31st Augt. 1883 aged 55 years. Also the said Samuel James Smiley who departed this life 13th Decr. 1884 aged 88 years. Matilda OWENS RENNIE records the death of her dear sister Annie CRAWFORD Smiley who departed this life 26th May 1905 aged 81 years, wife of the said Samuel James Smiley and daughter of the late Hugh Francis Rennie of Copenhagan and Belfast and Margaret Wilson Rennie.

[Letters of administration of the personal estate of George Baine, late of Larne, in the county Antrim, grocer, who died 1 October 1861 at same place, were granted at Belfast 21 December 1861 to Mary Anne Baine of Larne aforesaid, widow, the widow and relict of said deceased. Effects under £1,500.

Letters of administration, with the will annexed, of the personal estate of Mary Anne Baine, late of Larne, county Antrim, widow, who died 20 November 1880 at same place, were granted at Belfast 30 September 1881 to James Smiley Saunderson of Larne, master mariner, a legatee. Effects £355.

Letters of administration of the personal estate of Mary Smiley, late of Larne, county Antrim, spinster, who died 31 May 1883 at same place, were granted at Belfast 8 October 1883 to Samuel James Smiley of Main Street, Larne, farmer, the father. Effects £54.

Letters of administration of the personal estate of Samuel Smiley, late of Larne, county Antrim, of no occupation, who died 31 August 1883 at same place, were granted at Belfast 8 October 1863 to Anne Smiley of Larne, the widow. Effects £32.

The will of Samuel James Smiley, late of Larne, county Antrim, farmer, who died 13 December 1884 at same place, was proved at Belfast 8 January 1885 by Patrick Ramsay Hay of Glenwherry in said county, doctor of medicine, and Hugh Walker of Larne, auctioneer, two of the executors. Effects £159 17s.]

SMILEY

[Monument of dark granite, with a long draped urn. North side:-] In memoriam Jane Smiley who died 16th Sept. 1859 aged 76 years. Also her husband Robert Smiley who died 28th Feby. 1867 aged 88 years. [East side:-] In memoriam. Samuel Smiley, Dromaine, who died 12th Jany. 1903 aged 77 years. Also his son Alexander who died in South Africa 17th Nov. 1900 aged 39 years. Also his daughter Mary who died 9th Decr. 1902 aged 25 years. Also of his wife Mary Ann Smiley who died 11th March 1905 aged 71 years. [South side:-] Janie, wife of Hugh H. Smiley, born 23rd July 1884, died 1st October 1908. Hugh H. Smiley born 8th April 1875, died 12th August 1932.

[The will, with one codicil, of Robert Smiley, late of Islandmagee, county Antrim, farmer, who died 28 February 1867 at same place, was proved at Belfast 25 May 1867 by the oaths of Joseph Thompson Boyd and Hugh Huston Smiley, both of Larne in said county, merchants, the executors. Effects under £2,000.]

SMILEY

[Polished granite obelisk. North Side:-] Annie TAYLOR Smiley, only child of Robert Smiley and Mary Smiley, born 28th Septr. 1870, died 23rd Augt. 1888. Mary Smiley wife of Robert Smiley born 15th May 1845, died 5th May 1923. "Lord Jesus receive my spirit". [East Side:-] In memory of Ann Reid, beloved wife of John Smiley, who departed this life 3rd April 1868 aetat 64 years. And of John Smiley who died 5 April 1878 aetat 82 years. "Blessed are the dead who die in the Lord".

SMILEY

[Window in north wall of nave depicting the Annunciation and the Nativity. Arms:- per bend arzure and or, a lion rampant ermine between three pheons counterchanged. Crest:- a lion's jamb erased and holding in bend sinister a pheon shafted proper, head or. Motto:- Industria virtus at fortitudo (by industry, valour, and fortitude).] To the glory of God and in loving memory of his father and mother who rest beside this church this window is dedicated by Hugh H. Smiley of Drumalis. "My soul doth magnify the Lord. Glory to God in the highest and on earth peace. Emanuel, God with us."

[The will of John Smiley, late of Larne, county Antrim, gentleman, who died 5 April 1878 at same place, was proved at Belfast 27 January 1879 by the oaths of Hugh Houston Smiley of Drumalis, Larne, and Stewart Clark of Sea View, Cairncastle, Larne, both in said county, esquires, the executors. Effects under £1,000.]

SMILEY

[Window with tracery, depicting St. Patrick and St. Columba, in south wall of nave.] In memory of Sir Hvgh Smiley, Bart., of Drvmalis. This window was erected by his daughter Eileen, MCMXXIII.

[Hugh Houston Smiley (b. 5 Jan. 1841, d. 1 Mar. 1909), created baronet in 1903, married Elizabeth Kerr (d. 1930) of Gallowhill, Paisley, Scotland in 1874. Together they built the grand house of Drumalis (architect, S.P. Close, who also restored St. Cedma's), occupied by the Sisters of The Cross and Passion since 1930. H.H. Smiley's sister Anne married Srewart Clark, M.P. for Paisley, and uncle of Elizabeth Kerr. Sir Hugh's children were: the seond baronet Major Sir John Smiley, 6th Dragoon Guards (d. 1930); Major Peter Kerr Kerr-Smiley (1879-1943); Hubert Stewart Smiley (1883-1922); and Eileen

Margaret Kerr (b. 1895), who married Rev. Alfred James Edgar. Sir John was succeeded by his son Sir Hugh Houston Smiley (1905-1990), and by his son Lt. Col. Sir John Philip Smiley (b. 24 Feb. 1934), who married Davina Elizabeth Griffiths and has two sons and a daughter. See *Debrett's Baronetage*, 1964, 1995; Young and Pike (1909).]

Sir Hugh Houston Smiley, Bart, J.P., D.L. (from Young
and Pike: *Belfast and the Province of Ulster*, 1909).

SMILEY
    See ADRAIN, GETTY, HADDAN, McHENRY and SNODDY

SMITH
    [Sandstone concreted to the monument of Smyth of Duneira. The inscription is in a sunken panel framed by a wide margin.] Here lyeth ye body of Mary ALLAN, wife of Samuel Smith, who died Jan. the 7th 1722 aged 27 years.

SMITH
    [Low sandstone with corinthian columns carved in relief on either side of the inscription.] Here lyeth the body of John Smith who died Ap... 2(2) 1732 aged 28 years.

SMITH

[*U.J.A.* VI (1900), 100. Arms:- on a saltire between three crescents, one and two, a garb. Crest:- a dexter hand couped at the cuff holding a quill. Motto:- Ex usu commodum.] Here lyeth the bodies of 3 children of Adam Smiths viz. Hugh, Sarah, & Anabela. The last died June 14th 1786 & his grand child Eliza Smith died in Jan. 1800. Also the above named Adam Smith who departed this life 10th Jan. 1804 aged 59 years. Also his son James Smith who departed this life October the 8th 1811 aged 42 years. No man in his station lived more estem'd or died more regreted. Peculiar delicacy of morals marked the whole tenor of his life. Also (Agness) Smith, wife to the above named A. Smith, who died the 17th Ma(y) 1818 gd. 7(2) years.

SMITH

See BOYD and PATTON

SMYLY

[*M.D.* V (1901), 1, 2-3. Set against north boundary wall. Three female figures are carved on the stone.] Here lyeth the bodys of 3 children of James Smyly & Margret CALDWELL viz. Margret & 2 Marys 1761.

SMYTH

[Two panels flanked by three doric columns with a low surround, all in granite. On a white marble shield at the top are arms:- a saltire (azure?) between three crescents, one and two, in the base a leopard face, in the fess point an antique crown. Crest:- a dexter hand holding a sword. Motto:- With thy might.] Smyth of Duneira. In memoriam. John Smyth, son of Samuel Smyth of Larne and of Jane ALLAN his wife, born 7th June 1756, died 10th May 1823. And Anne CUBITT his wife died 3rd November 1847 aged 87 years. Their three sons:- James Smyth, born 7th Sep. 1792, died 5th Oct. 1821; Samuel Smyth, born 3rd Sep. 1795, died 1st April 1813; John Smyth, born 14th Feb. 1798, died 29th June 1883. Also three of the sons of the last named John Smyth, viz. George Watt Smyth, born 11th Dec. 1843, died 20th Dec. 1846. Samuel Smyth, born 6th March 1846, died 11th June 1847. James Watt Smyth, born 8th March 1833, died 6th August 1885 at Athy, Co. Kildare, where he is interred. Also Agnes WATT his wife, born 17th Feb. 1802, died 27th Dec. 1889. Annabella Charlotte O'BRIEN, wife of John Watt Smyth, born 31st Jan. 1847, died 20th Feb. 1907. [Robinson – Belfast.]

[The will of John Smyth, late of Duneira, near Larne, county Antrim, gentleman, who died 29 June 1883 at same place, was proved at Belfast 1 August 1884 by John Watt Smyth of Duneira, gentleman, one of the executors. Effects £516 9s. 4d.]

Letters of administration of the personal estate of James Watt Smyth, late of Model Farm, Athy, county Kildare, farmer, who died 6 August 1885 at same place, were granted at the Principal Registry 10 March 1886 to Elizabeth Ruth Smyth of same place, the widow. Effects £564 18s.

John Smyth of Larne, born 7 June 1756, had 3 sons:-
1. James Smyth, born 7 Sept. 1792. See above.
2. Samuel Smyth, born 3 Sept. 1795. See above.
3. John Smyth of Duneira, Larne, b. 14 Feb 1798, m. 8 Jan. 1830 Agnes Watt, daughter of James Watt of Ballycraigy. See above. They had 5 sons and 3 daughters:-
   1. James Watt Smyth, born 8 March 1833, m. 29 Oct. 1874 Elizabeth Ruth Hewson, daughter of the Rev. John Hewson of Kilmore Glebe, county Mayo. See above.

2. John Watt Smyth, of Duneira, Larne, B.C.L., B.L., Judge of Chief Court of Punjab, b. 1 March 1836, m. 14 Sept. 1871 Annabella Charlotte O`Brien, 2nd daughter of the Rev. Hon. Henry O`Brien (Inchiquin family). See above. They had 3 sons and 1 daughter:-
    1. Henry John Watt Smyth, b. 16 June 1872, d. 18 Aug. 1932.
    2. Lt. Col. Gerald James Watt Smyth, D.S.O., Royal Engineers, of Duneira, Larne, b. 27 March 1874, m. 5 Jan. 1917 Florence Mabel Graham, d. 28 June 1957.
    3. Norah Aimee Geraldine, b. 20 Dec. 1875, d. 8 Jan. 1963, m. 1908 Charles Francis Massy Swynnerton, C.M.G., killed in a flying accident 3 June 1938.
    4. Austin Watt Smyth, C.B.E., b. 28 May 1877, d. 9 June 1949, Librarian, House of Commons.
3. Thomas Watt Smyth, born 6 Jan 1839, Judge of the High Court of the Punjab, m. 18 Oct 1884 Amy Evans Massy, youngest daughter of Major Henry William Massy of Grantstown, county Tipperary.
4. George Watt Smyth, born 11 December 1843. See above
5. Samuel Smyth, born 6 March 1846. See above.
6. Elizabeth Smyth.
7. Anne Jane Smyth.
8. Isabella Smyth.
See *Burke's Landed Gentry of Ireland*, 1912 and 1958 editions; *Burke's Peerage and Baronetage,* 1936 edition.]

SMYTH
[One end of table stone set against south wall of chancel.] Sacred to the memory of James Smyth Senr. who departed this life 30th Septr. 1839 aged 69 years. Also his wife Anne Smyth who departed this life 20th Feby. 1840 aged 67 years.

SMYTH
[Sandstone laid flat, south of church.] Sacred to the memory of Alexander Smyth who died the 22nd day of June 1845 aged 38 years. Also his br(ot)her James Smyth who departed ths life 29th January 1858 aged 48 years. Sister Rachel KERR who departed this life 3rd February 1858 aged 63 years. Also their sister Jane HUNTER who departed this life 29th June 1863 aged 65 years.

[Letters of administration, with the will annexed, of the personal estate of James Smyth, late of Larne, in the county of Antrim, chandler, who died 29 January 1858 at same place, were granted at Belfast 23 April 1858 to Samuel Hunter of Larne aforesaid, gentleman, one of the executors named in the will of Rachael Kirk, spinster, deceased, the universal legatee. Effects under £200.]

SMYTH
See MANSON

SNODDY
[South-east of church.] Here lyeth the body of Joseph Snoddy who died Sept. ye 1(st) 1727 aged 51 years. Also Mary his daughter who died Apr. 30th 1749 aged 22 years. & Mathew Snody of Carnduf who died Feb. ye 4th 1760 aged 75 years. Also James Snody of Carnduf who died June 7th 1799 aged 78 years. Janet Snoddy died Oct. 1 1924 aged 79 years.

SNODDY

[Lying face down, south-east of church.] Here lieth the body of Andw. Snoddy who departed this life the 25th of Decr. 1783 aged 67 years. And also Martha McCOLOUGH his wife who departed this life the 7th of June 1780 aged 55 years. Here also is interred the remains of Sarah BEGGS, wife of Andrew Snoddy Junr., who departed this life the 6th of March 1833 aged 53 years. Also Margaret WHITE, daughter of Andrew Snoddy Junr., who departed this life 17th Nov. 1840 aged 44 years. Matthew Snoddy died July 11 1918 aged 75 years.

SNODDY

[Against south boundary wall.] Erected to the memory of (John) Snoddy who departed this life on the 1(4th) of April 17(.. ag)ed 36 years, and Mary hi(s wife) who died on the 16 ..... 1825 .... aged ...... Also John Snoddy, son to James Snoddy, whose youthful career terminated on the 10th of May 1828 in the 8th year of his age.

SNODDY

[Copied from a Lawrence photograph.] (In) memory (of) Samuel Snoddy who departed this life (July 20th 1806) aged 6(9) years.

SNODDY

[Copied from a Lawrence photograph.] Erected ... Andrew Snoddy in memory ...... wife Mary S(MILEY who .... this life on the 2nd .... 182 .. aged ....)

SNODDY

[Laid flat, south east of church.] Erected by Robert Snoddy in memory of his son Samuel who died 6th June 1856 aged 27 years. Also the above-named Robert Snoddy who died 8th Jany. 1874 aged 85 years. Also his wife Margaret Snoddy who died 9th June 1880 aged 79 years. And their son Matthew Snoddy who died 17th May 1900 aged 80 years. Also Jane Snoddy of Ballyrickard who died 4th Feby. 1934 aged 85 years.

[The will, with one codicil, of Robert Snoddy, late of Ballyrickardbeg, county Antrim, formerly farmer, who died 8 January 1874 at same place, was proved at Belfast 13 April 1874 by the oaths of Matthew Snoddy of Ballyrickardbeg (Raloo) and John Snoddy of Browndod (Larne), both in said county, farmers, the executors. Effects under £20.

Probate of the will of Matthew Snoddy, late of Ballyrickardbeg, Raloo, county Antrim, farmer, who died 17 May 1900, granted at Dublin 27 July 1900 to Robert Snoddy and Thomas Snoddy, farmers. Effects £738.]

SNODDY

See MOORE

SNODEY

See MANFOD

SNODY

See CHICHESTER and MEARNS

STAFFORD

[Label on lectern Bible.] Presented to Larne and Inver Parish Church by Arthur Willoughby Stafford, Gardenmore, in memory of his wife, Christmas 1900.

STARKIE

[Laid flat in south-east.] Erected by Thomas Starkie in memory of his beloved daughter Elizabeth Starkie aged 17 years. And other members of the family. The above-named Thomas Starkie died 1864. His wife Elizabeth died 1875.

[Letters of administration, with the will annexed, of the personal estate of Thomas Starkie, late of Larne, county Antrim, superannuated revenue officer, who died 8 December 1864 at same place, were granted at Belfast 28 July 1876 to Jane Starkie of Glenavy in said county, spinster, the daughter and the surviving residuary legatee. Effects under £100.]

STEVENSON

See GWYNN

STEWART

[White marble panel set into sandstone against west boundary wall.] In memory of Thomas Stewart, Magheramorne, who departed this life 23rd January 1870 aged 77 years. Also of his son Robert Stewart M.D. who died at Demerara, West Indies, on the 23rd day of February 1872 aged 34 years. Also Robert William, son of Ezekiel Stewart, who died at Southampton 2nd June 1874 aged 6 years. Also Mary, wife of Thomas Stewart, who died 24th Feby. 1876 aged 81 years. Also Sallie Stewart, daughter of Thomas Stewart, who died 29th August 1919 aged 77 years. Also Mary Stewart, daughter of Thomas Stewart, who died 2nd August 1923 aged 92 years.

[The will, with one codicil, of Robert Stewart, formerly of Larne, county Antrim, and late of Paradise, East Coast, Demerara, British Guiana, surgeon, who died 23 February 1872 at Paradise aforesaid, was proved at the Principal Registry 18 October 1872 by the oaths of Henry Montgomery of Downpatrick, county Down, general merchant, and the Reverend John Greenlees of No. 6 Landscape Terrace, Belfast, presbyterian minister, the executors. Effects under £800.]

STEWART

[In south-east of graveyard.] Erected in memory of Matthew Stewart of Curran who departed this life 7th April 1838 aged 39 years.

STE(...T)

[Broken into several pieces, but now reassembled with concrete backing against south wall of church.. Arms:- a lion rampant superimposed on a fess chequy. Crest:- a garb. Motto:- vi(r)... semper viridis.] Here lyet(h) ye bodies of (7 ..h)ildren of (..m)uel Ste(...t)s viz. Elizabeth, Hugh, Lydia, Agnas, Elizabeth, Mary, & Samuel. Ye last died May ye 4th 1753.

STEWART

See (SE)RVICE

STRAWTHORN

[White limestone with lead lettering against east boundary wall.] Erected by Fanny and William Strawhorn, in memory of their father William Strawhorn who died 9th Aug. 1895 aged 59 years. Also their sister Rosina who died 21st Aug. 1905 aged 28 years. Also their mother Rose Strawhorn who died 4th Nov. 1922 aged 90 years.

STRAWHORN

[Loose sandstone set against south boundary wall, with square and compass carved in roundel.] Erected by William Strawhorn in memory of his father Thomas Strawhorn who died 31st Decr. 1886, aged 37 years. Also his sister Charlotte Elizabeth & brothers Thomas & Bradford who died in infancy. His sister Jennie who died 7th July 1899 aged 18 years. And his dearly beloved mother Mary who died 7th March 1908 aged 52 years. "Gone but not forgotten".

STUART
[*U.J.A.* VI (1900), 101. Now lost. Arms:- a fess chequy surmounted by a lion rampant. Crest:- a garb. Motto:- Virtus semper viridis.] Here lyeth the body of James Stuart who died Jan. 31 1776 aged 33 years. Also his mother Agness Stuart who died 5th July 1796 aged 80 years. Also his father James Stewart who died 1st July 1799 aged 80 years.

STUART
See SIMPSON

SWEENY
[Mounted low on west boundary wall beneath Darcus tablestone.] Here lyeth the body of Catharine Sweeny who died 6th July, 1772 aged two years. Duncan Sweeny died 12th May 1798 aged 58 years. Also his wife Dorothea who departed this life 29th June 1806. [Inscription may continue below ground.]

TEMPLETON
[Set against south wall of church.] Erected by Robert Templeton in memory of his wife Rose Anne who departed this life the 20th Septr. 1819 aged 39 years. Also their daughter Anne who died the 25th of May 1819 aged 9 months.

TERBERT
[Decorated with cherub, set against south wall of church.] Here lyeth the body of Margret Terbert who died Decr. ye 16th (1796) daughter to John Terbert who also was lost at sea, March ye 1 1797. Also Helen CALDWELL who died 3d May 1774 aged 81 years, wife to John PEDEN who also died 7th April 1782 aged 78 years.

THOM
[*U.J.A.* VI (1900), 101. Southeast of church. Arms:- on a bend an estoile between two crescents. Crest:- stag's head erased. Motto:- Gardenter Amo.] Here lyeth the body of Robert Thom who departed this life 9th March 1793 aged 87 years.

THOM
[*M.D.* V (1901), 1, 3. Carved on the stone is a man reading a book and standing at a high desk. This "is evidently intended for a schoolmaster - a curious example of depicting the deceased in his usual occupation when alive". Outside the frame to the figure is an open book to the left and two closed to the right.] Here is interred the body of John Thom who died Mar. 16th 1767 aged 35 years. A man of great sincerity and virtue, obliging in his natural temper, wise in his proceedings. A lover of what is good he despised both evil company & bad practices.

THOM
[Present position unknown, upper part of stone could not be read but probably had same arms as the BURNEY stones.] ....ed .... April 1767 aged (.) 2 years. Also (Iso)bel Thom who died 14 (Oct.) 1773 aged 72 years. Also Isabella BURNEY who departed this life .... Feb. 1800 aged 23 years.

THOM
See PATRICK

THOMPSON
[Near south boundary wall.] Erected by William Thompson in memory of his parents Jane Thompson who departed this life 1st June 1836 aged 56 years. Also John Thompson her husband who departed this life 24th March 1844 aged 73 years. The above-named William Thompson died 1st July 1897 aged 85 years.

[Probate of the will of William Thompson, late of Larne, county Antrim, carpenter, who died 1 July 1897, granted at Belfast 23 August 1897 to Samuel Magill, draper, and the Reverend James Kennedy, presbyterian minister, both of Larne. Effects £88 . 10s. 3d.]

THOMPSON
[Table stone lying next to south boundary wall.] In memory of Mary Thompson born at Burgh(w)allis in the county of York, England, October 16th 180(5), died at Kilwaughter Castle August 4th 1850 after a few days illness.

THOMPSON
See WILSON

TURNER
[Sandstone south-east of church.] Erected by James Turner in memory of his beloved wife Margaret Turner who departed this life 31st Jan. 1856 aged 68 years. Here also lie the remains of the above named James Turner who departed this life 18th Oct. 1872 aged 84 years. Also their daughter Jane who died the 3rd April 1888. Also their daughter Ann who died 4th March 1897. And their son William who died at Beechworth, Australia, May 4 1897. Also their daughter Margaret who died 6th Oct. 1904.

TURNER
[Beside foregoing.] Sacred to the memory of Robert Turner who departed this life 4th Feb. 1862 aged 36 years. Also to James Turner his brother who died in Australia 24th Sept. 1859 aged 37 years. And their sister Matilda who died 17th Jany. 1906.

URIELL
[*U.J.A.* VI (1900), 103. Set against south wall of church. Arms:- a lion rampart with two tails, crowned. Crest:- a paw couped.] Here (lyeth) the bo(dy of) Lauran(ce Uri)ell who (departed) this li(fe) Sep. 29th 1788 a(ged 66 years). Also his wife An(ne Lamont) who died June 2(1st 1798 aged 64 years.

In thy fai(r book of life devine)
O God in(scribe our names.
There let us fill some humble place
Beneath the slaughter'd lamb.)

WALKER
[Thin white limestone, broken with frame missing.] Erected by Hugh Walker in memory of his fath... James Walker who died 18th Oct. 1(-5)8 aged (5)2 years. Also his brother James who died (20th O)ct. 18(64) aged (2)3 years. Also his brother William who died (F)eb. 1880 aged (3)6 years. Also three of his children who died in infancy. His mother Ellen Walker who died (9th) April 1884 aged 75 years. The above named Hugh Walker died 12th May 1888 aged 41 years.

[The will of Hugh Walker, late of Larne, county Antrim, auctioneer, who died 12 May 1888 at same place, was proved at Belfast 18 June 1888 by Elizabeth Jane Walker of Main Street, Larne, widow, one of the executors. Effects £63 19s. 6d.]

WALKER

Erected in memory of James Walker, Larne, who died 23rd Oct. 1830 aged 63 years. Also his son John who died 16th July 1877 aged 70 years. Also Margaret Walker who died 9th Decr. 1885 aged 75 years.

WALSH

[Set against south wall of church.] Here lie the remains of Mrs. Dorothea Walsh otherwise BUTTLER (widow of the late John Walsh Esqr.,) who died at Larne 5th October 1843 aged 74 years. This stone is erected to her memory by her son-in-law Solomon DARCUS who purchased this ground. Here also lie the remains of Anne Walsh sister-in-law of said Dorothea who died at Larne on the 19th day of Novr. 1841 aged 79 years. And of Anne Darcus, widow of the above-named Solomon Darcus, who died at Larne 22nd May 1881 aged 88 years.

WALSH

See DARCUS

WATE

[*U.J.A.* VI (1900), 101. Slate against north boundary wall. Arms:- a tree on a mount, on a chief an incresent between two mullets. Crest:- a crescent. Motto:- Gradatim.] Here lyeth ye body of James Wate who died Novbr. ye 29th 1751 aged 30 years.

WATSON

[Laid flat near gate.] Erected by David Watson in memory of his beloved wife Jane who died 29th Jany. 1877 aged 43 years. Also his daughter Anne who died 7th May 1876 aged 15 months. And his father Robert who died 19th Feby. 1856 aged 49 years. Also the above-named David Watson died 11th Octr. 1905 aged 70 years.

[Death: Nov. 10, at Black's Lane, Larne, Thomas, son of David Watson, aged 20 months. *Larne Weekly Reporter*, 18 Nov. 1865.]

WATT

[Sandstone and white limestone.] In memory of James Watt who died 7th Oct. 1849 aged 89 years and his wife Eliza HUNTER who died 6th Jan. 1850 aged 86 years. Also their daughter Jane who died 19th Nov. 1794 age 1 year and their daughter Eliza who died 22nd March 1884 aged 79 years.

[Letters of administration of the personal estate of Eliza Watt, late of Ballycraigy, county Antrim, spinster, who died 22 March 1884 at same place, were granted at Belfast 16 June 1884 to Jane Watt of Larne in said county, spinster, a sister. Effects £881 13s. 4d.]

WATT

[This stone is of the same pattern as that for James Watt (d. 1849).] In memory of Isabella Watt who died 19th January 1885 aged 85 years. Also her sister Jane Watt who died 8th July 1887 aged 91 years.

[The will of Isabella Watt, late of Larne, county Antrim, spinster, who died 19 January 1885 at same place, was proved at Belfast 27 February 1885 by Robert McNinch and Thomas Watt McNinch, both of Ballyboley in said county, farmers, two of the executors. Effects £913 . 5s.

The will, with one codicil, of Jane Watt, formerly of Ballycraigy and late of Larne, both in county Antrim, spinster, who died 8 July 1887 at Saint John's Place, Larne, was proved at Belfast 29 September 1887 by Robert McNinch of Saint John's Place, Larne, and Thomas Watt McNinch of Ballyboley, Larne, farmers, two of the executors. Effects £791 0s. 8d.]

WATT

[*U.J.A.* VI (1900), 103. Arms lost except for a mullet in the chief sinister point. Crest:- a crescent. Motto:- (g)radatim.] Here lyeth the body of Robert Watt who departed this life 27th April (.....a)ged 67 years. Also his wife (Ag)nes PATRICK who died 26th June 1813 aged 76 years. Also their son George who departed this life 26th Feb. 1840 aged 69 years. Also their daughter Jane who departed this life 18th December 1840 aged 76 years. And of their son James who departed this life 6th October 1849 aged 89 years.

WATT

[*U.J.A.* VI (1900), 102. Arms:- a tree on a mount, on a chief an increscent between two mullets. Crest:- a crescent. Motto:- gradatim. Now difficult to read.] Here lyeth the body of John Watt who died Dec. 22d 1758 aged 41 years. Also his son John who died Augt. 5th 1761 aged 2 years & his daughter Martha who died Novr. 6th 1767 aged (-) years. Also Jean Watt who died June 6th 1775 aged 22 years. Also Margaret MONTGOMERY wife (of) John Watt died April 24 1778 aged 5(-) years. Also Elizabeth Watt wife to Alexander PARK who died Jan. 17 1762 aged 25 years. The said Alexander Park who died 29th June 1786 aged 32 years. And his son Alexander Park died 11 July 1797 aged 17 years. Also his daughter Margaret Montgomery Park who died August 1(-)th 1854 aged 75 years.

WATT
See HUNTER and SMYTH

WEIR
[Very small headstone set against east boundary wall. Hourglass, skull, and crossbones carved on reverse.] Here lyeth the body of Edward Weir who died Feb. 8 1775 aged 20 years.

WEIR
[This appears on a Lawrence photograph as a substantial sandstone monument with two panels of inscriptions. Only fragments remains.] The family burying place of Samuel Weir, Belfast. Erected by Samuel Weir (.......r)y of his father (Dani)el Weir ....ted this life 20th ......855 aged 79 years. (...o) his mother ..... HUME Weir ....ed this life 23rd ....ged 86 year .... enn(y...................)
[On the second panel:-] Also in memory of his daughter Mary Eliza (who departed this life .... Jan. .... aged 23) years. [A fragment of white marble nearby may be the continuation of this:-] .... Sa(m..........) who depar............. 1893 .... Also his wi.......... who depar.. .... 189.......... And h.......... who..........

WHITE
[Laid flat east of church.] Here lyeth the body of Robert White who died May the 19 1722 aged 76 years.

WHITE
[Laid flat east of church.] Erected to the memory of David White who departed this life on the 6th Julie 1827 aged 19 years.

WHITE
[Laid flat east of church, next to foregoing.] Erected to the memory of James White who departed this life on the 25th Octr. 1828 aged 17 years.

WHITE
See GILLMER, SNODDY and WORKMAN

WIGLEY
[Set against east boundary wall.] Here lies the infant son of John G. and Catherine Wigley who departed this life the 11th of Augt. 1824 aged 8 months. Not lost but gone before.

WILLSON
See MEARNS

WILSON
[Red sandstone set against south boundary wall. Inscription on side:- "All the ground from this stone to the wall".] In memory of Mary Wilson who departed this life 16th of July 1777 aged 5 years. Also Jane Wilson who died the 1st Decemr. 1791 aged 19 years. Also their mother Sarah Wilson who died 4th May 1816 aged 66 years.

WILSON
[Set against south wall of church.] In memory of Elizabeth WORKMAN wife to John Wilson who died June 8th 1798 aged 26 years. Also their daughter Elizabeth Wilson who died Novr. 23d 1798 aged 5 months and 2 weeks. Also her father Wm. Workman died 20th June 1810 aged 80 years. Also Elizabeth CALDWELL, wife to William Workman, who died 16th May 1816 aged 77 years.

WILSON
[Set against south boundary wall.] Erected by Mary THOMPSON, La(rne), in memory of the following:- her grandfather John Wilson who died in 1829 aged 75 years. Her father James Thompson who died in 1841 aged 61 years. Her sister Sarah Thompson who died in 1845 aged 30 years. Her mother Margaret Thompson who died 12th May 1855 aged 73 years. Her two brothers James & William Thompson who died and her brother John Thompson who died 18th Feby. 1871 aged 63 years. The above-named Mary Thompson died 1st Decr. 1885.

WILSON
[Loose sandstone south of church tower.] Erected by Margaret Wilson in memory of her beloved husband John Wilson who departed this life 4th Jany. 1864 aged 30 years. Also the above Margaret Wilson who died on the 6th of March 1866 aged 27 years. And their daughter Lousia Wilson who died on the 15th of June 1865 aged 14 months.
    [Death: Apr. 24, Louisa, infant daughter of late John Wilson of this town, aged 14 months. *Larne Weekly Reporter,* 29 Apr. 1865.]

WILSON

[Set against south boundary wall.] Erected by Robert Wilson, United States America, in memory of his beloved sister Anne Wilson of Larne who departed this life 15th April 1865 aged 20 years. Also his mother Mary Wilson who died 10th April 1871 aged 68 years. Also his father Hugh Wilson who died 27th Feb. 1877 aged 80 years.

WILSON

[Loose sandstone in south-west of graveyard.] Erected by James Wilson in memory of his beloved daughter Hannah who died 11th June 1881 aged (12) years. [3 graves south.]

[Hannah, daughter of James Wilson, died 12th June at Mill Brae aged 18 years. *Larne Weekly Reporter*, 18 June 1881.]

WILSON

See GAWN, McCLOY and PORTER

WOODS

[Laid flat near east boundary wall.] Erected by Jane Woods in memory of her husband G.....e Woods who died 18(.)5 .... years. Also their six ch....... who died young, viz. Ann died 184(3), (...h) died 1847, Hugh died 1(8)4(9) (W.....m) died 1850, Henry Wm. M(.........Wo)ods died 1862 and M(............. 18)67. Also ....7.

WOODSIDE

[*U.J.A.* VI (1900), 104. Arms:- a tree on a mount between two crosses crosslet fitchee. Crest:- an oak branch. Motto:- Diu virescit.] Here lyeth the body of Margaret GRAHAM who departed this life in Oct. 1780 aged 76 years, wife to John Woodside who also departed this life July 2d of 1789 aged 81 years. Also his great-grand son Robbert KAIN who departed this life the 20th of May 1812 aged 6 years.

WOODSIDE

[Sandstone against west boundary wall.] Here are deposited the remains of David Woodside who departed this life 13th March 1844 aged 77 years. Also his wife Margaret LEE who died 23rd August 1844 aged 77 years. Erected by William & John Woodside as a tribute of regard to the memory of beloved parents. And of Margaret CRAWFORD, sister of the above-named Wm. & John Woodside, who died 26th Jany. 1869 aged 66 years. Also their sister Elizabeth Woodside who died 25th Jany. 1875 aged 76 years. The above-named William Woodside died 16th June 1875 aged 68 years.

[The will of William Woodside, late of Inver, county Antrim, farmer, who died 15 June 1875 at same place, was proved at Belfast 27 August 1875 by the oath of David Woodside Moore of 21 Gamble Street, Belfast, provision merchant, the sole executor. Effects under £300.]

WOODSIDE

See MEHARG

WORKMAN

[Arms (as depicted in *U.J.A.* VI (1900)), 104:- two dolphins haurient respectant, on a chief a cup between two castles. Crest:- a dexter arm embowed, in the hand a harpoon. Motto:- Curia omnia vincit.] Here lyeth the body of Robert Workman who died Jan. 17th 1737 aged 45 years.

[On back:-] Also his wife J. Cary WHITE who died May ye 20th 1747.

WORKMAN

[Smooth and mossy, now fallen.] Here lyeth the body of Samuel Workman who died Decmr. ye 24 17(4)0 aged 4(3) years & also (El)isab(eth) his wife who died July ye 28 17(-)4.

WORKMAN

[Sandstone with fan design at top, next to William Workman (died 1872).] Erected to the memory of Robert Workman who departed this life September 21st 1815 aged 62 years. Also his wife Margt. McCOLLOUGH who departed this life 5th May 1820 aged 68 years. Also their son George Workman who departed this life 6th April 1842 aged 52 years.

WORKMAN

Erected by Robert W. in memory of his children viz......................who died 10th June 18.... aged 3 months and Robert who died 12th March 1830 aged (3) years.

WORKMAN

[Low sandstone next to Robert Workman (d.1815).] Erected to the memory of Samuel Workman who departed this life August 15th 1845 aged 56 years. Also his wife Annjane who departed this life 11th of May 1852 aged 61 years.

WORKMAN

[Set against south wall of church.] Erected by Adam & Saml. Workman in memory of their beloved mother Jinette Workman who died 12th July 1880 aged 67 years and their sister Margaret Ann who died May 1847 aged 1 year. The above-named Adam Workman died 25th Sept. 1897 aged 56 years. Claimed by Janet Workman.

WORKMAN

[Set against south boundary wall.] Erected by John Workman, Ballyloran, in memory of his mother Jane Workman who died 24th Jan. 1891 aged 67 years. Also his brother James who died 6th June 1868 aged 4 years. And his sister-in-law Ellen Workman who died 18th October 1904. Also his father William Workman who died 20th May 1908.

WORKMAN

[Sandstone south of church next to Samuel Workman (d.1845.)] Erected by Jane Workman in memory of her daughter Isabella YOUNG Workman who departed this life December (5th) 1871 aged 32 years.

WORKMAN

[Black granite south of church.] Erected by Jane Workman in memory of her father William Workman who died 16th September 1872 aged 70 years. Also her mother Jane Workman who died 14th May 1888 aged 72 years. Also her brother John Workman who died 8th September 1912 aged 70 years. The above-named Jane Workman died 3rd June 1914 aged 70 years. T. Holden.

[The will of William Workman, late of Ballytober, county Antrim, farmer, who died 16 September 1872 at same place, was proved at Belfast 24 March 1873 by the oaths of Jane Workman, widow, and Robert Ritchie, farmer, both of Ballytober, and William Kerr of Ballywillan, farmer, all in Ballygally, Larne, in said county, the executors. Effects under £1,500.]

WORKMAN
[Capstone missing. Set against south wall of church.] ... in memory of his son John who died 17th July 1876 aged 24 years. Also his son George who died 12th March 1884 aged 34 years. Also his son James who died 27th Augt. 1887 aged 39 years. The above named John Workman who died 20th Dec. 1891 aged 80 years. Also his wife Margaret Ann Workman who died 18th July 1900 aged 80 years. Also his daughter Margaret Workman who died 20th July 1939 aged 80 years.
[The will of John Workman, late of Ballycraigy, county Antrim, farmer, who died 21 [sic] December 1891 at same place, was proved at Belfast 15 June 1892 by Robert Boyd of Ballycraigy, farmer, the surviving executor. Effects £429.]

WORKMAN
See WILSON

WRIGHT
[Sandstone laid flat in southwest of graveyard. The capstone is missing and with it the beginning of the inscription.] ... who departed this life 11th August 1876 aged 57 years. Also her husband William Wright who died 11th Dec. 1876 aged 52 years and two of their children who died in infancy.

WRIGHT
See McILROY

WRIGLEY
[Inscription on two brass lamp standards in chancel.] A.M.D.G. In memory of Barton, infant son of Barton and Margaret Wrigley, died January 19th mdccclxv. Erected by his sister Annie Moon Wrigley.

WRIGLEY
[Window in north wall of nave.] To the glory of God and in loving remembrance of Barton & Margaret Wrigley. This window is erected by their daughters, Margaret and Annie Moon, A.D. MDCCCLXXXIII. "Jesvs saith vnto him feed my sheep."

WYLIE
[Set against south boundary wall.] Erected by John Wylie to the memory (of his) father William Wylie (who) departed this life the 25th (May) 1832 aged 78 years. Also of Mary, wife of Wilm. Wylie, (who departed this life the .... 1810 aged .... Wylie .... departed this) life on (...............r)y 1829 (48 ......) And of Jane KANE their daughter who departed this life on the 21st of December 1832 aged 37 years. Also her daughter Elizabeth who died 26th Decr. 1873 aged 40 years.

WYLIE
See ESDEL

YOUNG
[Sandstone. An old crack was repaired with lead strips, but the stone is now laid flat and sunk below ground level to east of Macaulay enclosure.] Ere(ct)ed by (J) McC who holds too graves south. Erected in memory of William Young who departed this life the 15th of August 1789 aged 50 years. Also his wife Marey McCulloch who departed this life the 19th of February (18)11 aged 67 years.

YOUNG

[Set against east boundary wall.] Here lyeth the body of one child of John Youngs viz. Janet who died 12th May 1795 aged 9 months. Also Jenny who died Feb. 1810 aged (19) years.

YOUNG

[Sandstone laid flat in front of Johny Magill.] Sacred to the memory of Mary Young of Cairncas(tle) who departed this life on the 29th of July 1826 aged 23 years. Also her father John Young who died 17th Decr. 1838 AE 75 year(s).

YOUNG

[Lead lettering on white limestone, south of church.] Erected by Robert Young in memory of his mother Isabella Young who died 19 March 1865 aged 46 years. Also his aunt Agnes COWAN who died 29 Dec. 1890 aged 66 years.

   [Death: Dec. 29, 1890, at 35 Trafalgar Street, Belfast, Agnes Cowan, daughter of the late John Black, Inver, Larne, and relict of the late John Cowan, Bellahill, Ballycarry, aged 66 years. *The Larne Reporter,* 3 Jan. 1891.]

YOUNG

[Set against south boundary wall.] Erected to the memory of Mary Eliza Young who died 21st Decr. 1879 aged 4 years.

YOUNG

See WORKMAN

COATS OF ARMS

reproduced from
Ulster Journal of Archaeology, 2nd series, Vol. 6.

ALLEN
see page 47

BURNEY
see page 52

BURNS
see page 52

CAMPBELL
see page 53

CHICHESTER
see page 55

ESDEL
see page 63

FERRES
see page 64

FINLAY
see page 65

FINLEY
see page 65

FLECK
see page 66

GLASGOW
see page 68

HADDAN
see page 70

HOUSTON
see page 74

KELLY
see page 77

KIRKPATRICK
see page 78

LEARMOR
see page 80

McHARG
see page 88

McMUNN

see page 89-90

McTIER

see page 93

MANFOD

see page 93

MEARNS

see page 95

MONTGOMERY

see page 96

MURDOCH

see page 99

NAESMITH
see page 99

PATON
see page 101

ROBINSON
see page 104

ROGERS
see page 105

SHUTTER
see page 107

SMITH
see page 112

STUART
see page 116

THOM
see page 116

URIELL
see page 117

WATT
see page 119

WOODSIDE
see page 121

WORKMAN
see page 121

LARNE AND KILWAUGHTER NON-SUBSCRIBING PRESBYTERIAN CHURCH

O.S. Antrim 40. Grid Ref. D395025

This is situated between the Ballymena Road and Meeting House Street in the townland of Town Parks, the parish of Larne, and the barony of Upper Glenarm. It is also known as "Old Presbyterian" and "Head of the Town (HOTT)" to distinguish it from other Presbyterian congregations in Larne. The first meeting house on this site was built about 1668. The congregation divided in 1715 when another meeting house was erected beside the Inver Bridge. The present rectangular church with a classical frontage was built in 1828-29. A roundel bears the inscription "1625 rebuilt 1828". Classon Porter showed the earlier year to be an error when he established that the first Presbyterian minister to settle in Larne, George Dunbar, arrived in 1627.

There are two grave enclosures beside the church building, a number of mural tablets within, and a blue plaque in the grounds. All stones have been copied.

BAILIE
[White marble on east wall with arms:- azure a bordure wavy or a semee of estoiles. Crest:- eight pointed star. Motto:- Nil clarius astris.] Erected by his widow and children in affectionate remembrance of Hugh Bailie of Kilwaughter, born 18th March 1833, died 9th Novr. 1904. "Blessed are the dead which die in the Lord; that they may rest from their labours; and their works do follow them."

BAILIE
[Window depicting heavenly bodies and arms:- azure a bordure wavy argent a semee of mullets or. Crest:- a mullet or. Motto:- Nil claudius astris.] Presented to the Old Presbyterian Church of Larne & Kilwaughter by Mrs. Margaret MINNIS to the glory of almighty God, in memory of the Bailie family of Kilwaughter May 9th 1993.

BEATTY
[Mural tablet in vestibule, bordered by sixteen five-pointed stars and a rope, above is a crown and anchor.] Erected by Daniel McNeale Beatty, commander Royal Navy, in memory of Jane Stewart Beatty, for forty-five years his much beloved wife, who departed this life 21st Sept. 1874, in the 74th year of her age.

BEGGS
[Inscription beneath window depicting Christ in the prow of a boat and the legend "peace be still".] In memory of Arthur Gynn Beggs, presented by his wife Anna and family 10th May 1987.

BELL

[White marble in vestibule – the names are listed within a laurel wreath.] Our unforgotten dead 1914 - 1918. In grateful memory of the following members of this congregation who gave their lifes for right, freedom and honour in the Great War: Samuel Bell R.I.R., Arthur A. GAULT R.D.F., John GINGLES C.E.F., James A. HUXLEY C.E.F., Herbert T.F. MAGILL C.E.F., Hugh MONTGOMERY R.I.R., William McILROY R.I.R., Andrew NELSON I.G., David A. Nelson R.F.A., Samuel W. Nelson R.I.R., Robert ROBINSON R.I.R., Thomas Robinson R.I.R., William J. ROCKE R.E., Saml. SITTLINGTON R.N.R., Thos. COOKE R.I.R. David Nelson R.A.F., 1939 - 45. "Their name liveth for evermore."

BRECKINRIDGE

[BLUE PLAQUE mounted on undressed boulder near gateway.] Larne Borough Council American Heritage Trail. This plaque is erected in memory of John Cabell Breckinridge, American statesman and soldier, born January 16 1821 – died May 17 1875, Vice President of the United States 1857-1861 under the Ulster-Scot President James Buchanan, General in the Confederate army 1861-1865 and Confederate Secretary of War 1865, among those present at the last Confederate Council of War held at Abbeville, South Carolina, May 2 1865, and thereafter lived for a time an exile in Europe and Canada. On his return he endeavoured to reconcile his fellow Americans and his death was mourned across the United States, North and South. He was a descendant of the Breckinridge family who came as covenanting Presbyterians from Ayrshire and settled in the townland of Ballyrickard-Beg at Raloo. One of their line, Alexander Breckinridge, his wife and six children sailed as part of the Scotch-Irish migration to America arriving at Augusta County, Virginia. Alexander Breckinridge of Ballyrickard-Beg was the great-great-grandfather of John Cabell Breckinridge of Kentucky and the Breckinridge family were associated with this historic old Presbyterian congregation of Larne and Kilwaughter. Sponsored by Lamont U.K. Ltd.

CANNING

[Brass plaque on lectern.] In memory of Jeffery Canning, Given by his parents Mr. & Mrs. James A. Canning, dedicated 13th January 1957.

CHARLEY

See HOLMES

CRAWFORD

White marble on east wall with arms:- a fess ermine between three crows. Crest:- a garb. Motto:- Deus cornice pascit.] In memory of John Crawford of Larne, born at Raloo Sep. 4, 1810, died at Larne, March 9, 1889. This tablet is erected by his nephew Patrick Crawford, 1892. A. Jenkins.

[The will, with one codicil, of John Crawford, late of Larne, county Antrim, merchant, who died 9 March 1889 at same place, was proved at Belfast 21 June 1889 by David Nelson, merchant, James Morrow, bank manager, and Patrick Crawford, spirit merchant, all of Larne, the executors. Effects £22,035 . 17s.

John Crawford was a director of the Belfast and Ulster Banks, the Larne and Carrickfergus Railway Company, the Larne and Stranraer Steamship Company, and chairman of Larne Gas Company. He was a spirit merchant in Cross Street and, from 1871 to 1885, chairman of Larne Town Commissioners. McIlrath: *Larne Grammar School: the first 100 years* (1985), p.3.]

CRAWFORD
[Brass plaque attached to organ.] This organ was presented by John Crawford, esq., Larne, to the Old Presbyterian Congregation of Larne and Kilwaughter, with which congregation his ancestors and he have been connected for upwards of two centuries. 1886.

DRUMMOND
See NELSON

FLEMING
[Brass on wood, mounted on east wall depicting burning bush with motto:- Ardens sed virens.] In loving memory of Alexander Fleming and his family who were lifelong and devoted members of this congregation. Erected in 1951. Purdy & Millard, Belfast.

GAULT
See BELL

GINGLES
See BELL

HOLMES
In memory of Alexander Holmes of Larne who died in Rio de Janeiro on April 18th 1827. And his wife Margaret Holmes (nee CHARLEY) [sic] who died in Larne on April 16th 1836. Also of their departed children Jane Glasgow Holmes married to William MOON of Liverpool, Alexander Holmes, Elizabeth Holmes, Glasgow Holmes, Margaret Holmes, and Stewart Holmes. This tablet is erected by Isabella McKINNELL (nee Holmes)[sic] the only surviving child of Alexander and Margaret Holmes in loving remembrance of her parents and brothers and sisters. "Not dead but gone before". MDCCCLXXX.

HOLMES
Sacred to the memory of ALEXANDER Holmes of Larne who departed this life Octr. 16th 1844 aged 32 years and was buried in the bay of Bengal off Ceylon whilst returning to his native country after nineteen years residence abroad. Most dear to the memory of all who knew him.

HOLMES
See LEDLIE

HUXLEY
See BELL

JOHNSTON
Erected by the First Presbyterian Congregation of Larne in memory of William Johnston Esq., a native of this town but latterly resident in Demerara, who in addition to the other charitable legacies bequeathed the sum of one hundred pounds in aid of the funds of the worshipping society – with which he was connected in early life. A.D. MDCCCXXXIX.

KENNEDY
See McCULLOUGH

KIRKPATRICK

[Crest:- a dexter hand couped holding a dagger. Motto:- I mak sicker.] Sacred to the memory of Alexander Holmes Kirkpatrick who departed this life in Demerara on the 20th January 1857 aged 41.

KIRKPATRICK

[Crest:- a dexter hand couped holding a dagger. Motto:- I mak sicker.] Sacred to the memory of Thomas Kirkpatrick who departed this life in Larne 9th January 1864 aged 55 years.

[The will of Thomas Kirkpatrick, late of Larne in the county of Antrim, gentleman, who died 9 January 1864 at same place, was proved at Belfast 21 April 1864 by the oath of Sir Edward Coey of Merville near Belfast aforesaid, Knight, one of the executors (limited probate). Effects in Great Britain and Ireland under £35,000.]

LEDLIE

[Headstone within iron railings to south of church.] In memory of Jane Ledlie, daughter to the Revd. J.C. Ledlie D.D., who died 12th December 1830 aged 18 years. And also of his (wife Mar)y Ledlie died at Holywoo......(n) 30th Aug. 1871 aged 8(.) years.

[The will, with one codicil, of Mary Ledlie, late of Holywood, county Down, widow, who died 30 August 1871 at same place, was proved at Belfast 11 October 1871 by the oaths of William Harley of Belfast, county Antrim, house and land agent, and James Crawford Ledlie of Cork, merchant, the executors. Effects under £3,000.

Dr. Ledlie was born at Coagh, county Tyrone, in 1785, was ordained for Donegore in April 1806, and ministered in Larne 1808-32, and in Eustace Street, Dublin from 1832 until his death on 11th August 1852. He married Mary, daughter of Alexander Holmes of Larne, and they had a large family. Porter, McIlrath, and Nelson: *Congregational Memoirs*, pp. 92, 99-101.]

McCULLOUGH

[Headstone with iron railings to south side of church.] In memory of Rev. William McCullough who was for two years and ten months the beloved assistant minister of this congregation and who died on the 30th day of April 1878 aged 28 years. Also Rev. James KENNEDY, minister of this congregation 1878-1933, born 21st November 1842, died 14th January 1933. A. Jenkins.

[Mr. McCullough belonged to the Ballyclare neighbourhood, studied at the Home Missionary Board, Manchester and had been minister of the Old Congregation, Warrenpoint. He married a daughter of Rev. Joseph McFadden of Ballyclare. He was installed as assistant and successor to Rev. Classon Porter, but predeceased him. James Kennedy was then chosen to fill the vacancy. He was born in the Dromore district of Co. Down and ordained in 1869 as assistant minister for Rademon, were he served until 1878. Porter, McIlrath & Nelson: *Congregational Memoirs*, pp. 136-9, 153-189.]

McILROY

See BELL

McKINNELL

See HOLMES

MAGILL
[Brass tablet on wood on the south wall.] In loving memory of Samuel Magill, born 1846, died 1931, during his lifetime a devoted member of this church and for many years Senior Elder and Secretary of the congregation. Purdy & Millard.

MAGILL
See BELL

MINNIS
[Brass plaque on pulpit.] In memory of Richard Minnis, the pulpit and choir stalls of this church were presented by his wife Lily Kathleen to the Old Presbyterian Congregation of Larne and Kilwaughter on Sunday 11th September 1955 and dedicated by the Rev. J.A. WILLIAMS.

MINNIS
See BAILIE

MONTGOMERY
See BELL

MORROW
[Marble tablet on south wall. Crest:- a phoenix rising from the coronet of a marquis. Motto:- Utile et dulce.] In loving memory of James Morrow J.P., late manager Ulster Bank, Larne, for many years a faithful member of this congregation, fell asleep 6th May 1922. "Nearer my God to Thee." Purdy & Millard.

MOON
See HOLMES

NELSON
[Mural tablet of white on south wall with arms:- a bordure, three dexter hands couped. Crest:- a dexter arm coped at the elbow holding a spear. Motto:- His regi servitium.] To the memory of David Nelson J.P., Larne, who died 31st March 1896 aged 66 years. A lifelong and devoted member of this congregation. Erected by his nephew John DRUMMOND, Nov. 1912. T. Holden.
[The will of David Nelson, late of Inver Lodge, Larne, county Antrim, draper, who died 31 March 1896, was proved at Belfast 22 June 1896 by John Drummond, spirit merchant, David A. Nelson, draper, and John McNinch, grocer, all of Larne, executors. Effects £31, 304 . 7s. Resworn £31,676 . 1s. 6d.]

NELSON
[Brass plaque on font.] Presented by the Nelson family of Ballyhempton to the Old Presbyterian Congregation of Larne and Kilwaughter in memory of David Nelson, flight sergeant R.A.F., lost over Burma, 22nd February 1944 in his 27th year.

NELSON
[Brass on wood, north wall.] Thomas Nelson, 1889-1949. 1914-49 Clerk of the Larne Union and Rural District Council. 1921-49 Honorary Secretary of the Old Presbyterian Congregation of Larne and Kilwaughter, by whom this tablet was erected in affectionate remembrance of his loyal and devoted service. "I have fought the good fight, I have finished the course, I have kept the faith." II Tim. IV, 17. Purdy & Millard, Belfast.

NELSON
  See BELL

PARK
  In memory of Margaret Montgomery Park who living and dead was a benefactress of this congregation and of the schools connected with it. Born Oct. 6 1778, died Aug. 19 1854.

PORTER
  See WORKMAN

ROBINSON
  See BELL

ROCKE
  See BELL

SITTLINGTON
  See BELL

WILLIAMS
  See MINNIS

WORKMAN
  [Brass plaque on pulpit.] In memory of William Workman, 1906-1983, the sound system was presented to the Old Presbyterian Church of Larne and Kilwaughter by his wife Nettie on Sunday 11th December 1988, dedicated by the Rt. Rev. Desmond H. PORTER, moderator of the Non-Subscribing Presbyterian Church of Ireland.

LARNE: FIRST PRESBYTERIAN CHURCH

O.S. Antrim 40. Grid Ref. D390036 (presently), D399024 (formerly).

When Mr. Molyneaux and his wife died they were buried to the north of his church, which stood at the corner of Bridge Street and Point Street. Theirs was the only gravestone in the church grounds. In 1978 the congregation moved to a new site on the Inver Road and the Molyneaux grave was relocated to the municipal cemetery in the townland of Greenland. In the reconstruction of the headstone the flaming torches, which should be inverted to symbolise death, where positioned upright.

MOLYNEAUX
[White limestone panel framed in sandstone.] Erected by the First Presbyterian Congregation, Larne, in grateful and affectionate remembrance of the Rev. Henry William Molyneaux D.D. who was their faithful pastor from his ordination 9th June 1831 until his decease 23rd August 1871 aged 65 years. He was moderator of the General Assembly in the year 1853. Through life abundant in labours and although dead yet speaketh. Also his wife Sarah who departed this life 9th February 1867 aged 65 years. Blessed are the dead who die in the Lord.

LARNE, McGAREL CEMETERY

O.S. Antrim 40. Grid Ref. D402033.

This is in the townland of Town Parks and the parish of Larne and lies on the west side of the Old Glenarm Road. It was opened in 1867 because the parish graveyard was inadequate for the increasing population of the town.

ADAIR
[Lead lettering in white limestone, broken, with iron railings.] In memory of John Adair, who died 18th March 1907. Also his wife Margaret, who died 28th Feby. 1899. "Asleep in Jesus." Erected by his wife Elizabeth Adair 1907.

AGNEW
[Lead lettering in white limestone panel within sandstone surmounted by urn and enclosed by iron railings.] Erected in memory of Robert Agnew, Larne, who died 6th Nov. 1880 aged 52 years. Also of his wife Jane Agnew who died 18th Oct. 1881 aged 42 years. Here also are interred the remains of their son Joseph who died in infancy. Also their son Samuel who died 24th May 1890 aged 31 years.
[The will of Robert Agnew, late of Larne, blacksmith, who died 9 November 1880 at Richhill, county Armagh, was proved at Belfast 9 May 1881 by the oath of John Fullerton of Larne, grocer, one of the executors. Effects under £1,000.]

AICKEN
[White limestone.] Erected by James Aicken in memory of his father Henry Aicken who died 20th Feby. 1879 aged 47 years. His sister Sarah died 13th Jany. 1867 aged 2 years. His brother Samuel died 2nd May 1875 aged 2 years. His brother William died 1st April 1880 aged 2 years. And his brother David who was lost at sea August 1893 aged 30 years. And his mother Jane Aicken who died 23rd May 1909 aged 67 years. Also the above-named James Alexander Aicken who died 18th Novr. 1924 aged 59 years. Also his wife Mary Aicken died 12th April 1947 aged 79 years. Holden.

AICKEN
[White limestone.] Erected by Samuel Aicken in memory of his father Matthew Aicken who died 11th July 1887 aged 90 years. Also his mother Mary Aicken who died 4th July 1890 aged 84 years.

AICKEN
See LILLEY

ALEXANDER
[White limestone with lead lettering within iron railings.] Erected by Jane Alexander, Greenland, in memory of her beloved husband James Alexander who died 3rd Jany. 1881 aged 47 years. Also their son William, who died at Paterson, New Jersey, USA, 1st August 1895. Also their daughter Margaret, wife of Joseph BINGHAM, who died Lakeview, New Jersey, USA, 24th August 1902. The above-named Jane Alexander, passed away 16th September 1919 aged 85 years. "Let not your heart be troubled". John 14.I.

[The will of James Alexander, late of Greenland, Larne, county Antrim, farmer, who died 3 January 1881 at same place, was proved at Belfast 11 May 1881 by the oaths of Samuel Alexander of Redhall, Ballycarry, farmer, and Alexander Sloan of York Street, Belfast, carpenter, both in said county, the executors. Effects under £800.

Marriage: 31st Dec. 1890 at the residence of the bride's sister, No. 1 Madison Terrace, by the Rev. Alexander Smith, Joseph Bingham, Paterson, N.J., to Maggie, eldest daughter of the late James Alexander, Greenland, Larne.]

ALLEN
[White limestone in railed enclosure.] Erected by William Allen in memory of his father Robert Allen, who died 3rd July 1900 aged 62 years. Also his mother Jane Allen, who died 29th June 1913 aged 77 years. And his wife Susanna who died 28th August 1945. The above William Allen died 19th November 1955 aged 86 years.

ALLEN
[Flower holder of red granite.] In loving memory of Harry Allen, died 19th May 1986.

ALLEN
See CUTHBERT and DAVIDSON

ANDERSON
[Lead lettering in white limestone.] Erected by Agnes Anderson in memory of her son William Anderson, who died 28th January 1901, aged 32 years. And her husband James Anderson who died 17th June 1891 aged 60 years. And her son Thomas Anderson, who died 2nd April 1909 aged 47 years. The above-named Agnes Anderson died 6th Sep. 1909 aged 78 years. "Safe in the arms of Jesus." And her daughter Maggie Anderson who died 12th May 1916 aged 52 years. And her daughter Sarah Beggs who died 24th Dec. 1920 aged 62 years. T. Holden, Larne.

ANDERSON
See FULLERTON

ARMOUR
[Polished granite with low concrete enclosure.] Erected by Samuel Armour in memory of his grandfather Samuel Armour, died 21 June 1897. His aunt Rose HILL died 19 March 1924. His father John Armour died 7 Nov. 1937 aged 81 years. His mother Elizabeth Armour died 15 May 1943 aged 77 years. His sister Mary Hill died 17 June 1943 aged 48 years. Bell, Larne.

ARNOLD
[Polished granite headstone and enclosure.] 1890. William Arnold died 8th Feby. 1890 aged 24 years. John Arnold died 2nd Novr. 1899 aged 66 years. Sarah Arnold died died 26th Augt. 1912 aged 74 years. Joyce Ina Arnold died 4th Augt. 1943 aged 71 years. John HOLDEN, grand-son of John Arnold, died 29th Jany. 1911 aged 18 months. James Palmer Arnold died 30th June 1951 aged 77 years. James Palmer Arnold died 31st January 1967 aged 18 years. James Palmer Arnold died 16th June 1993 aged 79 years.

[Probate of the will of John Arnold, late of Browndodd, Larne, county Antrim, farmer, who died 2 November 1899, was granted at Belfast 2 February 1900 to John Alexander Arnold, merchant, and James Palmer Arnold, farmer, and John Holden, farmer. Effects £1,871 . 8s. 3d.]

ATKINSON
[Celtic cross and enclosure of granite.] Mary Atkinson died 29th Nov. 1890. "Let not your heart be troubled; ye believe in God, believe also in Me." Jane Atkinson died 24th Nov. 1908. Margaret Atkinson died 1st April 1915.

[Letters of administration of the personal estate of Mary Atkinson, late of Clonlee, Larne, county Antrim, spinster, who died 29 November 1890 at same place, were granted at Belfast 4 March 1891 to Jane Atkinson of Clonlee, spinster, a sister. Effects £2,898 . 9s. 8d.]

AUSTIN
[Lead lettering in white limestone headstone surmounted by urn.] Erected by Jane Austin and her sister Janette ROBINSON in memory of their father William Austin, who died 13th Oct. 1898 aged 70 years. Also their sister Lizzie who died 19th April 1899 aged 34 years. The above-named Janette Robinson died 7th Nov. 1902 aged 35 years and the above-named Jane Austin died 19th Decr. 1905 aged 45 years. Also their mother Margaret Austin who died 18th Feby. 1913 aged 86 years. And William Thomas Robinson who died 1st Oct. 1914 aged 18 years. Also of their aunts Jane & Janette FERGUSON who were interred in Inver Church-Yard.

[Probate of the will of William Austin, late of Ballyrickardbeg, Raloo, county Antrim, farmer and school teacher, who died 13 October 1898 at Larne, county Antrim, was granted at Belfast 15 September 1899 to William Austin of Larne, merchant, and Samuel Robinson of Ballyrickardmore, Raloo, said county, farmer. Effects £748 . 18s.]

AXON
See ROBINSON

BAILIE
[White limestone with lead lettering and low concrete enclosure.] Erected by Catherine Bailie in memory of her husband James Bailie who died 15th Dec. 1898 aged 57 years. Also their daughter Lizzie who died 1st July 1895 aged 14 years. Also their grand-daughter Cassie Eveline Bailie who died 24th Jany. 1901 aged 6 years. The above-named Catherine Bailie who died 28th Jany. 1924 aged 81 years. Also Margaret Ann, wife of John Bailie, died 27th April 1944 aged 73 years. The above John Bailie died 20th Aug. 1949, aged 80 years. "Asleep in Jesus." Jenkins.

BARBOUR
See THOMPSON

BARKER
[Small sandstone.] In memory of John Barker who died 1890, in infancy. Also his mother Elizabeth Barker died 20th March 1945.

BARKLIE
See MURRAY

BARR
See STEENSON

BARTON
See THOMPSON

BAXTER

[White limestone headstone and enclosure.] 1896. Elizabeth Evelyn Baxter, born 31st March 1889, died 7th November 1893. "My presence shall go with thee, and I will give thee rest." William Baxter, born 9th August 1853, died 21st October 1924. Jane Heron Baxter, wife of William Baxter, who died 11th September 1936. Agnes Gordon IRWIN, died 20th December 1967, daughter of William Baxter and wife of Thomas G.F. Irwin.

BEATTIE

See COBAIN

BEATTY

[Lead lettering on white limestone in a decorated frame of sandstone with a crowned anchor carved on an inset, all in a railed enclosure.] Erected by Daniel McNeale Beatty, Commander Royal Navy, in memory of Jane Stewart Beatty, for fortyfive years his much beloved wife, who departed this life 21st September 1874 in the 74th year of her age. Also in memory of the above-named Daniel McNeale Beatty, Commander R.N., who died on the 9th day of August 1879 aged 84 years.

[The will of Daniel McNeill [sic] Beatty, late of Hillmount, Carncastle, county Antrim, commander R.N., who died 9 August 1879 at same place, was proved at Belfast 24 January 1880 by the oaths of Harriet Leigh Beatty of Belfast, widow, and the Rev. Classon Porter of Ballygally, presbyterian minister, both in same county, the executors. Effects under £450.]

BEATTY

[Granite.] Erected by W.J. Beatty in memory of his beloved wife Ann Beatty who died 28th March 1897 aged 45 years. Also his daughter Lizzie, who died 5th Jan. 1903 aged 2 years and 7 months. Also his wife Catherine Beatty, who died 1st March 1909 aged 37 years. Also his granddaughter Margaret M. LOGAN, who died 9th Aug. 1927 aged 1 year & 2 months. The abovenamed W.J. Beatty died 23rd December 1938 aged 97 years.

BEGGS

[White limestone with lead lettering, in a low railed enclosure.] Erected by William Beggs in memory of his beloved wife Rebecca, who died 5th March 1910 aged 47 years. Also their son Thompson who died 23rd April 1895 aged 14 months. Also their son Thompson Beggs who died 15th Nov. 1927 aged 21 years. The abovenamed William Beggs who died 28th Feb. 1935 in his 69th year.

BEGGS

See ANDERSON

BELL

[Badly weathered red sandstone, fallen.] Erected by William Bell in memory of Mary who died (..) Nov. aged 1 year (..) months and Adam, died (..) Nov. 1865 aged 1 year (..) months .... William, died 11th Nov. .... in infancy .... who died .... years.

[Death: Nov. 1, at Kilwaughter Castle, Mary, daughter of Mr. William Bell, aged 5 years. *Larne Weekly Reporter,* 4 Nov. 1865.

Death: Nov. 11, at Kilwaughter Castle, Adam, infant son of Mr. William Bell, aged 12 months. *Larne Weekly Reporter*, 18 Nov. 1865.]

BELL

[White limestone, broken.] Erected by Samuel Bell to the memory of his beloved wife Susan Bell, who died 10th January 1898 aged 38 years. Also of their children, William Magee died 14th Sept. 1892 aged 8 years. Robert died 9th Octr. 1894 aged 1 year. Joseph died 19th April 1897 aged 6 months. John Magee died 13th June 1897 aged 7 years. William Robert Magee died 15th Sep. 1897 aged 2 years.

BELL

[White limestone on sandstone plinth.] Erected by Robert & Annie Bell in loving memory of their children, Thomas John died 27 Jan. 1893 aged 19 months. Robert died 26 May 1893 aged 11 years. Elizabeth Hyslop died 29 May 1893 aged 6 years. William died 26 May 1894 aged 4 years. Letitia McIlroy died 24 June 1894 aged 6 months. Edward H. died 19 Jany. 1899 aged 19 years. The above-named Annie Bell, died 4 Augt. 1900 aged 43 years.

BELL

[White limestone with lead lettering and concrete enclosure.] Erected by James Bell in memory of his wife Jamima Bell, who died 29th Aug. 1893 aged 43 years. Also their grand-child Lillie Bell, who died 22nd May 1893 aged 2? years. Their son John D., who died 31st Aug. 1898 aged 11 years. Also his wife Martha Jane, who died 4th Oct. 1905. And their daughter Martha, who died 18th March 191(0). The above named James Bell, who died 14th Oct. 1915. Also his grandson John Bell, who died 29th March 1905 aged 2 years. "Gone but not forgotten." Jenkins.

BELL

[Lead lettering in white limestone.] In loving remembrance of Rose Ann, wife of William Bell, who fell asleep in Jesus 21st March 1899 aged 62 years. Also their son Robert, who died 23rd Dec. 1910 aged 39 years. The above-named William Bell died 30th March 1911 aged 86 years. Susan Bell died 16th February 1967. "Until the day break, and the shadows flee away."

BELL

[Lead lettering in white limestone headstone, now broken.] In loving memory of Henry Bell, who fell asleep in Jesus 21st August 1901 aged 69 years. "Saved by Grace alone." T. Holden, Larne.

BELL

See BROWN and CRAWFORD

BINGHAM

See ALEXANDER

BLAIR

Erected by Eliza Blair in memory of her son Archie Blair, who died 25th Oct. 1874 aged 19 years. Also her daughter Mary Eliza Blair, who died 27th Jan. 1882 aged 19 years. The above-named Eliza Blair, who died 5th March 1901 aged 82 years. J.F. Pirie, 6 Emily Place, Belfast.

BLAIR

[White limestone, broken.] Erected by Alex & Martha Blair in loving memory of their daughter Jane Smiley, who died 14th May 1886 aged 15 years. Also their son James

Johnston, who died in infancy. Also the above named Martha Blair, born 10th May 1847, died 20th Nov. 1922. Also the above named Alexander Blair, who died 7th February 1927 in his 77th year. "Until the day break."

BLAIR
[White limestone with lead lettering.] Erected by John Blair, Cairnduff, in memory of his son Hugh, who died 12th Dec. 1890 aged 5 years. Also his wife Margaret Blair, who died 20th Jan. 1907 aged 52 years. Also his daughter Agnes Jane, who died 1st Dec. 1910 aged 31 years. Also his son Joseph, who died 11th April 1916 aged 29 years. Also the above-named John Blair, who died 13th Aug. 1922 aged 79 years. His son William Alexander who died 15th April 1945 aged 64 years, interred in Vancouver. T. Holden.

BLAIR
[Polished black granite headstone and enclosure.] In memory of John Blair, M.B.E., Cairndhu, Carnduff, died 9th April 1959 aged 76 years. And his wife Agnes died 14th January 1973 aged 89 years.

BLAIR
[No inscription except surname on concrete headstone.]

BLAIR
See CARMICHAEL

BLYTH
[Decorated with circle inside a keystone.] Erected by William Blyth, Belfast, in loving memory of his son Luke, who died 5th March 1897 aged 9 years & 8 months. And his daughter Annie, who died 15th March 1883. And his sister-in-law Nellie JOHNSTON who died 24th October 1900 aged 34 years. Also the above-named William Blyth, who died 20th Feby. 1906 aged 51 years. Also his mother-in-law Fanny Johnston who died 10th July 1909 aged 83 years. Also his father-in-law George Johnston, who died 4th October 1911 aged 88 years. Holden.

BOWMAN
[Granite headstone decorated with laurel sprays and surmounted by cross.] 1904. In memory of Martha Love SMILEY, wife of John Alexander Bowman, born 24 December 1833, died 1 January 1904. Also John Alexander Bowman born 8 July 1825, died 12 March 1909. "I am the resurrection and the life."

BOYD
[Flaking sandstone. At the top a hand holds an open book and a scroll bears the motto:- Amor ...ne timore.] Erected to the memory of Joseph (Thomp)son Boyd, who departed this life on the 7th of November .... years. Joseph Thompson .... of the above, who died at Bou.......... th March 1876 aged .... Samuel Bowman Boyd, fifth son of the above, who died 8th Dec. 1934 aged 78 years.
   [Death: March 25, at Bournemouth, J. Thompson Boyd, fourth son of the late Joseph T. Boyd of Larne, aged twenty-three years. *The Larne Weekly Reporter*, 1 Apr. 1876.]

BOYD
[White limestone tablet attached to railings.] In memory of Ann and James Boyd of Larne. Also their son-in-law Daniel MAGILL who died 26th December 1936.

BOYD
See FULLERTON and HIGGINSON

BRAITHWAITE
[Lead lettering on white limestone, broken.] Erected by Ann Braithwaite in memory of her beloved husband Samuel Braithwaite, who died 27th May 1903 aged 78 years. The above Ann Braithwaite, died 21st ....

BRETT
See McCLAUGHRY

BRIGS
See McKEE

BROWN
[Granite headstone and enclosure.] Erected by Samuel Brown in memory of his dearly beloved wife Mary Brown who died 6th Sept. 1909 aged 59 years. The above-named Samuel Brown died 27th April 1920 aged 74 years. Also his grand-daughter Mary CARMICHAEL died 1st May 1920 aged 11 days. His grandson William Brown Carmichael died 25 April 1931 aged 7 years. His grand-daughter Annie Brown Carmichael died 3 Sep. 1934 aged 12 years. His son-in-law David Carmichael died 21 Dec. 1943 aged 61 years and his daughter Annie IRVINE died 11th October 1961. "Blessed are the dead which die in the Lord. They rest from their labours, and their works do follow them." Rev. 14. 13. T. Holden.

BROWN
[White limestone with lead lettering on sandstone plinth.] Erected by John Brown in loving memory of his daughter Mary, who died 23rd Augt. 1911 aged 7 years. The above-named John Brown, who died 18th May 1925 aged 65 years. Also his wife Mary Brown died 28th Jan. 1951 aged 87 years. Their grand-son George died in infancy and their son John died 12th April 1966 aged 67 years. "Peace Perfect Peace". Thomas Nelson BELL, brother-in-law of above named John (Jnr.), died 27th May 1994 aged 80 years. Margaret Brown, wife of above named John (Jnr.), died 11th March 1995 aged 96 years.

BRUNTON
See ROBERTSON

CAMERON
See McMURTRY

CAMPBELL
[Decorated sandstone within railings with Capt. George Ferris.] In loving memory of Capt. Andrew Campbell, aged 38 years, who was lost at sea by the foundering of his ship on her voyage from Liverpool to China about the year 1852. Also his wife Jane Campbell who died 30th Novr. 1905 aged 90 years. Also their daughter Ann Jane Campbell, Waterloo, who died 30th April 1924 aged 82 years. "Erected by their daughters" Jenkins.
    [Marriage: June 10, in First Presbyterian Church, Rosemary Street, Belfast, by Rev. James Kennedy, Larne, William Teeling, Government Veterinary Department, Dublin, to Margaret Brown (Maggie), youngest daughter of the late Captain Andrew Campbell, Waterloo House, Larne. *Larne Weekly Reporter*, 12 June 1886.]

CAMPBELL
[Polished granite headstone and enclosure.] Daniel Campbell died 7th April 1924. And his wife Elizabeth Brown Campbell died 30th January 1941. And their son Hiram Adelbert Campbell, died 4th January 1953. And Elizabeth, wife of above Hiram Adelbert Campbell, died 8th January 1960. Also his daughter Margaretta Acheson Campbell died 3rd December 1880 aged 2 years. Also his sons, James Acheson Campbell died 12th March 1883 aged 1 year and James Acheson Campbell died 22nd October 1884 aged 2 months.

CAMPBELL
[Small cross of white limestone.] Hugh Campbell died 24th March 1895.

CAMPBELL
[White limestone in sandstone plinth.] Erected by James Campbell in memory of his wife Sarah Campbell, who died 17th May 1899 aged 52 years. Also his son William John who died 17th July 1883 aged 11 years. Also his son Samuel who died 2nd May 1901 aged 13 years. Also his son George who died 30th Sept. 1927 aged 57 years.

CAMPBELL
See DONAGHY

CANNING
See HAMILTON

CARMICHAEL
Erected by James Carmichael in memory of his beloved wife Susan who departed this life 2nd Nov. 1878 aged 66 years. The above-named James Carmichael departed this life 4th Augt. 1883 aged 84 years.
   [The will of James Carmichael, late of Ballyloran, county Antrim, farmer, who died 1 [sic] August 1883 at same place, was proved at Belfast 17 December 1883 by Thomas Holden of Larne, grain merchant, and Arthur Phillips of Larne and Ballyloran, printer, both in said county, the executors. Effects £626 . 1s. 6d.]

CARMICHAEL
[Sandstone.] Erected by Thomas Carmichael, Ballyloran, in memory of his beloved son John who died 25th Dec. 1882 aged (6) years. Also his wife Mary Jane who died 20th July 1896 aged 51 years. The above-named Thomas Carmichael died 28th Augt. 1911 aged 71 years. And his daughter Agnes BLAIR died 23rd March 1952 aged 70 years. Also his son-in-law William DOEY, died 18th Nov. 1963 aged 73 years. Jane Doey, wife of Wil(liam died) 19th Oct. 1965.

CARMICHAEL
See BROWN and McNEILL

CARSON
[Sandstone decorated with dove, within iron railings.] Erected by Thomas Carson, Larne, in affectionate remembrance of his beloved son Thomas who died 18th Dec. 1878 aged 4 months. Also his beloved mother Rachel who died 7th Feb. 1883 aged 73 years. And his beloved sister-in-law Ellen McFAUL, who died 12th Novr. 1885 aged 23 years. Also his father James Carson, Ballyrickard, who died 27th May 1905 aged (6)4 years. Also his son Capt. James A. B. Carson, R.A.M.C., died on active service in Alexandria 9th Aug.

1918. Also his son Lieut. Col. Herbert W. Carson, D.S.O., R.A.M.C. died on active service in Damascus 12th October 1918. Also his daughter Mary Carson who died 5th November 1918. Also the above-named Thomas Carson who died 26th April 1921 aged 69 years. Also his wife Mary Carson who died 25th Feb. 1925 aged 72 years. "Blessed are the dead who die in the Lord."

[Married: Apr. 11, in Raloo Presbyterian Church, by the Rev. J. Whiteford, Mr. Thomas Carson, Larne, to Mary, daughter of Mr. John McFaul, Glenarm. *The Larne Weekly Reporter*, 15 April 1876.]

CARSON
[Polished granite headstone and enclosure.] To the dear memory of R. Nelson Carson who passed away 8th June 1956 and his wife Martha E. passed away 11th December 1967. W. McElrath Carson died 27th December 1955. Margaretta Carson died in infancy. Herbert W. Carson died 3rd March 1903. Robert N. Carson died 14th April 1904. His wife Margaretta M. Carson died 25th April 1907.

CARSON
See REA

CASEMENT
See MAGILL

CLARKE
Erected by Elizabeth Clarke in memory of her husband William J. Clarke who died 14th Feb. 1892 aged 40 years. Also their dear son William John who died 17th Sept. 1891 aged 6 years. The above-named Eilzabeth Clarke who died 12th May 1917.

CLARKE
See KELLY

CLOSE
[Lead lettering in white limestone.] Erected by Charles Close in loving memory of his daughter Mary, who died 25th May 1904 aged 9 months. Also his aunt Sarah MOONEY who died 12th July 1905 aged 50 years.

COATES
See GIBSON

COBAIN
[Lead lettering on white limestone headstone within concrete enclosure.] In loving memory of Eliza Cobain, died 1901. And her daughters, Martha SAVAGE died 1896, Mary Cobain died 1922, Eilzabeth Cobain died 1934. Also her grand-daughter Elizabeth Ismay BEATTIE died 5th Feb. 1951. "Blessed are the dead which die in the Lord."

COEY
[Vault.
The will (with three codicils) of Sir Edward Coey, late of Merville, Whitehouse, county Antrim, Knight, who died 26 June 1887 at same place, was proved at Belfast 22 July 1887 by Thomas Sinclair of Belfast, merchant, George Smith of Craigoran, Islandmagee, county Antrim, gentleman, and Thomas Stewart Dixon of Belfast, merchant, the executors. Effects £31,876 . 19s. 8d.

Sir Edward Coey, D.L. was born in March 1805, a native of Larne. After some commercial experience in the West Indies he went to Belfast as a provision merchant, retiring in 1872 when he disposed of his interest to a joint-stock company. In 1845 he bought the mansion of Merville, Whitehouse, for £4,500 and in 1859 bought at least 1800 acres in Larne and to the north of it from Lord Antrim. In 1860 he became a member of Belfast Corporation, in 1861 was elected mayor and knighted by the Earl of Carlisle; Lord Lieutenant of Ireland 1867 and High Sheriff for County Antrim. He was an office holder in many charitable bodies, including the Belfast Charitable Society, the Royal Hospital, and the Seamen's Friendly Society. He gave £1,000 and the land towards founding Larne Grammar School. He was a member of York Street Presbyterian Church and then of Whitehouse, an original trustee of the commutation fund, president of the Presbyterian Orphan Society, and founded the "Sir Edward and Lady Coey Scholarships" in connection with Assembly's College. He married in 1836 Alice Cooper of Gateshead, county Durham. He died 26 June 1887 and was buried in the family vault in the McGarel Cemetery, beside Lady Coey who had died in 1876. See *Larne Weekly Reporter,* 2 July 1887; Heatley and Dixon: *Belfast Scenery* (1983); McIlrath: *Larne Grammar School: The First 100 Years* (1985) pp. 1-4;

COEY
[Large stone enclosure with 3 headstones with arched tops. The centre of headstones is inset with grey granite. Left stone] In loving memory of Eliza Coey (Aunt Eliza), born 18th March 1825, died 16th April 1904. Margaret Elizabeth Coey died 11th December 1944. "Until the day break and the shadows flee away."

[Centre stone] In loving memory of James Coey, born 7th Aug. 1823, died 14th July 1887. Sarah SMILEY, his wife, born 15th Nov. 1825, died 24th Feby. 1904. James Coey, born 17th May 1863, died 8th Feb. 1921. Annie Smiley Coey, born 12th April 1849, died 21st April 1939. "And so shall we ever be with the Lord."

[Right stone] In loving memory of John Smiley Coey, midshipman R.N., born 29th March 1898, drowned on active service 1st January 1915. Edward Coey, D.L., born 27th Dec. 1847, died 11th Nov. 1923. Edward Coey, Captain, M.C.O., born 11th April 1892, died 29th April 1927. Mary Hamilton, wife of the above Edward Coey, D.L., born 4th August 1860, died 17th March 1944.

[Letters of administration of the personal estate of James Coey, late of Ardeen, Larne, county Antrim, esquire, who died 14 July 1887 at same place, were granted at Belfast 24 August 1887 to Sarah Coey of Ardeen, Larne, the widow. Effects £95.

Death: July 14th, at Ardeen, Larne, James Coey Esq. in his 64th year. *Larne Weekly Reporter,* 16 July 1887.]

COMPTON
[White limestone within iron railings.] Erected by Robert Compton in loving memory of his father Henry Compton who died 17th Aug. 1900 aged 65 years. Also his brother Henry who died 1st July 1902 aged 22 years. Also his mother Martha Compton who died 21st Feb. 1911 aged 75 years. The above Robert Compton who died 14th April 1940 aged 71 years. And his sister Agnes Compton died 20th October 1954 aged 88 years. "Gone but not forgotten."

[Probate of the will of Henry Compton, late of Pound Street, Larne, county Antrim, labourer, who died 17 August 1900, was granted at Belfast 29 October 1900 to Richard Compton, farmer, and Hugh Compton, tailor. Effects £158 . 3s.]

CONOLLY

[Lead lettering on white limestone decorated with dove in roundel.] Erected by Samuel R. Conolly in loving memory of his mother Margaret McClure who died 31st August 1904 aged 66 years. Also his father Hugh Conolly who died 30th January 1909 aged 80 years. The above-named Samuel R. Conolly died 29th November 1918 aged 37 years. Also his sister Jane Conolly died 22nd May 1956.

CRAWFORD

[Sandstone.] Erected by John Crawford, Carnduff, in memory of his son Robert who died 16th March 1865 aged 4 years. Also his daughter Jane who died 1st March 1874 aged 20 years. Also his daughter Maggie Ann who died 9th July 1877 aged 20 years. Also his wife Mary Eliza Crawford who died 19th Augt. 1887 aged 62 years. The above-named John Crawford died 19th May 1890 aged 68 years.

[The will of John Crawford, late of Carnduff, Inver, county Antrim, farmer, who died 19 May 1890 at same place, was proved at Belfast 27 June 1890 by John Crawford and Joseph McCluggage, both of Carnduff, farmers, the executors. Effects £544 . 5s.]

CRAWFORD

[Decorative obelisk of polished pink granite.] John Crawford, born at Raloo 4th Sept. 1810, died at Larne 9th March 1889. Rose BELL died 17 March 1887 aged 89 years, for 35 years the faithful servant of John Crawford.

CRAWFORD

[Polished granite headstone and enclosure. Arms:- a fess crossy between three crows. Crest:- a garb. Motto:- God feeds the crows.] John, born Jan. 1882, died Feb. 1913. Janie, wife of H. H. SMILEY, buried in Inver Church-Yard, born July 1884, died Oct. 1908. James, born June 1896, died Dec. 1897. Patrick, born April 1850, died July 1932. Isabella, wife of Patrick Crawford, born April 1859, died Jan. 1945. Anna M. Crawford, born 1889, died 1973. Ruby Crawford, born February 1887, died January 1966. Vida I.G. Crawford, born 1891, died 1974. Margaret Crawford died 12th July 1992.

CRAWFORD

[White limestone with lead lettering and enclosure.] Erected by John Bell RAINEY in memory of his mother Mary Crawford, who died 17th Octr. 1910 aged 57 years. Also his wife Hannah Rainey, who died 15th Oct. 1925 aged 52 years. The above named John Bell Rainey who died 21st May 1932 aged 57 years.

CRAWFORD

See JEFFERY and RAINEY

CROOKS

[Two headstones in the same enclosure. (1) with lead lettering on white limestone.] Erected by Elizabeth PERRY in loving memory of her father Samuel Crooks, of Curran Farm, who died 29th March 1885, aged 84 years. Also her mother Elizabeth Crooks, who died 17th July 1890 aged 84 years. T. Holden, Larne.

[(2) White limestone in sandstone frame with anchor in roundel.] Erected by James Crooks, Curran, in memory of his beloved daughter Agnes Elizabeth, who died 1st Sept. 1881, aged 17 years.

With heav'nly weapons I have fought
The battles of the Lord;
Finish'd my course, and kept the faith

Depending on his word.

[Birth: Oct. 28, at Corran, Larne, the wife of Mr. W.A. Perry, a daughter. *Larne Weekly Reporter,* 4 Nov. 1865.

Marriage: Jan. 27, at First Presbyterian Church, Carrickfergus, by the Rev. James McGranahan, Gardenmore, Larne, Mr. James Stuart, Ballymena, to Miss Annie Crooks, daughter of the late Samuel Crooks, Esq., Larne. *The Larne Reporter,* 14 Feb. 1891.]

CROZIER
See LIDDELL

CRUIKSHANK
[Sandstone, broken.] Erected by Hugh Cruikshank in memory of his beloved wife Helen who departed this life 2(4th February 189)8. Also his son James who died 6th Dec. 1885 aged 9 years. The above-named Hugh Cruikshank died 23rd Sep. 1898 aged 54 years. And his da(ughter ...... Jane died 23rd) July 1907 aged 36 years.

[Administration of the estate of Hugh Cruikshanks, late of Main Street, Larne, county Antrim, house painter, who died 23 September 1898, was granted at Belfast 21 November 1898 to Jane Cruikshanks of Main Street, Larne, the widow. Effects £167 . 2s. 6d.]

CURRIE
See THOMPSON

CUTHBERT
[Sandstone with iron railings.] Erected by James Blair Cuthbert in memory of his dearly beloved child Susan who died 24th Decr. 1874 aged 14 months. Also the above-named James Blair Cuthbert who died 20th August 1925 aged 86 years. Also his son-in-law Hugh McGAVOCK (master mariner) who died 22nd August 1926. Also his wife Ann Jane Cuthbert who died 12th March 1931 aged 84 years. Also his son John E. Cuthbert died 4th February 1956. Annie, daughter of James B. Cuthbert and wife of Captain Hugh McGavock, died 17th October 1964. "Her children arise up and call her blessed." "Blessed are the dead that die in the Lord" A. Jenkins, Larne.

[Death: December 24, at St. John's Place, Larne, Susan, beloved child of James B. Cuthbert, aged 14 months. *Larne Weekly Reporter,* 2 Jan 1875.]

CUTHBERT
[White limestone in sandstone plinth in a concrete enclosure.] Erected by John Cuthbert in memory of his son John Cuthbert who died 29th May 1883 aged 19 years. Also his son Samuel who died 25th April 1897 aged 23 years. And his wife Ellen who died 2nd May 1902 aged 74 years. The above John Cuthbert died 1st May 1904. His daughter Isabella ALLEN died 1st Dec. 1905 aged 39 years. "Take comfort Christians, when your friends in Jesus fall asleep." T. Holden, Larne.

DANSKIN
[Granite headstone and enclosure.] 1897. Erected by the members of First Larne Presbyterian Church in memory of James Danskin, who was for many years an attached member and zealous christian worker in connection with the congregation, died 25th June 1892.

DARCUS
[White limestone panel in sandstone, surmounted by draped urn.] Erected by his wife and son to the memory of Solomon Darcus, lieutenant-colonel Prince of Wales` Own Donegal Militia, who died at Gardenmore, Larne, on 24th day of June 1881 aged 56 years.

[The will of Solomon Darcus, late of Gardenmore, Larne, county Antrim, lieutenant-colonel in Militia, who died 24 June 1881 at same place, was proved at Belfast 10 August 1881 by Henry Darcus of Londonderry and Thomas Lecky of Foyle Hiill, Londonderry, esquires, two of the executors. Effects £2,014 . 18s. 6d.

Solomon Darcus was born 30 November 1824, only son of Solomon Darcus of Larne, and Anne Walsh; educated at the Royal Refiner Grammar School, Houghton-le-Spring, England, King`s Inns, Dublin and Lincoln's Inn, London c 1843-7; never practised at the bar but entered the Donegal Militia as captain in 1855 and resigned as major; JP; married 1857 the eldest daughter of the Rev Henry Scott of Foyle Hill, Londonderry; father of Solomon Henry Darcus. See Keane, Phair and Sadleir: *King`s Inns Admission Papers*, (1982); *Larne Weekly Reporter,* 2 July 1881.]

DAVIDSON
[Heavy sandstone with iron railings.] Erected by James G. Davidson in affectionate remembrance of his wife Jane Allen, who died 10th April 1880 aged 46 years. The above-named James G. Davidson died 8th March 1884 aged 52 years. Also their daughter Mary Graham, who died 23rd August 1887 aged 15 years. A. Jenkins.

[The will (with one codicil) of John [sic] Graham Davidson, late of Larne, county Antrim, teacher. who died 8 March 1884 at same place, was proved at Belfast 2 April 1884 by John Marshall and Robert Allen, both of Ballyboley in said county, farmers, the executors. Effects £69 . 1s. 9d.

Death: Nov. 11, at Pound Street, Larne, Rosanna Biggarstaff, infant daughter of Mr. J.G. Davidson, teacher of Larne and Inver National School, aged 18 months. *Larne Weekly Reporter*, 18 Nov.1865.]

DAVIDSON
[Polished granite headstone and enclosure.] 1895. Erected by Mary Davidson in memory of her beloved husband. Mary Davidson died 9th August 1908. David Davidson died 27th January 1895 aged 76 years.

[The will of David Davidson, late of Clonlee, Larne, county Antrim, retired farmer, who died 27 January 1895 at same place, was proved at Belfast 31 July 1895 by James Kell of Slatady, Castlereagh, county Down, national school teacher, and the Reverend David Steen of Islandmagee, county Antrim, presbyterian minister, the executors. Effecst £3,556 . 4s. 1d.]

DAVIDSON
[Two slate panels in headstone of moulded concrete. Left] Erected by Wm. & Mary Davidson in memory of their four children viz. Sarah Jane, David, Bengamin, and David, who died in infancy. Also their son James Davidson, died at Delhi, U.S.A., 27th January 1923 aged 31 years.

[Right] William Davidson died 3 July 1934, his wife Mary Erskine Davidson died 12 April 1940, and their sons John E. Davidson died in Edinburgh 16th Feb. 1959, William Davidson died in USA Aug. 1959.

DAVIS
[White limestone with lead lettering.] Erected by James Davis in memory of his wife
Margaret Davis who departed this life 28th December 1892 aged 70 years. The above-
named James Davis, died 21st May 1899 aged 79 years.

DAVIS
See POWERS

DERMITT
[Lead lettering on white limestone with sandstone enclosure.] In affectionate
remembrance of Robert Verner Dermitt who died at Larne on the 31st March 1886 aged
59 years.
[Letters of administration of the personal estate of Robert Verner Dermitt, late of
Larne, county Antrim, flour miller, who died 31 March 1886 at same place, were granted
at Belfast 18 June 1886 to John McCullough of Royal Avenue, Belfast, accountant, the
nominee of some of the creditors on the estate. Effects £5,620 . 6s . 10d.]

DOBBS
[Sandstone with iron railings.] John Dobbs, late Captain 52nd Light Infantry, born 24th
March 1791, died 23rd August 1880. "Except a man be born again he cannot see the
kingdom of God." John ... Ch. 3rd Ve.
[The will of John Dobbs, late of Larne, county Antrim, esquire, who died 23 August
1880 at same place, was proved at the Principal Registry 29 January 1881 by Emily Jane
Dobbs of Ballycastle in said county, spinster, the sole executrix. Effects under £1,500.]

DOEY
See CARMICHAEL

DONAGHY
[The text is in lead around the sides of a grey granite enclosure.] In loving memory. John
Lyle Donaghy, minister of First Larne Presbyterian Church for 51 years, died 17th
October 1938. Also his wife, Jessie Meikle Donaghy died 13th February 1948. Also their
grandson, Lyle TURNER died 4th June 1932. Their son-in-law Hugh Alexander
CAMPBELL died 11th June 1966. Their daughter Margery Clare Donaghy died 14th
August 1986. And Jean Cecile Campbell died 2nd October 1989. Also his mother Anne
M. Donaghy died 16th March 1909.
[On the edge of a granite bird bath.] "The Lord is my shepherd."

DONALDSON
[Lead lettering on white limestone inside iron railings.] Erected by Henry Donaldson in
memory of his father Robert Donaldson who died 27th Novr. 1895 aged 76 years. Also
his mother Mary Donaldson who died 4th Feby. 1908 aged 74 years. And his sister Ellen
who died 13th April 1912 aged 49 years. Matilda, wife of John Donaldson, died 30th
April 1911 aged 38 years. Also their daughters Mary who died 15th May 1911 aged 12
years and Margaret who died in infancy. The above named John Donaldson died 29th
Sept. 1924. The above named Henry Donaldson died 26th October 1931. Also John, son
of the above named John Donaldson, died 18th Feby. 1939 aged 27 years. Emily
McCleverty Donaldson, daughter of the above named Robert Donaldson, died 13th June
1941. Also William, son of the above named Robert Donaldson, died 25th January 1952.
Emily, who died 17th September 1960.

[Letters of administration of the personal estate of Robert Donaldson, late of 3 Station Road, Larne, county Antrim, servant, who died 27 November 1895, were granted at Belfast 27 January 1896 to Mary Donaldson of 3 Station Road, the widow. Effects £180.]

DRISCOLL
[Lead lettering in white limestone headstone, in a limestone enclosure.] In memory of Thomas Hall Driscoll died 13th December 1896 aged 16 years and 6 months. Anne Driscoll died 27th August 1897 aged 79 years. Marianne Driscoll died 11th July 1909 aged 29 years.

ELDERS
See SPEERS

ELLIOTT
[White marble with lead lettering, on a sandstone plinth with a concrete enclosure.] Erected by Mary Ann Elliott in memory of her dearly beloved husband William J. Elliott who died 19th April 1900 aged 45 years. Also Mary Annie Elliott who died 9th May 1921 aged 31 years. The above-named Mary Ann Elliott, died 17th Nov. 1925 aged 68 years. Their daughter Agnes Elliott died 12th January 1982, interred in Larne Cemetery.
[Administration of the estate of William John Elliott, late of Meetinghouse Street, Larne, county Antrim, labourer, who died 20 April 1900 at the Royal Hospital, Belfast, granted at Belfast 25 June 1900 to Mary Ann Elliott, the widow. Effects £80 . 12s.
Birth: Nov. 11th, at Meetinghouse Street, Larne, the wife of Mr. William Elliott, a son. *Larne Weekly Reporter*, 17 Nov. 1883.]

ENGLISH
[Badly worn.] Sacred to the memory of David English who died .... 1851.

ENGLISH
[Sandstone topped by urn.] Erected by John English in memory of his daughter Jane who departed this life 20th June 1876 aged 26 years. Also his beloved wife Isabella SMILEY who died 26th Sept. 1895 aged 70 years. The above-named John English, died 10th Decr. 1906 aged 86 years. Also their daughter Isabella died 22nd Jany. 1927. Also their son John died 12th Jan. 1941. And his wife Mary died 15th Jan. 1951.

ENGLISH
[White limestone with lead lettering on sandstone plinth.] Erected by Capt. M.N. English in memory of his father Robert English, died 1st March 1897. His brother George Baine died 21st March 1902. His mother Margaret English died 22nd Feby. 1903. Also Daniel FERGUSON died 29th March 1926. And Mary Jane Ferguson died 25 Octr. 1943.

ENGLISH
See JENKINS and MEHARG

ERSKINE
[White limestone with lead lettering.] Erected by John Erskine, in memory of his mother Ellen Jane Erskine, who died 31st January 1875 aged 32 years. And his brother Thomas, who died in infancy. Also the above-named John Erskine who died 2nd Dec. 1912, aged 42 years. Deeply regretted. Also his wife Lizzie, who died 27th Sep. 1914, aged 44 years.

EVANS
[Lead lettering on white limestone.] Erected by Joseph Evans in memory of his father John Evans, who died 5th Jan. 1871. Also his niece Jane Guy who died 28th August 1905. Also his sister Maggie who died 22th June 1906. Also his mother Mary Evans who died 31st May 1911. The above-named Joseph Evans died 27th Oct. 1932.

[Letters of administration of the personal estate of John Evans, late of Glynn, county Antrim, mariner, who died 5 January 1871 at Paisley, Renfrewshire, in Scotland, were granted at Belfast 4 December 1871 to Mary Evans of Glynn, Larne aforesaid, the widow of said deceased. Effects under £100.]

EVANS
[Sandstone facing south within iron railings. The ornamental capstone has fallen.] Joseph Evans of Larne to the memory of his beloved wife Mary Jane who departed this life 8th May 1878 aged 32 years. Also their infant son William Thomas who died 12th March 1878 aged 4 months. Also his wife Jennie who died 13th January 1882 aged 23 years. The above-named Joseph Evans died 27th April 1887 aged ....
A few short years of evil past,
We reach the happy shore,
Where death-divided friends at last
Shall meet, to part no more." A. Jenkins.

EVANS
See KANE

FERGUSON
[Black granite "scroll" headstone and enclosure.] Erected by Annie Ferguson in loving memory of her mother who departed this life on 19th April 1934, her sister Madge McCOMB died on 3rd July 1930, her grandmother died on 29th July 1902, her father died on 30th December 1895, and her brother Albert (Bertie) died on 13th September 1967, cremated at Newport, I.O.W. The above Annie Ferguson died on 26th November 1972.

FERGUSON
See AUSTIN and ENGLISH

FERRIS
[Sandstone decorated with anchor and enclosed with Capt. Andrew Campbell.] Erected by Mary Ferris in affectionate remembrance of her husband Capt. George Ferris who died at Waterloo, Larne, 25th Feby. 1882 aged 35 years. The above-named Mary Ferris died 18th June 1910 aged 65 years.
They sleep in Jesus and are blest:
How calm their slumbers are:
From sufferings and from sins released,
And freed from every care.

FERRIS
[Cross of hammered granite.] In loving memory of Andrew Ferris, R.A.F. Squadron Leader, died 13th September 1954. Freeman, Borough of Larne. Served Belgium R.I.R. 1915, Dublin Rebellion 1916, France F.R.C. 1916, Mesopotamia R.A.F. 1921, Arab Rebellion 1921, Kurdistan 1923, India 1924, Palestine 1924-25, Egypt 1925. "Per Ardua Ad Astra"

FINLAY

[White limestone with lead lettering, broken.] Erected by Eliza Finlay, Belfast, in loving memory of her daughter Maggie who died 17th Dec. 1886 aged 8 years. And her daughter Maggie Gormal Finlay who died 28th May 1909 aged 20 years.

FINLAY

[Lead lettering on white limestone in same enclosure as Jane Holden d. 1901.] Erected by John Finlay in memory of his beloved wife Mary Elizabeth who died 28th March 1893 aged 21 years. Also his infant son Edward Fullerton died 16th May 1893 aged 10 weeks. The above named John Finlay died abroad. T. Holden, Larne.

FLEMING

In loving remembrance of the Flemi(ng) Family, (Ag)nes (a)nd Alexander and the(i)r c(h)ildren, (Ma)r(y) Wilson, William, Malcolm, (M)artha Jane (a)nd (M)arg(aret).

FLEM(MING)

[Broad granite stone and enclosure, with lead lettering.] In memory of the Flem(ming) family of the Nursery, Larne (1951).

FOSTER

[Lead lettering on white limestone headstone, in a sandstone enclosure.] Erected by James Foster in memory of his beloved wife Jemima who died 5th May 1891 aged 33 years. Also his mother Isabella Foster who died 1st Jany. 1900 aged 65 years. And his father Edward Foster who died 25th Decr. 1910 aged 83 years. Also his sister Harriett who died 27th Jany. 1922 aged 63 years.

FOX

[Lead lettering on white limestone on sandstone plinth with granite enclosure.] In loving memory of Thomas Wm. Fox, beloved husband of Maggie Fox, who died 16th Feby. 1905 aged 32 years. Also his wife Margaret McGHEE died 4th January 1953. "Peace Perfect Peace." Jenkins.

FULLERTON

[Limestone in sandstone frame with iron railings.] Erected by John Fullerton, Larne, in memory of his wife Jane BOYD who died 13th May 1880 aged 41 years. Also of their son James who died 3rd May 1875 aged 6 weeks. Here also rest the remains of their nephew John Fullerton Junr. who died 24th Feb. 1880 aged 19 years. Also his mother Jane Fullerton who died 6th Sept. 1892 aged 95 years. Also Rebecca ANDERSON who died 13th April 1898 aged 79 years. The above-named John Fullerton died 17th August 1911 aged 70 years. Also his wife Hannah Anderson died 27th January 1927 aged 81 years. May Sabina, wife of Joseph B. Fullerton, who died 7th April 1951. Joseph Boyd Fullerton, husband of May Sabina, who died 22nd October 1954. Jenkins.
[Marriage: January 16, at St. Mary's (Parish Church) Twickenham, by Rev. H.F. Limpus, M.A. (Vicar and Canon of Windsor), John Fullerton, Larne, to Hannah, only daughter of Joseph Anderson, Twickenham, England. *Larne Weekly Reporter*, 20 Jan. 1883.]

FULLERTON

[White limestone headstone and enclosure with lead lettering.] 1901. Erected by David Fullerton in memory of his dearly beloved wife Margaret Fullerton who died 11th Jany. 1901 aged 38 years. Also their son Joseph who died 21st Novr. 1894 aged 6 months. Also his mother Eliza Fullerton who died 31st August 1902 aged 74 years. Also his aunt Ellen REYNOLDS who died 6th Feb. 1911. Also his sister Ellen Fullerton who died 11th April 1929. Above named David Fullerton died 28th Nov. 1929. Also his son David Herbert who died in infancy.

GALT
[Granite headstone and enclosure.] In loving memory of Alexander Galt who died 28th January 1892 aged 72 years. Also his wife Matilda J. Galt, who died 2nd June 1910. Robinson, Belfast.

[The will of Alexander Galt, late of 96 Main Street, Larne, county Antrim, gentleman, who died 28 January 1892 at same place, was proved at Belfast 4 March 1892 by Robert Galt of 82 York Street, Belfast, lead merchant, and William Milliken of Ballyclare, county Antrim, the executors. Effects £1,537 . 18s. 2d.

GAMBLE
See HANNA

GARDINER
[Lead lettering on white limestone headstone, decorated with swags, now fallen.] Erected by John Gardiner in loving memory of his mother who died July 19th 1899 aged 60 years. Also his dear wife who died June 24th 1912 aged 38 years. The above named John Gardiner died 4th December 1944.

GARVEY
[Lead lettering in white limestone headstone.] In memory of Sarah Agnes Garvey who died 9th May 1901. Erected by Public Subscription.

GAWN
[White limestone headstone and enclosure.] In loving memory of Robert John Gawn who died 2nd December 1901 and of his mother Mary Gawn who died 3rd September 1930. Also his father James Gawn who was interred in Donegore.

GETTINBY
See McCAULEY

GIBSON
[Sandstone.] Erected by Arthur Hill COATES Esq. in memory of his faithful sailor, Samuel Gibson, aged 22 years, who was drowned in Larne Lough 25th May 1868.

GIBSON
[Two headstones together.] Erected by Alexander Gibson in memory of his father Robert Gibson who died 10th May 1888 aged 76 years. Also his mother Anne Gibson who died 8th April 1900 aged 89 years.

Erected by Robert & Sophia F. Gibson in memory of their father Alexander Gibson who died 23rd September 1924 aged 87 years. Also their mother Margaret Gibson who died 5th March 1929 aged 84 years. The above named Robert Gibson died 22nd May 1952. Sophia Ferguson Gibson died 11th May 1963.

[The will of Robert Gibson, late of Blackcave South, Larne, county Antrim, farmer, who died 10 May 1888 at same place, was proved at Belfast 17 December 1888 by Alexander Gibson of Blackcave, Larne, farmer, one of the executors. Effects £552 . 10s.]

GIFFEN

[Granite headstone and enclosure.] Erected by Robert Giffen in loving memory of his children, Bessie McFerran aged 5 years and James Moore aged 4 years. His youngest daughter Wilhelmina Morrison died 27th Sep. 1923. Robert Giffen, beloved husband of Annie Giffen, who entered into rest 24th Sep. 1924. The above named Annie Giffen died 7th August 1931. Their son Hugh Morrison died 6th January 1947, New York. Their daughters Mary Moore died 5th January 1960 and Annie died 27th March 1961. Their son Nathaniel died in Vancouver 27th Feb. 1973. T. Holden.

GILLILAND

[White limestone headstone and enclosure with lead lettering.] Erected by Ann Jane Gilliland, in loving memory of her husband James Gilliland, who died 24th March 1916 aged 70 years. Also their d(a)ughter Elizabeth who died 18th Nov. 1914. Also the above named Ann Jane Gilliland who died 28th Aug. 1929 in her 79 year. "Peace, perfect peace."

GILLILAND

[Broad white limestone headstone and enclosure.] In memoriam John Gilliland, died 2nd July 1931 aged 79 years. Also his beloved wife Agnes Gilliland died 23rd December 1942 aged 89 years. Sarah J. H. died 15th November 1887 aged 1 year. Margaret H. died 23rd March 1907 aged 27 years. James died 5th December 1922 aged 39 years. John (twin brother of James) died at Transvaal, South Africa, 31st March 1932 aged 49 years.

[Death: July 13th at the residence of his brother-in-law John Gilliland, Point Street, Larne, William J. Knox, aged 30. *Larne Weekly Reporter*, 16 July 1887.]

GILMORE

[Granite headstone and enclosure with much of the lead lettering missing.] (In memory of Robert Gilmore,) died (12th March .... Jane) C(rawford Gi)l(more died 2nd Se)p(t. 1935. Mary Gilmore Campbe)ll (died ..th .... Robert G)ilmore died (8t)h (August 192. El)l(en B)lair (W)e(bb di)ed 18th June (196.. Ag)es C(raw)ford (Gi)l(m)ore died (.)th March (...... Margaret Elizab)e(th Jane Sc)o(tt Gilmore d)ied 5th March (19)69.

GIRVAN

[Granite headstone and enclosure, where lead has fallen from lettering and black paint has been added.] In memory of John Girvan, his wife Isabel, and their children. James Wylie Girvan died 9th July 1920. Her daughter Isabel Violet WOODS, died 5th March 1977. Jennie Woods died 3rd Oct. 1926. And her son Francis Purcell Woods, M.B., D.P.H. died 5th Aug. 1925.

GIRVAN

See McDOWELL

GORDON

[Lead lettering in panel of white limestone in sandstone with railed enclosure.] Erected by Thomas & Mary Gordon in memory of their son James who departed this life 10 March 1882 aged 22 years. Also their daughter Jane died 24th April 1883 aged 20 years. The above named Thomas Gordon died 22nd June 1886 aged 58 years. Their daughters, Annie died 4th Aug. 1889, Ellen died 24th July 1892. The above Mary Gordon died 1(6)th Jany. 1909. Their son William died 12th January 1933. Their daughter Mary died 21st July 1942.

[Letters of administration of the personal estate of Thomas Gordon, late of The Rock, Antrimville, Larne, county Antrim, loftman, who died 22 June 1886 at same place, were granted at Belfast 7 January 1887 to Mary Gordon of 21 Walnut Street, Belfast, the widow. Effects £174 . 18s.]

GORDON
[Lead lettering on white limestone within iron railings.] In loving memory of Mary Elizabeth Gordon who died 13th February 1907 aged 57 years. Also her son John who died 15th March 1900 aged 20 years. Also her daughter Lily who died 27th March 1900 aged 11 years. Also her son-in-law Andrew GRAINGER, husband of Isabella, who died in Toronto, Canada, 23rd November 1912 aged 26 years, cremated in Montreal, urn interred here 8th August 1914. Also her daughter-in-law Elizabeth, wife of James Gordon, who died at Belfast 14th Oct. 1928. Also William John, the father, died 5th April 1935 aged 69 years. Also James, eldest son, died 8th Jan. 1950 aged 69 years. Erected by the surviving children. T. Holden.

GRAHAM
[Granite headstone and enclosure.] In loving memory of Patrick Graham, died 20th Jan. 1901. His wife Isabella died 9th April 1914. Their infant daughter Sarah Jane, interred at Inver Churchyard. Oswald, Robert, and Henry Kennedy, grandchildren, died in infancy.

GRAHAM
See McSEVENEY

GRAINGER
See GORDON

GRANT
[Worn sandstone with wheeled cross.] In affectionate remembrance of Mary Evelyn, the beloved wife of Robert Grant ....

GRANT
See REID

GRAY
[Low headstone.] In memory of Robert Gray, died 16th May 1890 aged 50 years. Also his son Robert died 14th Nov. 1895 aged 12 years.

GREENLEES
See McCAULEY

GREENWOOD
[Lead lettering in white limestone.] Erected by Matilda Greenwood in memory of her beloved husband William Greenwood, who died 18th Oct. 1910 aged 50 years. Her daughter Isabella died 29th Nov. 1899 aged 18 years. Her father-in-law James Greenwood died 19th Jan. 1903 aged 72 years. Her grand'daughter Isabella died 14th April 1907 aged 10 weeks. The above-named Matilda Greenwood died 16th March 1939 aged 85 years.

GREER

[Lead lettering in white limestone, fallen forward.] Erected by James Greer in loving memory of his wife Margaret Greer, who died 7th March 1897 aged 60 years. Also his son Joseph who died 10th April 1880 aged 2 years. And his grand-daughter Janette who died 5th October 1900 aged 7 years. And 2 grand-sons who died young. The above named James Greer died 27th July 1918 aged 85 years. Also his daughter Jane who died 8th April 1925 aged 66 years. Also his sons Robert died 27th July 1934, Arthur died 3rd Oct. 1939.

GREER

[Lead lettering in white limestone.] Erected by the employees of L.W.Co. to the memory of Jeanie, wife of Thomas Greer, who died 11th March 1904 aged 34 years. Also their son David who died 13th Feby. 1901 aged 5 weeks. Also their daughter Annie who died 23rd Decr. 1902 aged 7 months. Jenkins.

GUY

See EVANS

HAMILTON

[Granite headstone and enclosure.] In loving memory of William Hamilton who died 12th January 1903 aged 62 years. Also his wife Isabella Hamilton, who died 6th September 1890 aged 49 years. Their son James died 10th March 1889 aged 22 years. Their son Frances Joseph died in Melbourne, Australia, 24th May 1887 aged 19 years. Their daughter Edith May died 3rd March 1883 aged 10 months. Their daughter Isabella died January 1877 aged 5 years. Their son William died 2nd Jan. 1928, aged 50 years. "Gone but not forgotten." Erected by the surviving children, Nellie, William, Robert & Ethel.

HAMILTON.

[Polished granite headstone and enclosure.] Rosemary Hamilton died 13th March 1893. Also her sister Margaret CANNING died 12th Nov. 1924. John HOLDEN, beloved husband of Jane Elizabeth Canning (nee McNINCH), died 24th November 1967 aged 83 years. Norman died 20th July 1973 aged 84 years. Elizabeth Rose died 6th August 1981 aged 82 years.

[The will of Rose Mary Hamilton, late of Larne, county Antrim, spinster, who died 20 [sic] March 1893 at same place, was proved at Belfast 31 July 1893 by Margaret Canning of Larne, wife of John A. Canning, the sole executrix. Effects £136 . 16s. 10d.]

HAMILTON

See COEY and HOOKINGS.

HANNA

[Lead lettering on white limestone with concrete enclosure.] Erected by Patrick Hanna in loving memory of his daughter Annie Hanna, who died 19th May 1901 aged 13 years. His grandson Thomas GAMBLE died 19th October aged 3 months. The above-named Patrick Hanna died 24th April 1921 aged 67 years. His wife Agnes Hanna died 18th March 1938. His son Thomas Hanna died 19th October 1950. Holden, Larne.

HANNA

[Granite with concrete enclosure.] Erected by Thomas A. Hanna in loving memory of his father William J. Hanna, died 28th March 1936. His mother Margaret Hanna died 19th

February 1937. The above named Thomas A. Hanna died 24th Oct. 1944 aged 49 years. And his wife Margaretta died 22nd August 1975. "Love's last gift remembrance."

HANNAH
[Small headstone of white limestone, broken.] In loving memory of Ellen Hannah.

HARKNESS
[Lead lettering on white limestone headstone in a concrete enclosure.] Erected by William H. Harkness in loving memory of his wife Annie died 16th Dec. 1922, his father Hugh died 1898, his mother Margaret died 1914, his sister Jane died 1914. The above named William Hugh Harkness who died 7th Nov. 1954. And his son Hugh who died 31st May 1968. Also his daughter Jean died 2nd February 1994. J. Bell.

HART
[Lead lettering on granite.] In loving memory of James Hart who died 31st July 1941. Also his son Alexander Hart who died 31st January 1943. Jane, wife of James Hart, died 23rd January 1960.

HAVERON
Peace, Perfect Peace.
[On a small bronze plate in the centre of the grave.] Hugh Haveron, beloved husband of Mabel, fell asleep 22:7:75. Cremation at Chelmsford, Essex, England, ashes buried here.
You cannot come back, I know that's true,
But someday my dear, I'll come to you.

HAWKING
[Lead lettering on white limestone headstone.] Erected by Henry & Priscilla Hawking in memory of their beloved daughter Beatrice Martha, who died 31st Jany. 1895 aged 13 years.

HAY
[White limestone headstone and enclosure.] 1911. In loving memory of William Hay who died 19th December 1901 aged 70 years. Also his wife Elizabeth Peden Hay who died 16th January 1911 aged 66 years. Erected by their sons. Their youngest son Classon Porter Hay who died at New Orleans, La., USA, 22nd June 1924 aged 37 years. Their son John Crawford Hay died Cannock, Staffordshire, 13th March 1912 aged 31 years. William Thomas Hay died 20th November 1961.

HAY
See JAMIESON

HAYWOOD
Sacred to the memory of William David Morris, son of Isa & Ernest Haywood, born 2nd April 1897, died 24th Decr. 1900. And of two children who died in infancy.

HIGGINSON
[Lead lettering in white limestone, with sandstone enclosure.] Erected by E. Higginson in memory of his beloved wife Mary who died 6th January 1901. Also my devoted wife Jeanie, called home 12th March 1947, ever remembered by her loving husband and family. Also the above named E. Higginson, who passed to further service 2nd June 1958, leaving

cherished memories with the family. John Fullerton Higginson, son of the above Edward and Jeanie Higginson, united with his parents 13th April 1963, lovingly remembered by his brother and sisters. Also Agnes Boyd, second daughter of the above named, called home 7th Sept. 1965. "Worthy of everlasting remembrance". In memory of our beloved brother George Winston, who passed to higher service 24th July 1976, lovingly remembered by his sisters May, Kathleen, and Ethel. "Thy will be done." T. Holden, Larne.

HILL
[White limestone with lead lettering, broken.] Erected by Jane Hill, in loving memory of her husband Edward Hill, who died 16th March 1911. Also their daughter Mary who died in infancy. The above named Jane Hill who died 24th Sep. 1928 aged 70 years.
   [Marriage: Mr. Edward Hill, Larne, to Jane, daughter of the late James Boyd, Esq., Ballycraigy, Larne, on September 27th in First Presbyterian Church, Larne, by Rev. James B. Meek. *Larne Weekly Reporter*, 29 Sep. 1883.]

HILL
See ARMOUR

HOEY
Erected by John Hoey in loving memory of his son Agnew who died 17th March 1889 aged 7? years. Also his eldest and dearly beloved son William who died 21st July 1918 aged 44 years. The above-named John Hoey, who died 10th May 1928 aged 74 years. Also his wife Margaret Hoey died 4th April 1930 aged 78 years. Also his son Ernest Hoey died 1st Feb. 1948 aged 61 years. "At rest."

HOLDEN
[White limestone headstone and enclosure.] 1899. Sacred to the memory of Thomas J. Holden who died 9th November 1895 aged 7 years. Also his father Thomas J. Holden, died 14th April 1934 aged 72 years. Jane, wife of Thomas J. Holden, died 22nd May 1951 aged 87 years.

HOLDEN
[Granite headstone in same enclosure as Mary Elizabeth Finlay d.1893.] Erected by Thomas J. Holden in memory of his mother Jane Holden, who died 18th Sept. 1901 aged 66 years. Also his father William J. Holden who died 11th June 1905 aged 73 years.

HOLDEN
See ARNOLD and HAMILTON

HOOD
[Two headstones in same enclosure. Right stone lying flat with inscription hidden. Left:] Erected by Elizabeth Hood in memory of her husband James Hood, who died 12th June 1878 aged 68 years. Also her daughter Elizabeth Hood who died 20th August 1885 aged 25 years.

HOOKINGS
[Three stones in same enclosure. Polished granite:] In loving memory of Alfred J. Hookings, died 11th September, 1965.
   [White limestone with lead lettering in form of open book:] YOUNG - HAMILTON. Kirkwood, Belfast.
   [Polished granite:] In loving memory of Myrtle H. Hookings, died 24th May 1972.

HOWDEN

[Inscriptions along the sides of large granite enclosure.] Charles Howden, born Edinburgh 19th March 1821, died Larne 9th June 1887. Margaret Thompson SMILEY, wife of Charles Howden, born Larne 6th July 1827, died Larne 14th December 1907. Charles Howden, born Belfast 7th June 1855, died Larne 27th January 1900. John Smiley Howden, born Belfast 6th September 1853, died Paisley 30th April 1901. Matthew Howden, born Belfast 13th November 1851, died Belfast 11th June 1891.

[Probate of the will of Charles Howden, late of Invermore, Larne, county Antrim, merchant, who died 27 January 1900, was granted at Belfast 26 March 1900 to John Smiley Howden, merchant, and William Muir Mackean, manufacturer. Effects £3,717 . 8s. 3d.

The will of Matthew Howden, late of Alfred Terrace, Mountpottinger, county Down, grain merchant, who died 11 June 1891, was proved at Belfast 12 August 1891 by Margaret Thompson Howden of Larne, county Antrim, widow, one of the executors. Effects £7,510 . 2s. 11d.

Death: June 9th, at Cross Street, Larne, Charles Howden, aged 66 years. *Larne Weekly Reporter*, 11 June 1887.

"Death of Mr. Charles Howden, Larne" ... on Saturday last of Mr. Charles Howden of Invermore, Larne. The cause of death was acute pneumonia ... [He] received his early education in the Royal Academical Institution, Belfast, and afterwards served his time with Mr. James Moore, stationer, Donegall Place. The greater part of his life, however, was spent in Larne and neighbourhood ... With his brothers he engaged in the coal trade, under the style of Howden Brothers, but of late years his active share in the business of the firm was small, his time being largely taken up with various philanthropic and charitable schemes ... He had a large share in the promotion of the erection of the new Larne and Inver Schools and many other projects associated with the First Presbyterian Church ... A pianist of undoubted ability and prodigious powers of memory, with an exhaustive acquaintance with the works of the principal composers he was a rare acquisition in a place where at a time such attainments were comparatively unknown ... The funeral took place on Tuesday ... the remains, surmounted by numerous beautiful wreaths, were borne from his late residence along the carriageway to the public road by members of the local constabulary and those of adjoining stations ... Reverends D.H. Hanson and J. Lyle Donaghy conducted the funeral obsequies." *Larne Times*, 3 Feb. 1900.]

HUNTER

[Lead lettering on granite.] In loving memory of our dear mother Mary, died 7th Aug. 1955. Also our dear father Allan, died 13th Jan. 1958.

HUNTER

See TAYLOR

HUTTON

[Lead lettering on white limestone, framed in sandstone, decorated with rope, scallop shell, and anchor and topped with a draped urn.] Erected by James Hutton in affectionate remembrance of his beloved wife Jane, who died on board the ship "Earnock" at sea, 13th March 1880 aged 38 years. Her remains were brought to this country and interred here on 6th April 1880.

HYSLOP
[White limestone with lead lettering and low concrete enclosure.] In loving memory of
James Hyslop who died 31st January 1922, and his wife Emily Hyslop who died 28th
February 1929. Also their grand-daughter Emily Lynas who died in infancy.

IRVINE
[Headstone and enclosure of hammered granite, lead lettering.] In loving memory of
William Irvine of Jordanstown, Co. Antrim, died 25th July 1920. And his wife Sarah,
died 21st Sept. 1914, interred at Eglinton, Co. Derry. And Emily Martha, infant child,
died 7th April 188(7). Also his son James Potts, died 9th August 1946. Henry Joseph
West Irvine died 13th June 1968. "Thy will be done."

IRVINE
See BROWN

IRWIN
[Granite headstone with sandstone enclosure.] In loving memory of Thomas G. F. Irwin,
died 19th January 1960 aged 87 years. Also James Hamilton died (1956). Gordon Irwin,
son of Thomas and Agnes G. Irwin, died 6th May 1976 aged 65 years.

IRWIN
See BAXTER

JAMIESON
[White limestone obelisk with lead lettering on two faces.] Erected by Walter Jamieson,
native of Old Monkland, Lanarkshire N.B., in memory of his wife Annie Henderson
REID, who died at Glenarm 17th May 1880 aged 29 years. His daughter Maggie Grant
died at Glenarm 11th March 1880 aged 18 months. His daughter Mary Finlay Reid died
at Larne 8th June 1880 aged 6 weeks. The above-named Walter Jamieson died at Hobart,
Tasmania, 7th March 1893 aged 42 years.
    In loving memory of Marshall MELVIN, beloved wife of George HAY, who died 23rd
March 1896 aged 71 years. The above-named George Hay, who died 8th March 1901
aged 77 years. Also their daughter Grace who died 15th August 1936, widow of Walter
Jamieson.

JEFFERY
[Lead lettering in white limestone.] Erected by W.J. Jeffrey in loving memory of his son
Robert, who died 8th March 1900 aged 25 years. Also his daughter Miriam
CRAWFORD, who died in Indianapolis, U.S.A., 19th Sept. 1917 aged 35 years. The
above-named W. J. Jeffery died 7th Novr. 1920 aged 72 years. Also his wife Agnes Jeffery,
died 17th Novr. 1928 aged 81 years. Also his son William who died in Weymouth 4th
Oct. 1951 aged 64 years. Also his daughter Sybil E. NEWBURY, who died in Pasadena,
California, 6th September 1953 aged 76 years. T. Holden.
    [Administration of the estate of Robert Jeffery, late of 1 Clarence Terrace, Larne
Harbour, Larne, county Antrim, clerk, who died 8 March 1900, granted at Belfast 25
April 1900 to William John Jeffery, gardener. Effects £72 . 5s. 4d.]

JELLIE
[Lead lettering on white limestone with granite enclosure.] Erected by Jane Jellie in loving
memory of her son Joseph, who died 2nd April 1902 aged 15 years. Also her son Thomas
who died 7th Novr. 1907 aged 19 years. The above Jane Jellie who died 4th March 1943.

JENKINS
[Granite headstone and enclosure.] In loving memory of Robert John Jenkins, died 20th July 1942 aged 75 years. And his wife Annie died 19th Feby. 1952 aged [*blank*] years. And their son Joseph Jenkins, M.Sc., F.I.C.E. died 25th July 1968 and his wife Mary Kathleen (nee ENGLISH) died 28th May 1966.

JOHNSTON
[Polished pink granite headstone and enclosure.] In loving memory of James Johnston, died 16th May 1933. Also his wife Isabella Johnston died 14th February 1909. Their daughter May died 10th May 1964. Their son John died 28th April 1902. Their daughter Tennie died 20th May 1902.

JOHNSTON
[White limestone with lead lettering on sandstone plinth with granite enclosure.] Erected by George Johnston of Glynn in loving memory of his dearly beloved daughters & sons, Christena who died in infancy, James C. died 7th Feby. 1904 aged 3 years, George died 12th March 1906 aged 7? years, Martha Jane died 21st Oct. 1910 aged 16 years. Also his beloved grandson George J. SMYTH who died 6th Nov. 1928 aged 14 years. The above named George Johnston died 15th July 1945 aged 87 years. Also his beloved wife Sarah who died 28th June 1952 aged 93 years. Holden.

JOHNSTON
[Dark granite.] Erected by Agnes Johnston in loving memory of my husband John Johnston, died 8th April 1925 aged 54 years. Also my two sons died in infancy. Also her daughter Agnes (Nancy) died 9th March 1941 aged 29 years. The above Agnes Johnston died 11th July 1948 aged 72 years.

JOHNSTON
Erected in affectionate memory of a beloved husband, father, and grandfather, John called home 10th September 1986. "In the house of the Lord forever." Psalm 23, Verse 6.

JOHNSTON
[On an urn.] In loving memory of David & Annie Johnston.

JOHNSTON
See BLYTH and MUNDELL

KANE
Erected to the memory of Hugh Smiley Kane, M.D. who died on the 22nd June 1872 aged (33) years and his brother Dr John Kane, who died on the 22nd Sept. 1883 aged (42) years. Also their mother Eliza Ferres Kane, who died on (the 23rd April 1886 aged 78 years. And their daughter Margaret Kane, who died .... 1890 aged 35 years .... of ....th April .... aged ....) .
[Letters of administration of the personal estate of Hugh Smiley Kane, late of Larne, county Antrim, surgeon, who died 22 June 1872 at same place, were granted at Belfast 7 August 1872 to Ellen Kane, lately of Antrim, county Antrim, but now of Larne aforesaid, the widow of said deceased. Effects under £450.
Letters of administration of the personal estate of John Kane, late of Larne, county Antrim, M.D., who died 23 September 1883 at same place, were granted at Belfast 18 January 1884 to Isabella Kane of Larne, the widow. Effects £1,184 . 5s. 7d.

Death: June 22, at his mother's residence, Cross Street, Larne, after a brief illness, Hugh Smiley Kane, Esq., M.D., aged 33 years. *Larne Weekly Reporter*, 29 June 1872.]

Married: April 6, in Crosshill Presbyterian Church, by the Rev. George McCaughey, John Kane, Esq., M.D., Larne, to Isabella, third daughter of the Rev. James Whiteford, Ballyvernston Cottage, Raloo. *The Larne Weekly Reporter*, 8 Apr. 1876.]

Dr. John Kane died of peritonitis. "He was a native of Larne and belonged to an old and respected family who were connected for generations with the medical profession ... He was medical officer of health for the Larne Union since 1874 succeeding his uncle Dr. Ferris, who was medical officer of the Workhouse as well as medical officer of health ... He was buried at the new Cemetery on Wednesday morning ... On Monday evening last ... a subscription list was opened ... for benefit of Dr. Kane's widow and family ..." *Larne Weekly Recorder*, 29 September 1883. Hugh Smiley Kane was medical officer to Antrim Dispensary District.]

KANE

[White limestone, broken.] Erected by Martha Evans, Larne, in loving memory of her sister Elizabeth Kane, who died 28th April 1896 aged 66 years. T. Holden.

KANE

[White limestone set into concrete.] Erected by William Kane in memory of his children.

KANE

Erected by William Kane in loving memory of his daughter Mary, who died 13th Dec. 1893 aged 5 years. Also his son Samuel who died 20th February 1902 aged 7 years. Also his granddaughter Margaret Jane (Madge) who died 8th March 1914 aged 3? years. The above named William Kane who died 16th July 1929 aged 69 years. And his wife Margaret Jane who died 22nd Oct. 1952 aged 92 years.

KELLY

[Lead lettering in white limestone, enclosed with MACK.] Erected by Annie Kelly, Larne, in affectionate remembrance of her husband John Kelly, ex-sergeant R.I.C., who departed this life 12th Oct. 1902 aged 59 years. Also the above named Annie Kelly, wife of William CLARKE, who died 16th Feb. 1929 aged 65 years. "At Rest."

KELLY

See WRIGHT

KENNEDY

[Sandstone, fallen, badly weathered.] (Sa)cred t(o) the memory of The Rev. Archibald Kennedy, who departed this life on the 10th August 18(6)1 in t(h)e (-)1st year of his age and (2-) year of his Ministry. His infant daughter Martha Jane, who died 1(8)th October 1842.

[The Rev. Archibald Kennedy was born near Rathfriland in 1810, obtained the General Certificate at R.B.A.I. and was licenced by the Down (Secession) Presbytery. He was minister of Gardenmore Presbyterian Church, Larne 1839-61 and conducted at classical school there. He married a daughter of the Rev. George McCaughey of Larne. See McConnell: *Fasti of the Irish Presbyterian Church* (1951).]

KENNEDY

See GRAHAM

KING
See LOUGH

KIRKPATRICK
Erected to the memory of Margaret Kirkpatrick of Larne, who departed this life 31st March 1879 aged 83 years.
A few short years of evil past,
We reach the happy shore,
Where death divided friends at last,
Shall meet to part no more."

KIRKPATRICK
See McMURRAY and WRIGHT

KNOX
[In enclosure with McSeveney headstone.] Erected by Robert Knox in affectionate remembrance of his daughter Annie Graham, who died 24th Sept. 1893 aged 2 years. Also his son Gordon, who died 9th Sept. 1901 aged 1 year. Jenkins.

LADLIE
[White limestone headstone with concrete enclosure.] Erected by James Ladlie in memory of his wife Ann Ladlie, who died 7th March 1901 aged 68 years. The above-named James Ladlie died 15th December 1910 aged 72 years. "Blessed are the dead which die in the Lord."

LENNON
[Lead lettering on white limestone headstone and granite enclosure.] In memory of James Murdock Lennon, fifth son of William & Catherine Lennon, of Ballylaggan near Ballynure. He was born on 1st February 1861, and died at Larne on 13th March 1906, where for a number of years he carried on a successful business, and was held in high esteem by all classes of the community. Doubtless like all mortals he had faults, but "of the dead say nothing but good". "Him that cometh unto me, I will in no way cast out." "Rock of Ages cleft for me; Let me hide myself in Thee." Catherine Lennon died 20th March 1963.

LENNON
[Lead lettering on granite enclosure.] Martha Lennon died 9th July 1889. William James G. Lennon died 8th September 1889. Annie Allen Lennon died 10th December 1919. Nathaniel Lennon died 20th August 1939. Malcolm Macaulay died 5th April 1902.
[Birth: July 18th, at Point Street, Larne, the wife of Nathaniel Lennon, of a son. Death: July 9th, at Point Street, Larne, Martha (Myrtie) second daughter of Nathaniel and Annie Lennon. *Larne Weekly Reporter*, 20 July 1889.
Death: September 8th, at Point Street, Larne, William James Christie, infant son of Nathaniel and Annie Lennon, aged two months. *Larne Weekly Reporter,* 14 Sep. 1889.]

LIDDELL
[Sandstone with low concrete enclosure.] Erected by Mary Liddell in memory of her beloved husband Andrew Liddell, who died 10th Feb. 1880 aged 65 years. The above-named Mary Liddell died 19th August 1894 aged 63 years. Also their only son William Hugh, who died at New York 4th November 1923 and was interred in Mount Olivet Cemetery. Also their second daughter Jennie, who died 31st August 1931. Also their

youngest daughter Lizzie, who died 27th November 1935. And their eldest daughter, Margaret, wife of Samuel CROZIER, who died 10th June 1941. The above named Samuel Crozier died 28th May 1944. Isabel Rosborough Crozier died 24th February 1989 aged 87 years, beloved wife of Thomas Howard Crozier died 18th December 1989 aged 90 years. "Until the day break and the shadows flee away."

LILLEY
[Sandstone on granite plinth.] Erected by Robert Lilley in memory of his daughter Sarah McClure, who died 27 Decr. 1890 aged 4 years. His daughter Maggie died 10th March 1907 aged 23 years. His wife Jane Aicken died 21st Oct. 1909 aged 52 years. Also the above-named Robert Lilley died 9th Sept. 1929 aged 74 years.

LOCKHART
See MOORE

LOGAN
See BEATTY and McWILLIAM

LOUGH
[Sandstone.] Erected by Margaret KING in memory of her beloved mother Sarah Lough, who died 22nd Oct. 1877 aged 88 years.

LOWRY
See REID

LYNN
[Lead lettering in white limestone.] In memory of John Lynn who died 31st Jany. 1905 aged 63 years. Also his wife Margaret Lynn who died 23rd Jany. 1907 aged 64 years.
[Advertisement in *Larne Weekly Reporter*, 11 Nov. 1865: John Lynn, jun., (from Belfast) plain and ornamental painter, paper hanger, etc., etc., has established himself in business in Wellington Street, Larne (next door to Mr. Gawn).]

McAULEY
[Lead lettering in white limestone.] Erected by Robert McAuley in memory of his wife Maggie McAuley, who died 12th Jany. 1918 aged 69 years. Also their son George McAuley, who died at Buenos Ayres, 13th July 1909, aged 32 years. The above named Robert McAuley died 28th Dec. 1923 aged 78 years. Also their son James, who died 9th June 1929 aged 57 years. Also Robert, eldest son of above James, who died (as result of an accident) 14th Aug. 1955 aged 55 years. Martha, wife of James McAuley, died 17th August 1959 aged 85 years.

MACAULEY
See LENNON

McCAIG
[Polished granite headstone.] In loving memory of James McCaig who died 11th Feby. 1895. And his wife Sarah Jane died 22nd Jany. 1895.

McCAREY
[Sandstone.] Erected by William McCarey in memory of his beloved wife Margaret, who departed this life 22nd Jan. 1881 aged 78 years. Also his son William, who died 9th April

1883 aged 43 years. The above-named William McCarey died 31st March 1889 aged 88 years. And his son James, who died 10th Sept. 1905 aged 63 years. A.M. McBain, 68 York St., Belfast.

McCAUGHEY
[Lying flat, very badly worn.] Sacred to the .. .. in ....th .... For the ..o..g... .... orty o.............. He departed thi(s) life...............age .... The M........ also his wife Jane McCaughey (who departed this life on the 8th day of September ....) aged (81 years).

McCAULEY
[White limestone in railed enclosure with the next.] Erected by Samuel McCauley in memory of his youngest daughter Sarah Alexander (Cissie), who died on the 2nd September 1892 aged 4 years and 7 months. Also his beloved wife Jeanie who died 1st August 1923 aged 71 years and was interred in Elmwood Cemetery, Winnipeg. T. Holden, Larne.

McCAULEY
[White limestone with the above.] Erected by James McCauley in memory of his grand-daughter Annie Mabel Ross McCauley, who died on the 31st August 1900 aged 6 years. And his daughter-in-law Minnie GETTINBY died 14th May 1904 aged 26 years. Also his son Thomas who died 10th June 1913 aged 41 years. The above-named James McCauley died 3rd November 1920 aged 80 years. Also Anne Jane, wife of the above-named Thomas McCauley, died 24th April 1928 aged 55 years. Also Jane Greenlees, wife of the above-named James McCauley, who died 25th March 1929 aged 89 years.

McCLAUGHRY
[Polished pink granite stone and enclosure.] In loving memory of Susan C., beloved wife of A. McClaughry, who died 22nd December 1931. Also their two sons Wilfred and Cyril, died in infancy. Also Sarah Brett who died 18th October 1913. The above-named Claughry, died 22nd October 1950. Also Muriel, daughter of the above A. McClaughry, died 26th December 1982.

McCLUGGAGE
[Lead lettering in white limestone, now fallen and broken.] Erected by Edward McCluggage in loving memory of his daughter Lizzie, who died 27th July 1905 aged 3 years. Also his infant son Thomas, who died 12th May 1912. And his granddaughter Beth, killed by accident, 12th October 1936 aged 2 years. Also his son Sergt. Pilot Edward McCluggage, who died on active service 14th December 1939 aged 23 years. "In Everlasting Remembrance." The above named Edward McCluggage died 23rd August 1943 aged 74 years. Also Andrew, eldest son of above, died 14th October 1954 and cremated at Skipton, Yorkshire. And Jane, wife of the above Edward McCluggage, died 28th Feb. 1958 aged 85 years.

McCLURE
[Lead lettering on white limestone with sandstone enclosure.] Erected by Thomas McClure in memory of his father Samuel McClure, who died 4th December 1899 (ag)ed 86 years.

McCLURE
See CONELLY

McCLURKIN
[Two headstones in the same enclosure. Left, with lead lettering in white limestone decorated with dove.] Erected by James & Mary McClurkin in memory of their daughter Agnes, who died April 10 1879 aged 6 years. Their daughter Mary, who died Jan. 12 1892 aged 20 years. Their son John who died at Toronto, Canada, Sep. 19 1894 aged 32 years. Their son James, who died at Toronto, Jan. 5 1912 aged 43 years. The above-named Mary McClurkin, died Jan. 4 1913 aged 82 years. The above-named James McClurkin died May 17 1929 aged 91 years.
"The Lord gave and the Lord hath taken away: blessed be the name of the Lord." A. Jenkins.
[Right:] Erected by Thomas & Sarah E. McClurkin. The above-named Thomas McClurkin died September 11 1940 aged 80 years and Sarah E. McClurkin died July 15 1942 aged 81 years. Also their daughter Mary McClurkin died May 31 1996 aged 96 years.

McCOMB
See FERGUSON

McCONNELL
[Headstone and enclosure of polished granite.] 1903. Martha McConnell died 25th January 1913. Thomas McConnell died 27th June 1943 in his 89th year.
[On surround:] James Edgar McConnell, born 13th November 1879, died 14th December 1901. Thomas Walter McConnell, born 10th February 1882, died 29th March 1967. David English McConnell, born 14th May 1883, died 13th June 1928. Walter, born 6th June 1918, died 20th January 1919. Thomas Allan, born 16th April 1915, died 14th October 1915. Ronald Parr Pearson, Midshipman R.N., died 19th March 1941 aged 20 years. Lilla Pearson, born 2nd January 1878, died 3rd December 1941. Margaret McConnell, born 30th May 1881, died 2nd June 1969. T. Holden, Larne.

McCONNELL
[Sandstone.] Erected by Mary McConnell in memory of her dearly beloved husband William McConnell, who died 4th February 1894 aged 29 years. Also her dearly beloved daughter Mary, died 30th January 1901 aged 12 years. Also our dear mother, died 28th Nov. 1944. "Blessed are the dead which die in the Lord."
[Small inscription on vase.] In loving memory of a dear mother, Rose E. Paisley, died 7th March 1984.

McCORMICK
[Heavy sandstone within iron railings.] Sacred to the memory of James Miller McCormick, born 26th November 1816, died 23rd June 1873. Also his daughter Isabella Grey POTTS, died 20th April 1891. "He giveth his beloved sleep." Anne, widow of the above, died 12th April 1916. "Blessed are the dead, which die in the Lord." W. Graham, Belfast.
[The will of James Miller McCormick, late of Ardmore, near Larne, county Antrim, rent agent and farmer, who died 23 June 1873 at same place, was proved at Belfast 18 August 1873 by the oath of Anne McCormick of Ardmore, Larne aforesaid, the widow, one of the executors. Effects under £4,000.
Letters of administration of the personal estate of Isabella Grey Potts, late of Tyne Cottage, Whiteabbey, county Antrim, who died 20 April 1891 at Ardmore, Larne, in said county, were granted at Belfast 22 June 1891 to Robert Potts, gentleman, the husband. Effects £1,100.]

McCOUBREY
See SIMMS

McCRACKEN
[Lead lettering on white limestone headstone and enclosure. Headstone decorated with rope and anchor, fallen forward and broken.] Erected by Jane McCracken in loving memory of her husband James McCracken who died 5th Octr. 1911 aged 43 years. Also their daughter Jannie who died in infancy. Also their son James who died 14th April 1922 aged 22 years. Also their son Maurice who died 24th Feby. 1927 aged 24 years. Also the above Jane McCracken who died 19th March 1955 aged 89 years. Jenkins.

McCULLOGH
[Tall sandstone.] Erected in memory of John McCullogh, who died Nov. 8 1883, aged 76 years. Also his daughter Jane, who died Feb. 3 1855 aged 23 years. Also his son William, who died March 1 1871 aged 31 years. Also his son John, who died March 7 1884 aged 49 years. Also his wife Agnes McCullogh, who died April 5 1887 aged 82 years. Also their son Adam, who erected this stone, died 25th May 1897 aged 51 years. Also Matilda Jane, only daughter of the above-named Adam McCullogh, died 13th January 1908 aged 14 years. And his wife Margaret McCullogh died 18th November 1909 aged 58 years.

McCULLOUGH
[Sandstone.] Erected by Lizzie McCullough in memory of her beloved husband John McCullough, who died 27th Dec. 1878 aged 32 years. Also three of their children who died 1878. Sarah Ann aged 5 years, Lizzie aged 4 months, Mary Jane aged 3 years. The above Lizzie McCullough died 26th March 1923. "Blessed .... die in the Lord. ...."

McDOWELL
[Large enclosure of granite; two of the blocks rise above the others and carry the inscriptions. Left:] John McDowell died 19 Feb. 1906. Elizabeth McDowell died 1st Sep. 1914.
    [Right:] GIRVAN. Annie Girvan died 3rd June 1929.

McELHINNEY
[White limestone with lead lettering on sandstone plinth with low granite enclosure.] Erected by Catherine McElhinney in memory of her husband Thomas McElhinney, who died 11th June 1893, aged 50 years. Their son Thomas Henry, who died at Queenstown, 14th Nov. 1900 aged 20 years. Their son John who died 9th Dec. 1907 aged 37 years. Also their three grand-children. Their son Frederick William, who died 14th Oct. 1908 aged 23 years. Their son David Young, who died 30th April 1914 aged 31 years. The above-named Catherine McElhinney, who died 26th July 1916 aged 65 years. And their daughter Kathleen, who died 11th August 1935 aged 46 years. "Until the day break and the shadows flee away."

McELROY
[Lead lettering in white limestone panel in concrete headstone.] Erected by Samuel McElroy, Ballysnodd, in loving memory of his son Hugh Robert, who died 31st March 1903. Also his daughter Marion, who died 9th Oct. 1916. Also the above named Samuel McElroy, J.P., who died 27th September 1931 aged 71 years. And his wife Eilzabeth McElroy died 7th July 1944 aged 85 years. And their son Thomas George McElroy, who died 12th April 1945 aged 61 years.

MacFADDEN

[White limestone with raised carving of rope and ivy.] In loving memory of Robert Philip MacFadden, born 11th January 1868, died 24th October 1868. Catherine Patman MacFadden, born 26th February 1985, died 29th March 1871. Holden.

McFARLANE

[White limestone within iron railings.] Erected by Donald McFarlane in loving memory of his wife Mary McFarlane, who deid 24th Octr. 1899 aged 87 years. The above-named Donald McFarlane died 5th May 1904 aged 90 years.

McFAUL

[Sandstone.] In memory of Arthur McFaul, who died at Seaview, Cairncastle, on 11th February 1875 aged 73 years.

McFAUL

[White limestone headstone facing south.] Erected by John McFaul in memory of his wife Isabella McFaul, who died 7th Feby. 1884 aged 73 years. The above-named John McFaul died 3rd June 1887 aged 72 years. Also his grand-son Francis John McFaul, who died 28th March 1899 aged 5 years. Also his son Malcolm, who died 12th March 1905. Also his son James, died 1st Dec. 1944 aged 90 years. Agnes, wife of above James McFaul, died 9th April 1949. Also Charlotte McKay, daughter of the above named Agnes and James, who died 25th December 1971.

[The will of John McFaul, late of Drumaine, county Antrim, farmer, who died 7 [sic] June 1887 at same place, was proved at Belfast 5 March 1888 by Malcolm McFaul and James McFaul, both of Drumaine, farmers, the executors. Effects £64 . 15s.]

McFAUL

[White limestone, broken from plinth.] Erected by Eliza Jane McFaul in memory of her daughter Lizzie Jane, who died 2nd Feby. 1890 aged 6 months. Her daughter Enna, who died 5th Novr. 1900 aged 4 years, and her daughter Annie, who died 5th April 1902 aged 16 years. Her daughter Edith died 27th Dec. 1902 aged 2 years. Her twin babies Eva & Alfred died Septr. 1903 aged 7 months. Her son Hugh Whiteford McFaul died 8th Septr. 1905 aged 6 years. The above Eliza Jane McFaul died 23rd Septr. 1909 aged 43 years. And her husband John McFaul died 16th July 1927 aged 73 years.

McFAUL

See CARSON

McGAREL

[Sandstone with concrete enclosure.] Erected by Archie McGarel, in loving memory of his son Archie, who died 26th June 1911 aged 9 years. Also his beloved daughter Annie, who died 17th Sept. 1916 aged 17 years. Also his beloved wife Jane S. McGarel, died 14th October 1953. The above named Archie McGarel died 11th August 1955. And his son Thomas died 28th December 1985.

McGAVOCK

See CUTHBERT

McGHEE

See FOX

McGOOKIN

[No inscription except surname moulded in concrete headstone.]

McILROY

[Lead lettering on polished limestone, within concrete enclosure.] Erected by Charles McIlroy to the memory of his wife Hannah, died 19th April 1939. Also the above Charles McIlroy died 26th Jan. 1951.

McILWAIN

[Flaking sandstone.] Erected by Isabella McIlwain, in memory of her husband John McIlwain, who died 21st Augt. 1891 aged 42 years .... their daughter Chr(istina) w(ho) d(ied) 20th Aug. 18(96) aged (13 years).

[Letters of administration of the personal estate of John McIlwain, late of Larne, county Antrim, locomotive engineer, who died 21 August 1891 at same place, were granted at Belfast 25 September 1891 to Isabella McIlwain of Larne, the widow. Effects £213.]

McINTOSH

[Broken white limestone with concrete enclosure.] The family burying ground of Wm. R. McIntosh.

McKAY

[Sandstone.] In memory of Mary McKay, Ballymullock, who died 8th June 1888 aged 75 years. A faithful and beloved servant. Erected by Alexr. WILLIAMS, J.P.

[The will of Mary McKay, late of Ballymullock, county Antrim, spinster, who died 8 June 1888 at same place, was proved at Belfast 25 June 1888 by Alexander Williams of Larne, said county, bank manager, the sole executor. Effects £198 . 5s. 10d.]

McKAY

[White limestone with lead lettering, in a railed enclosure.] In memory of Thomas McKay, who died 16th Decr. 1897 aged 70 years.

[Probate of the will of Thomas McKay, late of Mill Street, Larne, county Antrim, clothier, who died 17 December 1897, granted at Belfast 19 January 1898 to William John Beatty of Mill Street, Larne, farmer. Effects £87.]

McKAY

See McFAUL and McMULLAN

McKEE

[Lead lettering on white limestone.] Sacred to the memory of Margaret McKee, relict of James McKee, Kildowney, and daughter of the late Rev. Alexander MONTGOMERY, Glenarm, entered into rest 10th March 1893 aged 74 years. "In my father's house are many mansions." Also her kinsman Robert James BRIGS, son of the late Henry Brigs of Belfast, who entered into rest on New Year's Eve 1902 aged 33 years. "Blessed are the pure in heart."

McKEE

[White limestone with lead lettering and concrete enclosure.] Erected by William McKee in memory of his daughters, Margaret, Emma, & Mary. Also his son Robert, born 11th Nov. 1871, died 24th May 1905. And his son George, born 20th March 1876, died 8th Dec. 1911. The above named William McKee died 22nd December 1925. Also his wife Annie McKee died 5th April 1930. His grandson Norman Rea died 25th October 1972.

McKEEVER
[Sandstone.] Erected by Neil McKeever and his sister Jane to the memory of their mother Jane, who died 6th April 1878 aged 76 years. Also his wife Jane, who died 17th June 1878 aged 40 years. Also the above-named Neil McKeever, who died 18th January 1906. And his granddaughter Mary McKeever, who died 3rd Nov. 1911. And his grandduaghter Agnes J. who died 5th November 1953. Also his grandson James, who died 30th May 1960.

McKENTY
[White limestone.] Erected by William McKenty in memory of his mother Nancy McKenty, who died 11th Jany. 1882 aged 51 years. Also his brother Daniel McKenty, who died 13th May 1889 aged 21 years.

McKEOWN
Erected by John McKeown in memory of his daughter Rebecca Jane, who died 1st May 1869 aged 13 years. His son John, who died 27th March 1873 aged 10 years. His son James, who died 22nd Octr. 1875 aged 10 years. His son Thomas, who died 4th Novr. 1875 aged 8 years. Also his wife Margaret, who died 7th June 1903 aged 73 years. The above-named John McKeown died 28th Novr. 1908 aged 78 years.

McKEOWN
[Polished black granite headstone and enclosure.] In loving memory of Edward McKeown, R.N. born 22nd June 1825, died 20th Feb. 1881. His wife Mary Ann McKeown, born 14th Feb. 1833, died 25th Oct. 1893. Their son James Phillip, born 28th Sep. 1863, died 8th April 1901. Their daughter Charlotte Jane, born 13th Jan. 1858, died 4th Jan. 1927. Their daughter Mary Ann, born 24th Dec. 1865, died 24th June 1935. Fell asleep in Jesus.

McKEOWN
[Lead lettering on granite headstone and enclosure.] In loving memory of John McKeown, master mariner, died 6th October 1899. And his wife Margaret died 30th June 1931. Also their daughters. Mary C. died 5th April 1894. Isabel died 6th October 1957. Constance died (5)th March 1959.
  [Probate of the will of John McKeown, late of Main Street, Larne, county Antrim, master mariner, who died 6 October 1899, was granted at Belfast 4 December 1899 to Margaret McKeown of Main Street, widow, and Thomas Carson of Pound Street, merchant, both in Larne. Effects £258 . 2s. 4d.
  Married: April 11, in the Raloo Presbyterian Church, by the Rev. J. Whiteford, Captain John McKeown, Larne, to Maggie, daughter of Mr. William Cuthbert, Ballyvernstown, Glynn. *The Larne Weekly Reporter*, 15 Apr. 1876.]

McKERNON
[White marble with concrete enclosure.] In memory of John McKernon, who died 18th May 1935, and of his wife Mary, who died 22nd Feb. 1936, interred in Cardonald Cemetery, Glasgow. And their children John and Hessie who died 15th-21st Jan. 1900. Erected by James McKernon.
  [Death: Jan. 21, 1900, at her residence, Pound Street, Larne, Hessie, eldest daughter of John McKernon. *Larne Times*, 27 Jan. 1900, p.2.
  Death: Jan. 15, 1900, at his residence, 32 Pound Street, Larne, John (Wee Johnny) dearly-beloved son of John McKernon. *Larne Times*, 27 Jan. 1900, p.4.]

McKILLOP
[Dark granite.] Erected by Robert McKillop, in loving memory of his wife Jane McKillop, who died 19th June 1908 aged 58 years. Also his daughter Elizabeth, who died May 1879. The above-named Robert McKillop died 14th May 1920 aged 70 years. T. Holden.

McMANUS
[Lead lettering on white limestone, broken, in concrete enclosure.] In loving memory of Ellen WALKER, died 13th Feb. 1929, widow of Alexander McManus (interred in Inver Churchyard) and their sons Hugh, Alexander and James. And their daughter Eleanor SEMPLE, widow of James Wilson Semple, died 13th March 1961.

McMASTER
[Tall sandstone within iron railings.] 1877. Erected by James McMaster, Larne, to the memory of his children who died at early ages, and to his son John, who died 20th Jany. 1875 aged 24 years. His loved wife Mary, who died 25th March 1880 aged 48 years. The above-named James McMaster died 21st July 1895 aged 75 years. A. Jenkins, Larne.
[Birth: October 26, at Mill Street, Larne, the wife of Mr. George McMullan, of twins – a son and daughter. *Larne Weekly Reporter*, 1 Nov. 1873.]

McMEEKIN
[Lead lettering on white limestone headstone, fallen and broken.] Erected by William McMeekin in memory of Agnes McMeekin, who died 21st July 1897 aged 74 years. Also his wife Isabella McMeekin, who died 26th Sept. 1918 aged 77 years. The above-named William McMeekin, who died 14th February 1928 aged 84 years.

McMULLAN
[White limestone with lead lettering, within iron railings.] Erected by George McMullan in memory of his son James who died infancy. Also his son James who died 20th August 1881 aged 4 years. And his son John, who died at Bombay, 30th June 1899 aged 32 years. Also his beloved wife Mary Ann McMullan, who died 14th May 1903 aged 65 years. The above-named George McMullan died 2nd July 1910 aged 78 years. Also his grandson George McWILLIAMS who died 21st March 1917 aged 19 years. Also his grandson Thomas Colvin McWilliams, who died 6th April 1920 aged 21 years.

McMULLAN
[White limestone "scroll" with granite enclosure.] In loving memory of John McMullan, husband of Mary McMullan, who entered into rest 10th Jany. 1897. "Be ye also ready."

McMULLAN
[Polished granite with granite enclosure.] In loving memory of Annie McMullan, beloved wife of John McKay, born April 1832, died March 1910. Also the above-named John McKay, who died 7th June 1921 aged 73 years. Also their daughter Bessie, beloved wife of James McSEVENEY, died 21st Nov. 1946 aged 76 years. The above James McSeveney died 30th October 1957. Peace, Perfect Peace.

McMURRAY
[Sandstone with iron railings.] Sacred to the memory of Rev. John McMurray for 1(7) years minister of 2nd Larne Presbyterian Congregation, who died 15th July 1879 aged 65 years. Also his wife Eliza Kirkpatrick who died 10th September 1886 aged 71 years. "Thanks be to God which giveth us the victory through our Lord Jesus Christ."

[The Rev. John McMurray came from Ballybay, county Monaghan, and began his ministry in Portlaw, Waterford. He later went to Seton Dalgeal in Northumberland and then to Canada, 1847-1859. He returned to Ireland and was installed in Gardenmore, Larne, on 24 September 1861. He inspired the building of the first manse, and the erection of a new church in 1870. See Bailie: *A History of Congregations in the Presbyterian Church* (1982).]

McMURTRY
[White limestone panel on sandstone.] In memory of Agnes CAMERON, wife of Matthew McMurtry, Glenford, she died 1st January 1882 aged 59 years. Also the above-named Matthew McMurtry, who died 6th November 1885 aged 69 years.
[The will of Matthew McMurtry, otherwise McMurtery, late of Glenford, Magheramorne, county Antrim, farmer, who died 6 November 1885 at same place, was proved at Belfast 22 January 1886 by Samuel McMurtery of Glenford, farmer, one of the executors. Effects £385 . 5s.]

McMURTRY
[Granite headstone and enclosure.] In loving memory of Captain William McMurtry, who died 4th June 1904 aged 45 years, interred in Sydney, N.S.W., and Agnes his wife who died 14th November 1945 aged 81 years. Their daughter Jane died 2nd Feburary 1964. Their son William died 8th July 1969, dearly loved husband of Edith. Edith, died 31st March 1977. Their daughter Mary Elizabeth died 21st Mar. 1895, interred in Acapulca, Mexico, aged 3? years. Their infant daughter Ellen McCready, who died 9th February 1891 aged 1 year 2 months.
[Death: Feb. 9, at Cairnduff, Ellen McCready, infant daughter of Captain William McMurtry, aged one year and two months. *The Larne Reporter,* 14 Feb. 1891.]

McMURTRY
Erected by Maggie McMurtry in loving memory of her husband William McMurtry, who died 21st Decr. 1891 aged 33 years. Their infant son John McCambridge, who died 26th Decr. 1891. The above-named Maggie McMurtry died 10th Decr. 1903 aged 43 years. Their elder daughter Elizabeth died 18th April 1967. Their younger daughter Mary Jane died 13th November 1980. "Blessed are the dead which die in the Lord."
[Letters of administration of the personal estate of William McMurtry, late of The Curran, Larne, county Antrim, writing clerk, who died 21 December 1891 at same place, were granted at Belfast 27 January 1892 to Margaret McMurtry of The Curran, Larne, the widow. Effects £95.]

McMURTRY
See CAMERON

McNEILL
[Tall sandstone.] Erected by James McNeill in memory of his daughter Mary Isabella, who died the 10th August 1870 aged 2 years 11 months. Also his son John, who died 3rd Sept. 1889 aged 18 years. Also his son Robert McNeill, B.A. who died 23rd Jany. 1897 aged 32 years. Also his grand daughter Mary Isabella Cameron Morrow, who died 7th Novr. 1899 aged 3 years. The above-named James McNeill died 12th Octr. 1902 aged 75 years. Also his wife Mary Isabella McNeill, who died 5th May 1917 aged 82 years. Also their son Archibald McNeill, who died 6th Octr. 1916 aged 55 years. Also their daughter Martha Jane McNeill, who died 30th Nov. 1938 aged 62 years. And his son Thomas Henry McNeill, died 1st August 1945 aged 85 years. Annie, wife of the above Archibald

McNeill, died 17th April 1951.
[Death: September 3rd at his father's residence, Blackcave, Larne, John, youngest son of James McNeill, aged 18 years. *Larne Weekly Reporter*, 7 Sep. 1889.]

McNEILL
[Polished granite headstone and enclosure.] Here lyeth ye body of William McNeill, born 1834, died 1914. Here lyeth ye body of Margaret McNeill, born 1839, died 1904. And in memory of their children, Willie, born 1865, died 1884. Janie Allen, born 1879, died at Winnipeg 1927. John, born 1864, died 1935. And their grandchildren Eleanor, born 1903, died 1904, Willie, born 1902, died 1921, Allan, born 1872, died 1945. Their daughter-in-law Nellie (nee WYLIE), wife of John, born 1876, died 1956.

McNEILL
[Granite headstone and enclosure.] In memory of Malcolm McNeill of the Corran, born 1832, died 1891, at Boissy St. Leger in France and interred there. Also of Hester, sister of the above, born 1840, died 1894. Also of Duncan McNeill, D.L., of the Corran, Colonel, Indian Army, born Jan. 25 1838, died June 29 1920 . Also his wife Mary Berthia, died 22nd March 1942. Also their sister Margaret McNeill, born 12 Jan. 1836, died 11 Nov. 1923. "For former records see Larne & Inver Church-yard."

Colonel Duncan McNeill, J.P., D.L.
(from Young and Pike: *Belfast and the Province of Ulster*, 1909).

[Letters of administration of the personal estate of Malcolm McNeill, late of The Corran, Larne, county Antrim, gentleman, who died 9 February 1891 at Boissy St. Leger, Leine et Elise, France, were granted at Belfast 6 April 1891 to Margaret McNeill of The Corran, spinster, a sister. Effects £9,660 . 2s. 6d.

Letters of administration of the personal estate of Hester McNeill, late of Larne, county Antrim, spinster, who died 14 September 1894 at same place, were granted at Belfast 12 November 1894 to Duncan McNeill of The Corran, Larne, retired colonel and J.P., a brother. Effects £9,301 . 4d. 11d.

Malcolm McNeill J.P. was the eldest son of Malcolm McNeill and Lucy, a daughter of John McNeill of Colonsay and sister of Duncan, Lord Colonsay. He was a trustee of Larne Town Hall, the McGarel Buildings, Larne Grammar School, and the Larne National Schools. He was agent for the Magheramorne estate and for the Agnew properties of Kilwaughter, Cairncastle, and Kells. Having gone to Paris to attend Mr. William Agnew's funeral he developed scarlatina and died on 9th February 1891 and was interred beside Mr. Agnew. *Larne Reporter*, 14 Feb. 1891.

Duncan McNeill: date of birth, 25 Jan 1838; ensign, 8 Dec. 1855; lieutenant., 5 Nov. 1858; captain, 8 Dec. 1867; major, 8 Dec. 1875; lieutenant colonel, 8 Dec. 1881; colonel, 8 Dec. 1885; placed on supernumerary list 25 Jan 1895; 26 Madras N.I. (2nd (Royal N. British) Regiment of Dragoons), 28 Mar. 1856; Madras Staff Corps, 12 Sep. 1866; District Superintendent of Police, Raepore, Central Provinces, 21 Jan. 1870 (later in Sumulpore, then Saugor in C.P.); Indian Staff Corps, 8 Dec. 1881. He served in the suppression of the mutiny at Seetabuldee in June and July 1857, and with the Kamptee flying column from 9th November 1858 to 26th January 1859; served also with the expedition to the Puchmurree Hills, and was present at the capture of Hurrakote in November 1859. Col. McNeill served on Antrim County Council, 1899-1920, and was a Deputy-Lieutenant of the county since 1911. He was chairman of Larne Urban Council, 1900-1903, vice-chairman of the Larne Board of Guardians since 1905 and chairman since 1915. He was also a director of Larne Markets Co. Ltd., occupying the chair since 1914, a trustee of the McGarel Buildings, and on the committee of the County Antrim Asylum (Holywell). Hart: *Army List*, 1862-1878; *Official Army List*, 1884, 1894, 1902; *Larne Times*, 3 July 1920. McKillop: *History of Larne,* p. 110. *Belfast & Province of Ulster Directory*, 1895-1920; Young and Pike (1909).]

McNEILL

In loving memory of Robert McNeill, died 6th August 1913. His wife Mary died 6th May 1920. Their daughter Isabella died in infancy. Their son Robert Wm. died 18th Sept. 1947. Also their daughter Margaret CARMICHAEL, wife of the late Alexander Carmichael of Neb., USA, died 29th Nov. 1950. Mary Jane McNeill died 31st March 1966.

McNINCH

In Memoriam James Watt McNinch, born 9th January 1845, died 30th September 1885. Robert McNinch, born 28th June 1809, died 19th Nov. 1899. Ellen Watt McNinch, born 14th May 1808, died 30th Dec. 1900. Nellie Watt McNinch, born 1st March 1893, died 27th Nov. 1912. Margaret Watt McNinch, born 19th August 1841, died 24th July 1917. Martha McNinch, born 4th December 1846, died 30th December 1923. Ann Jane McNinch, born 7th December 1848, died 26th May 1929.

[Administration of the estate of Robert McNinch, late of 14 Bedeque Street, Belfast, salesman, who died 13 November 1900 [sic], granted at Belfast 15 April 1901 to Thomas Watt McNinch, farmer, and Ann Jane McNinch, spinster. (Limited) Effects £763 . 15s.]

McNINCH
  See HAMILTON

MacPHERSON
  See SIMMS

McQUOID
  [White limestone with lead lettering.] In loving memory of John McQuoid, who died
  12th March 1906 aged 89 years. Also his daughter Catherine, who died 16th June 1932.
  "Blessed are the peace makers." A. Jenkins.

McREA
  [Small red sandstone.] In memory of William McRea, who died 10th July 1892 aged 11
  years.

McSEVENEY
  [Granite, propped against north boundary wall.] Erected by Robert McSeveney in
  memory of his wife Isabella GRAHAM who died 11th Jany. 1897 aged 64 years. The
  above named Robert McSeveney died 12th Dec. 1922 aged 81 years.

McSEVENEY
  [Lying flat, inscription hidden, in same enclosure as KNOX.]

McSEVENEY
  See McMULLAN

McWILLIAM
  [Obelisk of polished pink granite, with enclosure.] Erected by Margaret McWilliam in
  memory of her husband Robert McWilliam, who died at Larne 14th July 1891 aged 61
  years. The above-named Margaret McWilliam died at Larne, 16th May 1914 aged 85
  years. Also in memory of her sister Jane LOGAN, who died at Larne, 20th April 1910
  aged 74 years.
    [The will of Robert McWilliam, late of Larne, county Antrim, retired spirit merchant,
  who died 14 July 1891 at same place, was proved at Belfast 24 August 1891 by Margaret
  McWilliam of Larne, widow, one of the executors. Effects £8,579 . 1s. 1d.]

McWILLIAM
  [Polished granite headstone and enclosure.] 1896. James McWilliam, born at Raloo 1823,
  died at Larne 28th June 1895. Elizabeth Jane McWilliam died 17th June 1903 aged 26
  years.
    [The will of James McWilliam, formerly of Station Road and late of St. John's Place,
  Larne, county Antrim, R.I.C., who died 28 June 1895 at latter place, was proved at
  Belfast 9 August 1895 by James Donald of Ballyrickardbeg and John Holden of
  Ballyrickardmore, both in said county, farmers, the executors. Effects £695 . 13s.]

McWILLIAM
  [Polished granite headstone and enclosure.] 1896. In loving memory of Ellie Buchanan,
  who died 24th May 1896 aged 17 years. Also in affectionate remembrance of James
  McWilliam, who died 22nd June 1905 aged 56 years. Also his wife Ellen Jane
  McWilliam, who died 19th January 1923 aged 73 years.

McWILLIAM
    See BUCHANAN

McWILLIAMS
    See McMULLAN

MACK
    [Dark granite headstone enclosed with John Kelly d.1902.] Erected to the memory of
    Henry Mack, Ex-Head Constable, R.I.C., who died 7th June 1909 aged 68 years. Also
    Maria Mack, wife of Ex-Head Constable William Mack, who died 29th Feby. 1916 aged
    72 years. The above-named William Mack died 7th March 1918 aged 86 years. Also their
    daughter Harriette died 6th Aug. 1944 aged 76 years. "Gone, but not forgotten". T.
    Holden

MAGEE
    [Polished granite headstone with conrete enclosure.] In memory of E J Magee died 18-1-
    1880. A. Magee died 29-6-1895. T. Magee died 20-3-1910. M.J. Magee 9-11-1939. W.
    SIMPSON (Jnr.) died 10-5-1920. E. J. Simpson died 15-3-1964. W. Simpson (Snr.) died
    10-5-1973. "At Rest."
    [Inscription on concrete and granite vase:] Simpson, L.O.L. 1297, R.P.B. 47.

MAGEE
    [White limestone.] Erected by their loving children in memory of their mother Sarah
    Magee, who departed this life 16th November 1912 aged 39 years, and their father
    Michael Magee, who departed this life 27th November 1912 aged 44 years. Also of their
    sister Sarah who died in infancy. Gone but not forgotten.

MAGILL
    [White limestone in sandstone frame.] In memory of Matthew Magill who died 13th
    May 1876 aged 32 years. Also his wife Mary CASEMENT who died 23rd Decr. 1871
    aged 27 years. And their infant daughter Anna McKibbin. Erected by their son Thomas
    Magill. A. Jenkins, Larne.

MAGILL
    [Flaking sandstone.] (Er)ected by Charles Mag(ill), Larne, in memory of his wife
    Annabella Magill, who died 13 June 1877 aged 57 years. His daughter Annie MILLAR
    who died 13 Dec. 1878 aged 25 years. Also his grand-daughter Eliza Millar who died in
    infancy. His son (He)nry, who died 17 Nov. 18(83) aged 23 years.

MAGILL
    [Thick granite headstone and enclosure.] 1921. In loving memory of Herbert T. F. Magill,
    aged 23 years, Lord Strathcona's Horse, died in No. 5 General Hospital, Rouen, April 6th
    1918, from wounds received in action, and Matilda F. K. Magill, born January 14th, died
    July 16th 1887. Also in loving memory of their father Samuel Magill, born January 11th
    1846, died March 14th 1931. Also in loving memory of their mother Sarah Magill, born
    December 1st 1856, died February 9th 1942.

MAGILL
    [White limestone with lead lettering and low railings.] Erected by James Magill in loving
    memory of his children, Martin who died 8th November 1895 aged 6 months, also Lila
    who died 19th January 1901 aged 5? years. Also Eva who died 28th Octr. 1911 aged 8?

years. The above named James Magill died 15th Feb. 1931 in his 68th year. Also his wife Sarah Ann who died 24th July 1950 aged 88 years. And his son Campbell Johnston Magill died 10th March 1953 aged 61 years.

MAGILL
  See BOYD

MANUS
  [Lead lettering in white limestone, fallen on face and broken.] In loving memory of our dear mother Isabella M. Manus, who died 17th Decr. 1904 aged 61 years. "Until the day break, and the shadows flee away."

MAYNE
  [White limestone with lead lettering.] In loving memory of Sergeant John Mayne who died 12th September 1890. Also his mother Margaret Mayne who died 2nd June 1902 in her 89th year.
  [Death: September 12, at McGarel Town Hall, Larne, Sergeant John Mayne, caretaker. His remains will be removed for interment in the McGarel Cemetery. *The Larne Reporter*, 9 Aug. 1890.]

MAYNE
  See WAUGH

MEHARG
  [Sandstone.] Erected by Ellen English in memory of Joseph Meharg who departed this life 31st March 1877 aged 89 years. Also his wife Mary Meharg, who died 1st Dec. 1877 aged 87 years.

MELVIN
  [Sandstone ledger.] Revd. William Melvin died 8th April 1890. "Blessed are the dead which die in the Lord."
  [Inscribed at the bottom of slab:-] Revd. W. M. HENRY.
  [The will of the Rev. William Melvin, late of Larne, county Antrim, presbyterian minister, who died 8 April 1890 at same place, was proved at the Principal Registry 29 May 1891 by the Rev. William Montford Henry of Cootehill, county Cavan, presbyterian minister, one of the executors. Effects £641 . 9s. 6d.]

MELVIN
  See JAMIESON

MENEILLY
  [No inscription on headstone except surname.]

MILLAR
  See MAGILL

MILLICAN
  Erected by Samuel Millican in loving memory of his wife Margaret, died 11th Oct. 1928. His father John Millican died 11th Jan. 1903. His sons James died 21st July 1922. Thomas died 28th Nov. 1892. And his daughter Maggie died 28th Aug. 1890. The above named Samuel Millican died 28th July 1940. "In thy presence is the fulness of joy."

MILLS

[Lead lettering on white limestone.] Erected by Susan Mills in loving memory of her husband George Mills, who died 6th Nov. 1888 aged 57 years. Also her son Edwin, who died 18th August 1888 aged 6 years. Also her step-son Samuel, who died 16th May 1897 aged 31 years. Her son Robert died 28th July 1884 aged 16 years. Her son Frederick died 5th April 1886 aged 10 years. Her son David N. died 16th August 1911 aged 33 years.

[The will of George Mills, late of Larne, county Antrim, naval pensioner, who died 6 November 1888 at same place, was proved at Belfast 28 January 1889 by Susan Mills of Larne, widow, the sole executrix. Effects £29 . 17s. 11d.]

MONTGOMERY

[Sandstone, fallen.] Erected to the memory of Samuel Montgomery who died 17th May 1887 aged 89 years. Also his sister Ann WHITE who died 29th July 1889 aged 88 years.

MONTGOMERY

See McKEE

MOONEY

See CLOSE

MOORE

[Small sandstone, lying flat.] Erected by John Moore in memory of his son James, who died 24th Dec. 1871 aged 3 years.

MOORE

[Two headstones in same enclosure. Right: white limestone decorated with roses, passion flowers etc.] Erected by Ann Jane Moore, Ballysnodd, in memory of her beloved husband James Moore, who died 3rd January 1897 aged 77 years. Also her daughter Lizzie Jane, who died 4th January 1878 aged 3 years & 3 months. The above-named Ann Jane Moore, who died 2nd April 1920 aged 83 years. Also her son Thomas Moore who died 28th Jan. 1950 aged 93 years. Also Mary, the wife of Thomas Moore, who died 6th August 1953 aged 86 years. T. Holden, Larne.

[Left: polished granite.] Erected by Thomas Moore in memory of his daughter Margaret, died 22 March 1893 aged 6 years, his daughter Annie, died 18 April 1893 aged 4 years. His daughter Maggie Anne died 29 Oct. 1897 aged 1 year. His son Nathaniel died 31 Oct. 1897 aged 3 years. His grandson Thomas Moore died 8th Augt. 1903. Also his wife Margaret Moore died 7 Augt. 1906 aged 50 years.

[Probate of the will of James Moore, late of Ballysnod, county Antrim, farmer, who died 3 January 1897, granted at Belfast 5 March 1897 to William John Beatty, farmer, and Robert N. Carson, secretary, both of Larne in said county. Effects £1,173 . 6s. 6d.]

MOORE

[Cross-headed white limestone headstone with dove at intersection.] In affectionate remembrance of Martha Agnes Moore, Superintendent Nurse, Larne Union Infirmary, who died 27th Nov. 1899 aged 27 years. Erected by a few friends in Larne and neighbourhood who knew her work and worth.

MOORE

[Lead lettering in white limestone with concrete enclosure.] Erected by the family of Stewart Moore in memory of their mother Mary Moore, who died 20th May 1902 aged 48 years. And their father Stewart Moore, who died 2nd Jany. 1906 aged 55 years. Also their sister Letitia, who died 4th Jany. 1893 aged 15 years. Also their sister Margaret LOCKHART, who died 4th June 1911. Also Letitia RICE, sister of above named Stewart Moore, who died 23rd December 1915. Also their sister Grace WILSON, who died 26th July 1930. Their son William Stewart Moore, who died 30th June 1970 aged 79 years. Also their daughter Molly, who died 24th January 1971 aged 86 years. T. Holden, Station Rd., Larne.

MORRIS
See HAYWOOD

MORRISON
[Twin headstones on concrete enclosure.] In loving memory of Elizabeth Letetia Morrison, born 31st October 1852, died 26th December 1907. In loving memory of John Goudy Morrison, born 1st September 1852, died 29th October 1899.

[Administration (with the will) of the personal estate of John Gowdy [sic] Morrison, late of Larne, county Antrim, jeweller, who died 28 October 1899, granted at Belfast 17 November 1899 to Lizzie Morrison of Larne, widow, the universal legatee. Effecst £274 . 15s. 1d.]

MORROW
See McNEILL

MOUTRAY
[Enclosed with Murray stone.] M.A. Moutray in affectionate remembrance. Loved ones sleeping.

MULHOLLAND
[Dark granite headstone.] In loving memory of Jean C. Mulholland, born Jan. 7th 1899, died Jan. 28th 1900. Also her mother Martha VETTERS, wife of Capt. Henry Mulholland, died 17th August 1923 aged 60 years, interred at Cardiff. Henry Mulholland died 19th Nov. 1930 aged 66 years. T. Holden.

MUNDELL
[Lead lettering in white limestone headstone with concrete enclosure.] 1926. Erected by James Mundell in loving memory of his son James, who died 14th Decr. 1902 aged 2 years. Also his beloved daughter Agnes, wife of Lawrence JOHNSTON, who died 9th Sept. 1925 aged 28 years. Also his wife Margaret died 10th Aug. 1947. The above James Mundell died 11th June 1960 in his 98th year. His daughter-in-law Martha Mundell died 2nd Dec. 1977. And his son William died 24th April 1980.

MURPHY
[Sandstone decorated with a cross moline inside a roundel.] Erected by John Murphy in memory of his beloved wife Mary Anne, who departed this life April 5th 1873 aged 24 years.

MURRAY
[White limestone enclosed with Moutray stone. Ceramic urn broken from top of stone.] Erected by Jane Murray in loving memory of her husband John Murray, who died 13th Sept. 1907 aged 74 years. Also her brother William BARKLIE who died 16th Augt. 1899 aged 72 years. The above-named Jane Murray died 24th June 1922 aged 89 years.

NEWBURY
    See JEFFERY

NICHOLSON
    [Polished granite headstone with concrete enclosure.] In loving memory of Robert
    Nicholson, died 11th April 1949. And his daughter Jane Donald Nicholson, died in
    infancy. Also his wife Margaret Nicholson died 8th August 1971.

OWENS
    [Sandstone painted white.] Erected by William Owens in memory of his son Alexander
    Owens, who died 27th July 1881 aged 1 year.
        [Death: July 27th, at Mill Lane, Larne, Alexander, son of William, 15 months. *Larne
    Weekly Reporter*, 30 July 1881.]

PAISLEY
    [White limestone headstone and enclosure with lead lettering.] 1906. In loving memory
    of Eilzabeth Mary Paisley, who died 10th Nov. 1917 aged 69 years. Also her husband
    Samuel Paisley, who died 26th Jan. 1923 aged 65 years. Also their son Samuel James
    Paisley, husband of Elizabeth Jane Paisley, who died 2nd March 1932 aged 42 years Annie
    Paisley, born 1st May 1892, died 1st Octr. 1894. Lizzie Paisley, born Jany. 1887 died 24th
    June 1910. T. Holden.

PAISLEY
    See McCONNELL

PARK
    [Lead lettering on white limestone.] Jane Park died 5th December 1897 aged 80 years.

PEARSON
    See McCONNELL

PERRY
    See CROOKS

PICKEN
    [Granite headstone fallen from its plinth.] Erected by James Picken in memory of his
    beloved wife Harriet, who died 7th April 1885 aged 25 years. Also his mother Jane Picken
    who died at Larne Harbour 31st Octr. 1889 aged 57 years. Also Paulina, beloved daughter
    of Paul and Margaret Jane Picken, died 30th August 1917 aged 19 years. Also the above
    named Paul Picken who died 15th May 1926 aged 88 years. Also Margaret J. Picken, wife
    of the above Paul Picken, died 11th September 1932. "He giveth his beloved sleep."
    Margaret J. Picken died 13th Nov. 1944 aged 80 years. A. McBain, Belfast.
        [Paul Picken was managing director of Larne Shipbuilding Company. He was elected a
    town commissioner in 1891 and retired from the Larne Urban District Council in 1912.
    See McKillop: *History of Larne*, p. 135.]

PINKERTON
    [Limestone panel inserted in concrete.] In memory of Wm. Pinkerton died 16th May
    1917. His wife Janet Pinkerton died 5th Sept. 1916. Their son Wm. J. Pinkerton died
    21st Sept. 1921, interred in Kimberley, South Africa. Their son David Pinkerton died

11th Oct. 1942. His daughter-in-law Jeanette Ferguson Pinkerton died 25th August 1949. His grandson David Ferguson Pinkerton died 9th February 1951.

PORTER

[White limestone, broken.] Sacred to the memory of Nathaniel Porter, who died June 22nd 1905 in his 76th year. Also his wife Agnes Porter, who died at Hove, February 4th 1923 in her 93rd year. "God is Good."

POTTER

[White marble "scroll" with concrete enclosure.] Erected by Rachel C. Potter in memory of her dearly beloved husband John Richard Potter, P.K., Irish Lights Service, who died 5th April 1902 aged 39 years. Also their son Douglas Copeland, who died 30th December 1903 aged 2 years. The above named Rachel C. Potter died 14th July 1933 aged 73 years. And their daughter Charlotte Victoria died 12th May 1940 aged 52 years. T. Holden.

POTTS

See McCORMICK

POWERS

[White limestone with lead lettering, in sandstone plinth.] Erected by Sarah Powers in loving memory of her husband James Powers, who died 2nd Augt. 1881 aged 52 years. Also her daughter Eliza Powers died 27th May 1869 aged 1 year and 7 months. And her daughter Sarah Powers died 16th January 1884 aged 7 years. And her grandchild Robert DAVIS, died 25th May 1880 aged 1 year. Holden, Larne.

RAINEY

[Yellow sandstone.] Erected by James Rainey of Ballymullock in memory of his beloved wife Isabella, who departed this life 25th Nov. 1868 aged 64 years. The above-named James Rainey, who died 6th Sep. 1880 aged 66 years.

RAINEY

See CRAWFORD

REA

[White limestone with lead lettering, lying in two pieces.] Erected by John Rea in memory of his father William Rea, who died 29th November 1893 aged 66 years. Also Thomas CARSON, who died 9th Octr. 1897 aged 21 years. Also his mother Sarah Rea, who died 3rd Nov. 1914 aged 84 years.

REA

[White limestone with lead lettering, facing north, on sandstone plinth.] Erected by Robert Rea in memory of his wife Mary Rea, who died 12th Decr. 1893 aged 39 years. Also his grandson Archie, who died 21st Aug. 1896 aged 33 years & 5 months. The above-named Robert Rea, who died 27th October 1899 aged 49 years. Also his son Robert Rea, who died 12th July 1900 aged 31 years.

[Probate of the will of Robert Rea, late of Croft Lane, Larne, county Antrim, carter, who died 27 October 1899, granted at Belfast 2 July 1900 to David McQuillan, merchant. Effects £69 . 10s.]

REA

[Lead lettering in white limestone.] Erected by William John Rea, in memory of his beloved wife Mary, who died 29th Novr. 1900, aged 29 years. T. Holden, Larne.

REA

[White limestone panel set in concrete headstone.] Erected by R. Rea in loving memory of his wife Maggie Rea, died 25th Dec. 1948 aged 65 years. The above R. Rea, died 22nd Feb. 1964 aged 87 years.

REA

See McKEE

REID

[Dark granite with enclosure.] In loving memory of William Reid, died 6th October 1901 aged 77 years. Also his wife Margaret GRANT died 27th May 1914 aged 87 years. William Reid, son of the above, born 12th Dec. 1856, entered into the higher life 22nd Oct. 1932. Also Frances, wife of the above William Reid, died 12th March 1940 aged 82 years. "I will left up mine eyes unto the hills." Margaret Grant LOWRY died 27th September 1951. Purdy & Millard.

REID

[Lead lettering on white limestone headstone, now broken.] Erected by James Reid in memory of his father Neil Reid, who died 27th April 1902 aged 47 years. Also his mother Martha Reid, who died 8th May 1924 aged 69 years. "Gone but not forgotten." T. Holden, Larne.

REID

See JAMIESON

REYNOLDS

See FULLERTON

RICE

See MOORE

RICHMOND

[White limestone in sandstone plinth.] Erected by Elizabeth and Thos. Richmond in memory of Henry Richmond who died 25th Decr. 1880 aged 34 years. Also his wife Jenny, who died 24th June 1876 aged 36 years. And their son Samuel, who died 12th Decr. 1904 aged 32 years. The above named Elizabeth Richmond died 14th Dec. 1918 aged 79 years.

ROBERTSON

[Sandstone.] Erected by John Robertson in memory of his beloved son James Robertson who died at Kilwaughter 14th November 1871 aged 31 years. Also his beloved brother Richard Robertson died at Belfast 4th November 1872 aged 34 years. Also the above named John Robertson died at .... 1877 aged (..) and his wife Eliza BRUNTON who died 5th March 188(.) aged 79 years.

[The will of Richard Robertson, formerly of Miller House, Donaghadee, county Down, and late of No. 21 Waring Street, Belfast, county Antrim, mercantile clerk, who died 4 November 1872 at Belfast aforesaid, was proved at Belfast 12 February 1873 by the oath of Margaret Robertson of No. 21 Waring Street, Belfast aforesaid, widow, the sole executor. Effects under £200.

The will of John Robertson, late of Kilwaughter, county Antrim, land steward, who died 2 August 1877 at same place, was proved at Belfast 7 September 1877 by the oath of Elizabeth Robertson of Kilwaughter, Larne, same county, widow, the sole executrix. Effects under £200.]

ROBINSON
    [Polished granite.] In loving memory of Martha Robinson, who died 9th January 1890, and her father Thomas Robinson, who died 11th July 1934. Also her mother Martha Robinson, who died 30th April 1943. Jane Drummond AXON died 22nd November 1961. William Robinson died 28th June 1963.

ROBINSON
    [Granite, polished on front face, with low concrete enclosure.] Erected by Robert Robinson in memory of his son Robert, who died 29th June 1894 aged 5? years. Mary the dearly loved wife of the above named Robert Robinson, died 28th August 1952 in her 87th year. His son James died 26th October 1955 aged 58 years. The above Robert Robinson died 22nd December 1955 aged 93 years. His daughter Jeannie died 5th Dec. 1979. Martha died 9th April 1987. His son Robert died 23rd December 1989. T. Holden.

ROBINSON
    [White limestone with lead lettering, within low railings.] Erected by Daniel Robinson in memory of his beloved daughter Mary Ann, who died 29th September 1895 aged 5 years. Also his son Archibald, who died 27th Sept. 1896 aged 8 days. Also his wife Lena Robinson, who died 30th March 1912 aged 48 years. Also his mother Mary Robinson, who died 23rd Augt. 1907 aged 80 years. The above-named Daniel Robinson died 17th Dec. 1927 aged 73 years. And his son William John Orr Robinson, lost with H.M.S. "Princess Victoria" 18th May 1940 aged 53 years. And his son James Orr Robinson, died 13th Dec. 1944 aged 53 years. And his son Archie Robinson died 6th Aug. 1967 aged 69 years.

ROBINSON
    [Lead lettering in white limestone.] Erected in memory of James Robinson, who died 9th October 1912 aged 93 years. T. Holden, Larne.

ROBINSON
    [Lead lettering on white limestone panel in concrete headstone.] Erected by Fanny Robinson in memory of her husband Thomas, who died 24th March 1930. The above Fanny Robinson who died 14th February 1950.

ROBINSON
    See AUSTIN

ROSS
    [White limestone headstone with lead lettering standing in front of sandstone recessed in boundary wall. The sandstone has the same inscription except for the motto which reads "Gone, but not lost."] In loving memory of John Ross died 15th December 1882 aged 56 years. Arthur Ryder Ross died 9th August 1873 aged 3 months. Hugh Percival Ross died 15th September 1882 aged 7 years. Ethel Catherine Ross died 29th Jany. 1908 aged 31 years. "Not lost but gone before."

[Letters of administration of the personal estate of John Ross, late of Birch Hill, county Antrim, esquire, who died 15 December 1882 at same place, were granted at the Principal Registry 19 February 1883 to Catherine Georgina Ross of Birch Hill, the widow. Effects £3,283 . 17s. 2d.]

RUSSELL
[White limestone with lead lettering, now in three pieces.] Erected by Jane Russell in loving memory of her husband Thomas Roy, who died at Glengormley on 23rd July 1889 aged 25 years.

SAUNDERSON
[Granite, tilting.] Erected by William Saunderson in memory of her mother Margaret Saunderson who died 21st October 1886 aged 67 years.

SAUNDERSON
[White limestone with lead lettering.] Erected by Grace Saunderson in memory of her husband John Saunderson who died 30th Sep. 1910. Also her son Samuel, who died 8th Oct. 1903 aged 10 years. The above named Grace Saunderson died 12th March 1928 aged 68 years. Also their son John died 8th January 1954 aged 65 years. Also their daughter Martha died 6th March 1958 aged 66 years.

SAVAGE
See COBAIN

SEMPLE
[Sandstone decorated with square and compass.] Erected by James Semple in memory of his bel(oved) wife Sarah, who died 8th (S.......r) 1876 aged 56 years. Al(so) his daughter Martha, who died 12th Jany. 1871 aged 24 years. The above n(a)m(ed) James Semple died 12th June 1892 aged 70 years. Also their son James Semple, who died 20th April 1901 aged 46 years and his son (J)ames who died 2nd Decr. 1900 aged 19 years. Also his wife Jane Semple, who died 4th July 1919 aged 65 years.
[Letters of administration of the personal estate of James Semple, late of 110 Lindsay Street, Belfast, labourer, who died 12 June 1892 at the Royal Hospital, Belfast, were granted at Belfast 13 July 1892 to James Semple of Larne, county Antrim, stone mason. a son. Effects £32.]

SEMPLE
[Red sandstone obelisk decorated with palette and brushes in high relief.] Erected by a few friends in memory of Thomas Semple, artist, who died at Larne 18th Dec. 1874 aged 33 years.
[Nothing is known of the young painter Thomas Semple (1841-74) except that he practised in Larne for many years and was the son of another obscure artist, likewise Thomas Semple, who worked at little May Street and Corporation Street, Belfast, as a marine painter, gilder and picture frame maker between 1854 and 1870. To compound the mystery, it seems possible that there was a family link to another artist of the same surname – Joseph Semple – a Belfast painter of ship portraits, active in the town between 1863 and 1878. Only one work by Thomas Semple is known, namely an urban scene entitled *The late William Doughtertys Fowl Stores*, painted in 1869 and owned by the Ulster Museum. Whether the picture is by the elder Thomas Semple or the younger remains unclear; however, the fact that Doughterty's fowl stores were at 52-56 May Street, Belfast, suggests that the work is by Semple the elder. Examples of ship portraits by Joseph

Semple can be seen in Belfast Harbour Office. The standard of the works by the Semples indicate that they received little formal training before pursuing careers in art. (Dr. Eileen Black, Curator of Fine Art, Ulster Museum: personal communication.)]

SEMPLE
See WALKER

SHEPHERD
[White limestone in sandstone frame decoraed in high relief with Agnus Dei, an open book, and a dove bearing a leaf.] Erected by the Orangemen of Larne and vicinity in memory of Br. James Shepherd who departed this life 4th May 1874 at the early age of 28 years: much and deservedly esteemed by all who knew him. "The Lord Jehovah was his strength and his song; He is also become his salvation." Isaiah. Chp. XII.2. Jenkins, Larne.

SIMMS
[Lead lettering on white limestone within low railings.] Erected by William J. Simms in loving memory of his son James, who died 12th Novr. 1899 aged 21 years.

SIMMS
[Polished granite.] In loving memory of Robert Simms 1860-1945, Annie Simms 1866-1950, Jemima MacPHERSON 1864-1958, Letitia Simms (nee McCOUBREY) 1888-1949, William John Simms 1890-1968, Jean Simms 1907-1987. "Until the day break."

SIMPSON
See MAGEE

SLOAN
[Standard M.O.D. gravestone with regimental badge carved at top.] 18781 – Corporal S.F. Sloan. Royal Irish Rifles. 25th October 1918 aged 23. "Christ died for the ungodly." Romans 5.-6th. Mother: Sarah Sloan died 18th July 1898. Father: Samuel G. Sloan died 6th May 1929.

SMILEY
[Polished granite monument surmounted by urn, with iron railings.] Erected by Capt. Samuel Smiley in loving memory of his daughters, Jennie Louise died 1888 aged 17 months. Mary Isabel died 1894 aged 15 years. Also his son Samuel Thomas, Navigt. Lieut., who was killed by the torpedoing of H.M.S. Arabis in the North Sea on 11th Feb. 1916, aged 35 years. Above named Samuel Smiley died 12th June 1925 aged 81 years. Also his wife Jennie Smiley died 21st January 1926 aged 77 years. Their son Robert died 28th Jan. 1954 aged 80 years. Their daughter Elizabeth A. died 20th April 1954 aged 78 years. And their son David N. died at California, U.S.A., 29th August 1944. Jenkins.

SMILEY
See BOWMAN, COEY, CRAWFORD, ENGLISH and HOWDEN

SMITHIES
[Lead lettering in white limestone, fallen forward.] Emma, the beloved daughter of Thomas and Alice Smithies of Middleton, died 29th August 1899 aged 24 years.

SMYTH

[Lead lettering on white limestone, fallen and broken.] (E)rected by William S(m)yth in memory of his son Robert, who died 18th D(ecr.) 1879 aged 14 years. Also his son William, who died 18th April 1890 aged 13 years. Also his beloved wife Jane Smyth, who died 29th Oct. 1911 aged 74 years. Also the above-named William Smyth, who died 22nd Feb. 1913 aged 77 years. "Be ye also ready." Also his son John Smyth, who died 3rd August 1935 aged 74 years. Also his daughter Sarah Smyth died 2nd Nov. 1957 aged 76 years.

SMYTH

See JOHNSTON and TOWELL

SNODDY

[Lead lettering in white limestone.] Erected by James Snoddy in memory of his daughter Maggie, who died 4th April 1902 aged 21 years. The above-named James Snoddy died 29th November 1914 aged 74 years.

SPEERS

[Inscriptions of lead lettering on four panels of white limestone on four sides of concrete enclosure.] Robert Speers died 19th Jan. 1905 aged 62 years. Anna Speers died 17th Dec. 1913 aged 69 years. Anna Maria, wife of W.E. Speers, died 9th Jan. 1920 aged 44 years. The above W. E. Speers died 17th June 1946. Marian ELDERS died 2nd Jan. 1911 aged 91 years.

STEENSON

[White limestone, badly broken.] Erected by Agnes Steenson in memory of her daughter Eliza Jane, who died 6th August 1890 aged 20 years. Also her son William, who died 6th March 1902 aged 26 years. The above Agnes Steenson died 9th Feb. 1939 aged 96 years.

STEENSON

[Lead lettering in white limestone headstone.] Erected by William Steenson in loving memory of his daughter Maggie, who died 19th October 1901 aged 5 years. His son Robert died 24th Feb. 1915 aged 36 years. His grandson Robert died 18th June 1913 aged 2 years. The above-named William Steenson died 8th Nov. 1918 aged 74 years. Also his daughter Elizabeth Barr, who died 28th April 1920 aged 36 years. Also Isabella, wife of the above named William Steenson, died 7th Dec. 1932. Also his son John, who died 6th January 1939. His wife Bessie Steenson died 21st April 1980. Isaiah Ch. 53. T. Holden.

STEWART

[Granite headstone and enclosure.] Erected by Alexander Stewart in memory of his mother Margaret Stewart, who departed this life 8th February 1869. Also in memory of his father Hamilton Stewart, who was interred in Belfast City Cemetery. The above named Alexander Stewart, who departed this life 15th Aug. 1941 aged 82 years.

STRANGE

[Lead lettering in white limestone.] Erected by Andrew Strange, Larne, in loving memory of his sons, Robert who died 26th May 1895 aged 19 years, and William who died 7th July 1900 aged 27 years. Also his wife Sarah who died 16th Nov. 1912 aged 63 years. The above-named Andrew Strange died 25th Jan. 1922 aged 74.

[Administration of the estate of William Strange, late of Main Street, Larne, county Antrim, clerk, who died 7 July 1900, granted at Belfast 10 September 1900 to Andrew Strange, shopkeeper. Effects £269.]

STRAWHORN

[White limestone, lead lettering, sandstone plinth.] Erected by Agnes Strawhorn in memory of her beloved husband Thomas Strawhorn, who died 13th May 1883 aged 53 years.

STREIGHT

[White limestone panel in sandstone.] Erected by Jane Streight in memory of her beloved husband James Streight, who died 15th Feby. 1880 aged 27 years. A. Jenkins.

STREIGHT

[Tall granite headstone.] In loving memory of William Streight who departed this life 19th December 1916 aged 69 years. Also his wife Mary E. Streight, who died 2nd April 1926 aged 78 years. Their son Samuel M. who died 2nd Feb. 1927, interred in Edmonton, Canada. Also their son Thomas John, died 27th June 1962 aged 73 years. And his wife Mary Moore Streight, died 11th Dec. 1975 aged 85 years. Erected by his wife Mary E. Streight. T. Holden.

TATE

[White limestone with lead lettering in concrete enclosure, fallen.] Erected by Joseph Tate in loving memory of his family.

TAYLOR

[White limestone headstone and enclosure.] Isabella Taylor, in loving memory of her husband John H. Taylor, who died 25th Octr. 1901. Also George HUNTER, beloved husband of Winifred Hunter, died 1st December 1946. "Peace Perfect Peace." A. Jenkins.

TEARE

[Lead lettering on white limestone panel set into sandstone. A marble anchor is inset on the entablature. Iron railings.] Erected to the memory of Edward Teare who departed this life 2nd Octr. 1881 aged 63 years. Also Sarah, his wife who departed this life 13th Jany. 1905 aged 76 years. A. Jenkins.
[The will of Edward Teare, late of Larne, county Antrim, grocer, who died 2 October 1881 at same place, was proved at Belfast 29 March 1882 by Sarah Teare of Larne, widow, the sole executrix. Effects £895.]

THOMPSON

[Sandstone decorated in high relief with flying dove holding a branch.] In loving memory of Isabella CURRIE, wife of the late John Thompson, died 25th October 1880 aged 64 years. Also Sara Currie died 8th Octr. 1893 aged 80 years.

THOMPSON

[White limestone with lead lettering held in concrete.] Erected to the memory of his father Robert Thompson, who departed this life 23rd Nov. 1878, who was interred in Carnmoney. And his mother Mary Thompson, who departed this life 5th April 1895. And his daughter Ruth, wife of John T. BARTON, who departed this life 12th Dec. 1924. And my wife Margaret Barton, who passed away 25th Jany. 1937 aged 73 years.

"Was with us as one who served." Robert Thompson, son of the above, who died 17th Dec. 1949 aged 86 years. And his daughter Margaret C. BARBOUR died 13th March 1955.

[Death: August 12th, at her residence, Ballymena Road, Larne, Magaret, beloved wife of George Barton, aged 39 years. *Larne Weekly Reporter*, 20 Aug. 1881.

Marriage: January 20, at the Medodist Church, Larne, by Rev. Richard Cole, Robert, youngest son of the late Robert Thompson, Larne, to Maggie, eldest daughter of George Barton, Larne. *Larne Weekly Reporter*, 27 Jan. 1883.]

TODD

[White limestone.] Erected by James Todd in memory of his son Robert aged 11 years, and his daughter Martha aged 7 years, and his son John who died infancy. And his wife Margaret Todd died 5th July 1909 aged 81 years. The above-named James Todd died 8th Octr. 1918 aged 85 years. Also his beloved daughter Elizabeth Todd died 2nd Sept. 1936. "Gone but not forgotten."

TOPPING

[Polished granite.] In memory of Gardener Topping, died 14th August 1928 aged 69 years. Also his wife Margaret who died 4th Dec. 1957 in her 87th year.

TOWELL

[Square pillar of polished granite surmounted by an urn. Front face] Erected by David Towell of Dublin in loving memory of his daughters, Isabella Carson died in infancy 1880, Margaret Hawthorne died 1886 aged 8? years. Also his son Jackson Sinclair, as result of an accident on board S.S. "Crown of Castile", 23rd July 1910 aged 22 years.

[Left side] David Towell, J.P., loved husband of Isabella Carson Towell, died 25th November 1920 aged 73 years. Also the above named Isabella Carson Towell died 19th November 1926 aged 76 years. Also their daughter Jane Carson Towell R.R.C who died 26th July 1952 aged 70.

TOWELL

[White limestone with lead lettering.] Erected by Edward Towell in memory of his beloved daughter Susan, who died (8)th May 1897 aged 5 years. Also his wife Mary, who died 27th Feb. 1926 aged 66 years. The abovenamed Edward Towell, who died 1st May 1932 aged 67 years. Also his stepdaughter Mary C. SMYTH who died 6th July 1970 aged 79 years. A loved one sleeping.

TURNER

See DONAGHY

VETTERS

See MULHOLLAND

WALKER

See McMANUS

WALLACE

In memory of Lizzie Wallace, who died March 14 1893. Erected by her brother and sister. "Prepare to meet thy God." Jenkins.

WAUGH
[Lead lettering on white limestone with concrete enclosure.] Erected by Annie B. MAYNE in memory of her mother Ellen Waugh, who died 8th August 1903. Her father Robert Waugh, who died 4th March 1929. Also her children Thomas T. Mayne, who died 11th May 1906, and Ellen Waugh Mayne, who died 20th May 1907. And her son James Mayne, who was drowned in "Princess Victoria" disaster, 31st January 1953, and her husband Thomas Mayne, who died 14th May 1958. The above Annie B. Mayne who died 6th Sept. 1958.

WE(BB)
See GILMORE

WHARRY
[Very similiar to Hugh Campbell, but cross is broken off.] Maggie Wharry, died March 30 1893.

WHITE
See MONTGOMERY

WILLIAMS
[White limestone cross (now broken) and enclosure.] In loving memory of my father Alexander Williams J.P., born at Armagh 24th May 1827, died at Larne 4th August 1899. And of my little son Alexander Ernest Williams, who died 23rd Feby. 1901 aged 11? months. "Until the day break & the shadows flee away." Erected by W. W. Williams. Also my mother Annie Williams, who died 1st April 1924.
    [Probate of the will of Alexander Williams, late of Larne, county Antrim, J.P., who died 4 August 1899, granted at Dublin 12 September 1899 to Annie Williams of Larne, widow. Effects £3,299 . 17s. 11d.]

WILLIAMS
See McKAY

WILSON
See MOORE

WOODS
See GIRVAN

WOODSIDE/CRAWFORD
[No inscription except the two surnames on the headstone.]

WORKMAN
[Sandstone.] Erected by Isabella MAGILL in loving memory of her mother Mary Workman who died 21st March 1893 aged 64 years. Also her father Samuel Crawford who died 13th September 1897 aged 75 years. The above Isabella Magill died 14th Dec. 1946 aged 89 years.

WRIGHT
[Lead lettering on granite.] In remembrance of Susan Wright, who died 11th January 1897. Also her mother Mary E. Wright, who died 11th January 1946. And her father Thomas Wright, died 1st Feb. 1954.

WRIGHT
[White limestone with lead lettering and low concrete enclosure.] Sacred to the memory of Charles Wright, who died 4th March 1899 aged 72 years. Also his wife Mary Wright, who died 25th Decr. 1899 aged 78 years. Also their daughter Mary KIRKPATRICK, born 27th Dec. 1859, died 19th May 1938. And his niece Annie KELLY, who died 18th Dec. 1944. And William Kirkpatrick, husband of the above Mary Kirkpatrick, died 6th Sept. 1948 aged 82 years.

WRIGHT
[Lead lettering on white limestone panel inset on concrete headstone.] Erected by John Wright in memory of his wife Ellen, who died 5th Dec. 1928 and his children Charles, Crawford, & David, who died in infancy. And his son Crawford, who died 27th May 1967. Also his son Robert (Fergie) who died 7th Dec. 1969. Agnes, wife of Robert (Fergie), who died 4th Dec. 1991. Loved and remembered.

WYLIE
See McNEILL

YOUNG
See HOOKINGS

LARNE, McGAREL CEMETERY

Roman Catholic Section

AGNEW

[Limestone headstone decorated with sacred heart.] Erected by Mary McCAULEY, in loving memory of her grand-father Isaac Agnew, who died 2nd March 1871 aged 66 years. Her grand-mother Martha Agnew who died 3rd March 1897 aged 80 years. Also her dear mother Margaret Agnew died 15th March 1925 aged 75 years. Also her aunts and uncles. R.I.P.

BAINES

[Sandstone headstone with limestone panel inset, finial broken.] Erected by Philip Baines in memory of his beloved wife Mary who departed this life 26 June 187(4) aged 26 years. Also his two infant sons John died 24 June 1873, William John died 15 Aug. 1874. Requiescant in pace.

BLACK

[Polished granite headstone with concrete enclosure.] Erected by Rose Black in memory of her father and mother, brother and sister. Rose Black DUNNE died 6th Jan. 1962. R.I.P.

BOYLE

[Small fragment of headstone.] Erected by Francis Boyle, in loving memory of his son James, who died 23rd Aug. 1895 aged 3? years. Suffer little children to come unto me.

BUNTING

[Broken limestone statue and enclosure.] Saint Teresa of the child Jesus pray for the eternal happiness of Mary Ann Bunting who died 19th January 1892. Also her husband Samuel Bunting who died 21st May 1925. The little flower, pray for them.

CAMPBELL

[Limestone headstone with railed enclosure against north wall.] Erected by William Campbell in memory of his wife Ann Campbell, who died 2nd Sept. 1897, aged 45 years. R.I.P.

CAMPBELL

[Broken cross.] In memory of Hannah Campbell died March 1921. R.I.P.

CAMPBELL

See McLEOD

CAULFIELD

[Limestone headstone.] In loving memory of Anne Caulfield who died 2nd Augt. 1891 aged 82 years. Erected by her daughter. R.I.P.

COUPE

See KIVLIN

CROSSEY
[Polished granite headstone in railed enclosure.] Erected by Neal Crossey, in loving memory of his father who died 29th April 1877. His mother who died 12th July 1901. Also his dearly beloved niece Jeannie Magdalene O'BOYLE who died 9th Novr. 1912 aged 18? years. The above named Neal Crossey died 29th May 1944. His wife Margaret Teresa died 24th April 1953. On whose souls sweet Jesus, have mercy. Jenkins.

DALLAT
[Sandstone headstone enclosure.] Sacred to the memory of Ellen, the beloved wife of Christopher Dallat; she departed this life 9th Feby. 1883 aged 22 years. Also the above named Christopher Dallat; he departed this life 20th Feb. 1925 aged 71 years. Requiescant in pace – Amen. A. Jenkins.

DONAGHY
[Limestone Celtic cross in sandstone enclosure.] In loving memory of Michael Donaghy who died 1890. His wife Mary Donaghy who died 1896. Their grand-daughter Dora SHAW died 15th April 1910 aged 5 years. Also Francis Shaw who died 2nd Jany. 1912 aged 57 years. His son Francis Shaw who died 2nd Jany 1912, aged 57 years. His son Francis died in infancy. His son John who died 4th Augt. 1917 aged 37 years. Also his son Michael James Shaw who died at New York, U.S.A., 20th March 1927 aged 42 years. Mary, beloved wife of Francis Shaw who died 27th June 1931. On whose souls, sweet Jesus, have mercy.

DONAGHY
[Cross of white limestone, fallen and broken.] I.H.S. In loving memeory of William John Donaghy who died 29 March 1903 aged 53 years. Also his son Michael who was drowned at Belboa 7 March 1901 aged 23 years. Also his beloved wife Mary Ann Donaghy who died 12th March 1923 aged 81 years. "On whose souls, sweet Jesus, have mercy."

DUFFIN
[Limestone headstone.] Erected by Hugh Duffin in loving memory of his mother Ellen Duffin, who died 28th Dec. 1899 aged 81 years, the above Hugh Duffin, died 23rd May 1902. R.I.P.

DUFFIN
[Broken sandstone headstone.] Erected in memory of James Duffin who died 4th March, 1892 aged 57 years.

DUFFIN
O sacred heart of Jesus have mercy on the soul of Margaret Duffin who died 20th June 1942. And her husband Augustus Joseph Duffin who died 31st July 1947 aged 72 years.

DUNNE
See BLACK

FULTON
[Grey fossiliferous limestone decorated with sacred heart and broken cross on top.] In memory of Rose Fulton died 1st June 1906. James Fulton died 3rd July 1918. Rose Jane STURGES, *Regina Sask*, died 24th Dec. 1927. R.I.P. Walsh & Co., B'mena.

FULTON
[Polished granite headstone.] John died 20-10-43. Margaret 3-10-51. Their son John and three great grand children who died in infancy. R.I.P.

GARTLAN
[Granite cross in sandstone enclosure against south wall.] I.H.S. In memory of Elizabeth, the beloved wife of John Gartlan, died 26th May 1891 aged 70 years. Their nephew James Gartlan died 9th June 1889 aged 30 years. Requiescant in pace. "My Jesus mercy."

GARVEY
[Wheeled cross of white limestone, now tumbled, in a sandstone enclosure. The epithaph is on the base in lead lettering.] In memoriam Bernard Garvey who died 21st March 1891 aged 42 years. His daughter Margt. Christina who died in infancy. Also his wife Annie Garvey who died 5th March 1915 aged 59 years. Also their son John who died in New York, U.S.A., 18th April 1912 aged 33 years. Also their son Henry who died 21st Nov. 1918 aged 27 years. Also their daughter Emily who died 11th Dec. 1919 aged 35 years. Also their son Francis J. who died 4th Feb. 1922 aged 32 years. Also Bernard Garvey who died in U.S.A. 11th April 1947. "Requiescant in pace." A. Jenkins.
[Letters of administration of the personal estate of Bernard Garvey, late of Mill Street, Larne, county Antrim, spirit merchant, who died 21 March 1891 at same place, were granted at Belfast 29 May 1891 to Annie Garvey of Mill Street, the widow. Effects £770 . 7s.
Death: Aug. 8, at Mill Street – Margaret Christina, infant daughter of Annie and Bernard Garvey – funeral at 3 p.m. to-day (Saturday) in the McGarel Cemetery. *The Larne Reporter*, 9 Aug. 1890.]
Death: Mar. 21, at his residence, Mill Street, Larne, Bernard Garvey ... interment in the McGarel Cemetery Sunday 3 o'clock. R.I.P. *The Larne Reporter*, 21 Mar. 1891.]

GRAHAM
[Sandstone headstone.] I.H.S. In memory of Robert Graham, who died 11th Augt. 1887 aged 48 years. Also his grand-child, Rose Graham, who died 5th May 1892 aged 11 years. And his wife Rose Graham, who died 24th May 1904 aged 76 years. Also his son Robert Graham, who died, 24th May, 1904 aged 76 years. Also his son Robert Graham, who died 9th May 1931 aged 74 years. Also his wife Ellen Graham, died 23rd Sept. 1940 aged 83 years.

GRIBBEN
[Lead lettering in white limestone.] Erected by William Gribben in memory of his father William Gribben who died 18th Sept. 1906 aged 61 years. Also his mother Elizabeth Gribben who died 16th Octr. 1905 aged [blank] years. Also his sister Celia McDONALD who died 8th July 1902 aged [blank] years. R.I.P.

HAWKINS
[Sandstone headstone.] In memory of Cecilia Hawkins, who died 2nd August 1879, R.I.P., aged 70 years. Also her grand-daughter Alice M. Hawkins, who died 14th July 1907 aged 21 years.

HEANEN
[Small sandstone lying loose.] Erected by Mary Ann Heanen in memory of her son Daniel who died 1st Jan. 1873 aged 18 years. Her daughter Sarah Jane died 1st March 1887 aged 21 years. And her infant. And her grand-son John.

HOOPER
[Small headstone of white limestone with concrete enclosure.] Erected by Eliza Hooper in memory of her child Alice Maud who died 3rd Feby. 1901 aged 1 year. The above Eliza Hooper died 26 March 1946 aged 77 years. I.H.S.

JENKINS
[Sandstone headstone in a railed enclosure.] In memory of Thomas Jenkins born 2nd March 1811 died 16th July 1877. Also his wife Margaret Jenkins, who died 29th Oct. 1892 aged 77 years.

JENKINS
[Broken granite pillar enclosed by iron railings against south wall.] Dear wee Tom, died 11th Aug. 1894 aged 11? years and his brother Alexr. died 12th April 1888 aged 5? years. Their mother died 16th July 1914. their father died 17th March 1916.

KANE
[Polished granite headstone stone enclosure.] In loving memory of William Kane died 1st Septembr 1897. His wife Mary Anne, died 17 June 1938. Their daughters Katherine, died 21st July 1904. Susan, died 31st March 1909, and their son James, died 30th September 1925, and their daughter Elizabeth, died 19th Jan. 1959. R.I.P.

KEENAN
[Granite cross in rail enclosure.] I.H.S. In loving memory of James Keenan, who died 29th Jan. 1927. His father Henry, died 26th Dec. 1869. His mother Mary Ann, died 2nd Sep. 1878. His six children died in infancy. Also his brother Henry, died 13th May 1909. Also Jinnie, wife of above James Keenan died 14th March 1931. Eternal rest grant to them O Lord. R.I.P.

KEL...
[Worn sandstone headstone.] Erected by Henry Kel(... in) memory of his son ....ard, ... died 9th April 1873 ...... months.

KENNEDY
[Sandstone headstone in a railed enclosure.] Erected by Patrick Kennedy in memory of his brother Bernard who departed this life 17th Jan. 1874 aged 28 years.

KIVLIN
[Small limestone headstone.] Erected by Fred COUPE, in memory of his mother-in-law Bessie Kivlin who died 11th Oct. 1898 aged 78 years. R.I.P.

LAIRD
[Limestone headstone, cross broken off top.] Erected by William in loving memory of his mother Anne Laird, who died 23rd Sept. 1898 aged 84 years.

LEGG
See McNEILL

McALISTER
[Limestone headstone surmounted by Celtic cross showing Christ at centre and shamrocks in the arms, in a granite enclosure.] Erected by John McAlister in memory of his wife, Mary who departed this life 23rd April 1905. Also his daughter Annie who

departed this life 24th May 1891 and his children who died in infancy. Also the above named John McAlister who departed this life 11th Sept. 1915. Sacred Heart of Jesus have mercy on them. O'Neill & Co., Belfast.

McANALLY
   See TRAYNOR

McAULAY
   [Limestone headstone and enclosure, decorated with sacred heart.] In memory of Capt. Alexr. McAulay who died June 14, 1892 aged 72 years. Also his daughter Sarah who died Augt. 14, 1873 aged 7 years. His son John died at Rio De Janeiro March 24, 1873 aged 24 years. His son James died at sea Decr. 28 1881 aged 25 years. His son Patrick died April 23rd 1894 aged 37 years. His son Alexander died July 11, 1906 aged 56 years. Also an infant son of William. Also his wife Mary McAulay who died Oct. 17, 1923 aged 99 years. His son Francis Henry died at Auckland, New Zealand, 6th June 1925 aged 52 years. Neal died 16th Oct. 1936 William died 3rd Aug. 1937. Catherine died 9th Nov. 1947. Agnes died 5th Feby. 1956. R.I.P.

MACAULAY
   See NOUGHER

McBRIDE
   [Limestone headstone with enclosure.] Erected by Henry McBride R.I.C. in memory of his beloved wife Rose who died 25th Sept. 1892, aged 36 years. R.I.P.

McCAULEY
   [Limestone headstone in railed enclosure.] Erected by Samuel McCauley in memory of his youngest daughter Sarah Alexander (Cissie) who died on the 2nd Septembr 1892 aged 4 years and 7 months. Also his beloved wife Jeanie who died 1st August 1923 aged 71 years and was interred in Elmwood Cemetery, Winnipeg.

McCAULEY
   See AGNEW

McCAY
   [Polished granite headstone with iron railings.] In loving memory of Charles McCay born 12th June 1832, died 8th April 1906. Also his children John aged 4 years, Ellen aged 2 years, Charlotte aged 7 months, Martha Helen aged 4 years, and Charlotte Helen aged 14 years. Also his wife Hannah McCay born 29th June 1829, died 5th October 1912. Also his daughter Catherine McCay died 22nd September 1937. "May they rest in peace."

McCLARNON
   [Heavy sandstone.] Erected by John McClarnon in memory of his wife Ellen who died 26th Feb. 1882 aged 32 years. The above-named John McClarnon who died 17th Sept. 1918.

McCLEAN
   [Polished granite headstone, now smashed.] Erected by (Mar)garet McClean ....y of her parents ....d Nellie McClean. ....argaret McClean died 22nd Nov. 1968. R.I.P.

McCORMICK

[Sandstone, now fallen and broken into three pieces.] I.H.S. Erected by Duncan McCormick in memory of his father Charles McCormick died 11th Sept.1880 aged 57 years. Also his mother Ellen McCormick who died 14th Oct. 1901 aged 72 years. Also his brother William John who died 6th March 1921 aged 61 years. Also his sister Catherine O'NEILL died Dec. 1930. The above Duncan McCormick died 29 Sept. 1944. R.I.P.

McCORMICK

[Polished granite, fallen, with concrete enclosure.] Erected by John McCormick in memory of his mother Jane McCormick died 3 March 1919 aged 82. His brother Denis McCormick died 21 Jan. 1891 aged 26. His neice Jane McCormick died 16 Nov. 1897 aged 18. His sister-in-law Rose McCormick died 8 Jan. 1904 aged 41. John Henry McCormick died 9 July 1920 aged 9. His sister Mary O'NEILL died 22 Oct. 1924 aged 50. The above John McCormick died 28 Nov. 1943 aged 78. R.I.P.

McDONALD

[Polished granite headstone, with chalice, wafer and sacred heart, surmounted by a cross, in an enclosure.] Of your charity pray for the soul of Very Rev. Thomas J. McDonald, P.P., V.F., Larne, who was parish priest of this parish for nine years. He died on 26th March 1937. Dear Lord Jesus grant him eternal rest. "I beseech you, brethen, that you help me in your prayers for me to God." Romans XV, 30. Corr, Dungannon.

[He was ordained 8th October 1899 and served as Adm. of St. Peter's Belfast before coming to Larne.]

McDONALD

See GRIBBEN

McGOOKIN

[Limestone headstone with top broken and a granite surround.] Erected by Henry McGookin in memory of his daughter Alice who died 27th Sept. 1890 aged 1 year. Also his daughter Nellie who died 16th August 1922 aged 19 years. Also his son Thomas who died 14th May 1923 aged 23 years. The above Henry McGookin who died 2nd March 1930. Also his son James who died 2nd December 1965. R.I.P.

McGUGI(N)

See QUINN.

McHENRY

[Sandstone headstone.] I.H.S. Erected by Ann McHenry in memory of her husband John McHenry who died 17th October 1873 aged (.......rs.)

McILHERON

[Limestone headstone.] Sacred to the memory of Alexander McIlheron who died on the 1st June 1873, aged 73 years.

McILRATH

[Lead lettering on base of white limestone cross, now fallen.] In memory of James McIlrath died 6th Dec. 1940 aged 73 years. R.I.P.

McKAY
[Limestone headstone.] Erected by Michael McKay, in memory of his mother, Isabella McKay, who died 24th March 1899 aged 78 years. R.I.P.

McKEOWN
Erected in memory of Thomas McKeown died 7 March 1922. Also his wife Rose died 16 Oct. 1919. And their son Robert died in infancy. Also their son Patrick died 5 Nov. 1947. And their grandson Thomas McKeown died 26 Jan. 1929, infant son of Robert and Jane McKeown. And their daughter Ellen died 18th January 1954. On their souls, sweet Jesus, have mercy.

McKINTY
[Limestone headstone with a concrete enclosure.] In loving memory of Patrick McKinty who died 23rd December 1900 and his wife Margaret who died 7th January 1907. Also of their sons Patrick who died 15th March 1906, John who died 24th February 1917, Thomas who died 13th July 1926. R.I.P. Sacred Heart of Jesus Have Mercy on them.

McLARNON
[Lead lettering in white limestone with a concrete enclosure.] Erected by James McLarnon in memory of his son Thomas who died 29th Dec. 1904 aged 19 years. Also his son William who died in New Jersey, U.S.A., 5th Jany. 1927 aged 33 years. The above-named James McLarnon died 4th June 1931 aged 98 years. Also his wife Mary died 22nd May 1941 aged 91 years. His son Frank who died in New Jersey, U.S.A., 4th Oct. 1958. Also his son Robert who died 1st Jan. 1961.

McLEOD
[Broken and lying loose.] In memory of William McLeod, Cushendun, who died 9th July 1891 aged 70 years. Also his grand-daughter Mary RAMSEY who died 15th July 1917 aged 35 years. Also his daughter Mary CAMPBELL died July 1932. And her sons Patrick and Francis. On whose soul ....

McMANUS
Erected by Alexr. McManus in memory of his wife Agnes who died 6th June 1939 aged 53 years. Also their daughter Elenor died Oct. 1911 aged 2 years. The above Alexander McManus died 28th May 1955 aged 73 years.

McNALLY
[Limestone headstone, with broken top.] Erected by Sarah McNally, in memory of her husband Hugh McNally who died 10th Jany. 1900 aged 56 years. The above-named Sarah McNally died 1st July 1903 aged 58 years. Also their son Charles killed in action 18th July 1916, interred in France. Also their son Patrick J. who died 1st July 1925, aged 50 years. R.I.P.

McNEILL
[Granite headstone in railed enclosure.] In memoriam, Alexander McNeill, who died 29th Augt. 1874 aged 80 years. Also his wife Ann McNeill, who died 30th May 1897 aged 95 years. Their son Daniel who died 28th Augt. 1900 aged 74 years. Their son Henry who died 11th March 1904 aged 68 years. Also Bernard LEGG, who died 8th Novr 1908 aged 79 years. Also his wife Ann Legg, who died 14th February, 1929 aged 95 years. Requiescant in pace. Jenkins.

[Administration of the estate of Daniel McNeill, late of Larne, county Antrim, farm steward, who died 28 August 1900, granted at Belfast 19 October 1900 to Mary McNeill, the widow. Effects £96 . 11s.]

MAXWELL

[Lead lettering on tall limestone headstone, leaning steeply in concrete enclosure.] Erected by Catherine Maxwell in memory of her beloved son Adam, who died 22nd October 1894 aged 24 years. Also her beloved daughter Elizabeth Ann who died 9th September 1895 aged 20 years. Also her grandson who died in infancy. Also her dearly beloved husband Hugh Maxwell who died 15th August 1909 aged 77 years.

MURPHY

[Large statue against wall in railed enclosure.] I am the immaculate conception. Our Lady of Lourdes pray for them. Erected in loving memory of John Murphy who died 17th Feby. 1914. Also his dearly beloved wife Mary, who died 13th Jany. 1898. Their sons Joseph who died 23rd Jany. 1896, John died 9th March 1900, James who died in infancy. Their daughters Katherine died 9th Augt. 1907, Minnie died 29th Sept. 1921, Martha died 3rd July 1928. "O Jesus through thy sweet mother have mercy on them."

NOUGHER

[Small limestone, broken at top.] In memoriam Thomas Nougher who died 8 Decr. 1891. For 27 years the coachman and faithful friend of John MACAULAY, Red Hall, by whom this is erected.

[The will (with one codicil) of Thomas Nougher, late of Main Street, Larne, county Antrim, coachman, who died 8 December 1891 at same place, was proved at Belfast 13 January 1892 by the Reverend Francis Cornelius Henry of Larne, R.C.C., one of the executors. Effects £600 . 4s. 2d.]

O'BOYLE

See CROSSEY

O'NEILL

[Granite headstone and enclosure.] Of your charity pray for the souls of Philip O'Neill who died 1st Jan. 1922, Nora O'Neill who died 11th Aug. 18(9)9, Eileen Mary O'Neill who died 30th Nov. 1939. Agnes, wife of above Philip O'Neill, who died 3rd January 1956. Philomena O'Neill who died 1st Nov. 1983. In Thy sacred heart dear Jesus let their previous souls find rest.

O'NEILL

I.H.S. Of your charity pray for the souls of Philip O'Neill who died 7th August 1909 and of his wife Elizabeth who died 19th October 1922. Also of their daughter Sara who died 21st March 1925. "Sacred heart of Jesus, have mercy on them."

O'NEILL

See McCORMICK (2)

QUAYLE

[Sandstone monument topped by sandstone cross with arms supported by twin colums having grape vine capitals, in a railed enclosure.] Erected by Sarah Ann in memory of her dear and only son Helenuss James Quayle, born 29th Octr. 1860 died 7th Sept. 1879.

Also her husband Timothy Quayle, born 25th Sept. 1830, died 7th Feby. 1862.
May they rest in peace.

QUINN
[Sandstone, fallen and broken.] Erected by Hugh Quinn in memory of his son Hugh
Quinn who died 20th Nov. 1877 aged 4 years and 8 months. Also his beloved wife
Catherine who died 5th Feb. 1885 aged 33 years. Also his (....... w)ife Annie who di(ed
..)th July 190(6 ....)

QUINN
[Broken limestone headstone.] .... Mary McGUGI(N) in memory of her mother Rose
Quinn who died 16th Sept. 1893 aged 80 yea(rs). Also her husband Felix McGug... who
died 13th Sept. 1895 aged 34 yea...
[Letters of administration of the personal estate of Rose Quinn, late of Ballyedward,
Magheramorne, county Antrim, widow, who died 16 September 1893 at Redhall, said
county, were granted at Belfast 4 October 1893 to Sarah Noble of Carrickfergus, married
woman, a daughter. Effects £222.]

QUINN
[Limestone headstone next to yew tree.] Erected by Randal Quinn in memory of his
father Charles Quinn who died 1st Dec. 1896, aged 80 years. Also his mother Margaret
Quinn who died Jany. 1882. R.I.P.

RAMSEY
See McLEOD

READ
[Sandstone headstone enclosed with Quayle stone.] 1878. Sacred to the memory of James
Read, born at Liminary near Ballymena 9th May 1817, appointed postmaster of Larne in
the year 1857 and died 5th August 1871. Also his son Robert born 18th June 1858 died
at D...... Us 16th Feb. ..... Also his son Patrick born 2nd Oct. 18(.. die)d (..h) Oct. 18...
Requiescant in pace. Amen. A. Jenkins.
[Letters of administration of the personal estate of James Read, late of Larne, county
Antrim, postmaster, who died 5 August 1871 at same place, were granted at Belfast 16
October 1871 to Sarah Anne Read of Larne aforesaid, the widow of said deceased. Effects
under £450.
Death: May 9, Grace Anna, daughter of James Read, postmaster, aged 5 years. *Larne
Weekly Reporter,* 13 May 1865.
Death: at Dunluce Street, Larne, Fri. 20th inst., Grace Anna, infant daughter of Mr.
James Read, Postmaster, aged 14 weeks. *Larne Weekly Reporter,* 28 Oct. 1865.]

RICHARDSON
[Polished granite headstone with enclosure.] In loving memory of Arthur Richardson died
26th March 1899. Also his wife Mary died 31st January 1918. Their daughter Jane died
30th Dec. 1939. "May they rest in peace."

ROBIN
[Sandstone headstone.] I.H.S. Erected by Hugh Robin in memory of his wife Jane who
died 17th March 1880 aged 28 years. Also two of their children who died in infancy.

SHAW
　See DONAGHY

SHIELDS
　[Low granite headstone with concrete enclosure.] In memory of Agnes Shields died 18th
　April 1940. R.I.P.

STEWART
　[Sandstone headstone in rail enclosure.] Erected by William Stewart in memory of his two
　children Thomas, who died 11th May 1882. Annie who died 31st May 1884.

STURGES
　See FULTON

TRAYNOR.
　[Limestone headstone.] Erected by Isabella McANALLY in memory of her father Michael
　Traynor who died in 1877. And her mother Martha Traynor who died in 1881. Her
　husband James McAnally who died in 1880, and her four children who died in infancy.
　Also her brother William Traynor who died at Glasgow 24th April 1895 aged 40 years.

WILLS
　[Polished granite headstone and enclosure.] In loving memory of Francis Wills died 31st
　July 1948 and Elizabeth Wills died 29th March 1958. Also their daughter Elizabeth died
　11th Aug. 1976. R.I.P.

(.......)
　[Worn sandstone headstone] Erected ..... he..... in memory ....who died 5th May
　1886 .... His wife Mary Agn..... who died 15th Oct. 1895 aged .... The above
　named Henry .... died (.1st July 1901 aged ...).

LARNE, ST. MACNISSI'S ROMAN CATHOLIC GRAVEYARD

O.S. Antrim 40. Grid Ref. D404027

St. MacNissi's Church is on Agnew's Street near the corner with Victoria Road, in the townland of Town Parks and the parish of Larne.

In 1807 a disused slaughter house on Mucket Hill became the first Roman Catholic chapel in Larne since the reformation. Twenty-four years later Father Arthur O'Neill had it demolished and a purpose-built chapel raised on the site. In 1859 it was replaced by a larger structure and transepts were added in 1905.

Only priests who served the parish have been buried in the grounds. The earliest date of death given is 1895, but all headstones have been copied as well as a blue plaque and memorial windows.

BURNS
[Low stone of polished granite and enclosure.] Pray for the Very Rev. J. Canon Burns P.P. V.F. died 18th Dec. 1927 aged 66 years. Parish Priest of Carnlough 1905 - 1919. Parish Priest of Larne 1919 - 1927. Erected by the people of Carnlough and Larne. R.I.P.
[Joseph Burns was born 30th May 1861, educated at the Irish College, Paris, and ordained 29th June 1884. *The Parish of Larne*, pp. 41, 96.]

CONWAY
[Tall wheeled cross of fossiliferous limestone decorated on the west face, in a low granite enclosure.] Pray for the happy repose of the soul of Very Rev. John Conway P.P., V.F., Larne who died 30th Jany. 1909 aged 59 years. Requiescat in pace.
[He was born in Rasharkin 13th July 1850, educated at St. Malachy's College, Belfast, and Maynooth, was ordained 26th July 1873 in St. Malachy's Church, Belfast, was Dean in St. Malachy's College 1876-1887, P.P. of Ramoan 1887-1902, P.P. of Larne 1902-1909. *The Parish of Larne*, pp. 32-39, 95.]

FALLOONA
[Wheeled cross of fossiliferous limestone, decorated on west side.] Pray for the soul of the Very Rev. Bernard Falloona P.P. V.F. who died 18th March 1919 aged 65 years. Requiescat in pace.
[He was born in the parish of Ballee, educated at St. Malachy's College and Maynooth, ordained 25th March 1877 in St. Peter's, Belfast, P.P. in Newcastle, P.P. in Ballycastle 1902- 1910, P.P. in Larne 1910-1919. *The Parish of Larne*, pp. 39-41, 96.]

McCARTAN
[Tall wheeled cross of polished granite with shallow interlace pattern.] I.H.S. OCRUX + AVE + SPES UNICA. Orate pro anima Adm. Rev. Eugenii McCartan P.P. V.F. Larne Qui Omnibus Sacramentis devote susceptis, anno vitae suae 74to anno sacerdotii 50mo die 25to augusti 1902. Spiritum creatori reddidit. Requiescat in pace, amen.

[He was born in Bryansford, county Down, 20th March 1829, educated at St. Malachy's College and Maynooth, ordained in Dublin in 1850 or October 1852, P.P of Cushendun 1871-1883, Antrim 1883-1895, Larne 1895-1902. He published a book *Reminiscences of Rome* in 1883. *The Parish of Larne*, pp. 30-31, 95.]

McFAUL
[Three lancet windows in the gable of the south transept depicting the Resurrection.] In memory of James and Mary Heffernan McFaul, parents of Right Rev. James A. McFaul, Bishop of Trenton, N.J., U.S.A. Mayer u. Co., Munich. [*The Parish of Larne*, pp. 100, 121, 138.]

McFAUL
[Blue circular plaque attached to rough stone.] Larne Borough Council American Heritage Trail. Erected to the memory of Bishop James Augustine McFaul 1850-1917 of Rory's Glen, Kilwaughter, whose family left their native land to go forward in faith.

After studying at Pennsylvania and New York, James McFaul was ordained to the priesthood at Seton Hall College, New Jersey, on May 26, 1877, a devout cleric, he was elevated to the position of Bishop of Trenton, New Jersey, in 1894 and was known from Maine to California for his writings and high moral views.

In 1906 when visiting the land of his birth, he donated stained glass windows in his church in memory of the parents who had guided his path and handed down a strong enduring faith. Sponsored by Jamont UK Ltd.

[He was baptised in St. MacNissi's by Rev. John Garland on 2nd July 1850. *The Parish of Larne*, pp. 35-36, 100, 138.]

McKENNA
[Tall wheeled cross of polished granite with shallow pattern of interlace.] I.H.S. Very Rev. Francis McKenna, parish priest of Larne for 43 years, died January 7th 1895 aged 70 years. Requiescat in pace. This memorial cross is erected by the people of Larne to testify the esteem and affection in which he was held by them.

[The will of the Reverend Francis McKenna, late of Larne, county Antrim, parish priest, who died 7 January 1895 at same place, was proved at Belfast 6 February 1895 by the Reverend Peter McKenna of Bangor, county Down, parish priest, the sole executor. Effects £25 . 17s. 6d.

He was born near Castlewellan 25th March 1824, educated at St. Malachy's College and Maynooth, ordained in Maynooth by Archbishop Murray 29th May 1847, P.P. of Larne and Ballygowan 1859-1869, P.P. of Larne 1869-1895. *The Parish of Larne*, pp. 26-30, 95.]

MULVENNA
[Three lancet windows above the altar depict Christ's crucifixion.] Erected by Mary Mulvenna, Station Road, Larne, in memory of her father John Mulvenna died 18th Dec. 1904, her mother Catherine Mulvenna died 27th Sept. 1901, her brother John Mulvenna died 5th Nov. 1905. May they rest in peace. [*Parish of Larne*, p. 121.]

[Death: 11th inst., at the residence of her son, Mr. John Mulvenna, Newtown, Larne, Mrs. Mary Mulvenna, aged 84 years. *Larne Weekly Reporter*, 14 Oct. 1865.]

MURPHY
[Dark headstone and surround of polished granite.] In memory of Very Rev. Joseph Murphy P.P. V.F. ordained 22nd June 1924, died 29th April 1972. You are a priest forever ... Psalm 109. R.I.P.
[He was educated at St. Malachy's College, Queen's University, Belfast, and Maynooth, ordained in Maynooth, and served as P.P. in Ballymoney from 1955 to 1961 when he came to Larne. *The Parish of Larne*, pp. 64-67, 97.]

O'NEILL
[Dark headstone and surround of polished granite.] Pray for the soul of the Very Rev. Sean O'Neill, parish priest of Larne, who died 13th March 1986. Christ has died, Christ is risen, Christ will come again.
[He was ordained 18th June 1933, and was P.P. of Killough before coming to Larne in 1972. He retired due to ill health in 1982. *The Parish of Larne*, pp. 67-74, 97.]

SUMMARY GUIDE TO DOCUMENTARY SOURCES FOR THE FAMILY AND LOCAL HISTORIAN

PARISHES OF INVER, KILWAUGHTER AND LARNE

Presented here is a brief introduction to documentary sources available for the parishes of Inver, Kilwaughter and Larne. A more detailed guide to County Antrim sources will be published in due course by the Ulster Historical Foundation in its *Researching Ancestors* series.

CIVIL REGISTRATION

Civil or state registration of all births, deaths and marriages began in Ireland on 1 January 1864. Non-Catholic marriages, including Protestant and Jewish marriages as well as those conducted in a government registry office, were required in law to be registered from 1 April 1845.

Civil registration followed the administrative divisions created by the Poor Law Act of 1838. This act was an attempt to provide some help for the most destitute in Ireland. The country was divided into Poor Law Unions. Each of these had a workhouse where paupers were accommodated. The Poor Law Unions were subdivided into dispensary districts, each with its own medical officer.

Under civil registration the area covered by a Poor Law Union was used as the basis of each superintendent registrar's district, while the dispensary districts corresponded to the registrar's districts. In some cases the medical officer also served as the registrar. In overall charge of registration was the Registrar General in Dublin. Certified copies of all registers compiled locally were sent to his office and, from these, indexes covering the whole of Ireland were produced.

BIRTH CERTIFICATES

Birth certificates record the date and place of birth of the child. Normally the name of the child is also given, but in some cases only the sex is given, i.e. the child had not been given a name by the time the birth was registered. The name and residence of the father is given. Usually this will be the same as the place of birth of the child, but in some cases it will show that the father was working abroad or in another part of Ireland when the child was born. The father's occupation is also given. The mother's maiden name is provided as well as her first name. Finally, the name and address of the informant is given, together with his or her qualification to sign. This will usually be the father or mother or someone present at the birth, such as a midwife or even the child's grandmother.

MARRIAGE CERTIFICATES

Civil records of marriage normally give fuller information than birth and death certificates, and are the most useful of civil records. Information on the individuals getting married includes their name, age, status, and occupation. The names and occupations of their fathers are also given. The church, the officiating minister and the witnesses to the ceremony are named. In most cases the exact age of the parties is not given, and the entry will simply read 'full age' (i.e. over 21) or 'minor' (i.e. under 21). If the father of one of the parties was no longer living, this may be indicated in the marriage certificate, but in many cases it is not.

DEATH CERTIFICATES

Civil records of death in Ireland are rather uninformative. The name of the deceased is given together with the date, place and cause of death, marital status, the age at death, and occupation. The name and address of the informant is also given. Usually this is the person present at the time of the death; this may be a close family member.

THE INDEXES

Indexes to civil marriages 1845–63 are handwritten, but thereafter all indexes are printed. From 1864 to 1877 indexes for births, marriages and deaths consist of a single yearly volume covering the whole of Ireland. From 1878 the annual indexes are arranged on a quarterly basis. In each index the surnames will be arranged alphabetically, followed by the first names. The name of the superintendent registrar's district is also given, followed by the volume number and page number of the master copies of the registers in Dublin.

GENERAL REGISTER OFFICE, BELFAST
AND DISTRICT REGISTRARS' OFFICES

The General Register Office (GRO) in Belfast holds the original birth and death registers recorded by the local district registrars for Northern Ireland from 1864. Marriage registers for Northern Ireland are available from 1922. The following computerised indexes to the civil registers are available:

- birth indexes – 1864 onwards
- death indexes – 1864 onwards
- marriage indexes – 1845 onwards.

Only the indexes are available for public inspection, not the registers themselves. Visits to the GRO to view the indexes have to be arranged in advance. An index search costs £8 for a period not exceeding four hours. This includes four verifications of items found in the indexes, with the option of further verifications at £1.50 each. An assisted search service is also provided. This can be a much quicker method of extracting information from the civil registers, especially if a specific location is known, but costs £19 per hour. A full certified copy of a birth, death or marriage certificate costs £9.

The General Register Office is located at Oxford House, 49–55 Chichester Street, Belfast, BT1 4HL. Applications for certificates can be made in person, by post, by telephone (028 9025 2000) or online (www.groni.gov.uk). Searches will be made in the year quoted plus the two years either side unless a wider search is requested. A further fee will be required for each extra five years searched. Personal applications are processed within three working days; postal or telephone applications are processed within eight working days. The GRO also holds adopted children registers from 1931 and marine registers of births and deaths on ships at sea from 1922.

CHURCH OF LATTER-DAY SAINTS

From 1948 the Church of Latter-Day Saints (LDS), or Mormons, began microfilming documentary material in Ireland. The most important resource acquired at that time was the registers of births, deaths and marriages as well as the indexes to these records held in the Registrar General's Office, Custom House, Dublin. Unfortunately the Mormons were not able to complete the filming of all registers before work was suspended.

This is a vital resource, because in the General Register Offices in Dublin, Belfast and London the public have no right of access to the original records. The LDS collection of microfilms of civil registers and indexes is as follows:

- birth indexes 1864–1959
- birth registers 1864 to first quarter 1880; 1900–13
- marriage indexes 1845–1959
- marriage registers 1845–70
- death indexes 1864–1959
- death registers 1864–70.

An excellent introduction and guide to civil registration in Ireland is Catherine Blumsom's *Civil Registration of Births, Deaths and Marriages in Ireland: a Practical Approach*, published by the Ulster Historical Foundation.

The Mormon holdings also include some baptismal and marriage registers for Roman Catholic parishes and some other denominations. The Mormons have indexed many of the two million reels of microfilm that they hold, and these indexes have been made available as the International Genealogical Index (IGI). This index is arranged both by county and by surname and is available in many libraries and record offices and also on the Internet. Access to the IGI is free of charge, as is the viewing of films held in Mormon Family History Centres. A microfiche version of the IGI is available at PRONI (MF/1/6/C).

CHURCH RECORDS

Prior to civil registration the most important sources for basic family information are the registers of baptisms, marriages and burials kept by individual churches. The records available for Larne and district are set out below together with the PRONI references. The abbreviations are as follows: CI Church of Ireland; M Methodist; NSP – Non-Subscribing Presbyterian; P Presbyterian; RC Roman Catholic; RP Reformed Presbyterian.

INVER PARISH

CI Inver and Larne (Connor diocese)
Baptisms, 1806-71; marriages, 1817-20 and   MIC/1/49; T/679/38,
1826-45; burials, 1826-1905; vestry minutes,   58-9, 78, 80
1763-1870, cess applotment book, 1833
P. 1st Larne
Baptisms, 1813 and 1824-1902; marriages,   MIC/1P/335
1846-1902
Stipend and other account books, 1828-89   D/2009/1

KILWAUGHTER PARISH

CI Kilwaughter and Carncastle (Connor diocese)
Earliest registers destroyed in Dublin
Baptisms, 1883- ; marriages, 1845- ; burials,
1883-   In local custody

LARNE PARISH

M Larne (Weslayan Methodists)
Baptisms, 1878-1915, marriages, 1863-1906;   MIC/1E/39
circuit schedule books, 1879-93 and 1908-23;
printed history of Larne Methodist Circuit, 1885-
1985

NSP Larne and Kilwaughter
Baptisms, 1720-69, 1796, 1801-03 and 1826-   MIC/1B/6
1929; marriages, 1721-69 and 1826-1908; session
minutes, 1720-48, 1800-01 and 1828-30; session
and committee minutes, 1864-1929; discipline
cases, 1721-49; poor accounts, 1720-57
P 2nd Larne or Gardenmore
Baptisms, 1861-1906, marriages, 1946-1906   MIC/1P/263
RC Carrickfergus, Larne and Ballygowan (Down
and Connor diocese)   MIC/1D/68, 90
Baptisms, 1821-83; marriages, 1821-82; indexes
to baptisms and marriages, 1828-1960
RP Larne
Minutes, 1898-1930   CR/5/10

SCHOOL RECORDS

In the early years of the nineteenth century there were numerous schools in
Ireland. These included some 'charter schools', which were established by
royal charter in 1733 for the education of the poor, receiving grants from the
Irish parliament and built by private subscription. There were also a large
number of pay or hedge schools for Catholic children. These were usually set
up by itinerant schoolmasters, who were paid according to the size of the
school. They were sometimes, as their name suggests, held in the open air,
but more commonly they were established in a local barn or cabin. The
Society for the Education of the Poor in Ireland, better known as the Kildare
Place Society, was founded in 1811 and aimed to provide a system of
interdenominational education. The Established Church remained
suspicious of these attempts to remove its influence over the education
system, and, ironically, the Roman Catholic clergy remained suspicious of
what they saw as a proselytising organisation.

A state-run system of education was not established until 1831. These
national schools were built with the aid of the Commissioners of National
Education and local trustees. Between 1832 and 1870 about 2,500 national
schools were established in Ulster. Of particular interest are the registers of
attendance. These record the full name of the pupil, date of birth (or age of
entry), religion, father's address and occupation (but unfortunately not his
name), details of attendance and academic progress and the name of the
school previously attended. A space is also provided in the registers for
general comments, which might tell where the children went to work after
leaving school or if they emigrated. Some have an index at the front that can
greatly ease searching.

As they include the age of pupils, school registers can be cross-referenced to other records such as baptismal records or birth certificates. Many of the schools, particularly in the early part of the century, were cross-denominational, with the religion of the child listed as RC (Roman Catholic), P (Presbyterian) or EC (Established Church, i.e. Church of Ireland).

A series of calendars listing the registers available at PRONI are available on the shelves of the Public Search Room. Each school is given the prefix SCH and then a separate reference number. The schools for Larne and district with surviving registers of pupils are listed below. Unless otherwise indicated the registers cover both male and female pupils. Nat. stands for National, while PE means Public Elementary.

Name of school	Date of registers	PRONI references
Larne & Inver Nat./PE	1837-1942	SCH/81/1/1-9
Larne Parochial	1908-57	SCH/903/1/1-4
Larne no. 1	PE 1908-52	SCH/905/1/1-2
Larne North End Nat./PE (McKenna Memorial)	1865-1958 (male only)	SCH/1200/1/1-3
Larne Infants	1901-26	SCH/904/1/1-2
Larne Model Agricultural	1841-1901 (male only)	SCH/80/1/1-3
St Mary's Convent	1903-50 (female only)	SCH/1191/1/1-2
Olderfleet	1884-1951 (male register only from 1911)	SCH/289/1/1-3
Toreagh	Loose pages of a register Roll books, 1859-68	SCH/259/1/1 SCH/259/2/1-5
Larne	1921-32	SCH/206/1/1-2

1901 CENSUS

On 31 March 1901, a census was taken of the whole island of Ireland. The original returns of the 1901 census are deposited at the National Archives in Dublin. The census records: name; relationship to the head of the household; religion; literacy; occupation; age; marital status; county of birth; and ability to speak English or Irish. The 1901 census is available on microfilm at PRONI under reference MIC/354.

The PRONI references to the 1901 census for Larne and district are as follows:

MIC/354/1/129-30 – Inver and Larne

MIC/354/1/129 – Kilwaughter

TITHE APPLOTMENT BOOKS, 1823–38

The tithe was not a tax but a charge upon land. The tithe system, which nominally earmarked one-tenth of the produce of the land for the maintenance of the clergy, was introduced in England as early as the eighth century. It was introduced to Ireland during the reign of Henry II, although it was not paid outside the area around Dublin until the reign of Elizabeth I.

In Ireland, because the tithe system was used for the upkeep of the Established Church only, it caused a great deal of unrest among Roman Catholics and Presbyterians.

In 1823 the Tithe Applotment Act was passed, which stipulated that henceforth all tithes due to the Established Church were to be paid in money rather than in kind, as they previously could have been. This necessitated a complete valuation of all tithable land in Ireland, the results of which are contained in the manuscript tithe applotment books for each civil parish.

The tithe applotment books are unique records giving details of land occupation and valuations for individual holdings prior to the devastation brought about by the Great Famine and the resulting mass emigration. They list the occupiers of tithable land and are not a list of householders, as is the case in a census. Therefore, landless labourers and weavers were omitted, in addition to all purely urban dwellers. In 1838 the tithe payment was reduced by 25 per cent and transferred from the tenant to the landowner. Tithes were finally abolished in Ireland in 1869.

The PRONI references to the tithe applotment books for Larne and district are as follows:

FIN/5A/158 – Inver (1833)
FIN/5A/192 – Kilwaughter (1834)
FIN/5A/197 – Larne (1834)

VALUATION RECORDS

The levying of a rate in Ireland, to raise money to meet the costs of local government, dates from 1635. An Act of that year gave Justices of the Peace power to levy certain sums, known as the county cess or grand jury cess, upon the inhabitants of a local area for the execution of public works such as roads and bridges. By 1824, parliament recognised the need for a more equitable method of measuring liability for cess and rates. The 1st Valuation Act was introduced in 1826 and a valuation of the whole of Ireland was prepared.

THE TOWNLAND VALUATION OF THE 1830s

Though often dismissed as being of fairly limited genealogical value, the townland valuation carried out in the 1830s can be an important source for those searching for their ancestors, particularly if those ancestors were urban dwellers. The bound manuscript returns are arranged by barony and parish and those for Northern Ireland are available at PRONI under reference VAL/1B; the accompanying annotated maps are listed under VAL/1A and VAL/1D. Although the townland valuation was primarily concerned with the agricultural value of land, it also included details on houses valued at £3 or over (in 1838 this was raised to £5 or over). In the rural areas the names of only a few householders were given, and these tended to be of the gentry or the better class of tenant farmers. In towns, however, many more houses were substantial enough to reach the valuation, with the result that a large number of householders are recorded.

The PRONI references for the townland valuation for Larne and district are as follows:

VAL/1B/117 – Inver
VAL/1B/152A-B – Kilwaughter
VAL/1B/153 – Larne

THE FIRST GENERAL VALUATION (GRIFFITH), 1848–64

By contrast, the 1848–64 valuation gives a complete list of occupiers of land, tenements and houses. This Primary Valuation of Ireland, better known as Griffith's Valuation after the Commissioner of Valuation, Sir Richard Griffith, is arranged by county, within counties by Poor Law Union division, and within Unions by parish. It includes the following information: the name of the townland; the name of the householder or leaseholder; the name of the person from whom the property was leased; a description of the property; its acreage; and finally the valuation of the land and buildings.

Griffith's Valuation is of particular interest to anyone wishing to trace their family tree, due to the fact that so little of the nineteenth century census returns has survived. It is available in manuscript form at PRONI (VAL/2B). A bound and printed summary version is available on the shelves of the Public Search Room, PRONI, and at major libraries. These volumes are arranged by Poor Law Union within counties, and then into parishes and townlands. There is an index at the front of each volume which enables searchers to identify the page or pages in which a specific townland may be found. The Householders' Index can be used as a guide to the surnames listed in the Griffith's Valuation. The valuer's annotated set of Ordnance Survey maps showing the location of every property is available at PRONI (VAL/2A).

The valuer's manuscript books, held by PRONI, were updated on a regular basis and these books up to *c.*1930 are available under reference VAL/12B. The so-called 'cancelled books' consist of manuscript notebooks kept by the valuation office and updated to take account of changes in tenure. When a change of occupancy occurred, the name of the lessee or householder was crossed off and the new owner's name written above it, while the year was noted on the right-hand side of the page. This helps to establish significant dates in family history, such as dates of death, sale or emigration. By the closing years of the nineteenth century most of the occupiers of land had become landowners, thanks to a series of land purchase acts. This explains the initials L.A.P. (Land Act Purchase) that may be found stamped on an entry in the revision lists. The corresponding maps are also available, reference VAL/12D.

The PRONI references to the manuscript valuation books for Larne and district are as follows:

VAL/2B/14 – Inver
VAL/2B/43 – Kilwaughter
VAL/2B/44A-C – Larne

The PRONI references to the valuation revision books for Larne and district are as follows:

VAL/12B/7/14A/G; /15B-M – Inver
VAL/12B/7/13A-F – Kilwaughter
VAL/12B/7/14A-G; /15A-M; 16A – Larne

LANDED ESTATE PAPERS

Landed estate papers are an invaluable source of information for the family and local historian. Leases, rent books, correspondence and maps can all be used to further one's research. There are several collections of estate papers relating to Larne and district in the Public Record Office of Northern Ireland. The most important will be dealt with first.

ANTRIM ESTATE

The papers relating to the earl of Antrim's estate in County Antrim form one of the largest landed estate archives in the Public Record Office of Northern Ireland. The Antrim estate extended as far south as Larne and there is a large amount of material relating to the town and its hinterland in the archive. The main categories of record are listed below.

Leases for Larne including Gardenmore, 1624-1945 (D/2977/3A/4/81/1-433). The first item is a copy memorandum of a fee farm lease dated 14 March 1624[5] between Randal McDonnell, earl of Antrim, and Hugh

Miller, maltman, of 40 feet of land, being a whole tenement in the 'New Town of Enver' [Larne].

Rentals, 1814-1934; rent books, 1816-1963; rent ledgers, 1751-1956 (D/2977/7B, 8, 9).

Maps of Larne, 1735-1928 (D/2977/36/2/1-15). The first item is a map of 1735 by Archibald Stewart showing the 'Old Town of Lairn alias Gardenmore'. This list the names of the occupiers of the tenements in the town. There are also bound volumes of estate maps. The most important date from 1734 and 1782 (D/2977/35/3 and /5)

Records of the manor court of Glenarm, 1755-1845, including court books (D/2977/23/1/1-9). Records of the court leet of Glenarm, 1765-1845, including court books (D/2977/23/2/1-3). Both sets of records cover Larne.

Large plans of buildings in Larne, 1838-1936 (D/2977/37/2/1/1-11). Small plans of buildings in Larne (D/2977/37/2/2/1-10).

AGNEW ESTATE, KILWAUGHTER AND LARNE

Papers including deeds, leases and wills etc., 1703-1879 T/502/2-62); conveyances, leases etc., c.1800-c.1840 (T/528/2/31); volume of maps by James Williamson, 1788 (T/2309/1); estate papers including leases, assignments, mortgages, rentals and conveyances, c.1647-c.1880 (D/282/2-160); estate correspondence of agent Knox etc., c.1800-c.1900 (D/668).

ARMSTRONG ESTATE, BLAIRMOUNT, LARNE

Deed, 1792 (T/1065/5); accounts and mortgages, 1797-1811, c.1812 and 1820 (D/618/19, 26, 30); c.35 title deeds, 1779-1896; testamentary and legal papers, c.1800-c.1900; family and estate papers, 1803-94 (D/2838/A-F).

CHAINE ESTATE, BALLYCRAIGY, LARNE

Details of shipping, railways and harbours, no date (D/1326); Irish Land Commission papers and letters relating to Larne harbour, 1889 (D/1905); bundles of correspondence, 1869-1911 and 1892-1911; miscellaneous deeds, notices, forms etc, c.1870-c.1900 (D/2448/12-13, 32, 43, 57/68-69).

COEY ESTATE, LARNE

About 50 copy and draft leases for Larne, c.1900-c.1930; Irish Land Commission sale papers, c.1900-c.1940 (D/971/13/1-2).

JOHNSTON ESTATE, GLYNN, LARNE

Two volumes of receipts and payments, 1798-1923, 1864-78; rentals, c.1865-c.1930; five volumes of house, farm and garden accounts, c.1900-c.1920; account books, c.1910-c.1920 (D/971/19/1-2); letter books, 1867-72; account books, 1875-1935 (D/1783).

WILLS AND TESTAMENTARY RECORDS

Once the date of death of an ancestor has been discovered, it is worth finding out whether they left a will. Wills contain not only the name, address and occupation of the testator, but also details of the larger family network, such as cousins and nephews. Many wills also include the addresses and occupations of the beneficiaries, witnesses and executors. It must be borne in mind, however, that the vast majority of people did not make a will.

WILLS BEFORE 1858

Prior to 1858 the Church of Ireland was responsible for administering all testamentary affairs. Ecclesiastical or Consistorial Courts in each diocese were responsible for granting probate and conferring on the executors the power to administer the estate. Each court was responsible for wills and administrations in its own diocese. However, when the estate included property worth more than £5 in another diocese, responsibility for the will or administration passed to the Prerogative Court under the authority of the Archbishop of Armagh.

Unfortunately, most original wills probated before 1858 were destroyed in Dublin in 1922. However, indexes to these destroyed wills do exist and are available on the shelves of the Search Rooms at PRONI and the National Archives in Dublin. These are useful, for although the will cannot now be produced, the index contains the name and residence of the testator and the date that the will was either made or probated. Occasionally the testator's occupation is given.

Larne and the surrounding area falls within the diocese of Connor. Wills relating to the parishes of Inver, Kilwaughter and Larne have been extracted from the index to Wills probated in the diocese of Connor and are listed over.

CONNOR WILLS FOR INVER, KILWAUGHTER AND LARNE

Adams, James, Ballysnodd, Inver, 1853
Adams, Robert, Larne, 1782
Agnew, Daniel, Kilwaughter, 1827
Agnew, Capt. Francis, Kilwaughter, 1681
Agnew, James, Kilwaughter, 1814
Agnew, John, Kilwaughter, 1852
Agnew, Patrick, Kilwaughter, 1686
Agnew, Patrick, Kilwaughter, 1855
Agnew, Patrick, Larne, 1841
Alexander, John, Larne, 1807
Allan, Samuel, Inver, 1726
Allen, John, Larne, D 1775
Allen, Joseph, Larne, 1814
Allen, Samuel, Larne, 1812
Ballantine, Margaret, Kilwaughter, 1850
Ballantine, William, Kilwaughter, 1850
Barklie, Thomas, Inver, 1811
Beers, Isabella, Larne, 1834 & 1843
Berry, John, Larne, D 1686
Black, Mary, Larne, 1837
Black, Rose, Larne, 1837
Blair, Elizabeth, Inver, 1841
Blair, James, Larne, 1777
Blair, Jane, Larne, D 1760
Blair, Randal, Larne, 1837
Boll, John, Larne, 1819
Boyd, James, Larne, D 1755
Boyd, John, Larne, 1675
Boyd, John, Larne, 1840
Boyd, William, Larne, 1842
Brown, Charles, Larne, 1744
Brown, James, Kilwater, 1724
Buchanan, William, Kilwaughter, 1828
Burns, Samuel, Larne, 1781
Caldwell, Abraham, Larne, 1769
Caldwell, William, Kilwaughter, 1831
Callwell, David, Larne, 1738
Callwell, Hugh, Larne, 1741
Campbell, David, Larne, 1837
Corley, Alexander, Larne, 1814
Casement, George, Inver, 1835
Casement, Martha, Inver, 1842
Casement, Mary, Larne, 1845
Cassidy, Thomas, Larne, 1812
Chichester, Isaac, Inver, 1851
Chichester, William, Inver, 1843
Clark, Fanny, Larne, 1796
Clark, William, Larne, 1827

Clements, Andrew, Kilwaughter, 1852
Cooth alias, Larne, 1784
Cooke, John, Larne, 1842
Corney, John, Kilwaughter, 1818
Craford, John, Inver, 1661
Craig, Hugh, Larne, 1842
Crawford, John, Larne, 1729
Crawford, John, Kilwaughter, 1851
Crooks, Sergt Thomas, Enver, 1675
Cuddy, Margaret, Larne, 1827
Curell, James, Larne, 1828
Curry, Hugh, Kilwaughter, 1841
Curry, John, Inver, 1808
Davis, Robert, Inver, 1854
Drummond, Samuel, Larne, 1795
Dunbar, Alexander, Larne, 1800
Dymond, John, Larne, 1834
Egleson als Alexander, Kilwaughter, 1710
Esler, William, Kilwaughter, 1819
Esler, William, Kilwaughter, 1852
Fairies, Charles, Larne, 1795
Fairies, James, Larne, 1805
Fareys, John, Larne, 1746
Ferguson, Mary Ann, Larne, 1842
Ferguson, Samuel, Kilwaughter, 1838
Fife, David, Inver, 1663
Findlay als Kerr, Janet, Enver, D 1696
Finlay, William, Larne, 1833
Fisher, Mary, Larne, D 1758
Fleck, Jane, Larne, 1753
Fleck, Jennet, Larne, 1729
Fleck, William, Larne, 1729
Forless, John, Larne, 1701
Fullerton, Samuel, Kilwaughter, 1845
Fulton, John, Larne, 1719
Getty, Helen, Larne, D 1746
Getty, James, Enver, 1673
Getty, Robert, Enver, D 1698
Getty, Robert, Larne, 1766
Getty, Samuel, Larne, 1724
Gillis, Isobel, Larne, 1728
Gillis, John, Enver, 1695
Gingles, Andrew, Kilwaughter, 1841
Gingles, Andrew, Kilwaughter, 1856
Gingles, John, Kilwaughter, 1814
Gingles, Patrick, Kilwaughter, 1840

Gingles, Samuel, Kilwaughter, D 1739
Glasgow, James, Kilwater, 1727
Glasgow, James, Larne, 1803
Glasgow, Jane, Larne, 1846
Glasgow, William, Larne, 1783
Glasgow, William, Larne, 1816
Greenlees, Andrew, Kilwaughter, 1842
Haddan, John, Larne, D 1728
Hair, James, Larne, 1728
Hamilton, Alexander, Larne, (Commdr RN), 1807
Hare, William, Larne, 1805
Harper, James, Kilwater, 1841
Hart, John, Larne, D 1729
Harvey, Samuel, Inver, 1850
Harsson, John, Kilwaughter, 1839
Havron, William, Larne, 1834
Highton, James, Larne, 1848
Hill, Arthur, Larne, 1788
Hill, John, Inver, 1753
Hockenhull, George, Larne, 1806
Holden, James, Kilwater, 1841
Holmes, Alexander, Larne, 1800
Houston, James, Larne, 1725
Houston, Samuel, Larne, 1828
Hume, John, Larne, 1790
Jackson, James, Larne, 1766
Jafferies, William, Larne, 1820
Johnston als Finlay, Elizabeth, Enver, D 1684
Kane, Alexander, Larne, D 1727
Karr, James, Larne, D 1719
Kearney, John, Larne, 1802
Kerney, Brice & Janet, Larne, 1730
Kerr, Isabell, Larne, D 1728
Kilpatrick als Tweed, Larne (lodged) 1845
Knox als McMurtry, Susanna, Larne, D 1721
Laughlin, Agnes, Larne, 1728
Lilley, Thomas, Larne, 1745
Lind, John, Larne, 1805
Linn, Davin, Larne, 1827
Livingston, Jane, Larne, 1822
Macauley, Jane, Larne, 1829
Magill, Neal, Larne, 1717
Magill, Patrick, Kilwaughter, 1812
Maginis, Arthur, Kilwaughter, 1827
Maxwell, James, Kilwaughter, 1812
Miliken, Jane, Inver, 1841
Miller sen, Alexander, Kilwaughter, D 1702

Miller, Alexander, Kilwaughter, 1853
Miller, Elizabeth, Larne, 1780
Miller, John, Larne, (will missing), 1820
Miller, Joseph, Kilwaughter, D 1716
Montgomery, Anne, Larne, 1813
Montgomery als McNeill, Larne, 1775
Montgomery, Hugh, Larne, 1775
Montgomery, John, Larne, D 1780
Montgomery, John, Larne, 1811
Montgomery, Neal, Kilwaughter, 1743
Montgomery, William, Inver, 1808
Moon, John, Larne, D 1740
Moore, David, Larne, 1816, D 1795
Moore, John, Larne, 1779
Moore, John, Kilwaughter, 1837
Moore, Thomas, Larne, 1824
Moore, William, Larne, 1813
Moore, William, Kilwaughter, 1835
Morrison, John, Larne, 1758
Morrow, Samuel, Larne, 1795
Morrow, Samuel, Larne, 1846
Mountgomery, Hugh, Larne, D 1701
Murchy, Margaret, Larne, 1729
Murdoch, James, Larne, 1781
Murphy, Thomas, Larne, 1824
Murray, Jane, Larne, 1758
McAlister, Daniel, Larne, 1824
McCalmont, William, Larne, 1846
McCambridge, Alexander, Larne, 1823
McCambridge, Alexander, Larne, 1855
McCambridge, Alexander, Larne, 1855
McCambridge, Daniel, Larne, 1825
McCaughey, George, Larne, 1841
McCleverty, Rev Wm, Larne, 1799
McCloy, William, Larne, 1814
McCormick, James, Kilwaughter, 1854
McCracken, Margaret, Inver, D 1696
McCulloch, John, Larne, 1815
McCullogh, John, Kilwaughter, 1814
McCusack, Robert, Larne, 1830

McDowell, Hugh, Kilwaughter, 1787
McDowell, John, Kilwaughter, 1815
McDowell, John, Kilwaughter, 1857
McDowell, Robert, Kilwaughter, 1829
McDowell, Joseph, Larne, 1828
McDowell, William, Kilwaughter, 1802
McFall, Daniel, Kilwaughter, 1802
McFall, Shane or John, Kilwaughter, 1831
McGlatchery, Anne, Kilwaughter, 1856
McGlatchery, John (sen), Kilwaughter, 1822
McHenry, Agnes or Ann, Larne, 1825
McKee als Murray, Margt, Larne, 1770
McNick, Ellinor, Larne, 1770
McNinch, John, Kilwaughter, 1845
McNish, William, Larne, 1800
McSwine, Charles, Kilwater, 1731
McWilliam, Hugh, Larne, 1833
Nelson, Robert, Kilwaughter, 1853
Nelson, William, Kilwaughter, 1855
Netterville, Nicholas, Larne, 1777
Ogilvie, James Blair, Larne, 1785
O'Neill, Daniel, Kilwaughter, 1787
Owens, William, Inver, 1840
Park, John, Larne, 1746
Park, Margaret, Larne, 1854
Patrick, John, Larne, 1773
Pedan, Daniel, Larne, 1821
Pool, John, Larne, 1846
Pool, John, Larne, 1854
Rea, John, Larne, D 1787
Read, Hugh, Larne, D 1772
Richey als Boyd, Elizabeth, Envermore, 1686
Ritchey, Alexander, Larne, 1812
Ritchey, Robert, Kilwaughter, 1857
Robinson, John, Larne, D 1728
Rock, Jennet, Kilwaughter, 1825
Ross, Ann, Inver, 1802
Ross, William, Inver, 1802
Rowan, Eliza, Larne, 1856
Russel, Jennet, Larne, 1788
Russell, John, Inver, 1727

Scott, Andrew, Larne, 1794
Semple, Hugh, Larne, 1729
Semple, John, Larne, 1846
Service, James, Kilwaughter, 1835
Service, Jane, Kilwaughter, 1856
Service, John, Kilwaughter, 1829
Shaw, Collin, Enver, 1720
Shaw, Eliza, Larne, 1816
Shaw, George, Larne, 1815
Shaw, Rev Joseph, Larne, 1830
Shutter, Hugh, Larne, 1751
Simpson, William, Larne, 1848
Smeally, John, Envermore, 1749
Smiley, James, Inver, D 1815 (lodged 1814)
Smith, Ann, Larne, 1840
Smith, Hugh, Invermore, D 1741
Smith, James, Inver, 1749
Smith, John, Larne, 1742
Smith, John, Larne, 1743
Snodd, Andrew, Larne, 1843
Snodd, James, Larne, 1835
Snodd, Joseph, Larne, 1737
Snodd, Matthew, Enver, 1760
Snodd, Samuel, Larne, 1846
Speide, John, Enver, 1639
Stanhouse, James, Larne, 1744
Stanhouse, William, Larne, HMS Deptford, 1742
Steel, Hugh, Larne, 1768
Stevenson, Mary, Larne, 1834
Taylor, James, Enver, 1669
Thompson, William, Inver, 1764
Thomson, Hugh, Larne, 1729
Wallace, Arthur, Kilwaughter, 1851
Watt, John, Larne, 1759
Watt, Nathaniel, Inver, 1753
Wharey, Matthew, Larne, 1830
White, James, Larne, 1746
White, John, Larne, 1803
White, Margaret, Larne, 1819
White, Patrick, Larne, 1728
White, Robert, Larne, 1727
White, Robert, Kilwater, 1722
White, William, Larne, 1789
Willie, William, Larne, D 1730
William, Thomas, Enver, 1750
Wilson, James, Larne, 1751
Wilson, John, Larne, D 1707
Wilson, Robert, Larne, 1759
Wilson, Samuel, Kilwaughter, 1806
Winnart, John, Kilwaughter, 1812
Winter, Gilbert, Larne, 1730
Workman, Mary, Inver, 1752
Workman, Robert, Larne, 1816

WILLS, 1858–1900

The testamentary authority of the Church of Ireland was abolished by the Probate Act of 1857. Testamentary matters were brought under civil jurisdiction and exercised through District Probate Registries and a Principal Registry in Dublin. The registries covering Ulster were at Armagh, Belfast and Londonderry: County Londonderry was covered by the Londonderry Registry. The wills of wealthier members of society tended to be probated at the Principal Registry. The district registries retained transcripts of the wills that they proved and of the administrations intestate that they granted before the annual transfer of the original records (20 or more years old) to the Public Record Office of Ireland in Dublin. The original wills were destroyed in Dublin in 1922 but the transcript copies in will books survived. These are now on deposit in PRONI and the National Archives, Dublin. Those for Northern Ireland are available on microfilm at PRONI for the period 1858–1900 (MIC/15C). Each volume contains an alphabetical index.

There is not a comprehensive index to these post-1858 wills and grants. However, there are bound annual indexes called 'calendars' on the shelves of the Reception Room. These calendars are of value to genealogists since they provide the name, address, occupation and date of death of the testator as well as the names, addresses and occupations of executors, the value of estate and the place and date of probate. Each calendar covers a single year and the entries are in alphabetical order. Even if you have only an approximate date for the death of an ancestor it is worth looking through a number of volumes in the hope of spotting an entry giving details of their will.

When using these calendars to gain access to a will or transcript, the vital date to note is not the date when the will was signed or the date of death. It is the date of probate, i.e. the date when it was officially proved in a probate registry. This date of probate is normally a few months after a person died. However, it is well to bear in mind that a significant number of wills were probated ten or more years after death. Such delays may have been more common where probate was in the Principal Registry in Dublin.

A consolidated index to the calendars, 1858–77, is available in the National Archives, Dublin and at PRONI. This gives the year and the registry where the will was probated. The Ulster Historical Foundation has an index to the calendars covering the period 1878–1900 on its website. This index gives the date of death and county of residence. Access to the index is available to members of the research co-operative, the Ulster Genealogical and Historical Guild.

PRONI also has a card index to post-1858 surviving wills and will abstracts. This index is most useful when looking for a copy or abstract of a will probated at the Principal Registry in Dublin, which would have been destroyed in 1922 without a transcript being made.

WILLS FROM 1900

PRONI has in its custody all wills for the districts of Belfast and Londonderry from 1900 to, at present, the mid-1990s, and Armagh from 1900 until it closed in 1921. After 1900 the original wills and their associated papers are available filed in a separate envelope for each testator. If the person did not make a will there may be letters of administration that give the name, residence and occupation of the deceased as well as the name and address of the person or persons appointed to administer the estate. Post-1900 wills are found by using the annual will calendars located in the reception area at PRONI.

BOARDS OF GUARDIANS RECORDS

The new English system of Poor Law administration was applied to Ireland in 1838. Destitute poor who were previously granted relief at parish level were to be accommodated in new workhouses, where conditions were to be as unpleasant as was consistent with health.

Ireland was divided into 137 Poor Law Unions. These ignored traditional divisions, such as the county, barony and parish, and were centred on a market town where a workhouse was built. In County Antrim workhouses were built in the towns of Antrim, Ballycastle, Ballymena, Ballymoney, Belfast, Larne and Lisburn. Each workhouse kept registers of those admitted to it; these give the name, religion and residence of each the inmate.

It was a fundamental rule of the workhouse system that 'no individual capable of exertion must ever be permitted to be idle in a workhouse and to allow none who are capable of employment to be idle at any time'. The men were employed breaking stones, grinding corn, working on the land attached to the workhouse or at other manual work about the house; the women at house duties, mending clothes, washing, attending the children and the sick, as well as manual work including breaking stones.

The average day in the workhouse started at 7 a.m. when the inmates had to rise, dress in their workhouse clothes and then attend the central dining hall, where they waited for prayers to be read. The roll was called and they were inspected for cleanliness. They then lined up for their stirabout and milk. After breakfast the inmates were allocated work until late in the afternoon, when they had dinner of either potatoes or brown bread and soup. Inmates could not go to the dormitories until bedtime at eight o'clock. Even their leisure time was strictly monitored. They were not allowed to play cards or any game of chance, smoke or drink any 'spirituous or fermented drink'. They could see visitors only when accompanied by the Master, Matron or other duly authorised officer.

The management of the workhouses was the responsibility of the Boards of Guardians composed of elected representatives of the ratepayers in each union, together with *ex officio* members including Justices of the Peace. The names of those attending weekly meetings are to be found in the minute books. Also included in the minute books are details of the day-to-day running of the workhouse, including information on many of the inmates and those employed in the workhouse as teachers, nurses, chaplains, etc.

There is a large archive of Larne Board of Guardians records on deposit at the Public Record Office of Northern Ireland under reference BG/17. The main items of interest to the local and family historian are listed below.

Minute books, 1840-1948 (/A/1-159)

Rough minute books, 1862-81 (/AA/1-3)

Outward letter books, 1893-1946 (/B/1-9)

Contracts and tenders, 1878-1929 (/BJ/1-20)

Statement of salaries and additional salaries paid to sanitary officers, 1875-1920 (/CQ/1)

Return of paupers in the workhouse, 1847 (/DC/1)

Outdoor relief registers, 1848-1947 (/EA/1-2)

Indoor register of workhouse, 1845-1944 (/G/1-20)

Medical officer's relief register, Ballycarry dispensary district, 1852-1948 (/JA/1-8)

Medical Officer's report book, Ballycarry dispensary district, 1872-1910 (/JF/1)

Attendance and prescription papers, Ballycarry dispensary district, 1852-68 (/JG/1-2)

Record book of births in Larne workhouse, 1843-1900 (/K/1)

Register of successful vaccinations, districts of Ballycarry, Ballynure, Carrickfergus, Glenarm and Larne, 1864-1948, including indexes (/L/1-46)

LOCAL GOVERNMENT RECORDS

Local government records are a neglected source of genealogical and historical information. A large collection of records relating to Larne Urban District Council have been deposited in the Public Record Office of Northern Ireland (LA/43). The more interesting items are listed below.

LA/43/2B/2-5 – Minute books of Larne Town Commissioners, 1880-99. Each book is indexed. Although some bodies of town commissioners had already been established under an Act of 1828, most came into existence under the Town Improvement (Ireland) Act, 1854. The commissioners were responsible for the provision of lighting and cleaning services and water supply for all towns with a population of more than 1,500. Later town commissioners were given powers to establish and regulate markets, and promote housing schemes.

LA/43/2CA/1-17 – Minute books of Larne Urban District Council, 1899-1943. County councils and rural and urban district councils were established in 1899, superseding the grand juries and taking on many of the functions of the Board of Guardians.

LA/43/2D/1-12 – Minute books of Larne Borough Council, 1843-1973.

LA/43/4DA/1 – Ledger of Larne Town Commissioners, 1852-86.

LA/43/7CB/1 – Census register compiled by Larne School Attendance Committee recording names of parents and children and schools where educated, [1893].

LA/43/9C/4 – Free milk register, 1919-20.

Larne Rural District Council records are also available at the Public Record Office of Northern Ireland (LA/44). Records of interest are listed below.

LA/44/2FA/1-53 – Minute books of Larne Rural District Council, 1899-1973.

LA/44/12E/1 – Labourers' cottages register, 1908-57.

LA/44/8J/2 – Map of Kilwaughter graveyard, c.1879.